Antipodean Antics

A travel story about driving around
Australia and New Zealand

First published in 2010 by Priory Publishing

Priory Publishing, 147 Corhampton Road, Bournemouth, Dorset, BH6 5PA

ISBN 978-0-9565260-0-7

A CIP catalogue record for this book is available from the British Library.

Typeset and covers design by CuCo Creative, www.cucocreative.co.uk
Printed and bound by PressPlus, www.pressplusltd.com

Antipodean Antics

A travel story about driving around
Australia and New Zealand

Ken Cook

Priory Publishing

Bournemouth, England

AUSTRALIA ROUTE

Taken in 2004/05 & 2007/08

NEW ZEALAND ROUTE

Taken in 2007

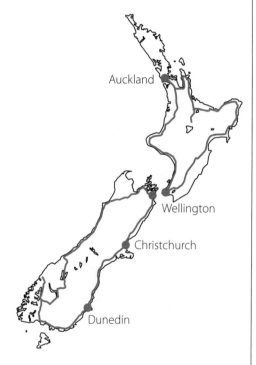

Auckland

Wellington

Christchurch

Dunedin

CONTENTS

Part 1

Chapter One

Forward and introduction.
A silver surfer goes to Aussieland.

In 2004 I decided to go to Australia to revisit a land that I had already lived in twice before. These were stays of four and six and a half years, in length. The first was made in the sixties when I was in my mid twenties. I had not long been out of service in the British armed forces, and was restless and wanted some excitement. Living then, in London, I met an Aussie who wanted someone to share expenses and drive overland back to his Ozland.

Well I thought you cannot get better excitement, than to do just that. Also another thing that was prompted me, was that I had recently done a runner from my first wife, and I thought that Oz was about as far away as I could get from her! So that alone was enough to make my mind up, and pretty damn quick too!

I arrived in Darwin after having spent five months driving overland from London via Europe to Turkey, then Iran, Afghanistan, Pakistan (Mumbai), where we sold the old Combi van. Then a ship to Bombay, a train journey across India to Madras, another boat trip to Penang in Malayia. We trekked through Thailand, Malaysia and finally to Singapore, where a flight to Darwin was our quickest and cheapest way to touch down in Oz. I then spent my four years partly in Sydney, then Perth, and back to Sydney again. From there, in November 1969 I caught the Oriana cruise ship for a voyage of a lifetime, back to cold old Blighty via New Zealand, Fiji, California, Mexico, Panama, Bahamas, Miami, and Bermuda.

My second visit was as a business immigrant and this time I brought my second wife, (me being a glutton for punishment, I had remarried!) I arrived this time by air, in late 1979, from Los Angeles where I had been in business. I stayed for the six and a half years, but due to the fact that my boat building business was not making me a fortune and my second marriage was going down the plughole and not helped by the fact that the ball and chain took an instant dislike to Oz as soon as she stepped off the plane. But that is women for you, and to compound that, she once said to me years later that she had been wrong and she should have stayed in Oz as she now realised how much better it was compared to the UK! After I had stopped myself from strangling her, I told her not to mind as it was too late now, unless she wanted to emigrate again, all on her own.

So in total I spent over 10 years in Oz and had seen a lot of the country already and I had lived on the Gold Coast, in Sydney and in Perth and I guess I had seen at least two thirds of the place. However I had not seen anywhere near all of it as I was too busy in business and work to take travelling holidays. Now that I was recently retired and getting bored, I needed to do something and as I had seen most of Europe, and a lot of the USA, I thought I may pass some time away with an extended trip to Oz and travel all the way round. See the places I had never seen before, and really get to explore the places I had lived in, but never had the time to do so.

Now, in the UK these days, many people in my position are doing just this, not to mention young back packers etc. Some like me sell their homes to fund such trips on the premise that they should still have enough left to rent, if they return to Blighty. They may even return to a cheaper European country where they could afford a small place. Or they could live in a motorhome or caravan. There are many ways to live without having loads of money tied up in bricks and mortar. In my case I had a cheap retirement flat which if I sold it, would not give me enough money to travel, then come back and buy anything else. But so what, I would rather spend some time enjoying myself while I was still able to do so.

Why would anyone want to go to such a far off place like Australia? Many reasons I would say. The World nowadays is not the place it used to be in my twenties. It is a very dangerous place with places I personally would now not dream of going to. I would never do the trip again that I did in 1966 as many of the countries I passed through then are too dangerous to travel through now. Many other countries that I would have gone to in those far off days I wouldn't dream of visiting now.

All this means that a country like Oz has many things going for it. It is cheap to get to, it is very safe in comparison, they all speak English, and their way off life is very British in many of its facets, coupled with some American style influences. So Brits feel very much at home there, just like Aussies feel at home when they come to the UK. We all know about the country from TV and films, so it's a country we feel we know before we go there. We have much in common and a common shared history. It has a very different countryside and feel about it compared with the UK and Europe. The weather is generally very good and pleasant and the wildlife can be fascinating. So it will prove, I am sure, a trip of a lifetime for most.

I am an experienced traveller but I realise that many people who may think to do such a journey, have either never travelled much or have never done such an extended trip as this. Where do you get some info on such a trip to

Australia. I know there are many books on Oz, but I have never seen one that deals specifically with a complete around Australia road trip with either a caravan or motorhome. I felt that I could answer many questions that would not be easily found in one place, and questions that relate to the older generation who need to know things that younger people would never even think about. Like what happens if I have a heart attack? Now there I have practical experience, having had one in Spain, out of the blue! So it is a question that concerns me too. I will try and touch on as many topics that relate to older people.

I will deal with as many subjects as I can think of that I feel people will want to know about, at the beginning of this story, and then I will relate what happened to me on the actual trip and what I saw and what there is to see. Some may find the day to day ramblings of my trip, when I was on the move, as boring. I have done it this way so the reader can see exactly what life is like, on a day to day basis, whilst doing a trip like this. If I dealt with say the section of my trip from Perth to Cairns as a whole, commenting on various aspects in general, one would not get the real flavour of what that trip was actually like to undertake. So for better or worse, I think writing about each section of the overall trip on a daily basis, gives the reader a fair reflection of what it was all about. After reading about it in this way, one may come to the conclusions that it would all be too boring, or hectic, or whatever. But at least you would be able to make a decision for yourself. If you are with me?

GETTING PERMISSION TO VISIT AUSTRALIA

Now here, this immediately raises issues that I feel strongly about. When I went to Oz in the 60's, Brits did not even need to ask for permission. You just arrived. The second time round, all the rules had changed and even Brits had to jump through hoops. I had to prove I had enough money and business experience etc. As I went through the LA Oz Embassy where they did not get many applications, I found them very easy going and helpful, and the process was quite quick. However had I been in the UK I think I would have ended up tearing my hair out and probably telling them where to stick their country.

What has this got to do with travelling there as a visitor I hear you ask? Well what I am saying is that if you think that the Brits are too bureaucratic and full of red tape, then you aint had to deal with Oz civil servants etc. They have got a hundred times worse over the past 40 years, I can tell you.

So in their wisdom, I found that unlike before, when you could visit their Embassy either in London or Manchester and talk to a human being and get all your questions answered, now they in their wisdom have decided that everyone has to do this on the web. Now I don't know about you but I think the World Wide Web is overblown, and websites NEVER contain all the answers to questions you have. Also to make a good website you need to spend a lot of money and know what you are doing. I find them a constant pain and their site is no different. For instance, I wanted to make a prolonged visit of up to a year in duration. What do I find? First of all instead of just one site, they have TWO. One run by London and one by CANBERRA. Both are convoluted to get around and NEITHER DEAL with the specific question of 'how do I get a visa lasting for a year'?

Such a simple question you would think, but nowhere could you find the answer. What you do find out is that the Aussies in their lack of wisdom seem to think that EVERYONE who wants to visit their country only wants to stay for a maximum of three months. If you fall into that category, you can get your visa on line. Fine for those who are only taking a quick holiday for a few weeks or even a month. ABSOLUTELY NO USE WHATSOEVER FOR SOMEONE WANTING AN EXTENDED STAY VISA. The Aussies simply do not want anyone writing to them, or ringing them or calling on them. They specifically tell you not to call on them and they do not provide a telephone number… I ask you, they aught to get real.

Well I searched through the web on Australia and got onto a site that listed all their Embassies and was able to get a number for the London one. I rang, and could not even get past the awfully rude belligerent young woman who answered the phone. I explained that I simply could not get an answer to my question, and was bluntly told in as many words to get lost. I thought to myself 'they haven't changed much, have they'? Even though I was fast running out of time, as I had already sold my place and needed to get my visa within a few weeks, I decided to write in. I posed my question and asked for a quick answer. I got no answer and after two weeks I resorted to going laboriously over their inadequate websites again. I decided to look at a copy of their visa application form which you would fill in for a 3 month visa. I had not bothered to look before as I thought, that being as I wanted a visa for over 3 months, the form would ask different questions. Anyway tucked away in small print at the top of the form, it said for those wanting longer visas, use this form and supply a letter giving your reasons Hallelujah! Why did they not put this somewhere on their website? I filled it in made up a letter telling them the OBVIOUS and posted it off via recorded delivery with my money and a note explaining the ABSOLUTE need to get it back within the timescale they said it would take them, and no longer.

After that time which I think was 7 working days, I had not got it back, and they had my passport as well. What happens if they had lost it? I knew they had received it as I checked with the Post Office, but how could I ask the Aussies as to where the damned thing was? They did have an email address to which you could send in a request to find out where your application was. Hurrah I thought, I sent in an email noting the extreme urgency that I was going to be out of a house soon and I needed my passport back and my visa. No answer, so a second email, still no answer. This time I sent a recorded delivery urgent letter to their Ambassador, no reply. Now I was hopping mad, so I sent an email to the Minister for Tourism in Canberra giving them what for. I got lucky with that as I then got a phone call off the head of their visa department full of apologies, and the assurance that I would get it back with the visa in a couple of days. It had been sent to the wrong department. I did lecture her on the need for a decent site and a way people could get answers, and stressed that her country made billions a year out of tourists and they needed to treat them a lot better than this. I was assured they were looking at a new website and procedures. Well I have learnt never to believe politicians or civil servants, but I hope anyone reading this book does not experience the trouble I had and that they have cleaned up their act by now.

You see, you cannot even book an airline ticket until you know you have got a visa, unless you are only going for the three month maximum deal, and then the travel agent will do it all for you. So if you plan to go for more than the three months, give yourself plenty of time to deal with getting a long term visa. The visa can be stamped to start from the time you arrive, and does not start from the date it is made, which is what I thought it would do. So you will have no problem even if you do not arrive until say two months after you got your visa stamp in your passport.

THINGS YOU MAY WANT TO KNOW ABOUT IN ADVANCE

GETTING TO AUSTRALIA

In this day and age there is no other way to get there than to fly. It is cheaper to fly now than when I went there in 1979. I paid £575 return and that is ridiculously low when you look at how much it costs to fly to other parts of the World. To get the best prices look up the adverts in the National newspapers and or book on line. I would strongly urge you to fly with an airline that goes via Japan or Taiwan or Korea and gives you a stopover of say five hours or so. This breaks up the long flight, and you can have a kip on a bench seat while you wait. I went via Seoul and had four hours kip and never felt any jet lag when I got to Oz.

Prices obviously vary during the seasons so try and go when it is at its cheapest and not at the height of the Summer season. It is no problem to get a ticket with a years gap before return.

WHAT TO TAKE WITH YOU

You only get so many kilos that you can take with you as baggage, and I think it will be about 20 Kilos. My advice is to travel as light as possible, but if you want to take more than your allowance then the cheapest way to do it is to do as I did. I took quite a bit of equipment with me because I intended to be away for up to two years and to do some sailing and I had quite a lot gear that I had bought already and why buy it again. So I had and extra 50 kilos which I sent independently via airfreight. The cost was only £130 and had I bought what I sent it would have cost much more than that.

Do not take too many clothes as you do not need as much clothing in a place where the climate is generally much warmer than the UK. Unless you intend to spend time up in the Snowies in the Winter in amongst the snow. Summer clothes are quite cheap there and most of the time your only in flip flops, shorts and T shirts and the like. If you buy a used motorhome from a hire company, they usually sell them with all the gear like bedding and cutlery and pots and pans etc.

So be sensible as to what you cart over there as you will have to pay to take it and it may be cheaper to buy it there. If you intend to buy a scooter or motorbike and you already have wet weather gear, then take that as that gear is more expensive. I took my expensive UK wet weather gear and I was glad I did as I got to use it a lot. I also took my hand held GPS which would be handy when I was off the beaten track. It is always handy to be able to work out your coordinates if you need to. If your not into sailing yourself then you may not have such gear, but you may if you do a lot of walking or trekking.

HOW DO YOU GET AROUND AUSTRALIA WHEN YOU GET THERE?

There are obviously a number of ways you can use to see Australia. The most expensive way if you are rich is to use only Public transport and airlines. Buses run round Oz and even the American Greyhound Bus has a service there. Then there are trains, but they do not traverse absolutely all of Oz, especially in Western Australia and Northern Territory.

The Airlines are quite cheap to use to get between major cities and towns. They of course will not allow you to explore off the beaten track. So I think most people are going to want to have the freedom of having their own wheels, which will enable them to go anywhere they like, when they like, and will be in the end the cheapest way to do it. I will therefore list all the different types of wheels you can buy and deal with each type:- Car/campervan/car with caravan/ car with trailer and tents/standard van/estate car/four wheel drive vehicle/Motorhomes/Caravans.

1/ SALOON CAR. Obviously a car will get you from A to B and with the right type of car, that can be in comfort. What it will not do is allow you somewhere to sleep and cook. Unless it is a very large car into which you can stow the necessary tents, sleeping bags and gas cooking gear and pots and pans and crockery etc. That can mean little space left for you and giving you very basic standard of life. Most people who are retired and say over 50 will want more than just basic standards as they are more suited to the young.

2/ ESTATE CARS. You will get much the same standards with an estate as you get with a large car. All you will get is some more floor space. Some youngsters in Oz favour the Estate car or panel van and will use the large flat floor in the rear to sleep in, but again if your older you will not favour this method of travel.

3/ CAR OR ESTATE WITH TRAILER. Pulling a trailer will give you more space with which to carry more equipment and that can be bigger and better tents etc. You see many younger Oz families travelling this way, but again I think it is more suitable for trips that last for only weeks rather than many months and is more suited to the younger. Anyone willing to travel this way can pick up older Oz cars like the big Holdens (Vauxhall), and Fords both of which are made in Oz. You can find quite cheap rust free examples. As they usually have big 6 cylinder or V8 engines, they can do very high mileages and still not have been stressed too much, so can still have many more miles left in them. They will use more petrol than the usual Euro 4 cylinder type cars, but in Oz petrol is half of what it is in the UK. (2004 prices, so check current prices.)

4/ CAMPERVANS. These are just small vans that have been adapted to make what are basically very small motor homes. They usually involve an expanding roof to enable you to stand up, will have seats that make up into a double bed, and will no doubt have a small fridge and sink and small gas cooker. They are what they say they are, vans turned into campers, but they are very small and basic and in my opinion somewhat claustrophobic. However whenever I am in a caravan park they can be seen in large numbers, but are used mainly by the young who don't mind the lack of space and are on a small budget. Many can be seen for sale or can be hired. (More about the cost of hiring these and motorhomes, later on.)

5/ CARAVANS. Now we are talking business, because you obviously can get decent sized caravans. You can also get small ones, and I could never get over how small some of these can be. They make smaller caravans in Oz than I have seen anywhere else, but these are really only if you have a small car that will not pull a big one, or your only going on short trips.

Bigger caravans with decent interiors can give you decent living. However any caravan means also buying a car. The bigger the caravan, the bigger the car or pulling vehicle you will need. One plus for all this is that you will also get a vehicle in which you can, when in large towns and cities, use to explore in. Many caravans can be seen for sale so you will not have any problem getting used ones at various price ranges.

6/ FOUR WHEEL DRIVE VEHICLES. The 4WD vehicle is even more popular in Oz than in the UK. Like in the UK, many are bought by the big city posers and women school run mums, and these will never see off road use. But many are used to travel outback because when you go off road in Oz, a lot of the non tarmac roads are terrible and there are many tracks which are not even proper roads. So if it is out of the way and bush and outback travel your looking to do, then a 4WD is a must. Any wet conditions will also mean 4WD is a must. They will not be as cheap as cars and will use more petrol or fuel, even if a diesel. If you are going to go the big caravan way, then a big engined 4WD will be needed, over a car.

7/ MOTORHOMES. Like caravans, there are a wide variety of motorhomes from titchy small ones based on little more than small van chassis/cab units, to medium sized ones based mainly on either the Transit Cab/chassis or the Mercedes chassis, bigger ones based on same, to much larger ones based on mainly ex buses that have been converted. A few very large American homes can also be seen for sale but these are rare and usually have huge V8 engines and use huge amounts of fuel. Even though fuel is cheaper why pay more than you need. Also a lot of Yankie jobs are auto boxes and they too add to fuel usage. Some of these may have been converted to run on cheaper gas, which is much more easily available than in the UK.

I think any Brit will want to buy the minimum, of a medium sized motorhome. There are magazines that are for motorhomers which carry adverts for used and new motorhomes and a cheap weekly magazine like 'Exchange and Mart' called 'The Trading Post', which has a caravan/motorhome section. This paper is a local one so the adverts will relate to your area, and this is where I found the advert for the home I finally settled on. I found that in all the other magazines, Oz being a big place they will carry adverts from all the States. You will need to concentrate on the ads in the city your in. Prices range from say $15,000 to $150,000 depending on age, and size. You can buy a medium sized motor home of about 6/7 years old from $30,000, or a 3 year old ex rental home which has done say 150,00K's, for $60,000 I looked at many homes privately and at dealers around Sydney, and was getting fed up looking at many over priced homes and many grot boxes. Eventually I found one advertised in The Trading Post which sounded what I wanted and at the right price. So I ended up buying it privately off an older couple. It was a 7 year old Transit based home of medium size, with a 2.5 Turbo diesel engine, manual box, fridge, shower, hot water, water tank, Grey water tank, sink, cooker, and microwave with two double beds (one over cab). Good enough and big enough for me and costing $35,000, which was lower than average for the year of the vehicle. I did get done in a small way as later on I found that the turbo wasn't working which was for me, hard to tell as I had never driven a turbo diesel before. Then I found that the fridge was not working and this is hard to know when you look at a home, because they will not have it switched on. So do check out fridges and turbo's and aircon units. The fridge did not cost very much to repair, but the turbo did, some $1700. So if buying, my advice is get it well checked over by the NRMA. (Like the RAC)

Do not buy a new one as you will never get your money back. (unless you are rich) Buy one as cheap as you can because remember, you will have to sell it when you want to leave and this can be tricky and time consuming. So the trick is to buy a good one at the best lowest price possible, be prepared to lose some on it and you will then, a year later, stand the best possible chance to get rid of it as quickly as possible, as a low price will hopefully attract buyers quickly.

However the one negative to buying is as I have just said, is getting shot of it when your finished, no matter what the price. On this score I found a lot of travellers in the caravan parks, from Europe, who were trying to offload their vehicles of various types, and were having a hard time finding buyers. This was the case even for cheap vehicles at less than $5,000. I met a couple in Brisbane, he was Aussie and she was Danish and they lived in Denmark and were now going back after a long trip around Oz. They had bought for $27,000 a 1986 Isuzu based home much the same size as mine and in very good nick for its age. They had been trying to sell it for a couple of months and were now getting desperate with all the tyre kickers and time wasters messing them about. They were now looking at taking offers and talking about accepting $10,000 and at that price would take a $17,000 loss. I advised them to take the vehicle back with them and use it in Europe or sell it in the UK.

For myself I did not get serious about the business of selling my home, until I arrived back in Sydney in the eighth month of my stay. This is when the frustration started and this is when you start to learn, that anything you want to do that involved the Aussie government and its multi level bureaucracy, it will be guaranteed to get you tearing your hair out. You would think that the act of wanting to sell a vehicle would be a simple thing. Not in Oz!

When I bought my home it had six months of road tax still left on it and that included the compulsory third party personal injury insurance (which the Ozzies call the green slip) that the Government insist you get when you register the car in your name, and an MOT. I am told that many people who sell a vehicle pass on that insurance to the new buyer. So I had no need to worry about it at all until the time came when I wanted to sell.

When that time came at the end of my trip it coincided with the road tax and therefore the MOT and the green card insurance, running out. If I had the time to sell I would have to sell it with those items in force. However I wanted to find out more about the costs and the ins and outs of this green slip insurance. So I went to the local Road Traffic Authorities office to get the answers, and the fact I had lost one of my number plates, which fell off on one of those dirt roads. All the screws holding it on loosened with the vibration from corrugations. I found that I would have to be issued with a brand new set of plates with a new number, at a cost of $30 (12 pounds) A bit stiff for two new plates when in the UK I would have been able just to go to a number plate maker and buy ONE plate! Here you will also have to fill in the usual long form and deal with a government department where you will hang around waiting to be served etc for hours. Then I get told about this green slip which I will have to get, not from the RTA but from a private insurance company. I pointed out that I had got comprehensive insurance which should cover injury and death to third parties and damage to third party property as well, so why did I need another layer of insurance for an area already covered? The reply I got was woolly and did not entirely satisfy me, as the person dealing with me did not come over as really knowing the full facts.

I was given a list of insurance companies who specialised in green slip insurance, some seven in all. These included the NRMA motoring association with I was a member of. So I thought that being a member may give me an advantage and I went into their local office in Chatswood, only to be served by an Asian lady who again did not answer my question with any authority. She did work out that I would have to pay $296 for it. As I had paid $528 for fully comprehensive insurance I thought this was a complete rip off. So I left just as sceptical as before, and feeling she cannot have got it right. I resolved to contact some more of these insurance companies. Not as easy as you would think. I looked in the yellow pages to get their addresses and almost all of the listed companies only gave their telephone numbers and no address of their Head Office in Sydney centre. Somewhere I would be going the next day and could call on them in person and talk for as long as necessary to get an answer as to what is EXACTLY included in this insurance and if it is a duplicate of what I have already paid for and why is it that I have to pay again for what I thought I already had? I then thought 'I know I will ring my own insurance company in Melbourne and ask them' What a waste of time and money, as the girl I spoke to obviously didn't have a clue.

The next day I went to Sydney city centre on the train, and called personally on three companies that had given their addresses in the phone book. The first company SGIO quoted $325 and that was based on my age, my no claims, vehicle type and my address. I found out that this green slip applies to only third party personal injuries or death, and not to third party property.

Second company I called on was the NRMA, to double check. Here I got some arrogant bossy know all Ozzy female of later years. She did not even ask my age or vehicle or anything. 'Hang on' I said 'how can you give me a quote off the top of your head without knowing any details? I know the rates off by heart she told me. No amount talk would budge her even when I told her of the quote of $296 from her branch in Chatswood. I left none too pleased. Another example of Ozzy madness.

Next it was a visit to QBE and there I got a quote of $425, also based on age, NCB, and I found out here that you cannot get a refund if you sell the vehicle and do not want to pass on this insurance. So it looks as if I export it, also no refund. More madness, because I am quoted on MY details, then if I sell, it could be to a young driver of 18 who cannot have a record the same as mine.

So it will be back to the NRMA at Chatswood to see what they say again. When I did this I got yet another story from what I got the first time I visited them and the story I got at their Head Office. Now under questioning I find that if you already have insurance of your own, this insurance should be cheaper. Quite what this has to do with things as even if you have fully comprehensive insurance of your own, none of that covers what this green slip insurance covers and you could be using a completely different insurance company. What a way to run things, duplications of insurance and differing stories and quotes wherever you go. So now NRMA at Chatswood are quoting $567, after they had quoted $296. So the quotes I get all differ and no one quotes with any air of certainty. I am glad I am not now going to have to go along with this charade.

The MOT would be no problem (I think), as like the UK it is just down to an inspection by an independent garage. The years road tax would have cost me $527 (about £210) which is a lot more than the UK. (2004 figures.)

Another point which anyone going to Oz and buying any vehicle should know about, is their ludicrous system with relation to the fact that there are six separate States. All of them like six separate countries. Say you buy a vehicle that had, like mine, under a years road tax/MOT/and green slip insurance, on it? You will no doubt be out of the State when it comes to renewing things. How will you go, getting an MOT in a different State? Will that MOT be accepted in the other State? Are all the green slip insurance companies covering all the States and how can they give you a quote when your not living in one place as your travelling? Remember the quotes I got depended on the address of where I lived. My lost number plate posed me a problem as I lost it in the middle of nowhere in the Queensland outback. There was no way I could get another one, until I got into NSW. All questions you should get answers to before you start travelling.

Another problem that arose with relation to shipping it back. This concerns, how do you ship it if you decide not to sell and lose lots of money? Normally most vehicles smaller than the larger motorhomes would go into a 20' or 40' container, and would cost $2,500 to $6,000 depending on who you use, and what size you use. The problem is that most motorhomes are too high to get into a container. This means that it would have to go RoRo and I was quoted twice for that, for the massive figure of $11,000. Just getting a shipping company or agents to give you a quote is frustrating too. I rang a number of companies and only got an uninterested attitude and I had to keep chasing them all, to even get them to get back to me with a quote. All typical Aussie behaviour I am afraid. I always had this problem when I lived there. So I contacted my UK agent to see what he could do. I got given his agents contact email, and I sent him a message, but true to the way Aussies seem to work, he never contacted me. Eventually I managed to get a couple of agents to answer my queries and if I can get the height down to the maximum height of a 40 foot container, the cheapest quote was $6K. I had worked out that if I ran the motorhome into the container on wheels, minus their tyres, it may work. This is all showing you the problems you will have if you buy a normal sized motorhome and cannot afford to lose heaps on it, so you think about shipping it back, as you feel you could use it back home in Europe.

Quite frankly based on my experiences I would now advise anyone not to think about buying a motorhome that will not easily fit into a container or rack, if you think about taking it back with you. If you think that you will sell it anyway then my advice is that from my experience of watching who is in caravan parks, the overwhelming number of Aussies use caravans and not motorhomes. Most motorhome use is by overseas visitors who mostly hire, by the looks of things. They either do not hire for extensive periods or are rich enough not to be bothered by how much it costs. If you are like me and have to watch each cent and penny, then hiring is simply throwing money down the drain. So if you do not want to buy a car or 4WD and a caravan, then you will have to buy a motorhome on the cheap because if you buy over say $10,000 you will undoubtedly have more problems getting it sold at all and if your up against a time limit in which to sell, then you could end up giving it away to get rid of it and losing lots of money. If you buy a very cheap motorhome it will be older and maybe not in good condition. So all in all it is a very complicated subject and one which you will have to weigh up CAREFULLY, taking into consideration all your requirements and financial position. (Also see the POSTCRIPT on what problems you could have receiving it back in your country)

One thing that I have not covered to date about buying any vehicle in Oz, and that has to do with rip off tax on all car purchases. Even secondhand ones! This is called Stamp Duty. I call it a TAX and nothing more. How the Ozzies put up with that blatant rip off I do not know. They are as apathetic as the Brits! If you think about it, the Government collects the TAX on the car when it is new, then every time it gets sold over its lifetime they get a cut with their grubby fingers in the till. I had to pay $924 tax on top of the purchase price. If I had bought a new vehicle and paid the equivalent of VAT (their GST) I would get that back if I exported within 12 months. Yet I cannot get a zack back on the $1,000 I paid in tax. What a rip off.

On top of this, if you like me, intend to take the vehicle onto New Zealand the NZ Customs will charge you 12 and 1/2% customs on the value. Only if you export it out again do you get it back. But no refunds if you sell it in NZ, before leaving.

If all this is not enough to put anyone off, there is more. I have already told you that when I got my home, I insured it fully comprehensively with a company in Melbourne. This was done through the joining of the Motorhome Club as I mentioned. They had a deal going with this company where you could not only get insurance, even though you were not an Ozzie, but at a reasonable price. I rang this company from Sydney before I had set out in October. They quoted me and said I would have to supply details of my UK No Claims Discount and show what I paid for it. It was arranged that I would call into their office when I got to Melbourne, with all this and they could take copies. This I did and paid for it all with my credit card. They posted me the policy and invoice/receipt and I carried on round Oz thinking that no matter what happened I was covered every which way.

Then I received a phone call from this insurance agent, some SIX MONTHS after I had fixed up the insurance. (Quite frankly I think that me ringing them up and asking questions about what my insurance covered, had set them thinking) I was asked if I still wanted this insurance and when I asked what the hell were they talking about, I was told that as they had no evidence of my no claims or price paid, there had been no insurance. They had sent letters to the caravan park in Melbourne, obviously long after I had left, even though they knew my phone number and I had been at the park five weeks. I do not know what you think but this is yet another example of just how staggeringly incompetent Aussies can be, as the girl who dealt with me took copies of my NCB and purchase receipt, but of course this girl no longer worked for them. Naturally I told them that I was livid and that if I had not paid for it, which is what they say happened as they had not debited my card, then at this stage they could stick it. How they could actually send me my policy etc if I had not paid, is beyond me. I had not had the amount debited, but with me on the move all the time I had not noticed this as I could not check my bank balances.

If you think the above is incredible, I have more!! This home I bought, whilst it has done the job OK from a mechanical point of view (apart from the turbo), that was only down to the fact that the base for the home is a Ford Transit, the coachbuilt home part has left a lot to be desired. It has not been well designed and the quality of the fittings have been of poor quality. The biggest fault is that it has been built just like a colander. That is… it is full of holes in places you cannot see, around the floor pan, the side panels and other parts of the body that join the chassis, that have just not been joined up in a totally sealed way. So when I went over a dirt road, which in Oz is hard not to do, dust has got into the home through a multitude of gaps and holes. A MAJOR BAD DESIGN AND LACK OF QUALITY BUILD. Other faults are:- poor quality cooker, poor sealing of the major air vent over the stove and the fresh air hatch which both let in hordes of insects at night through gaps, rattling vibrating step below door, no wiring diagram for 240Volt setup, smells coming into the home from the toilet unit due to more gaps in the toilet shower cubicle, leaking window over bed that drenched the mattress, window rubbers that are severely stained and unsightly and difficult to clean off, toilet door keeps opening because no way of locking it whilst in motion, poorly designed home entry door which also lets in dust, and has no fly screen, (which most homes have) poor quality furniture, storage lockers whose doors open when in motion and let the contents out, poor quality table fitments that broke, poorly designed upper bunk base, the outside panels are made with a soft and extremely poor quality board which has absorbed water and come out in blisters and bumps and you cannot attach anything to the walls using screws, as they cannot grip on the soft board, and other faults that I will not bang on about as what I have listed so far, are bad enough.

I tried to find who the manufacturer was in order to see if I could get some spare parts off him. These were parts that had got damaged en route. The nearside rear mudflap had been torn off when the tyre in front of it disintegrated, due to poor design again. The offside indicator lens had cracked when I reversed into a pole I could not see. Plus I wanted to know who made the home so I could tell them what a heap it was.

In the footwell there was a compliance plate put there by the Queensland Government saying it had passed their design rules. It listed the maker as Leisureport. I reasoned that this meant the manufacturer was in Queensland. So I left it until I got to Brisbane to see if I could locate them there. No such luck, and I tried everywhere and found nobody listed. So I reasoned that it could be a foreign manufacturer and it was imported.

Now I had noticed on my travels that there were homes belonging to hire companies, that had been obviously made by the same manufacturer as mine, as all the fittings on those homes were the same as mine. So when a home turned up on the caravan park I was staying on, in Brisbane, I talked to the owner. He told me that he had had it specially made by a New Zealand company. Then another hire home that was the same as mine turned up and that had a sticker on it naming this NZ company as C.I.Munro.

I went onto the web and found their site and sent them an email asking if they could tell me where in Oz I could get a wiring diagram, a rear lens and a mudflap. Imagine my anger when they sent me a reply saying they could not help me and I would have to ring their Oz agent and gave me his number. I rang, he was not in, I left a message with my number and I haven't heard a dicky bird from him. Typical! I tried the Association of RV Vehicle Manufacturers of Australia to see if they belonged to them. No they did not. I wrote back listing all the problems I had had with this home and the list of faults and said that they may like to know of this for their own information, and I asked if they could oblige me by telling me where I could get a replacement rear light, and I named the manufacturer of the light unit. No reply! So I hope you are gradually getting the picture of what Aussies can be like in situations like this. Totally and utterly, bloody unhelpful and incompetent.

I'm not finished yet either, because when I tried to let the Motorhome Club know about all this, their reaction was abysmal. (See my notes on Motorhome Club below.)

All the faults I can rectify using my 40 years of manufacturing expertise of making boats and cars, but this is not the point. Your average Joe Blow who will buy one of these ex hire motorhomes will be entirely ignorant and not know what to look for to see if it is up to scratch. Until like me they start driving it and using it. Then all the faults and poor design will manifest themselves and it will be too late. Now what you aught to know is that the manufacturer C.I Munro is part of a group in New Zealand that also owns two large motorhome hiring companies namely Maui and Britz, and these people regularly sell off their two and three year old homes to the general Public in Oz. So beware if your buying any Aussie or New Zealand home, go over it with a fine tooth comb, use my list of faults as a guide. Take your time, don't be rushed. (Also note the comments the motorhome club woman said to me about other Oz makes.)

Quite frankly if you really decide to buy instead of renting you will have to work it all out very carefully in my opinion. That is if you will want to have decent sized place to live in over a long period. Of course you can buy much cheaper than I did, but what will you end up with, and as I have stated even with lower priced homes you may still have a problem selling. You could go and buy something real small like a Campervan at a super low price, but then you have a small vehicle, or you are into tenting it. You makes your choice. Or if you have so much spare money then hiring a decent sized motorhome will not worry you one bit and bully for you.

So there I was in the position of, shall I try to sell this home or shall I ship it back? Because if I sold, I will have to pay $300 or more for a green slip, then get an MOT and that will no doubt mean I will have to replace two tyres and maybe the windscreen because of the little crack I got in it when that truck sprayed me with stones, near Norseman. On top of that the cracked indicator lens on the rear lights may need to be replaced and I could not find who sells that particular make of light. So naturally I start to think I would be better taking it back to the UK as it is worth at least what I paid for it, maybe more. If I get $30,000 for it in Oz, I have paid $35,000 plus the $2500 cost of a new turbo and doing the new cambelts etc, making a total of $37500. I will therefore lose $7500 on the home plus the costs of tyres and windscreen, etc in order to pass the MOT . Bringing a minimum loss of over $8,000 plus, and that is IF I MANAGE TO SELL IT AT ALL, and for $30K. Many decisions to make, and the type of decisions you will have to make as well. I shipped mine back.

ALTERNATIVES TO BUYING

Obviously this is to hire. It is a BIG business, hiring out Motorhomes, in Oz. You see many hire homes plying the roads and in the camps. However they are VERY expensive and I think most sensible people will if they intend to stay for up to a year, will do their arithmetic and see it is too expensive to hire. The big names in hiring are:- BRITZ, MAUI, APOLLO, AND KEA. You will no doubt be able to easily find them on the net. So look up their websites and get their latest hiring prices and do your working out and compare to the costs of secondhand units.

I have done my own homework on their costs and here is what I have found:- (2006 prices) Maui has a daily rate of $336 in the high season (Dec to Jan) and down to $160 (May to June) and various prices in between these at other times of the year. Apollo quote a high of $221 and a low of $109. So even on the low prices you can see if you want to stay here for three months it's going to cost you $9,000 plus, and you cannot really see in Oz, what I have seen, in three months. I would say the absolute minimum you need is four months, and that would mean not spending much time in all the Capital cities and not really hanging about anywhere.

DRIVING LICENCES

If you have a full Brit licence that is all you need. On this you can drive any car, 4WD, car with caravan, and any motorhome up to 6 metres in length. Over that and especially the larger bus conversions will need a truck licence. If you do not have one of those don't even think of getting an Oz one as it is so convoluted to get one and expensive and more importantly, lengthy.

A Scooter or bike licence; if like me you want to carry a bike or scooter on the back, this is another thing to think about, thanks to their rules. If you do not have a UK bike licence, forget it if you want to ride a scooter over 50cc in engine size. Or get a UK licence first for all sized bikes, as to do this will be easier than doing it in OZ. Here you have to take a written test first, then after getting that you have to apply to take a riding test. You cannot ride round on a bike with L plates whilst you teach yourself as in the UK. So it costs too much money and is a hassle. This is why I bought a 49cc scooter which you are allowed to drive on your UK car licence. Mine only cost $2,000 new and costs no more than $10 a week in petrol and is fast enough for city work. It will carry two people as well and has storage under the seat, and with the box I have added to the back, you can do a good shop for a weeks food, and carry it all.

INSURANCE

For fully comprehensive Motorhome, car and or caravan insurance, you will no doubt like me, start tearing your hair out, as I have recounted above. All the Insurance companies I contacted, and I contacted all the big ones, did not want to know as I was not an Aussie. Even some of the Brit insurance companies (operating in Oz) had the same attitude. Racial discrimination if you ask me, and another example of the frustrating ways of Oz.

I was advised that the only way I could get insured was to join the Campervan & Motorhome Club and use their insurer who will insure you even if you are a Brit, no problem. Who will be much cheaper and will accept your Brit 'no claims entitlements' So take your driving evidence and insurance NCB evidence with you to Oz.

With the scooter I also had no luck to find anyone willing to insure me due to my being a Brit visitor. However as I have pointed out above, with either cars or bikes, when you pay your road tax, it you have to get the green slip 3rd party insurance and it is not all that expensive for a scooter and the dealer fixed that up. So I never bothered with fully comp on the scooter and if it gets nicked or I damaged it, then I would have had to take the loss.

MOTORHOME CLUB OF AUSTRALIA

I have above told you that in order to get comprehensive insurance at all, you should join the Campervan and Motorhome Club of Australia who are based in Newcastle, just North of Sydney. Normally I would not join any club whatsoever, however I had no choice here, if I were going to cover myself for the eventuality of suffering a massive accident or total loss of the home and possessions. This club bring out a monthly magazine and have what they call chapters around Oz. (Sounds a bit like the Hells Angels lot, with their chapters etc.) They all get together and swop travel stories and all that kind of stuff, which I would not have a bar off. I could see no other benefits to being a member other than getting insurance and at a reasonable rate. So I joined.

When I got back to Sydney I thought that it would be a right thing to do and let them know about all the problems I had had with this home, of which there would be hundreds and hundreds in circulation, having been sold onto the Oz market by the two associated motorhome hiring companies.

I sent a copy of the email I had sent the Oz association of RV manufacturers in which I detailed the 12 faults I had endured. The Club then actually rang me about questions I had previously asked them re advertising a motorhome in their magazine. I mentioned I had sent them the email detailing the problems over the home build quality and that they may wish to warn their members. I was very curtly and abruptly told that they would not do this as they could never print such things because they would get sued. I asked if this meant that in Oz there were no such thing as consumer protection, and how would their members know about such poorly made motorhomes being sold on their market, if they could never read about it. She then went into a tirade of how I should have practised buyer beware and I should have talked to members to find out if they had had problems. I tried to point out that I at first did not even know who the manufacturer was, as no name was evident on the home. That I had to buy quickly and had no time to contact anyone. That in any case how could I contact members as at that stage as I wasn't a member and did not even know of the existence of the club, etc etc. Whatever I said she was not interested in listening, and when I tried to just show her how bad it was and that one couldn't see that the faults would be there until one drove the home for some time. This by telling her about the home filling up with dust (which I did not drive on until I had had it some months), she said she didn't even want to listen to what I had to say, and that every home on the Oz market were riddled with faults and had to go back to manufacturers for rectifications. Apart from being massively negative and rude, she showed that buying any make of home in Oz could be fraught with danger and you could end up with a lemon. Which doesn't say much for Oz manufacturers. So I repeat once again the need to go over all the pros and cons of buying motorhomes and caravans and to get them thoroughly checked out by someone who knows about such vehicles, if you feel you cannot do it yourself.

I also told the club in a further email about what had happened with regards to THEIR wonderful association with the incompetent Mr Ken Tame, insurance agent extraordinaire, recommended by them. Guess what?… they ignored my email… So they acted par for the course… again!

As for the value of belonging to the club, well that is debatable, as apart from the insurance you obviously get no real benefit at all, and maybe if you spend more time than I did and look at more insurance companies you may come up lucky and actually find an insurance company who is not racially biased. It certainly is obvious that it is not a club that looks after the benefits of its members and consumer protection is a no no as far as it is concerned. It is more interested in being totally PC and not saying Boo to anyone, and appears to be just a gossip shop. Also it may make money from all the trades adverts on its website and no doubt in its magazine, and that is why it can't be bothered upsetting those money earners.

WHERE TO STAY WHILST TRAVELLING

If your not buying a caravan or motorhome or such like, and you intend to stay in hotels or similar, that is going to cost you more, as I am sure you will appreciate.

Obviously there are many expensive hotels, and hotels in every price bracket. What I have not seen are B&B places run in peoples homes as in the UK. There are plenty of B&B places advertised in country places, but I do not recollect seeing any in the big cities. The ones I called on when I was travelling around on my scooter and waiting for my Transit to be repaired, were as expensive as staying in a cheaper hotel.

There are many cheaper hotels and many pubs in Oz have rooms that do not cost more than $25 to $30 a night. There are many Backpacker hostels which are very cheap. (photo1a). You can get a dormitory room for $15 or a double room for $40 total cost, a night. They are not just for young people either as people of all ages are accepted, and every town and city will have many of these places dotted around.

When you first arrive in OZ you will need somewhere to stay while you sort yourself out and look for a motorhome or other means of transport. If like me hotels are too expensive and you do not want to stay in a backpackers place, because they are full of noisy youngsters, then there are plenty of other types of places you can rent. These range from simple bedsits to flats or houses. There are no shortages of such places and it won't take you long to get fixed up. How do you find these places? The newspapers have adverts but even though you do not get newsagents shops with cards in the windows, you do see adverts pinned on notice boards in all sorts of places. Most Internet cafes have such advertising notice boards and some supermarket shopping malls do. Libraries can have such boards as well, especially in the beach areas.

Some holiday resorts have cabins you can rent, but in the summer periods they are expensive, probably more expensive than hotels. Most caravan parks have such cabins or even caravans that can be rented. However if you start off in Sydney, it is the worst city for caravan parks and what there is, are all out on the extreme outer limits of the city. Melbourne, Adelaide and Perth all have caravan parks well within the city limits.

HOW TO FIND OUT ABOUT AUSTRALIA

There are many books that have been written about the country and deal both with the history, and the places to visit. You will find books on what camping sites there are and where there are Caravan Parks. So visit your library or bookshop if you want to read up and get information that is not included in this book. (However if you have libraries that are as bad as my local libraries you may not find many, if any books on Oz) As Australia is such a large place, books tend to concentrate on certain parts of it as it would be impossible to have a book that covers absolutely every aspect and in depth, of the country and travel within it.

There are also some books written on the safety aspect of travel in such places like the outback. Most are written by ex SAS guys and deal with all the things you need to know about wilderness travel and safety. Then there is the net, but I always find the net isn't what it is cracked up to be.

CARAVAN PARKS

There is no shortage of these ANYWHERE in Oz. Even the most remote town or hamlet seems to have its caravan park. They range from the very basic to the excellent and the overnight prices range from a low of $12 a night to $27 a night. The quality of the site does not necessarily determine what you will pay as I have stayed in fantastic sites for only $12 and paid top dollar for abjectly crap dumps. All provide toilets/showers and water and 240V electricity which you can plug into and power your home electrics. Most motorhomes have systems that automatically will switch the 240Volts into 12V. Some electrical items only operate on 240, such as microwaves, but some fridges will operate on either. The cost of the electricity is included in the price in most of the places. I only came across one site, which was the one I stayed at in Freemantle, that if you stayed on their long term sites, had an electric meter and you paid for what you used. My months stay only cost about $6.00.

Some sites have access to Internet machines operated by a coin. Usually costing $1 or $2 per 5 minutes. (expensive) Many sites have lots of trees under which you can park and they will provide much needed shade on hot days, but they can host hoards of noisy twittering birds which can crap on your home and wake you up at 5am in the morning. The absolute worst offenders are the little gaily coloured parakeets who just NEVER stop making a racket, delightful though they are on the eye. The big black crows are the other noisy bird with their mournful calling.

My main grouse about Oz parks is the vast majority are not kept clean and tidy. The roads are in poor condition and some are just dirt tracks, and the pitch on which you have to park on can be a dirt patch. This means that you end up treading dirt and leaves etc into the home every time you step outside, especially when it rains. In many places it is just not possible to grow good grass sites for you to park on. So they degenerate into dirt patches with a few bits of measly grass here and there. They should, in these cases, make tarmac or concrete pads on which to park. With the trees they do not sweep up the droppings of dead twigs and leaves, so that also treads into your home. They certainly could do with cleaning up their act and I do not know why the authorities can't categorise caravan parks like they do with hotels and rate them. However these remarks can equally apply to sites in the UK and Europe.

FOOD IN AUSTRALIA

When I lived in Oz in the 60's large supermarkets were unknown and the range of food stuffs you could buy was not up to UK Standards. By the late 70's and into the 80's they were now building large shopping malls with some supermarkets, but still lagging behind the UK ones. Now I would say that whilst they are still behind they are almost there. There are many more shopping centres and malls with large supermarkets within them and they offer a wide range of foods, both fresh and manufactured. Even relatively small towns have got a supermarket and very often it is one of the big ones like Coles or Woolies. On the ready meals side, they still do not offer the range of meals you can get say in Tescos, Sainsburys or Marks, but it is good enough for a lazy cook like me. You can buy good quality fresh produce the same as in the UK, which includes all meats and fish. Although I have to say that I was very often disappointed with the quality of fruit. Sometimes it was good, many times it was poor, and all the time I felt it was too expensive. Especially considering it was grown in Oz. One thing I will say, and this surprised me, is that my weekly shopping bill was slightly higher than the UK. I am also surprised that fresh veg and fruit was as high if not higher in price than the UK. This in a country that should be self sufficient with the sunny climate they have. We in the UK import much of our fresh fruit and veg and yet I would say it is cheaper. Bread and milk are both quite a bit more expensive than the UK. A wholemeal loaf costs $2.00 to $4 plus, and a litre of milk starts at $1.60. Maybe this has to do with the buying power in the UK due to its higher population. So do not think it's is all going to be cheaper. In out of the way places like in the country and in the bush, the prices go up because of the cost of getting the produce and provisions to there. Plus you will find less choice. So do like I did and stock up on as much as you can prior to leaving a big conurbation whilst you have the choice and at the best prices.

Eating out is also more expensive than some holiday programmes will have you believe. From the basics like a cup of tea or coffee and maybe a small cake, then they are about the same. A Latte which I always favour, is in a big city around $3 and in some areas of Sydney I was having to pay $3.50. In some smaller places it could drop to $2.50 or $2.70. A slice of cake can cost $4 to $5 or even up to $6 for a fancy piece of cake like a piece of Gateaux. ($3 = £1.25, $8 = £3.30). Meals in cafes and restaurants I think may work out slightly less expensive than in the UK, which I have always thought were rip off prices. Wine is not as cheap as I had expected nor is beer, a midi glass which is half a pint can cost $2.50 plus which is over a pound. (All 2004/5 prices but probably the differences are still there.) I had a chicken and mixed salad sandwich with a huge amount of salad, in Sydney centre, for $3.80 which is about £1.50. So I would say this was slightly cheaper than in the UK.

There are plenty of cafes for a quick coffee in the cities and bigger towns and I would say they have become obsessed with the European pavement cafe style of life. For instance in Fremantle there must be more cafes, coffee shops and restaurants than you can shake a stick at. On a Saturday they are crowded all day long. Darling Harbour in Sydney has a huge choice of places to eat. So if you like eating out you will love it in Oz and the variety is enormous. Food from every country you can think of. Sea food meals are big too, thanks to the abundance of fish etc caught off the coasts. However the posher eating places are as expensive as the UK or even more.

HEALTH ISSUES

Now this will be a big question especially for people over 50. Some may have had problems and may be put off doing a trip like this. Britain and Australia have a reciprocal agreement for emergency treatment. This means what it says… if you suddenly fall ill, you can get free doctors visits and if you end up in a hospital it will be free, including the medicines. However if you are taking regular medicines like I am (for cholesterol and heart) you will have to pay for them.

You can get travel insurance, but every company I called in the UK would not insure you for a year. Quite why this is, I could never get an answer to this question. As I had left it to the last moment, I did not have time to go into it more. So look into this one long before you intend to go. I decided that as I was now quite fit. (I had had a heart attack due to artery blockage which in turn was due to very high cholesterol.) My Doctor told me that my chances now of another heart attack were extremely low as my weight was fine, my lipids were also fine and I was exercising regularly and felt great. Actually for most the need to get travel insurance because of the reciprocal agreement, is not necessary. Except for one thing; If you need to be repatriated back to the UK, then if you have no insurance it would be very expensive.

You can get private insurance in Australia, but I can't say at what price or what cover, as I did not look into this subject. One thing you must do as soon as you arrive and that is go to a Medicare shop, which are to be found in most areas and usually in large shopping centres. Tell them you have arrived for an extended holiday stay, show your passport and visa, and they will give you a Medicare card which is like a credit card. You show this to any Doctor or hospital (Australia wide) when needing attention.

If you need a prescription for your medications, go to a Doctors surgery show your card and you can see the Doctor and tell him what you need. In Oz they have a system of what is called bulk billing and what this means is that it is like our dentists, so called system. Some Doctors will not touch bulk billing where they bill the Government for all the visits made to them by people who cannot afford private health care. However even though in Perth there were hardly any Doctors who would do bulk billing, I found that when you told them you were a Brit on holiday, they did not charge you.

If you do have to pay for a Doctors visit it will be around $40, which you will have to claim off Medicare. You will have to pay for your medicines, which can work out very expensive. You do if you have your Medicare card, get a reduction, but it is not much. It was costing me for my three types of heart pills about $65 for a months supply (£26) However should you need to visit a specialist, as I did, they do not bulk bill, and you will have to pay in full and claim the costs back from Medicare. Medicare will need to see a letter saying the attention was necessary, and an invoice or receipt. A lot of bull as far as I am concerned and pretty one way too, as Aussies in the UK do not have to jump through hoops when they require ANY medical attention, even from a specialist. Of course one big problem to getting money back is if you are on the move all the time, and Medicare being a bureaucratic organisation, it is going to take them ages to process your claim.

It is apparent that in Australia they are having EXACTLY the same problems with their Health system as we do in the UK. IE long waiting lists, dirty hospitals, lack of Doctors and nurses, cockups by Doctors and everything else you can think of. So do not expect to get any better than you get in the UK. Maybe their private Health care system will give better quality than their State systems. On top of this do not forget that when in out of the way places, you are NOT going to get an ambulance in five minutes, if at all. The nearest Doctor may be hundreds of miles away. So if you have any health issues BE REALISTIC IN YOUR DELIBERATIONS.

It is mainly North of Perth and in the centre of Oz, that you will have the lack of healthcare due to the lack of towns in these areas. Have no illusions, parts of Oz are very remote and lacking in population. That is the lure for many, to visit those places and experience the lack of people and civilisation. I have just read a book on bush survival where the writer trekked for over a month up in NT and arriving at the Timor sea, and never saw a person, nor any sign whatsoever of humans or human habitation or signs of humans past or present. He was totally on his own apart from the flies!

COMMUNICATIONS IN OZ

From what I have said above about emergencies over health in remote places, this raises the issues of how do you communicate with the emergency services in times of trouble. I mean trouble from crashes, accidents of all sorts, and health emergencies. One way we all use in the UK and Europe to contact emergency services is the mobile phone. Although I have to say the service in the UK is rubbish in my opinion. I cannot even get a signal in the CENTRE OF BOURNEMOUTH!! I took a complete trip around Scotland and for much of the time I was out of signal. So what do you think it is going to be like in OZ?

Well I can tell you… it's even worse than the UK. Even in coastal areas which are quite near towns and cities, and you are on a MAJOR highway, you have no signal. Even in and around Major cities you are always running out of signal. So you have ABSOLUTELY NO CHANCE OF A SIGNAL IN THE MIDDLE OF NOWHERE!

The only way you can be assured of a constant way to phone, is to use a satellite phone. These can be bought at a cost of about $2500 or hired. If you are into paying for one of these, start by going to a Telstra shop as they are dealers in sat phones (Telstra are the equivalents to BT) Maybe a phone bought in the UK will be cheaper. Also the calls and monthly line costs are quite high. Certainly higher than a normal landline. You takes your choice on this one.

Another cheaper way to have communication is to buy a CB Radio which I am sure you have all heard of. Cost for a good set is about $300 and you will find that many caravaners and 4WD people have these sets and they communicate on Channel 18. Also all truck drivers (Truckies in OZ) have these sets and they use channel 40. However I found that when I listened to truckies talking, I could never understand a word of what they said, their Oz accent being accentuated on the air. So should you have to use channel 40 and get talking to a truckie, tell them to talk slowly and clearly otherwise you will not understand anything. If it is an emergency tell them it is and it is essential they speak clearly so as to save time, nor mistakes and misunderstandings. I am sure they would understand. On top of this, dotted around the country they have volunteers who listen in, on their emergency channel 6. So you stand some chance of getting in touch with someone, if you keep trying. All modern sets have a device that will automatically scan all the channels and when it comes upon one that has someone on it, it will stop on that one and you can then break in and announce yourself and that you seek help. Another set is the High Frequency transmitter which will send signals long distance, however these are expensive and not many travellers have them.

Using a mobile as a general phone is EXTREMELY expensive in Oz. As you will have no address you will have to use, as I did, a pay as you go system. I took my UK Nokia phone with me and was able to just put in their simcard at a cost of $90 with about $60 free calls. However thereon it is costly, is the cost of the calls which are in my opinion very high. The only way to get cheap calls is to ring after 8pm. I called the UK at 11pm and spoke for about 3 minutes for a $1, which is fine. However, many of your calls within Oz will have to be done during working hours and then a $30 dollar refill will fly away!

One thing that makes mobile calls expensive is the heavy use of automated answering machines. If you ring just about any company you will have to spend minutes going through the endless steps, (just like in the UK) then when you think you will be put through to a human being, they put you on hold, as the human is busy! In the meantime your phone has just used up $3 of credit and you still haven't spoken to anyone.

Using the Internet. Many caravan parks have internet machines, which in some places can cost $1 for 10 minutes, which is too much. In the big cities, the suburbs will not have internet cafes or lounges unless it is an area where many students are or backpackers, or it is a seaside/beach area.

In country towns, some will have an internet place, many will have nothing. All libraries have computers which they will sometimes let you use for free and some will charge. Most backpacker hostels have access and to non residents too. So mostly you will have it, but sometimes at a price. I found that in big cities I was able most of the time to piggy back on someone else's wireless connection, as a lot did not have a secure system. So I saved a lot of money this way.

RADIO AND TV RECEPTION

As in the UK, radio transmissions are on Medium Wave and FM. Aussies stations are either commercial and mostly rubbish in my 'oldy' opinion. Aunty ABC is their equivalent of our BBC, although not as good. I say this not to knock them but it is a fact. There are several regional ABC services and they transmit from each area. In my opinion on their ordinary ABC stations, there is not enough variety such as you get in the UK. If your like me and only listen to Radio 2, because it plays music from your younger days and it has many interesting announcers who change during the day and a few interesting programmes, you will not get that in Oz. Mainly it is non stop talking about subjects you will find totally boring, like the local price of feed or sheep. Or callers who ring in and twitter on about local issues that even Aussies cannot possibly be interested in, and little music seems to get played. The outside World doesn't exist, so you will not hear much about international things. Forget about the commercial radio stations. For as I have said, they are for youngsters. When I was there in the sixties they played lots of good music. Now it is all sport and endless talk on sport, talk shows, rubbish music, when it gets played, and endless manic commercials.

I found that the ONLY station I could listen to was ABC's 24 hour news programme. Whilst you may think that to listen to a news station solidly for hours, would be too boring. This station has regular inputs from BBC, United States, Holland and Germany so you are getting not just news from them, but general interest stories covering the whole World. The BBC has several hour and half hours slots throughout the day and you get to know what is going

on not only from the UK, but Worldwide. However I found it totally frustrating that they only transmit this station in the capital cities. So when outside these and in the country or bush, you will not get this, their best programme.

If you want music, my suggestion is take your own CD's and tapes and play your own. This is also because you will not get any stations in many areas of Oz, even in places on the East Coast where you would think you were near enough to civilisation to still be able to pick up radio. Not good enough for any country in the 21st Century, even if it is a big place. If nuclear war broke out, you would never know if you were in Oz and not in a city area. Radio is the medium that governments use to warn their citizens in times of emergencies, except in Australia.!! I found it very frustrating that if I was listening to a station while in a town or city, as soon as I moved to about 30 K's away from it, bang went the station. Also I found that the ABC stations got transmitted on different wavelengths in different parts of the country. Quite why this is so I can't work out, as in the UK no matter where in the UK you are, radio 2 is pretty much on the same frequency wherever you are.

TV has only five stations ABC, Channels 7,9,10 and SBS. You see very few satellite dishes and there are hardly any companies that deal in satellite TV. You can buy satellite dishes for caravans which will enable you to pick up the channels I have already mentioned above. These cost around $500 so if you are a desperado for a diet of TV then this will be a must. You cannot pick up Sky news or sport or BBC World or a lot of the satellite channels that you can in the UK or Europe. You will see in the lists of TV programmes on each day, that there are about 20 odd channels you can receive in Oz, but they can only be picked up via cable. I can assure you they would not really be worth it even if you were to rent a house or flat for a long time. In the pubs you will see many have the large screen TV's as they do in the UK and they are showing sport. These do pick up Sky Sports and show the UK matches. However the pubs have to have extremely large screens that need a licence to erect and they do not allow householders to erect such large dishes.

What I can say about TV in Oz is that like radio, the reception can be very poor, even when your in towns. So all in all I think that in Oz they are light years behind Europe and the US. On top of this I found all the commercial TV channels were really all rubbish and not worth looking at. The saving grace is ABC TV which luckily seems to be an offshoot of BBC and other Brit TV channels. So you can see decent programmes most nights even if some of them you will have seen a few years back. Some of you will not mind about whether or not there is or isn't good TV as you will want to get away from it. With me, I love TV in the evening as being on my own, it fills in the evenings. But not to spending $500 just to watch ABC, Aussie wide.

AUSSIE ROADS AND FREEWAYS

The roads in Oz vary a lot from great, to terrible. From modern world class Motorways to dirt tracks. Due to the distances, you do not get Motorways that connect the capital cities. All the motorways or Freeways as they call them, are in and around the big cities. They are designed to get commuters in and out of the dormitory suburbs and into the city centres. So the highways that connect all the major towns and cities are either dual carriageway or just what we would call 'A' roads. Some are not up to scratch, some are good. The roads in the Northern Territory are not up to scratch and also the NSW roads are debatable. Sydney has the worst city roads, followed by Melbourne. Perth roads were very good, Adelaide and Brisbane are not bad. Non highway roads equivalent to our 'B' roads can also range from good to poor. Non sealed roads can range from well looked after, that is to say graded frequently and not too loose or suffering from corrugations. They can be two lanes wide or one lane wide. Some can be little more than tracks which are windy and uneven with ruts, holes and other horrors. Those are best traversed with a 4WD vehicle and not cars, vans, motorhomes or caravans.

In areas where they have wet seasons, some sealed roads can suffer from flooding in dips and hollows. Bridges over creeks, can get washed away in the worst circumstances. It is surprising how many Aussies get swept away in vehicles and drowned, trying to ford a small river that has burst its bank or where there is usually a shallow ford which becomes a deep raging torrent with a flash flood. So do not try to drive through water you do not absolutely know how deep it is, especially if there has been a lot of rain recently. Unsealed roads can become impassable even to 4WD, as they become quagmires.

Buy yourself good road maps which show clearly all the roads and tracks, their type and where you can get petrol in the outback. If going into the deep bush where most will not be going, it is wise to have maps that show Longitude and Latitude, so with your hand held GPS you can at any time work out exactly where on the map you are.

Road signs in Oz can be very good or very bad, and almost non existent at many junctions. I found Perth to be particularly bad in this respect. Many junctions simply did not exhibit ANY road name signs, so it made it very difficult to know when to turn or where you were. Many signs when they were there, are either small and unreadable or stuck on poles where you couldn't see them, or where you would necessary look. Signs telling you which direction a town or suburb was as you came up to junctions were either absent or stuck somewhere silly or right on the junction and your in the wrong lane to turn. Out on the highways the direction signs were generally OK and it was mainly in cities and towns I found them poor. So you will need to have a GOOD navigator who is quick and observant, when in towns and cities. For those who will have a wife doing navigation… my commiserations! Alternatively she drives and you navigate!

AUSSIE DRIVERS

Here I have direct and relevant experience of what Aussie drivers are all about and I have spent a lifetime in the auto fields and have driven in over 50 countries often driving high powered very fast cars. Not to mention I spent three years teaching young Aussies how to drive, both in Perth and in Sydney and ran a driving school in London. I was taught to drive by the Metropolitan Police Driver Training School at Hendon when I was in the RAF Police.

So throughout this tome I will be commentating heavily on all matters to do with driving, cars, roads and safety issues, as you the reader will be making your way round Oz by some sort of vehicle. So this subject is the most importance to you. So I make no apologies for this.

I am afraid to report that things do not appear to have improved too much during the past 40 years. Although in some areas things have improved, but judging by what I read in the papers and on TV they still have the same problems now as they were talking about 30 to 40 years ago.

In the 60's Aussie drivers were rated as being only slightly better than the Belgians at driving, (the Belgians then had no driving test) and they were rated the Worlds worst. This is taking into account the number of accidents, injuries and deaths. I do not know where in the Worlds rating they are now, but I would think and hope they have got better.

The main reasons for the horrendous accident and death rates 30/40 years ago were…. very poor roads, easy driving tests, poor road layouts, some stupid laws like always giving way to the right, drunken drivers, young kids able to pass an easy test and then jump straight into a 500 horsepower V8 engined killing machine. The mindset of the average Aussie male, especially the young ones, the boredom when driving hundreds of miles a day on generally straight roads and losing concentration or going to sleep. All these things contributed to the high death toll.

Some things have improved, but by the look of it, some haven't. So I will deal with the points raised in the above comments:-

Roads have improved. In the cities and even in small towns some junctions have improved and many of the intersections, which you get a great deal of with their grid pattern layouts, have now got small roundabouts, in them. You see before when there was just a straight forward intersection, many did not even have a stop line or even a give way dotted line. It was dog eat dog. Result, many bad collisions caused by aggressive drivers not even slowing down let alone giving way. Also as I mentioned above they had this stupid rule that you always had to give way to the car coming from your right. This even applied if you were driving along on a main road and a car wanted to join off a side road, you had to give way to it even if you were too close and doing 30mph +. I do not have to tell you how many accidents that caused. That law has gone. There are more Freeways now and they are safer as we all know. However many of their freeways are not up to the standard of ours. Many do not have the central barriers or barriers where they should have them, say at the sides, and next to deep drops.

Many connecting highways outside cities and towns which were gravel, are now wider and tarmacked. Speed limits have been brought down and they are using speed cameras and guns. So there is not quite the rampant speeding I used to see before. But it is still there and 99% of all cars drive at, at least 10K's over the limits.

One thing that aids speedsters and nutcases is that in Oz you are legally able to undertake, and the brainless who seem to think that even in heavy traffic, if they weave in and out they will get there quicker. You can undertake in the USA, but there unlike in Oz, you can be done if a policeman thinks you are overdoing it in order to speed. The Aussies should do likewise.

Driving tests have raised their standards but not enough I believe. This is because you still see a general poor standard of driving from young drivers who haven't had their licences long.

Then there is the Aussie male with his macho mindset, especially the younger ones. Many are pure Neantherdals and drive as such, plus a love of showing off and speed. They have this absolutely stupid lack of any law to stop these blockheads from immediately after getting their licence from going out and buying a high powered car. In Oz many Fords and Holdens are V8 powered. They always were and they are still churning out high powered standard saloons for the idiots. It was a bone of contention in the 60's and it still is there now. They talked about it endlessly in the papers then and they are still just talking about it. Young Aussie males are killing themselves and others with monotonous regularity. They hit other cars, come off the road, turn over, hit trees etc etc. They do not wear seat belts and are ejected.

You see in Oz in their lack of wisdom over these matters, you can buy a car and you do not even have to approach an insurance company to get insurance. Because as I have said, when you pay to register the car in your name, you are obliged to pay for the compulsory third party insurance, which young kids get easily. Hey presto the young idiot with his hotted up Holden V8 which he has just bought is now a lethal killing machine. It is bad enough in the UK with young male drivers, but it is much worse here. This because in the UK you have to get insurance through an independent insurance company who just price kids off the road and from buying higher powered cars. Although in the UK lots of the yobbo's do not even get insurance. The answer for both countries is to combine the best of both countries. Make it compulsory for ALL drivers under 25 to get compulsory third party through the State at registration time, and compulsory comprehensive insurance through a independent insurance company, who will make the rate so high on high powered machines that they will not be able to afford it. In Oz it is compulsory to carry your car documents with you so when stopped you have to show your 'rego' documents. They should do that in the UK as well, to stop people from not registering the cars in their name and taxing it. You will have to do more roadside checks in both countries. To wrap it up in a nutshell, when in Oz beware of young drivers in their noisy V8 engined hot cars (and they are everywhere) Avoid driving at night as well, because it is at night that they come out (they call them HOON drivers in Oz, but I do not know where they got that expression from and I always laugh when I see Hoon, MP on the telly.

In Oz a new driver has to show a P plate on their car after they have passed their test, and show it for a year. I cannot get over the number of P plate cars I see that are V8's and hot cars, like modern Supras, and Subaru Imprezzas which are seriously fast, and being driven by some young pimply kid with no more brains than a big toe.

Another thing that is rampant with the Oz males, is drag racing and doing wheelies. Smoking the tyres and losing many dollars as they lay down on the tarmac, inches of tyre rubber. You will see very quickly just how rampant this practice is as soon as you arrive, and start driving. All over Australia the roads are COVERED with wavy black rubber lines. Even in the middle of the Nullabour they were there. It is a gross case of highway tyre graffiti and I hate it every time I see it. Mostly this is done at night and it is against the law and if caught they can lose their cars, but of course they still do it. They are showing on TV, cases of people who are sick of the noise etc of these Hoons wrecking the peace and safety of some of the suburbs. It's a hoot man...you know what I mean man? Cool baby!

'God give me patience' as me Mum used to say when exasperated.

However I have to also point out that older Oz male drivers can be a pain too especially in country towns and in the outback. Many of these like back home, have never taken a test or if they did, it was so long ago it was a joke. Because of the lack of traffic they are not traffic wise and drive in a dream or half asleep. They simply are not aware of other cars. Beware especially on long straight, two lane roads. Head-ons are always happening in the outback and remote roads, as drivers lose concentration, and wander about or nod off. BE VIGILANT AT ALL TIMES AND WATCH ONCOMING CARS LIKE A HAWK. ESPECIALLY TRUCKS! Truckies drive too fast and for too long, without rests, and take speed etc to keep awake. It is rampant in Oz. In fact I would urge you to drive all the times, outside towns, with your headlights full on. I have noticed that Aussie drivers are doing this a lot now.

Lastly, the big issue about drunken drivers. If you think that it is bad enough in the UK with drink drivers, 'you aint seen nuttin yet' Well in Oz it is a rampant disease, and always has been, and it does not appear to have diminished. It was on the TV that a well known minister has lost his licence for drink driving, not to mention just recently a well known Judge and a well known solicitor. The Police do stop more drivers at night to check for drinkers, but it obviously does not have the effect they are looking for. Of course it is a well known fact that Aussies are big drinkers and this is why there is the problem. If you think that we have a big enough drinkers problem in the UK, then it is exactly the same here with city street fighting etc and drunk drivers.

You may think I am painting a grim picture of life on the Oz roads. You may think Bloody Hell I am not going to bother going now... I will end up in hospital or dead. Well calm down, (as the famous scouse said) because I am only painting the picture for you at its worst. You know the saying 'Forewarned is forearmed' well that's quite true. If you know the worst facts about life on the roads here, you can drive defensively to avoid trouble. Listen, I have driven in and on the worst roads on the planet. Including ten years in OZ! I am still here and I have NEVER had an accident abroad... only minor bumps in English heavy traffic, at low speeds. DEFENSIVE DRIVING IS THE KEY WORD. Also do not drive at night, especially in the country, take regular stops, do not drive if drowsy, under no circumstances drink and drive or take drugs and you will survive.

After I had been right round the country and experienced all the different roads and drivers, I can report a few more observations. Truly, the sign posting as I have said can be very frustrating, especially street name signs in the cities. Too many intersections with no names whatsoever. As for drivers, I have come to the firm conclusion that 99.99% of them, including women, are habitual speedsters. In the UK about 50% observe the limits, but here no one does. My motorhome would not do much more than 100kph. I averaged 85kph. Even when I was on a motorway and went up to 100 if I wanted to get a move on, I would be passed by 100% of the drivers coming up behind me, all of them tailgating like mad.

As far as I am concerned allowing trucks to do 110kph is absolute lunacy. Many do over this, and I am talking here of trucks that are much bigger generally (see photo 1b), than the UK or European ones. They are at least in general; twice as big and longer than ours, and it is quite frankly frightening when one of these monsters roars past you at 120kph. Do they not realise how long it must take to stop one of these heavyweights? Coming down the motorway past Newcastle I watched in my mirror one lunatic truckie came roaring down the third lane, then swerve into the middle lane, and then pass a whisker away from me, at about 125kph! And they wonder why all the time, why there is such a horrendous accident and death rate, in Oz?

WEATHER

Now I am sure a lot of people will have erroneous ideas of what weather is to be found in the whole of Oz. Many I am sure will think it is always sunny and warm, even in their Winters. Let me put you right. Sure all States with the exception of maybe Tasmania, have plenty of sunshine. However Oz is a country of extremes. The weather whilst I was there has highlighted this fact. I arrived in Sydney at the end of their Winter and was there during their Spring. We had days that were really sunny and quite warm. Warm enough for the beaches to be packed and people swimming. Then the next day would be overcast, cold and windy and it may rain quite a lot. Days when it would be cold and you needed a heater on in the evenings, and days when it would rain buckets all day. Boy when it rains in Oz no matter where you are it can absolutely pour down in torrents. So you get flash flooding and on hillsides you can get mudslides as they give way. Trees can get blown over if there is wind at the same time. Hail storms with hail the size of tennis balls can happen at any time even in the Summer and it happened one day in mid Summer, whilst I was there. Also on another Summers day IT SNOWED A HEAVY SNOW FALL up in the Snowies, in Victoria/NSW. In Queensland especially, you can get tropical storms that wreak havoc with the winds and rain. North Western Australia you also get monsoonal weather with lashings of rain and wind. Huge lightning storms are another thing and they set off bush fires. You can get earthquakes (I have been in two quite big ones) and you can get the odd whirlwinds. Not as big as in say Texas, but big enough.

Have I put you off? Well don't panic as the worst of what you can experience does not happen all the time, and you would have to be unlucky to experience something as bad as the worst you can get. Let's not forget that even in the

UK you can get all sorts of bad weather at unusual times. Generally the weather will be OK with reasonable temperatures and lots of sunshine, and the Winters are milder in most places, than in the UK. Even in the colder Winters, you will have to use a good duvet and pyjamas and maybe even a small heater in your room at night. But you are not going to absolutely freeze, except if you are several thousand feet up in the mountain areas or in Tasmania with winds coming in directly from the Antarctic. Up in the dry Northern areas of the Northern Territory and North Western Australia, it can be extremely hot in the Summer months and here I am talking temperatures in the 40's and even 50's. In and around the Darwin areas, it is also humid. So best to visit out of Summer months. Also, as I have said, it is the rainy monsoon season in their Summer.

WHAT ARE THE AUSSIES LIKE AS PEOPLE

Well I could be very contentious here, but I will resist the urge. I do think that they have changed for the better somewhat, to what they were like in the 60's, or even the 80's. The younger ones especially. There was quite an underlying anti British feeling and Pom bashing in those days. I put it down to what went on in the first and second World Wars. They felt our generals treated them badly especially at Gallipoli. Of course here they were right and I could never stand the British Officer set myself, when I was in the Forces. So much so that I tried to not salute any officer if I could get away with it. Some Aussies are still trying to get over Jardine (the 30's bodyline Brit bowler who sorted their batsmen out and being bad losers they had to blame him) even though their current bowlers give no quarter themselves. A lot of older Aussies are of Irish stock and they are still trying to forgive us over the potato famine of the 1800's, or for sending their great, great, Grand Fathers out there for stealing a piece of bread in the early 1800's. I get the impression that a lot of that has died out now, and so it should have, too. I never once on this trip heard the name Pommy being used in the anti way it had been used to me when I was here previously. We the Brits, are their closest kin even today, and we have the most in common with them out of all the immigrants they have let in their country. We can be relied on to be on their side in times of strife, more than anyone else in the World. One has to ask why so many of them still come in their droves to the UK for working holidays, and why so many young Brits go to OZ for the same reason. It is because we both feel instantly at home in each others countries because of the bonds that tie us together.

This is why it is such a good place for we Brits to visit, a country that we feel at home in, amongst a majority of people we are really our kith and kin. A country that has freedom and wide open spaces with endless blue skies and warm sun and wonderful seas, all in relative safety, compared to many places that I could mention, where I would have been happy to visit 30 years ago, but wouldn't touch with a bargepole now.

We do have banter with them over such things like sport, but I believe it is all in good spirit, for the most anyway. We secretly wish that Brit sports men and women could be as good as they are, but we can forgive them when they beat us, because what the hell, they are almost British and they are playing games that we invented and taught them anyway!

Are they welcoming and friendly, these natives? I think that generally most Aussies are very friendly and ready to strike up a conversation, especially if you instigate one. In the service industries that you will mainly come into contact with, you will find them mostly very helpful and friendly, although I have found in out of the way places in the outback, or even just out in the country areas, you will still find grumpy unfriendly types who are not so nice and helpful.

Obviously when you are travelling, you may not come into contact with so many of the ordinary citizens who are not in the service industries who rely on tourists like you to make a living off. You will only get a true picture as to how friendly Aussies are towards us Brits if you were working and living amongst them. However I get the feeling that you would find the majority of them will be still be kindly disposed to you.

That is not to say that everyone is just great. On my trip I did come across some stinkers and one thing you have to watch out for is the Oz 'rip off merchant'. You only have to watch their politicians and the way they are always getting involved in graft. Not to mention their businessmen ripping off the Public and shareholders. They have had some big cases whilst I have been here. Then there are their Police and here I am not a lover of any Police, even UK Police. But here they are a shower. Most are built like brick dunnies (shithouses) and have brains to match. Again whilst I was there, there were high profile cases of their wonderful Police shooting dead people (3 in Melbourne in 3 months), practicing their national pastime of killing Aborigines whilst in custody. Take the Police ratbag that pulled me over in Adelaide and accused me of using my mobile phone whilst driving. I was listening to my little mobile radio which was clipped to the side window and I had its ear piece in my ear. I was pressing it into my ear with my left hand as the engine was making a racket due to the fact I was going slow in heavy traffic. When stopped, I pointed out I was wearing an ear piece and I went and got my phone and keyed in the record of calls received and made, and showed her that I had not made a call in days, nor received one. No, I had been on the phone… just could not admit she was wrong. I went to the Police HQ on that one and got it scratched, but what a pain. So take my advice and keep away from them if you can.

Whilst I was in Oz several Policemen were being done for corruption, and other matters, and just before I left all five of the highest coppers in the NSW police force, bar the top man, were being investigated and had been suspended. I think that tells all. All in all they are bad news.

I was watching the Police when I was in Sydney just before I left. You see more there on street patrol and what a scruffy lot they are. Baggy workman like dungaree trousers, stupid Yankee like baseball caps, and awful looking boots. Then they have leather belts within a million things hanging off them, just like the awful Yankie police do. (Ours are following suit too.) They did not fill me with any confidence and I thought they looked like a bunch of third World military police.

One thing that I do feel I have to warn travellers about especially, and that is, when travelling in the country and in the outback. There are many weirdos knocking about in Oz and I found this phenomena also in the USA, in similar out of the way places. Both countries because of their size and the fact that they have States which are mini countries with borders, with huge areas of nothing, they attract the weirdos, the criminals, the fugitives from the law etc. It is easy for someone who is a total bum, and who has committed crimes (sometimes serious crimes) to escape out into the bush. To blend into small communities where it is the norm for people to mind their own business and not ask questions. Where there are so many scruffy looking weirdo males anyway, that they blend in easily. There are countless shifty Oz males with a 'ute' or old panel van, who drift from one place to another. Picking up odd jobs here and there.

My advice is do not try to make friends with such weird looking drifters, keep them at arms length. Keep out of the pubs in grotty outback towns if they look dubious even if you are dying for a cold drink, especially at night. Whatever you do not stop for anyone when you are in the middle of nowhere. If you are confronted with what looks like a crash, be very, very careful. Do not get out of your vehicle unless you are absolutely sure it is 'dinkum' as they say in Oz. It could be a way to get you to stop and lure you out of your vehicle. (On this subject read a book not long out called 'Left for dead in the bush'.)

Keep a weapon of some sorts handy in your cab. I kept a very hefty wheel brace in my drivers door pocket plus a decent sized kitchen knife which I used for general DIY, but very sharp. Keep your doors locked if you come across what looks like an accident, before you decide it is safe to get out, and if there are two of you, one stays in the cab with the doors locked. Always keep the side door locked as well when on the move in lonely places, so no one can hop in that way.

One has only to remember what happened to the UK couple in the Northern Territory when one of these criminal/ drifters got them to stop by intimating there was something wrong with their vehicle. They were trusting and stopped and the male got out. We know how fatal that decision he made was. As he ended up being shot. (Peter Falconio) Plus the young nutter who threw a young English woman backpacker off a bridge recently. You have to use as much common sense as possible, and do not trust anyone at face value. But then this is the same anywhere these days. We live in dangerous times and it can happen in the UK or Europe or anywhere. However there are more chances here for them to melt away, due to the vastness of the place and these scum know that help can be non existent, if you cannot even get a phone signal to summon it, and even if you could it would take a long time to reach you. I do not want to scare you off, but many people who have not travelled a lot can be too trusting and naive, no matter where they are.

WILDLIFE

I don't mean the hairy weirdos that I have been warning you about above. I mean the real wildlife of Oz, which is what a lot of people want to see when they come to Oz. The most well known animal is of course the Kangaroo. They will not be in every field and I travelled from Sydney to Perth and had not seen one live kangaroo. Plenty of dead ones

though. You will see them mostly in the evening and night times, and for that reason it is why I have said you should not drive at night. They get blinded by the headlights and freeze on the road. Or they bound out in front of you unexpectedly. Hitting one will cause much damage, even with a roo bar. It can put your vehicle out of action. So why risk it if you are not in a hurry? Wallabies are just smaller kangaroos and can still mess your vehicle up. In the Northern Territory Camels and Water Buffalo are another menace to watch out for on the road.

Do not swim in waterholes or creeks in the North of Western Australia , the Northern Territory or Queensland because of saltwater and fresh water crocodiles. You have been warned! Just lately in Queensland near Brisbane the kiddies were swimming in the LOCAL MUNICIPAL SWIMMING POOL, and a croc had got into it! Luckily it was a small one. Tourists regularly provide crocs with food by stupidly ignoring all warnings and swimming in infested waters. A croc can travel at 60Klm an hour for short bursts, you cannot outrun it!

It isn't even safe to camp near waterholes, rivers or even on sea shores where there may be crocs. When I was there a family were camping in Northern Queensland on the sea shore and a large seawater croc entered a tent whilst people were asleep and latched onto the husband. His wife bravely jumped on it and managed to get it off by poking it in the eyes. She was badly bitten.

Oz has the biggest selection of poisonous spiders and snakes. You will probably never see any of them, but be aware, and if you walk in the bush, wear good boots and keep your senses awake and be alert. It would be a good idea when you get to Oz to buy a book on snakes and spiders etc that has plenty of pictures, so you can identify them if you did come across any. Mostly they will want to get away from humans, so do not panic. Again it is down to following rules and being sensible.

Nice wild life can give you lots of pleasure. Oz is a bird watchers paradise with hundreds of varieties. You will not see anywhere near all of them but what you will see is fantastic. I spent hours just watching the common birds that you get around towns. These can include Brit birds like sparrows, blackbirds, swallows, crows, Oz magpies (a little bigger than ours) and starlings. Then there are honey eaters, parakeets, galahs, cockatoos, (black and white) Ibis, black Swans, Currawongs, blue wrens, red capped robins, curlews, etc.

Out on the road you will see Emus, Alpacas, lizards of all sorts, skinks, dingoes (do not treat them as if they are like household dogs) wild cats, echinidas, wombats, and so on.

Off the coasts you can see whales, seals and dolphins and in certain places penguins. Plus a wide variety of sea birds. If it is of great interest to you then I suggest you read up on all the wildlife of Oz plus their vegetation, as the subject is too extensive a one for me to adequately cover here.

MUSEUMS

You will find many museums all over Oz. Some large, many quite small and specialised. Some are quite good and many I found to be amateur and not up to scratch, especially if they charge admission, as many do. Even a lot of the bigger museums run by Councils in the big cities are mainly in my opinion not up to World standards. I believe they could do much better than they do. However you have to take what you are offered, and make do. So visit them and see for yourself what they have to offer and make your own conclusions. You will learn something anyway.

SAFETY TIPS FOR GENERAL TRAVEL

Mostly it is all common sense as with most things. I have already covered the health aspect of things, but will reiterate that you should be in good health, not perfect health, but generally good and not liable to come down at any time with some horrendous medical problem. Of course those of us who have had a heart attack could always have another one. But generally you will know how you are and if you like me have not suffered from a heart that itself is diseased, and merely had an attack through a blockage, but now the reason you had a blockage has been dealt with and is under control, then go for it.

Make sure you take a good emergency first aid kit. Include all the usual things like aspirin or paracetamol, bandages of all sorts, antiseptic creams, TCP, sleeping tablets, acidity tablets, tablets in case you get a dose of the runs, tablets in case you get constipated, rolls of elastoplast or similar, insect bite sprays or creams, gastrolyte tabs for dehydration, surgical gloves, surgical dressings, cotton wool, alcohol swabs, cotton balls and tips, sterile surgical blades, scissors, tweezers, splinter probe, zinc oxide cream, sunscreen, adhesive blister pads if you intend to do a lot of walking, medicated soap, and anything else you feel may be of use. You cannot take enough, but on the other hand you cannot take a whole pharmacy with you.

It may be a good idea to take a first aid course if you have never done one. What you will learn can't be bad. Basically on the subject of safety and first aid, it all depends on exactly what kind of trip you intend to undertake. If you are going to do like 90% of all travellers do in Oz and that is stick to the main roads, then you are not going to need as much in the way of safety gear. However once you deviate off the beaten track especially if you are going to do any walking in the middle of nowhere, then you need to have more and know more. If you break down on a tarmacked highway then it's not going to be too long before someone happens along, even if you do not have any means to raise an alarm. If it is a medical emergency then you should know how to deal with as much as possible, in order to be able to last until the alarm can be raised and real medical help can arrive.

Other safety aims are to make sure your vehicle in good order and not likely to break down. Have a good tool set, be able to take a wheel off, have two spare wheels with tyres, if possible, or like me carry four inner tubes so if you get punctures and run out of spare wheels, you have the ability to put in a tube. You will need tyre levers and know how to use them. One tip on how to break the tyre off the rim is to jack up the hub high enough to set the wheel and tyre under the hub, then lower the weight of the vehicle and the hub, down onto the tyre at the point where it joins the rim. This should push it off. Make sure you have a decent wheel brace that is strong enough and long enough to give you leverage. Nuts can be very hard to shift if they have been on for ages. Also carry an air pump that is operated off the battery. It is also a good idea to carry a battery charger as well, especially one that allows you to turn the motor over to start it without waiting for the battery to fully charge. I also carried a 240 Volt generator, so if I had to stop anywhere were there was no mains, I could operate everything and use the charger. Expensive, but can be used in so many other areas such as on a boat, or back at home in case of blackouts.

Specific safety devices such as hand held VHF radios are OK as if you are near the coast you could raise a ship or boat and aircraft use VHF. A GPS is handy, as then you will always know exactly where you are. A compass, and be able to know how to use one, and especially if you are going off track, an EPIRB beacon which when set off will send a signal to a satellite giving your exact position. If you take a UK EPIRB then you stand the best chance as that signal will be picked up by Falmouth which is monitored 24/7. I have heard of EPIRBS being set off in the Southern Hemisphere that were not picked up, so maybe in this area if the EPIRB is Southern registered one, the service isn't so great, who knows. Luckily with me doing my sailing, I had all this gear and took it with me, and thankfully never had to use it.

Always carry plenty of spare fuel, and water is a BIG must. You will see from the photos of my home that I fitted a large aluminium box onto the back. In this I carried two 25 litre cans of diesel, a 25 litre plastic container of drinking water, a hydraulic floor jack to easily lift up the vehicle, a winch to pull me out of any situation, if I went off road or got bogged down, and this with a long strap. Plus a spare 9Kg gas bottle, a plastic 10 litre container for unleaded fuel for my scooter. A large container of diesel oil, some oil for the two stroke scooter, brake fluid, various straps and bungies, a ground sheet, and an air pump. Couldn't get the gas stove or kitchen sink in though!

Inside the home I carried another two plastic containers of drinking water totalling 25 litres, which I kept in the toilet/shower cubicle. I reckon I had two months worth of drinking water (for one person), as many places inbetween the big cities have awful water and if the worst happened in the bush I would not run out of the elixir of life for quite some time. I filled them all up in Perth before I left for the great wide open spaces of the unknown! I also carried a sleeping bag just in case I ever had to leave the home, and a back pack of reasonable size. Of course in my case my scooter would have been a good secondary way of being able to move on, but that was limited to how much distance it would go as the petrol tank only held 5 litres which would give me 230 Kilometres, but my spare scooter petrol container would give me extra mileage. So I reckon I was covered every which way.

During my time in Oz and near the end of the trip, two youngish men died in the WA outback from breaking down in an old Landrover that was knackered to begin with, right out on a little used track. They were hopelessly prepared and had little water, tools or anything. They tried to find water with no success even though they were close to a well, and they died where they broke down due to no one coming along, and in 50 degree heat. They were not found for a week. Mind you I have always said that there are some incredibly stupid people around.

Always have a good sharp knife and maybe carry a stone to keep it sharpened, have water proof matches and or lighters and a good flashlight. Water purification tablets are also a must, just in case.

But do get to know how you can treat water and find water or catch it from condensation or dew.

BOOKS YOU COULD GET TO READ UP ON :-

Australian Bush Survival Skills, *Kevin Casey. Kimberley Publications. Mt Gravatt, Qld.*
Australias Reptiles, *Steve Wilson, Angus & Robertson.*
Bush Food, *Jennifer Isaacs, Ure Press.*
Bush Medicine, *Tim Low, Angus & Robertson.*
Camping & Caravanning across Australia, *Ian Read , Little Hills Press.*
Camps Australia wide, *Philip Procter,*
Caravanning Outback Australia, *Lloyd Junor, Aussie Outback Publishing.*
Dangerous Australians, *Bay Books.*
Explore Wild Australia, *Les Hiddens. 4WD in remote Oz places.*
Safe Outback Travel, *Jack Absalom, Five Mile Press.*
SAS Survival Handbook, *John Wiseman, Harper Collins.*

There will be other books in addition to this and many books of maps and specific trips worked out for you. Books like the Lonely Planet which deal with Oz in detail and is invaluable for doing the trip, plus books on the individual States, and many books on the history of Australia. The sky is the limit as to just how much you want to swot up on. Then of course you can hunt about on the net and see what you can find as well.

Chapter Two

Sydney: Sights and History

When you talk to anyone outside Australia about the country, Sydney is the one place that people identify as being Australia. Of course it isn't, as it is merely a city within Australia. However it receives so much media attention that anything to do with Australia is going to heavily include Sydney. After all it was Sydney that was the first place where settlement took place and it was in being for some 30 years before any of the other four big cities even got started.

On top of all this Sydney is undoubtedly the most photogenic of all the cities of Australia, the one with that lovely big beautiful harbour and two of the most photographed monuments of Australia, namely the Harbour Bridge and the Opera House. It is also the largest of the capital cities and the most vibrant.

Certainly I like the place more than all the other cities and I have lived in during the time that I have spent in Australia. It is my most favourite city in the World, and I have been to most of the big important cities of the World. So it had to be the place where I would start my tour of Oz, and where I would spend most of my time exploring and re-exploring.

Captain Cook on his visit to Australia during his voyage of exploration of the World, first stopped in Botany Bay in 1770, but it was Port Jackson as Sydney Harbour is officially called, that was to be the place to start any settlement in this new land. So it was on Jan 18, 1788, that the first fleet arrived at Botany Bay commanded by a Captain Philip, with 586 Male convicts and 191 females and 13 children, but unlike the time when Cook was there, which was during the Winter when there was some water and green grass around, when Captain Philip arrived it was mid Summer and dry and uninviting. So he upped sticks and moved up the coast to where he knew there was probably another harbour. Capt Cook had seen the double headlands entrance after he left Botany Bay and surmised that this was an entrance to another harbour. But he was in a hurry to get on to Pacific Isles to view the passage of Venus that was about to happen. What a wonderful harbour it turned out to be and which Philip named Port Jackson. They chose to land at a Cove, at what is now Sydney Cove, and the mighty city was to have its humble beginnings here. There was reasonable soil and good water from a stream which they called the Tank Stream. A few weeks later a ship with some convicts on set off up the coast to eventually find Norfolk Island which had abundant water and good soils, and they settled there. In fact life there was so much better than the early beginnings at Sydney, so for some time Norfolk had a higher population than Sydney.

Capt Phillip did some exploring and came across a good site some 30 kilometres west and up a river that fed the harbour. It was decided that this area would be good for farming and it was named Rose Hill and later renamed Parramatta. In 1790 a second fleet arrived with more convict settlers and what is more important, much needed further provisions. The third fleet arrived in 1791. So the settlement of Australia got off to a slow and difficult start.

Conditions were hard with the settlement constantly running low on the provisions that they had brought with them. The convicts were not farmers, and did not make willing workers to get down and get things up and started and to become self proficient in food. The British plants they brought with them did not fare well in the harsh Oz sun. So it took many years of toil and trials and experimentation with the new conditions in order to successfully get farming up and running. Plus there were the constant skirmishes that took place with the local Aborigines who rightfully resented the white people pinching their land.

Over the next 30 to 40 years other settlements were started up and were to become what we now know as Brisbane, Melbourne, Adelaide and Perth as well as Tasmania. All these places experienced the growing pains due to the terrain, weather, isolation and the general poor quality of the early settler stock, who were let's face it, unwilling settlers. Many tried to escape and were never heard of again. One group in Sydney thought that China was not far away to the North, and they escaped on foot to try to reach China and were never seen again.

All these five major cities of Australia do not have the same wealth of history that major cities and towns have in Europe, so do not expect to be able to see and flavour masses of historical places. Although Sydney because it was the first to be settled and from where all else emanated from, it does have a reasonable amount of history in the form of places and buildings. Many of the first structures that were put up were of poor quality and so did not last and it is only the Government buildings in the first instances that were built of any lasting quality. In 1789 the foundation stone was laid for Government House and was finished very soon afterwards. It was not a substantial building and was later pulled down and the site of the now Sydney Museum is on that spot.

In 1811 Governor MacQuarie laid the foundation of a building that was known as Rum Hospital. This was completed in 1816 and was later to become two buildings namely the Parliament House taking up two of the house wings and the remainder became the Mint Building. Both survive to this day. A new Government house was started in 1837 and finished in 1845 and still stands, and is situated next to the Botanical Gardens. MacQuarie was also responsible for the building of Hyde Park Barracks in what became known as MacQuarie Street. This street became a very fashionable street and still has many of the surviving 'grand' houses' that were built in early days. The oldest surviving residential house called Cadmans Cottage built in 1816 is still to be seen in Sydney Cove, down at the Circular Quay area of the Rocks. It was originally at the waters edge, so you will see how much of the original Cove has been infilled, as it is now some way back from the water.

Other notable buildings started in the early 1800's are the two Cathedrals, Anglican in1819, the Catholic Cathedral in 1821.

The Wentworth family who arrived on the First Fleet (may I point out here that Sydneysiders who can trace their ancestry to someone on that first fleet, think of themselves as Oz Royalty.) If you actually have a convict in your family your definitely IN!) Wentworth's father was a surgeon on the fleet and he married a woman convict who was also on that fleet, after they arrived at Sydney. They had a son called Charles and he became a well known barrister and was amongst the first of the high class people in Sydney's upper classes. He built Vaucluse House and it belonged to that dynasty for many years until after the last War, when it was finally bequeathed to the Nation. You can visit this house.

Sydney Cove is now where the Harbour Bridge, the Ferry Terminals, and the Sydney Opera House are. So it is in this area that the oldest Sydney houses and buildings of worth, that survive. The area around the Southern end of the bridge is called the Rocks, presumably as this area is very rocky, and this is were the houses for the early settlers and convicts were built, and today it forms a tourist attraction because of the older buildings and early history to be found there. It certainly has a flavour about it and it contains many pubs, restaurants, hotels and street markets.

On the East side of the Rocks, which abuts the Cove, is now the large passenger ship wharf along which all the big liners who call on Sydney, tie up to. On the other side of the Cove is the peninsular on which the Opera House was built on, and the part of the Cove which is the ferry terminal is called Circular Quay. It is all this area that is so familiar with peoples of the World and of course superimposed upon the Cove is the famous Sydney Harbour Bridge which was built by a British company in the thirties and which became the first iconic image of Sydney known to the World at large.

The city of Sydney and all the streets that housed the merchants and shops and shipping businesses, that ran to the West of the quay, and was built like all subsequent Oz towns and cities on the grid pattern of parallel streets. The second Governor, MacQuarie, was responsible for getting some order to the way the new town was laid out.

In 1791 coal was found in and around what is now Newcastle, just North of Sydney, and by 1804 convicts were taken there to start mining it, and to this day it still is a coal producing area and it is exported from that port.

Of course since the end of the last war, many of the old buildings were torn down and replaced with many tall skyscrapers and they add to the image of what Sydney looks like from the Harbour. Undoubtedly they did away with many fine buildings only to replace them with sterile lumps of concrete and glass, but I think they have realised this and will keep the better older buildings that are left, in order to give a sense of history and some lasting quality. You will see this repeated throughout all the five major cities.

Fifty years after the first fleet arrived the population of NSW was 98,126. Most of these people were in the Sydney areas and the rest scattered around the fast growing State. As a matter of interest from 1788 to 1840 just over 50 years, 161,500 convicts were brought to Oz, (so they had been quite busy) of which only 16,000 were women.

So what is worth looking at in Sydney? Well of course each to his or her own. I think the following should be worth a visit:- Governors House, the Botanical Gardens which are adjacent, Parliament House, the Old Hyde Park Barracks, the Mint, the Cathedral (Anglican), State Library, Australian Museum, the Catholic Cathedral, the Queen Victoria Building with its arcades, Hyde Park, China Town, Darling Harbour Complex with its Aquarium etc, Paddy's Market, The Power House Museum, The Bridge, (you can walk over the top of it if you can afford the $160 cost), and last but not least, the Opera House.

Other places outside the city itself worth visiting are the beachside areas of Bondi (of course), but also of Coogee (see photo 5) and Manly on the Northside. (take a ferry across to there) Also the Aquarium at Manly. Also take a ferry to Taronga Zoo and see indigenous Oz wildlife. If you can make it, get up to the Pittwater area and if you can afford it, hire a boat and explore all the nooks and crannies of this magnificent area.

Paramatta is well worth a look and a good way to get there is to take the ferry from Circular Quay all the way up the Paramatta River. Further to the west of Paramatta are the Blue Mountains and they are terrific. I will deal with both these places in detail, later on at the end of my trip as that is when I will visit those places.

Of course again if you can afford it, you could always hire some sort of power craft, and explore the whole of the Harbour. This harbour has to be seen to be believed with its many fingers and rivers and creeks, going off it. You could spend days doing this.

Take a trip to the Heads, as they are called. That is to say the eastern entrance of the Harbour, North of Bondi Beach and at Watsons Bay. A bus goes specifically there from Circular Quay. It is a National Park and Military reserve and it offers spectacular views of the entrance and the harbour at its sea end. Visit the Gap as well. A sheer cliff where many poor souls end their lives by jumping off into the boiling sea and rocks, hundreds of feet below. (This will interest the ghouls out there.)

Botany Bay to the South is worth going to see especially if you have a car or wheels, because you can visit both the North and South sides. The North side is known as La Perouse after the Froggy Captain who visited the Bay with two frigates a couple of days after the first fleet arrived. When they left a month or so later, they were never seen again as their ships were wrecked off Vanuatu. But he has lived on in name. The South side has the site of where Captain Cook landed. While you are in that area you may want to take a visit also to the most Southerly Sydney beach area of Cronulla which is very up and coming, and the nearby Royal National Park where you can get an early taste of what Oz bush is like. The North side of the park butts onto the miniature Sydney Harbour which is called Port Hacking. For spectacular inland bays, the Sydney area has FOUR truly magnificent bays or inlets, call them what you will. To the North of the Pittwater/Broken Bay there are even more similar bays and inlets of Tuggerah Lake, Lake Macquarie, the River Hunter upon which sits Newcastle, Port Stephens, Myall Lakes, The Broadwater, and Wallis Lake. These numerous places are what makes the coast of NSW for me, and I have mentioned but a few of them, as there are more further North and to the South of Sydney.

During my first stay in Sydney I saw during one of my walks around the Circular Quay area, a nice old four masted barque (see photo 4) tied up on one of the quays. A sign on it proclaimed that one could take three day trips up the coast on it. I thought this would be a good adventure so signed up for a trip. The day it started was a stinker of a day. Low rain clouds, with some rain, a strong wind blowing and an extremely choppy sea. I thought it would all make for an interesting start to the trip.

We motored through the Harbour and to the Heads (see photo 6) where you then meet the full force of the bad weather. A strong fairly high swell made for a nice up and down motion with some rolling. My being used to sailing and well togged up in my full weather gear which I had brought with me, was relishing all this. The other members of public on this trip were not taking this weather too good and there were plenty of them going to the ships side to meet 'Hughee'! We proceeded to motor away from the coast until we were about three miles out and then turned North to make our way up to our destination of Pittwater, which is a large inlet where the Hawesbury River exits to the ocean. However due to bad visibility the coast is now not visible at all, which means that the Captain who was a somewhat laid back Aussie, probably in his late thirties lets it be known to me that the ships GPS was on the blink. As I had brought my own hand held GPS I offered the use of it to him. So I put in the coordinates of where we were heading for and we navigated on that. OK he could have navigated in the old fashioned way and we would eventually come closer to shore in order to get sightings of where we were, I thought it was typical of how Aussies are a bit slap dash and laid back.

Towards the end of the day the wind started to abate and visibility picked up and we made the entrance to Pittwater OK. We sailed around for some time and then made our way up one of the many fingers that went off the main route of Pittwater. This took us into a sheltered bay near a spot called Brooklyn (see photo 2) where we anchored up for the night.

We had originally intended to make the next large Bay further up the coast past Newcastle, called Port Stephens, but due to the bad weather which had meant a later start and slower progress, we would not be able to go that far so the next day we would explore the whole of Pittwater (see photo 3) and its many bays and inlets or fingers. So as the weather was brilliant the next day, that's what we did, and very enjoyable it was too, and I got to steer the ship for quite some hours, as he could see I was used to steering ships. (I was also in the M.N) The food was excellent and my fellow passengers were all good company.

The next day it was a slow trawl under sail back down the coast to the heads and back up the mighty Harbour and back to our berth at Circular Quay. A fantastic three days I wouldn't have missed for anything.

As I said before Sydney is a huge city covering an area maybe as big as London or bigger. The endless suburbs have nothing really to recommend you to visit them. You will pass through some of those suburbs in order to get to some of the places I have mentioned above, and they will give you some sort of idea how the Aussies live and what their house are all like. However I would not tell you to spend any more time seeing any particular suburbs, unless you want to gawp at how the rich and super rich live. If that is your cup of tea, then visit the suburbs of Double Bay, Rose Bay, Vaucluse, Watsons Bay, and they will give you an idea of what you haven't got.

So Sydney is not a city where you can spend ages looking at many historical buildings and huge Museums. It is more a place to soak in the beautiful vistas and the harbourside delights, plus some of the fabulous beaches. On the subject of beaches BEWARE. They are not like your benign Brit beaches because they invariable have strong waves beaching on them and are ridden with rips and currents. Also it is surprising how cold the water can be. They are not like the Med with calm waters where you can enjoy a leisurely swim out to sea. Here you have be sensible and swim only between the life savers flags and know what to do in the event of being carried out on a rip. Do not fight it or panic, but go with it calmly until it dies out and maybe head parallel to the beach and come back further down. Also be careful of being dumped on your head by trying to body surf in on a big wave. People are always getting broken necks, with all the strife that can bring. A lot of the beaches have calm sea water swimming pools on the beaches, made by low walls to trap the sea water and to make up a pool.

To the South of Sydney, the town of Wollongong is a nice little place to visit, and to the North the town of Newcastle. Waragamba Dam to the South West provides water for Sydney, and if you are not intending to drive through to Canberra, a trip there by coach or train is a must. If you visit a travel agents or a hotel, they carry lots of brochures, see what tours and trips are on offer.

Chapter Three

Sydney to Melbourne

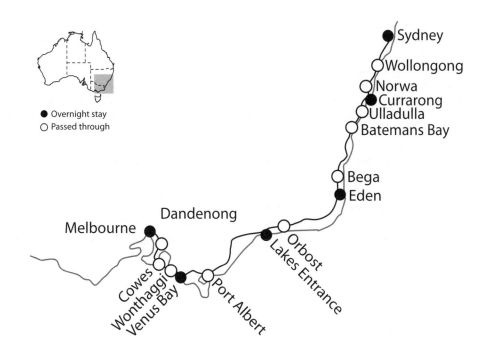

● Overnight stay
○ Passed through

Sydney
Wollongong
Norwa
Currarong
Ulladulla
Batemans Bay
Bega
Eden
Dandenong
Melbourne
Orbost
Lakes Entrance
Cowes
Wonthaggi
Venus Bay
Port Albert

Saturday came and all is ready to commence my trip. The motorhome has the toolbox fitted and the scooter ramp/ bracket and I have managed to get a lot of the bits and pieces I think I will need for the trip. At least to get started anyway, and I can use this first section of the trip to work out what else I need in equipment and how things are working all round. Then when I get to Melbourne I can spend time fixing things better and getting any equipment I think I need in addition to what I already have.

It's a fine day, at least no rain. I get all my belongings out of the room I have called home for the past two months and into the home on wheels. I get away for about 10 am and head Southwards out along the Princes Highway. This hugs the coast more or less all the way to Melbourne. Before I leave Sydney I must call on the Caravan Parts and Accessories place in Kogarah because the TV I bought off them doesn't work. I tried it and there are no instructions and I can't get any picture. When I reach them it turns out that this set has to tune itself into the frequencies of the local transmitters, and how to do that is in the instructions. I get those and am given a quick rundown on how to do this, and then I am off again.

As you get out of the Southern most suburbs of Sydney, namely Sutherlandshire, where I used to live in the early eighties, the road skirts the large Royal National Park. It was here a few years back that they had some disastrous fires which destroyed many homes. This is a constant fear in Oz, bush fires, which start and spread so easily. Some are started deliberately by the usual nutters one gets in society, but many start on their own or are started by lightning. Even a small piece of broken glass can be responsible or a discarded ciggy butt thrown out of a passing car by some moron.

Not long after you leave Sutherlandshire, the road is running along a quite high escarpment which is 3 to 4 kilometres inland from the coastline. There are numerous lookouts in the Bulli area and stopping for a look is a must. (p.7.) The views along the coast to the South and to the nearby town of Wollongong are stunning. I took a road down the hillside which is called The Bulli Pass, and into the little town of Bulli. I then drive into the big 'W' along the coast road.

Wollongong is quite a large industrial town and is clean and tidy and I have lunch in a car park on the sea front. I had visited this place several times when I lived in Sydney and I fondly remembered the dirty weekend I had spent here in 69 with my blonde Aussie nurse lover of the time in a seedy motel. After my dreaming of old times, as it does not have anything of worth visiting to see, once I'd eaten I got on my way out of town.

A short trip along the coast and you soon come to the very pretty seaside town of Kiama. I am quite taken by the place as it is not only situated in a picturesque place, namely a small horseshoe bay, but it is a place that they have obviously taken some pride in. Very neat and clean and I saw that they had won a tourist award for their endeavours. I park up and have a coffee and then take a walk to look around the little harbour where I come across a group of pelicans waiting patiently in front of visitors who are sitting outside a cafe, for scraps of food. (see photo 8)

Nearby on a headland is a blowhole, so I wander off to see if this is a good one. It wasn't up to much and I wasn't impressed, had the waves been stronger it would have been better, so didn't stay around for long and as the day was getting on, I was anxious to move onto the next town of Nowra and see if this would be an OK place to stay overnight. Passing through wooded land I quickly reach Nowra but it didn't seem to have a town centre and I found I was quickly at the other end of the town and heading out, so had to turn round and go back. After looking at the map I decided to head towards Jervis Bay to a small place called Currarong which had a caravan park and was at the mouth of the bay. This bay has an Oz Navy training base and I was curious as to what I would see. I imagined a Dartmouth (Devon) sort of place.

Well Jervis Bay itself is a very large bay and it was absolutely deserted. No boats moored anywhere, nobody on the water and no sign of Navy activity. The road to Currarong went through solid forests, and the village was all tourist cabins and second home type places. At least it was all quiet and semi deserted due to the time of year and not yet summer. So it was a quiet night and my first taste of an Oz caravan park and it only cost me $12 so I was very surprised and hoped they would all be as cheap.

I had to take the road back to Nowra as the more direct road back to the highway which would have brought me onto it south of Nowra, was too rough and unsealed. The road South ran through green farmland mixed with forests and undulated up and down shallow hills. I went through a small the town of Ulladulla, and onto Batemans Bay. (p.9.) By now it was raining heavily and was pouring down when I got there. I stopped in a car park next the river that the town is on and outside a small shopping mall. I needed a few provisions and a coffee.

After this it was on through Moruya, then Narooma, and into a little place on the coast, called Bermagui. Here I decided to try out pitching up in a place other than on a caravan site. I wanted to try out the new Honda generator I had bought. What I needed to know is how long would it run for on a full tank. I needed to keep the largish portable freezer, running all night. To allow it to run on purely the battery would along with the running of the smaller fridge, would severely drain it. So I looked around for a suitable spot to park where I would not draw the attention of nasty police or council officials who may want to say overnight parking of motorhomes is Verboten, Ya! Like in the UK, councils do not like motorhomers and caravanner's to cheat them out of revenues by getting free parking. The little Council Hitlers abound, the World over.

Anyway I found a nice little spot along the coast road going out of town, which was near the road but hidden. It was right next to Lake Wallaga so a nice pretty spot and quiet. I found that the generator ran all evening and night on a full tank, but only just.

The next day took me through Bega and onwards towards Eden, which I have heard is a pretty and interesting place. So it turns out to be, although the town itself is much like all the other small towns I have already passed through and aesthetically nothing to shout about. It is its location and history that is of interest. Set at one end of a large bay which affords it some good shelter, it was started in the early 1800's primarily as a port to serve whalers. Of course nowadays no whaling is done, but it still serves as an important fishing port for the South East coast region. Its little port section is set separately from the main town at an aptly named Snug Cove, and here I saw that a catamaran was offering a whale watching trips. So I booked for the following day.

The caravan park I booked into was situated along the shoreline called Aslings Beach, just out of town on the North side. Due to the time of year, it was practically empty. I checked my emails at the Council Offices and took the Transit to the local Ford dealer for a check on why the engine was smoking. They confirmed that the Turbo wasn't working and suggested it may need replacing, but they didn't have the parts in stock and they would have to be ordered and that would mean it would take up to three days. I decided to get it seen to in Melbourne.

The next day it was an early start as the boat left at 7.30am. The boat was only half full, but the weather was very good, and we motored out past a headland and out to sea. It wasn't long before we saw our first sighting of a Southern Right whale. I don't know what it is about whales and dolphins but they evoke strong feelings among most people. They really are awesome wondrous creatures as they slowly make their way down the eastern coastline of Oz and on their way back to Antarctic waters. They spend summer months in Antarctic feeding up on the enormous amount of krill that abound there. Then with good reserves of body fat they make the long run up the eastern coast of Oz to warm seas North of Oz where they mate and give birth. When the calves are big enough after a good feed of Mothers milk, they come back down the Oz coast and back to Antarctic. It is these trips up and down the coast that enables people to watch their progress. Starting in October / November they head south and the females are accompanied by their calves. Males travel in separate pods.

We spend a whole morning travelling around trying to locate whales and are very successful. The whales have to come up every now and then for air and the first thing you see is the mist of water as they exhale, accompanied by the hiss of exhaled air. Then you see the black back and then as they go back under their great tails come vertically out of the water, to then disappear below. Sometimes they leap straight out of the water, to then flop back with a great splashing of water. Other times they will crash their tails down onto the water, and no one knows really why they do this. (see photos 10, 11 & 12)

We also see dolphins who come up to our boat and accompany us by swimming alongside our bows. They do this for some minutes until they tire of this frolic and head away to play elsewhere. (see photo 13) Also sighted are small penguins and seals and petrels who are on their migration South from Siberia. So a really enjoyable and eventful morning out. I strongly recommend you take such a trip if your in this area, or anywhere else where whale watching trips are carried out. I promise you an unforgettable experience.

After my boat trip I visited the Whaling Museum which is very near to the harbour. Very interesting, and here I learnt that Eden was started by a Scottish family and they set up the first whaling company and they became very successful and powerful.

The next day back on the road I head for the nearby Victorian border. I am travelling through green farming lands and forests. Once you leave Eden the road goes away from the coast and once over the border it is thick with forests. You travel through a number of small towns of no real note. Going through a place called Cann River an almighty thunder and lightening show suddenly starts accompanied by a very heavy downpour. I reach Orbost which is where the famous Snowy River is almost at the sea. This of course starts up in the nearby Snowy Mountains which was made famous by the film 'The Man from the Snowies' starring one of my favourite American film actors. (Kirk Douglas)

The land is becoming more farmed and this area to Melbourne is known as Gippsland and was settled fairly early on in the early settlement of Australia and Victoria. The early settlers quickly realised that the land here was prime farming land, so it quickly became settled by farmers. Inland from here are two great areas of mountain ranges. To the East and up to the NSW borders you have the Southern Tablelands and more to the West are the Great Dividing Ranges. These areas can afford many enjoyable trips and they can be either explored on a separate inland trip or undertaken in a series of trips out of Melbourne if you use there as a base.

I press on to a town called Lakes Entrance where I will stay overnight. This is right on the coast and at a spot where a great series of inland waterways, Australia's greatest stretch of inland waterways in fact, and they consist of a series of narrow waterways, lakes and rivers and are extensively used by holiday makers. (see photo 14 & 15) Just off the coast, by a few yards in fact, there is a strip of land made up of sand dunes which is something like what you see in Dorset on the Chesil Bank. Only here instead of a shingle bank you have a sand dune bank. On the sea side of this strip of land you have a beach which stretches for ninety miles and is known by that name, and is Oz's longest unbroken straight stretch of beach.

After an overnight stay and a quick check of my emails, I set off again. Through a largish farming town of Bairnsdale (Scottish maybe?) through to Sale where instead of taking the more direct route to Melbourne, I take the South Gippsland Highway, so that I can follow the coast. I travel to Port Albert which was settled even earlier than Melbourne and was used as a principle port until the latter overtook it. So at one stage it was a bustling and busy port and it took out the produce of the farmlands for sale in Melbourne and Sydney. Now it is a quiet and mainly a holiday area. I press on and past the turn off to the Wilson Promontory, which is Oz's most Southerly point. I want to get on as it is getting late and I want to make Venus Bay where there is a park.

This is another holiday settlement, hardly a town, just a large collection of holiday type homes and none of them cheap either, judging by the prices displayed in the three real estate offices. Seeing as they were mainly shacky type buildings and not solid city type houses, and you couldn't get one under 80K's pounds.

Next day I'm on my way to the next place I want to look around, namely Philip Island. This is at the entrance to the smaller bay to the East of Port Philip Bay on which Melbourne sits, called Western Port. It has a second island in it, called French Island. I reach a little town called San Remo which is nothing like the real San Remo which I hazard a guess must have been started by a homesick Italian. From here there is a modern concrete bridge spanning the narrows and to the island. It reminds me a bit of the newish bridge in Scotland going across to the island of Skye. However crossing this one is free unlike the Scottish one. Once on the Island I am reminded of the Isle of Wight. It is roughly the same shape, although smaller and some of the names of the little towns are, Cowes and Ventnor. Wales is even represented by Rhyll. Cowes is a nice little place and I arrived at the same time as they were holding a welcoming parade for one of their own, namely a young girl swimmer who had done well at the recent Athens Olympics.

Pushing on, I wanted to visit the Western most point of the Island where they have an equivalent of the Isle of Wight Needles, this they call the 'Nobbies' (see photo 16) This promontory is a nature park with lighthouse and plenty of rocky outcrops in the sea off it. There are some little cliffs and it is in the cliff faces that thousands of sea gulls nest (see photo 17). They have built board walks along the cliff face and onto the rocks and these birds are totally unfazed when you walk past where they are sitting on nests only a few feet away.

The rocks are volcanic black, so unlike the Needles, and on those rocks there is what they say is the largest colony of Australian fur seals to be found in Oz. Funnily enough, they are called 'Seal Rocks' and because they have all these seals the area also boasts the largest Great White sharks, presumably feeding off these juicy seals. No place to swim then!

Also on the cliffs they have a large modern building with a huge car park in front of it, so I went over to investigate. I found that this section of cliffs has a large colony of small penguins and they are such a visitor draw that this building and car park was build to handle all the visitors. These penguins or at least the males, spend all day out in the sea searching out fish, for food. They will journey many miles, even as far as the next bay of Port Philip to find this food. Returning at sunset, nicely full up with fish, they seem to all arrive at the same time and it is a real spectacle to watch them coming out of the sea and making their way up the sandy cliffs to their various burrows on the cliff faces and tops. Coach loads of parties arrive to watch all this. They have built into the walls of the main building, little boxes in which some penguins are nesting. The entrance to the box is on the outside wall and the box has a perspex top, so you can look inside without disturbing the sitting female. As I was there during the afternoon this was what I had to be satisfied with.

Leaving the Island I made my way to the North and towards the Eastern outskirts of Melbourne. I had seen that there was a caravan park at a place called Narre Warren just off the Princess Highway which I had left way back. Unfortunately this was a park that only had permanent residents. However the girl there gave me the name of one further up the Highway which I rang, and they had a vacancy. So off I went towards that and it was in a better position as it was nearer to the centre of Melbourne. So on the seventh day after leaving Sydney I was ensconced in Melbourne and ready to explore it.

Chapter Four

Melbourne: Sights and History

This city is like Sydney in that it covers a very large area, but it feels quite unlike Sydney. They like to boast that Melbourne has more of a European feel about it, and to an extent I suppose it does. However it can never compete with the many European cities, that have many more older buildings and a much more history. It does have nice wide tree lined boulevard streets and a tram system, (see photo 18) and this makes it feel different from Sydney. A slower pace also helps. They also like to boast that it has a more cultural life with theatres and opera etc, but I do not believe it has more than Sydney in this respect. Like all the main Oz State cities, it hasn't many fine old buildings or an old section and this is due to the youth of the country.

It has more parks and open spaces than Sydney and these are close to the city centre, and the River Yarra (see photo 19 & 20) runs through the centre, which adds to the ambiance of the place. The centre like Sydney has many modern skyscrapers, with building still going on.

The city is situated at the Northern end of Port Philip Bay which is a very big horseshoe bay some 40 kilometres wide at the widest and about 45 kilometres long. Whilst standing say on the east shoreline you cannot see the West side. Similarly when at the mouth of the bay, you cannot see the Northern shoreline. The River Yarra flows into the bay, at the Northern end and it winds eastwards and into the city area.

The bay was found by the British in March 1802, when a Lt John Murray landed on the Southern shores at what is now Point King, which is near Sorrento. A year later a small fleet was sent out to start a settlement in the area, and this was started at what is now called Camerons Bight. The settlement was made up of a mixture of convicts and non convicts. There is a monument to the first settlement and a few graves of those who died in the first year. However the whole exercise only lasted a year as it was found to be unsuitable for settlement as there were no trees growing in this area which could be used for buildings. So they upped sticks and carried on by ship to the Island now known as Tasmania, but then known as Van Diemans Land, after the Dutchman who found it. Some of those (a John Bateman was one of them) who settled there later came back to the Port Philip area to start a settlement which grew into Melbourne, (named after the then Lord Melbourne).

The settlement grew quite quickly after its start in 1830 and a surveyor mapped out the grid pattern of streets which now form the Melbourne city centre. A port also grew on the banks of the Yarra as boats were able to come in as far as the settlement. As the years went on this port grew and was developed into the series of docks you see now. However as with all ports around the World these docks are now no longer used as containerisation has taken place. So they have been and are continuing to be developed into other uses, like entertainment complexes and high rise flats for the rich. (Who are the only ones who can afford to live next to water, as in London etc.)

The caravan park I had got into was the nearest one to the town centre and yet it was some 25 kilometres away. So exploring the city centre involved a long drive on the scooter taking at least half an hour in good traffic. Over the four weeks I was in Melbourne when the weather was good enough to allow it, I gradually visited all the places of interest in the city, and I explored the coast line of the bay looking at the various beach suburbs. The rest of the time was taken up with doing shopping, emailing, and upgrading the home. I fitted a rear view camera set up, towel rail, various hooks for cups and bits and pieces, a TV wall bracket that swivelled and so on. I do not know how previous owners managed with such a poorly fitted out home. I found the same with my sailing boat which was 30 odd years old and lacked many gadgets and gizmos that can make living in a confined space more tolerable and organised.

The first place I visited of historical interest was Melbourne Old Goal. They built this in short order and was probably one of the first official buildings in the new city. You have to imagine all the dregs of British life that were out there, in those early days. Law and order was hard to keep, especially if after arresting a miscreant, there was nowhere to put him. Anyway a goal was designed on the latest pattern as used in the UK and was built out of local limestone. What is left of the whole original complex, is one building of three stories. Typical of goals, in having two rows of cells facing each other with a passageway in between. A second and third story above. What was interesting was the fact that Ned Kelly, their iconic hero of the working classes, was kept here after his capture and, hanged here. They have one of the three suits of armour that he made (I learnt something there) on display, plus much info on boards, about the rascal. Also the trap door through which he departed, is still there.

In the early 1850's, gold was discovered nearby at Ballarat and this helped enormously to kickstart Melbourne in to rapid growth and prominence. All the gold that was dug out was brought down to Melbourne for storage and shipment to other parts. This meant that a place to receive it and store it was needed to be built, and they started in 1840 to build a building that would be used for the Parliament of Victoria and as a treasury and place to store gold. This is a lovely building of typical Victorian style and worth a visit.(see photo 21) One thing that tickled me was that it was designed by a Scouse, (native of Liverpool) and a very young one at that, being only 23 years old. He certainly was a talented young man. They displayed a map of Liverpool which he drew at only 13 and I could identify with streets and places on that, being a Scouse myself. It looked very professional, especially bearing in mind the age of the lad doing it.

Later on in the 1870's they started a better building for the Victorian Parliament just up the road and although it looks finished, it is hasn't actually been finished off as per the design. You can go round this on a guided tour so long as Parliament isn't sitting. I was lucky as the lazy dogs were on one of their many holidays, just like UK politicians! I liked this building. It is modelled on the two chambers, as are the UK chambers, with green leather upholstery for the peasants and red for the Lords, or in this case, the Senators of the higher house.

Much REAL gold leaf is in evidence and the guide told us that there is 3 million dollars worth of the stuff in the building. It was because of the huge amount of wealth that was very quickly generated by the 'Gold Rush' that enabled this show of wealth to take place. In fact Melbourne became so wealthy that it rivalled many a European capital city and it imported all the very best on offer from the old World to pour into its new buildings and way of life.

On this theme they decided to hold a big exhibition and built a great exhibition hall near the centre, and this was completed in 1879. (see photo 22) Again, this can be looked at by a guided tour. You have to book for this in the nearby modern Museum building and it starts once a day, at midday. A splendid building and well worth a visit. It is extensively decorated inside, with lovely wall and ceiling paintings. It has received a World Heritage award, and is so far the ONLY Oz building to have achieved this. When Australia got its independence or Confederation status in 1901, the ceremony was held in this building.

When Independence was obtained they were obviously going to have to have somewhere to have a national Parliament and they of course, as we all know, decided to build Canberra and have it all there. Whilst this was being done, the country was run from the Victorian Parliament House (see photo 23) and the Victorian Parliament had to be operated out of the treasury building on a temporary basis.

Another very early building is the old Customs House which can be found on Flinders St. It shows very well how officials can organise themselves very quickly in order to collect taxes.(presumably so they can pay themselves, so they were no different then than are current modern robbers) This building is now used as the Immigration Museum and is interesting enough to visit. It deals with all the inflow of people from early days and including immigration that took place after World War II.

Being interested in all things to do with boats, I had to take a visit to look over the 'Polly Woodside' clipper which is in a small dry dock on the South side of the River Yarra, and just down from Melbourne's Exhibition Centre. This dry dock was the only dry dock in use throughout the years, but as it became defunct, they decided to use it to show off a typical clipper type boat of the steel variety, which were responsible for much of the early trade between Oz and the UK and elsewhere. This is a boat that was built in Belfast in the late 1800's and named after the daughter of the eventual owner. It is very similar to the Cutty Sark in its looks, but that ship I believe is mostly wood. The rigging has all been restored as has much of the interior, but it has not been completed yet. Next to it is a large shed which houses the Maritime Museum. This deals with all the different types of ships which plied between Europe and Oz and the Americas.

On one of my many trips into the city centre I was turning right at an intersection, and the traffic was very light. A police car was coming the opposite way to me and I stopped as one does in the middle of the intersection to let him through as he had right of way. He stopped me and started to berate me for making an illegal type turn. Nonplussed I told him I did not know what the hell he was talking about, as turning right was not banned at that intersection. He waffled on about I should have turned from the left lane and gone to the far top of the middle of the intersection, then waited until the lights went red and then completed my turn. Well I thought he was mad and more or less said so. It turns out that ONLY in Melbourne is this way of turning right, done. I asked that if this was the case how the hell was a visitor supposed to know this? I think the question was too hard for him and he insisted on taking down all my details even though I told him I was not at a permanent address as I was travelling. I hinted when he told me I may get a ticket, that that was fine by me as I had no intention to pay it as I would be long gone and would not even receive it. He was about 6'6" and that was just the measurement around his head! What a Wally and that is Oz Police for you!

In the gardens next to the Treasury Building which are called Fitzroy Gardens, can be found a cottage called Captain Cooks Cottage. (see photo 24) Not entirely true as it was his parents cottage that they built back in the UK. It was bought and transported to Melbourne to celebrate that great mans achievements and is filled with furniture and fittings of that era. Of course Capt Cook would have visited his parents house, but it was built by them after he started his naval career. I thought it was a good idea to have done what they did but I think the cottage would have been better in Sydney as at least he had a connection with that city. He did not have one with Melbourne.

One thing that happened to me whilst visiting this cottage which I thought was indicative of what has happened to Oz in the last 25 to 30 years, which I believe has changed the two major cities forever. You had to pay to go round the cottage and they had a little ticket office on the boundary of the garden which is around it. There was a young Asian manning it, and as a joke I said I was going to look at my ancestors house. He looked mystified and I told him my name was Cook. He really thought I was an ancestor and I could see him watching me as I went round and in and out into the gardens. Then when I had finished and was taking a photo of the place he rushed up to me and excitingly asked me if I had liked it. He spoke in such a way as if he was talking to a real ancestor of Cook. I felt I had to tell him that Cook was my adopted name and so I couldn't really be an ancestor. He looked somewhat puzzled as if he didn't quite get it. My point being is that in the past 25 plus years, the Australian government has let into Oz millions of Asian, African and Middle Eastern immigrants who do not know anything of the history of Oz and the traditions and way of life. This little incident was indicative of this as this young guy who did not speak very good English and didn't really understand the nuances of the history of this particular person named Cook. So I felt disconnected with him and had it been an Aussie we would have had a bit of a laugh and joke about it all.

Sydney a city I know the best, has changed out of all proportion and I feel it is really no longer an archetypical Oz city. I was shocked at the percentage of Asians who seem to have taken over much of the city including many of the suburbs. The same is to be said of Melbourne and I feel the government has made the same mistakes as the British government, because there are cities in the UK that I as a Brit feel I am an outsider in my own country in certain areas. I have talked about this to a few Aussies and they also feel the same. So be prepared that you will find these similarities between Oz (in certain places) and the UK. You will find that the only places where Oz feels like Oz, is out in the countryside, and the more remote it is, the more Oz it will be. Adelaide is nowhere near as populated with these later arriving immigrants, but then it is not as vibrant and the employment chances are not as high as the two main cities of Sydney and Melbourne, so less immigrants.

Other places you can visit if you wish, are the bay areas, like Brighton, (which is a snobby rich area). I followed the road from Frankston in the South, right up to St Kilda in the North section and past there and past the dock areas and into the west of the city centre. I also went up into the eastern hills area around Narre Warren and the reservoir called Lysterfield Lake. Then there is the Cardinia Reservoir, the Dandenong Hill National Park. These are all within striking distance of the centre and are all in the Metropolitan area. Of course you can strike out as far as you want and go to other places. It is up to you.

The last place I wanted to visit was the Mornington Peninsular. This is South of the Metro area and forms the Eastern arm of the horseshoe bay of Port Philip. On its most Southerly end there is a park which used to be a no go area for the general Public as It was used by the Army as a firing range, and since settlement began they had used the extreme tip of the peninsular which forms the Narrows of the Heads of the Bay, as a gun emplacement and Fort. Called Fort Nepean, it was initially set up so as to deter those nasty Frenchies who may still harbour thoughts of pinching our (The Brit empire) new possessions. Then a little later it was the threat from the nasty Russians who were getting too big for their boots too. Then the First World War, and then the Second World War and the nasty threat from the nasty Japs. So all in all the Brits and Aussies used their various paranoia's to keep the Public out, and it was only in the last 20 years that it opened up as a park.

I drove the home down there and there is a motorway most of the way, so it doesn't take long to get there. South of Frankston the land is mostly virgin and what is built on seems like it may be expensive. The park is not free and you have to pay as you enter it! The road does not go all the way, you have to stop and walk the last three or so kilometres.

This isn't such a big deal, but this is Oz and this particular day was nice and warm and sunny. This park is not a park in the European sense, but just raw Aussie heavy solid bush! So immediately on getting out of your vehicle, you are set upon by flies. The walk was an exercise for the right arm, and I got some good exercise in doing the 'Aussie Salute'. That is to say your right hand constantly moves from the right, across your face to the left and back again. Repeat this ad nauseum. If your left handed it is the opposite. Your given a brochure explaining the historical bits and pieces about the place, and this made a handy addition to my hand which is really too small to do an effective fly swotting job.

There are a number of concrete gun emplacements, fort structures and the like, which you can wander around. At the end of walk you are at Point Nepean (see photo 25) and can look across the narrows at the opposite Point Lonsdale. This narrow strip of water is fast moving and reminds me somewhat of the similar narrow channel at the entrance to Poole Harbour, only wider.

On my way back I see a helicopter which is hovering over a rock on the beach, (see photo 26) at the very point where the Aussie Prime Minister Harold Holt, stupidly went swimming in December 1967, on a day when the water was too rough for swimming, and was never seen again. I wondered if they were still looking for him, but it was evident that they were just practising lowering a rescue tray.

Next to the car park where I had left 'The Home' there is a cemetery where they buried the people who died in the Quarantine Station that they had there in the early days. (see photo 27) Anyone arriving from Europe who had got sick on the boat during the journey, would be put into quarantine here. Some obviously did not make it and the cemetery was managed like many of the historical cemeteries that I have so far visited and would go on to visit in the future. Namely run down and sadly neglected, and this is their history which does not seem important to them.

So I reached the end of my stay in Melbourne, having seen all I wanted, the time came to pack in, and get ready to move on to the next stage of, 'to Adelaide'. I have booked in the Transit into the local Ford dealer for the Monday next.

Chapter Five

Melbourne to Adelaide

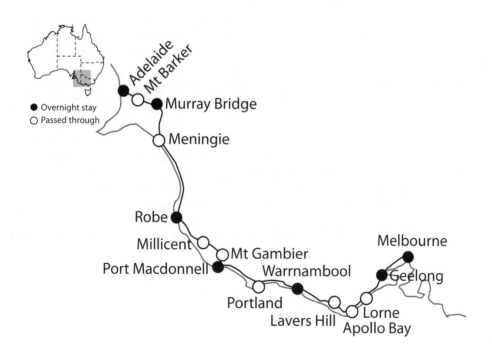

Monday comes and I take the Transit to the Ford dealer expecting them to take at least two days to fix the turbo/ EGR problem. So it was a pleasant surprise when they rang me at 3 in the afternoon to say it was all done, it meant I could get on my way instead of having to book into a hotel. Turns out all it was, was a loose and blocked EGR valve and the cost was only $120. Or in real money about £50.

I decided to get quickly on the road and out of Melbourne and as far down the coast to Adelaide as I could before night fell. I knew that after Geelong, which is the next decent sized town West of Melbourne there were plenty of caravan parks. By the time I got into Melbourne city centre to go over the West Gate Bridge which goes over the River Yarra and over which the freeway to the West and Geelong goes, it was rush hour and traffic was slow. However once over the bridge it quickly eased off. Before I took this freeway I wanted to visit the western suburb of Williamstown as this was the place where there was a bit of history and the shipyards that built the RAN Navy ships.

A nice place with neat little town centre adjacent to the marina area and the Tenix shipbuilding yards. Had a quick walk around and along the short jetty to have a quick look at an old RAN minesweeper of WW11 vintage. Then back onto the freeway which is 4 lanes wide and gave me a quick run down to Geelong. This is the place where they build all the Aussie Ford cars and it is a typical industrial type town with all the factories and chemical industrial complexes. It had that whiff of chemicals that reminded me of Runcorn in Cheshire where there are also loads of chemical industrial plants and you smell them as soon as you start to enter the place.

The road to the Bellarine Peninsular, where I was heading went right through the town centre and it was all neat and tidy and in nice order, which for the type of industrial town it is, was surprising. I was quickly through and onto the Geelong to Port Arlington Road and out to the south. It wasn't long before I came upon the first of the caravan parks, off the main road to the left and down to the Western shores of the Bay of Port Philip. Exotically named 'Pelican Shores Caravan Park' it was a nice and clean place.

I didn't see any Pelicans, but I did see a very large flock of black Swans just off shore in shallow waters all seeking whatever Swans eat, that is to be found on the sea floor. (see photo 28) I had not seen any black swans anywhere up to now so I was surprised that suddenly here they should be. Quite why they were not to be seen on the Eastern shore of Port Philip, I don't know.

Next morning I was out by 9am and on my way driving along the coastal road towards the Great Ocean Road. All the land West of Melbourne is very flat and I went through lots of little towns which were obviously all holiday type places. I suppose Victorians from the inland areas come here just as we flock to the seaside in the UK. Eventually I reached Queenscliff where they run a catamaran ferry service over to Sorrento on the Eastern side of the entrance to Port Philip Bay, where I had been only last Sunday. Not much there to see but I checked out the cost of taking a car across, and it was more expensive than our cross Channel, Dover to Calais, so a rip off service I would say. A little further on is Point Lonsdale which is exactly opposite Pt Nepean.

On this headland they have the usual lighthouse which is on a little cliff. (see photo 29) Right underneath the lighthouse is a small cave called Buckleys Cave. It had to be looked into. It turns out that according to the information board displayed, that when the first ship load of settlers that I talked about when visiting Sorrento on the other side of the bay, settled in 1803, a felon called Buckley had escaped with some others. Most of whom were never seen again. Well this bloke it turns out got in with the local Aborigine tribe and at some stage he managed to get over to this side of the bay to this cave, where he is supposed to have stayed for a while and lived off the fish and other marine life to be found on the rocks. Later in 1834 he turns up at a new settlement at Queenstown and turns himself in. He had spent 32 years living with Aborigines and it is said he looked like a wild white man and had to be taught how to speak English again. The new Governor of Victoria pardons him and he becomes one of the very early settlers of the new beginnings of what turns out to be Melbourne, and apparently does well. Anyway the best bit is that there is a well known saying in Oz which goes like this; if you have two chances; the first is a no chance and the second is 'Buckleys' Which means that, because he was lucky and survived 30 odd years living wild in the Oz bush after he ran away, you may too, be lucky or you may not. These Aussie sayings are profound, don't you think?

Continuing along the coast, the next town of any size, is good old Torquay, and like the original it is a seaside holiday town, only this one doesn't have the palm trees and is a lot smaller. Then we have a bit of Wales with the seaside town of Anglesea. Must have been a Taffy settler who started this place, only one who couldn't remember how to spell his old town. It is after Anglesea that you come onto the interesting bit of the 'Great Ocean Road'. (see photo 30 & 31) This road was built by returned soldiers after WW11, so as to be able to give them work when that was in short supply. It was built along a stretch of coastline that has behind it a range of mountains called the Ottway Ranges and these sweep right down onto the ocean. So this road had to be hacked out of solid rock and it would wind its way along the rugged coastline, in and out of little bays. The day that I was travelling along this stretch had turned a bit horrible with low cloud and squally showers. The mist was coming down the steep mountainsides to my right and I was wishing it had all been nice and sunny so I could enjoy the views a bit more.

The first decent sized town you come to is Lorne and it is set amongst a quite spectacular backdrop of heavily wooded mountainsides. It is a pretty little place and a popular tourist destination and also obviously popular with the surfing fraternity as they were all over the place. Had the weather been good I would have stopped off here for a while and looked at some of the scenic sights, such as Mt Defiance Lookout, Teddy's Lookout, Cumberland River, the Erskine River and Falls. So as it was I stopped only briefly for a coffee and got on my way.

Apollo Bay was the next little town and another seaside place. (see photo 32) But by now you were out of the spectacular section of the road and the Ottway Ranges were behind you. They say that this place is Australia's most Southerly town. However if you look at the map there are more Southerly towns around the Wilsons Promontory which is between the Lakes Entrance and Philip Island, east of Melbourne. Maybe these place names of Yanakie, Walkerville and Walkerville South and Waratah Bay are not classed as towns as they may not be big enough.

After Apollo Bay the road turns inland and goes through the Ottway National Park and very scenic it was too because after you come out of the forest you hit a lovely plain with rolling grassy grazing farmland which was very green. I could have been in the UK somewhere. Then you hit the coast again at a place called Glenaire and after this the road turns inland again and steadily climbs upwards and into heavily wooded forests. The low clouds meant that I was soon driving through   mist, and it was quite surreal for a place like Oz. Eventually on reaching the top of the hill or small mountain I reached my destination for the night, Lavers Hill. (see photo 33) My touring book told me there was a place called Lavers Hill Roadhouse where there was supposed to be a caravan park. The only place I could see was a pub of sorts but no signs saying caravan park, and as I drove slowly past I saw a small scruffy sign on the end of a shed which proclaimed 'overnight parking'. So had to turn back and ask, but there was nowhere what looked like an office, to be seen. Went inside the pub which had a few locals and waited ages for the guy behind the bar to attend to me. Yes, they had two patches of grass upon which I could park and there was electricity on a pole next to them. For this I had to fork out the princely sum of $21. I felt they were taking a liberty, as basically what I was doing was parking on their back lawn and being charged the same as if I were in some spanking great caravan park with all the best facilities. There was a run down looking building nearby that had a small toilet and shower of dubious quality. Anyway I hunkered down for the evening and night and boy did it rain. It pelted down most of the night but luckily it stopped just after I got up at 8am, so when I got going at about 9 it was bravely trying to clear up.

The road was downhill from there and it went on for miles (see photo 34) down and down, round and round and not too good a surface either. Heavy forest on either side, but eventually it got to the bottom and rolled on to the next town/village of Princetown, a small farming place. From hereon this stretch of coastal road is probably the most famous and noted stretch in Oz. It is dramatic and stunning and definitely the most photographed stretch in Oz. Out of Princetown the land is now not so green and fertile looking. A bit brown and I wondered what they did use it for as there wasn't a lot going on. It was fairly flat but we were on a plateau which was obviously quite a bit higher than sea level. You could see to your left and seawards, that there were cliffs. The first sign you come across tells you that you are approaching a parking place for viewing Beacon Steps. These turn out to just be a run of steep steps which drop down onto a stretch of beach. Apparently a guy called Gibson decided to hack these steps out of the rock in the cliff face so he could enjoy this deserted beach. Who knows why as there is no explanation as to their history. So I didn't stay long.

The next site of interest is the famous stretch of coast called the Twelve Apostles. (see photo 35) This stretch has twelve outcrops of rock that are left some distance away from the current line of cliffs. As the cliffs which are made of soft sandstone, they got worn away over thousands of years of wave action, some sections of harder rock never got worn away. They are now left out on their own and this collection of twelve rocks are said to be the most photographed section of Oz coast. This is what some tourists were doing just recently, and before their very eyes one of the Twelve Apostles just collapsed into the sea. So now there are only about six left. (Since then I hear another has fallen to the same fate.)

Next we have what I thought to be the most interesting section of this coast is called The Loch Ard Gorge, (see photo 36) and around it are several other interesting sites all of which can be seen by walking from the one car park. So here you can spend a couple of hours quite easily. Loch Ard Gorge called because in 1878 a sailing boat bound for Melbourne from England was wrecked on nearby rocks. Forty nine people lost their lives and there were only two people who survived. Both were youngsters, one Eva Carmichael and one Tom Pearce. They were washed into the large gorge that ate itself far into the cliffs, and which at its end, had a nice little beach onto which they could drag themselves. Had this not been there they would have had a job to save themselves as elsewhere, all there is are tall insurmountable cliffs. Tom managed to scale the gorge face and get out and went looking for any people he could find. Luckily the area was well settled with farmers, so he quickly came across some farm workers who rescued the girl. They only found four bodies and these were buried on the cliff top and for some reason unknown to me, since then, other early settlers from the surrounding areas have also elected to be buried there too. So there is a little collection of graves at this spot.

Nearby is another gorge and at the end of it a tunnel has been worn out by the constant wave action. (It is calculated that on this coast there is a wave every 8 seconds. As they have come uninterrupted all the way from the Antarctic, so they have some power in them, and their action on these soft limestone cliffs is there to see in the incredible formations.) This tunnel goes on for a 100 metres and a sink hole has manifested itself right at the end, so every time a big surge of water is pushed down this tunnel it forms a blowhole up this sinkhole.

Another gorge has a large cave at its end and when each large wave is pushed into it, it makes a noise like thunder. Hence it is known as 'Thunder Cave' (see photo 37) Also nearby there is a small gorge which at its end has a tunnel formed which is 8 metres above sea level and the roof of this short tunnel looks like an arch which makes the whole formation look similar to a grotto with a rock pool under it, hence known as the 'Grotto'(see photo 38)

Nearby a local river runs out to a beach known as Sherbrooke Beach (see photo 39) which is part of a large bay. There are a couple of large formations of rock which form small islands just off the cliffs. One is called Razorback Island due to the row of sharp rocks running along the top of the island. (see photo 40)

Further along the coast you can find London Bridge, an island which was off the cliffs and had a rock bridge connecting it to the mainland.(see photo 41) This was called London Bridge probably by some local homesick cockney! Anyway the arch fell into the sea in 1990, so it was a case of London Bridge did fall down… out here, anyway! Another similar archway still exists nearby. Other sites to see are the Bay of Islands and the Bay of Martyrs, although I could find no explanation as to who the Martyrs were. These are West of a small fishing and tourist town of Peterborough.

The road now turns inland and at a small country town called Allansford it rejoins the main Princes Highway which runs from Geelong on an inland route and is not as an interesting route to take. The only thing of note at Allansford is a huge factory that makes cheese, and if you are a cheese lover you can stock up with the stuff at their shop. There is also a cheese museum and restaurant where you can gorge on it. As I am on orders from my doctors to avoid cheese, I just drove on by and onto my next overnight stop of Warrnambool.

A nice town of reasonable size, being a regional centre for the surrounding farming areas. The caravan park I decided to use is situated down by the shores of Lady Bay, and is well ordered and of good standards. The next day after booking out I used the nearby Council Library at the Town Hall, to check my emails and afterwards a coffee before hitting the road out of town.

The countryside since the Great Ocean Road left the coast and went inland a bit after Peterborough, has been parched looking. No sign of the land being used for growing crops, only for grazing. But unlike the land nearer to Melbourne or in Gippsland, where it was green, it has been land covered in a yellow dry looking grass. So it is on the way to the next town on the map, Port Fairy, which is described as an historic port town.

When places in Oz are thus described, what they mean is that it would have been started as a settlement in the early 1800's. Thus it is here, and it is one of Victoria's oldest settlements and once, believe it or not, Australia's second port. Set on a river called the Moyne. Not very big but a nice little place and I saw a sight I have not seen often along the coast all the way from Sydney, some sailing boats moored. They were on the river along with a number of fishing boats. A number of old Victorian buildings are dotted around the town. However there was nothing of great interest, so didn't stop for long.

The road is following the coast around a bay called Portland Bay and eventually I reach Portland itself. This is described as Victoria's first permanent settlement by a chap called Edward Henty, in 1834. Again quite a pleasant place, with a large breakwater forming a large port area, and described as the only large deep water port between Adelaide and Melbourne. Be that as it maybe, but it wasn't a busy place. It only had one medium sized ship berthed there on the day I was there. After looking around and trying to find the road out of the town that I wanted to go along, cursing the lack of adequate sign posting, I eventually got onto the coastal road that would take me onto Port MacDonnel, which was were I would spend the night. The countryside was the same as I had passed along for many a mile now. Flat and parched grazing land and passing through only a few very small villages/hamlets or settlements, call them what you will. I find it difficult to quantify these small Oz places as to me the name 'village' conjures up the typical English village or even the Continental village. In Europe they are places of real age, not a small collection of shacks and or bungalows. There are invariably too small to be called towns, and sometimes if you blink whilst driving, you miss them completely.

I pass through one of these places called Nelson, and a few miles after I pass through the Victoria South Australian border. A series of signs warns me of this momentous occasion is about to happen. I wonder if there will be guards and a pole across the road, and will I have to present my passport?

I am warned that I must get rid of any fruit I may be carrying so that I do not carry into South Australia the dreaded fruit fly. There will be spot checks and if I am caught, I could be fined up to $5,000. Wow! Of course I have my fruit which I bought in the supermarket in Melbourne, but I am damned if I am going to throw out what's left. Darn it, I am a pensioner and can't afford such luxuries. It is back again to some of the Aussie petty fogging rules that they have. Their civil servants are as bad or worse than our Brit ones. They used to spray the insides of all aircraft that arrived in Oz from abroad, so that we didn't bring in bugs. I see they have stopped this stupid process. I mean the fruit in Oz is grown in many states and transported in big semi trailers over state borders to their markets. They obviously don't have to stop at borders and get rid of their load, so why should I have to dump my two bananas and three apples? They even have a solitary wheely bin sitting at the side of the road for the dumping. So I sail through and ignore it all, and hope I will not be jumped on by an army of cops waiting round the corner. Luckily I lived to tell this tale to you and wasn't banged up in some fetid police cell for gross cross border fruit smuggling. The Police were all too busy watching footy or cricket or otherwise engaged.

Port MacDonnel is another one main street wonder, with a few houses and shops. It is situated right on a large sheltered bay with a long jetty and many boats moored in the bay. They are all medium sized fishing boats, no sailing boats at all. The caravan park is small and I am the only visitor that night. No wonder it is up for sale. The place is absolutely dead, nothing happening at all. I am glad that at places like this I can spend the evening looking at the gogglebox and ABC, which shows many BBC programmes. Some I have already seen back home, but I am quite happy to see them a second time as mostly I have forgotten what they were about. I have been able to get TV reception at all the places I have stopped at, but this will stop, I know, when I get into the more remote places.

Disaster last night. On writing up my journal on this trip something happened with my secondhand laptop when I went to move down to a new line, it went to a new page. I happily typed on, writing two lines, then I wanted to go back to the previous page to check something and couldn't get up there with the cursor. Then I noticed that the page numbering was reading 1/1, which meant that somehow the computer had started a new document without my asking it to. The original 30 odd pages I had carefully written over the past five weeks or more, had disappeared. I hoped that it hadn't gone for good and could be retrieved as I did not fancy rewriting it all again and trying to remember everything. It had crossed my mind that I could lose a whole document and was thinking about what I could do to safeguard this eventuality. If I were at home I would print out pages at regular intervals, so at least I would have it on paper. I would have to buy a cheap printer.

Anyway back to the action… lovely day, so back to the road by 9am and along the short distance to the next large town of Mt Gambier. (see photo 42) This turned out to be a nice interesting place. (see photo 42a, b, c & d.) It is built on an old volcano site or should I say the site of a couple of them, and in geological terms, a fairly recent made one, as it blew its way into being only 5,000 years ago. The local Aborigines can even still remember it happening as they have stories about it erupting!

Driving into the town on the right hand side of the road you see a beautiful bright blue lake in what is obviously the crater of an old volcano. (see photo 43) There are three such lakes all next to each other all in volcanoes. The water in them supplies the town with all its water requirements.

Apparently a lot of Australia, millions of years ago before the big freeze, was under water. The skeletons and bones of all the sea creatures that died, dropped to the bottom of the sea and over millions of years compacted to form limestone. When the big freeze came the sea levels dropped and the limestone is now left as dry land. Over long periods of time rain water fell onto the land and mixing with the soils and leaves etc, turns acidic. This eats into the soft stone and permeates down into the lower layers of the land. It meets with hot lava in certain places, turns into superheated steam, high pressure, big bang. Hey presto a volcano spewing forth lots of volcanic ash which falls on top of the limestone. So after everything cools down we have a landscape with layers of lime and volcanic stone with some nice big craters. Rain water permeating through the layers of stone and eating its way through the stone horizontally, then runs into the volcanic craters making lakes of very pure water.

Also in certain places the rock is eaten away so much that it forms into underground caverns. Some of whose roofs get weak and collapse downwards making a hole in the ground which is called a sink hole. (see photo 44) Off these sink holes run underground rivers in tunnels eaten out of the rock. So all around this town and into the surrounding countryside are many caves and ponds and lakes, all formed in this way. Right in the centre of town is a sink hole and another one not far away from the town centre which has an underground river running off it through which divers regularly swim along as a training exercise.

Well after viewing all these interesting holes and caves, which I find dead interesting because I think I definitely must at one time been a caveman, as they have always fascinated me, it's time to move on. (see photo 45 & 46)

The countryside is still fairly flat and given to grazing of cattle and sheep. I take the coast road again towards a place called Beachport. I pass more dense man made forests of pine trees and a very large wood mill which is obviously turning the huge mounds of wood chips into paper. Bog paper to be exact and the company Kimberly Clarke makes Oz bog paper. On this subject beware as Oz bog paper isn't a patch on the Brit stuff. Its miserly thin and dangerous and has to be used three or four folds at a time to be on the safe side. Thought you may like to know that!

Beachport is an archetypal Aussie small town as most of the small towns are in Oz. By this I mean they are all built on the square grid pattern which makes it easy to get around but dull and boring as they are all similar in their style. As most are built on fairly flat land, this also lends them to being boring. On top of this all are built within the past 150 years and many of the buildings are pretty plain. The buildings that were going to be used by local government departments are usually the best built, and out of local stone. Built in pleasing Victorian styles, they are always the nicest building in these towns. Of course some towns are hideous and have no decent buildings at all and are what I call one horse towns with one main street with a few other streets off that, if you are lucky. Mostly these type of towns are found in the bush, so far most of the towns I had gone through to date were not too bad.

Beachport had few shops and I saw hardly any people. So had a quick coffee at the local general shop which sells everything, and got going towards the seaside town of Robe. Drove through flat land of a mixture of grazing, bush trees and shrubs and lakes of quite a decent size. Some of the land looked boggy and unproductive. Saw two emus in one field, I wondered if they were running wild around there? I wondered if they were an oddity, as an Aussie couple had stopped their car to look at them. (see photo 47)

Robe is yet another small place, but quite pleasant and full of caravan parks, so it must be a holiday place where no doubt amongst others, people from Adelaide spend weekends there. It is on a horseshoe shaped bay so the waters are nice and calm as they are sheltered. I book into a nicely laid out caravan site next to the waters edge.

The site is quite well occupied by weekenders staying in the fixed cabins and in their caravans, plus a couple of Motorhomes. I find that at these sites most of my fellow travellers in Oz seem to favour the caravan, mostly pulled by some stonking great 4 wheel drive unit. The guy next to me is one of the few who owns a Brit 4wd, namely a Discovery, and I get talking to him. He is a professional fisherman based at Kangeroo Island which is near Adelaide. He didn't fish himself anymore but took the Public out on his boat on fishing trips. He was about my age and we quickly get into a deep conversation about the state of immigration in Oz as at present. Which due to today's extreme political correctness, I will not be able to report verbatim! Whilst we were talking it started to get dark and we were quickly enveloped in a swarm of mossies. As I was wearing shorts, I did an imitation of a Red Indian war dancer trying to stop the wretched creatures from settling on me. I thought I was winning, and then he suggested for my sake (he was wearing longs) that we stop the conversation and get into our homes. I thought I had been successful and all the next day I was fine, no scratching. How wrong I was because it started about 4pm in the afternoon, and by evening I had about half a dozen red spots that were itching like crazy. Motto, do not stand outside in the evening unless you cover all exposed skin in anti mossy spray!

One thing I had noticed with all these towns on the Southern coasts and even a lot of those down the Eastern coast from Sydney, and that is many of them have either no boats moored by them, even when they have a breakwater. If there are boats they are usually all power boats of the fishing type.

The use of sailing boats seems to be almost non existent. I wonder why? I will try and find out from the guy in the caravan next to me to whom I spoke with before retiring. I waylaid him the next morning before I booked out, but could not elicit a sensible answer out of him. Quite why I don't know as being on the seas full time as his business you would have thought he could have answered such a simple question.

This caravan site cost me $25 which is in the upper echelons of prices. But it is really quite cheap because even this high figure equates to only £10. The drive all the way from Robe was through ever drier looking country. Quite flat with many hills present, which were low and really only hillocks. Dry looking grass, few signs of grazing cattle, no signs of crop growing. So I don't know how the farmers made a living around there. I did go past one area that was given over to wine grape growing, and some pine forests, but in the main it was all looking parched.

The road was well maintained but there were few towns, in fact I passed through only four on the whole 307 kilometres trip, so that means you are driving along a fairly boring straight road for mile after mile with boring countryside. This to warn you is what driving in Oz can be like. It's not all like the day I had along the lovely coast, day before yesterday. This brings me to mention one big negative aspect about driving in Oz. That is ACCIDENTS. The accident rate in Oz is horrendous compared to the UK and it always has been. It hasn't changed much from when I was here in the mid 60's. They are still going on about the same old subjects to do with it, as they were then. So it seems to me they have learnt little in the last 40 years. The problem in cities is somewhat different than on the open road so I will comment only on the open road probs. Which is; because of the boring straight roads, and the lack of traffic on them, and the boring scenery for hundreds of miles, some drivers just nod off. This means that you get a sickening death toll from head on accidents. Couple this with the fact that the average Oz truck is a humongous American rig with two trailers or more behind it, and usually going well over their speed limit which I think in Oz is 100K's. In the UK they are limited to 60mph. 100K's is equivalent to 66mph, so at that speed they are going far too fast and when they are doing 110 as most are, they are madness personified. On top of this they are going on in the Oz newspapers and in Parliament, about truck drivers taking drugs to keep awake. So you see it is all a bit dodgy. (I know that I have covered all this already, but just reminding you.)

In South Australia they are putting red steel pole markers at the side of the road at spots where a death has occurred. On this stretch of road from Robe, along one particular stretch I counted six red poles all within 5 miles and all this on a stretch which is quite straight and one wonders just how anyone could have an accident. Well it can only be the type of accident I have outlined, which happen on Oz roads. Sleepy drivers, drivers being inattentive, and so on. So what I am saying is when in Oz you just have to be 100 percent on the ball when driving. I have driven many, many thousands of miles in Oz and all over the place, and so far I have never had an accident. Whereas in the UK I have had many minor bumps in cities due to density of traffic. So do not be alarmed, just be careful and aware of the possible dangers.

All along on this days trip you pass many shallow lakes, if you can call them lakes. It appears that water collects in shallow depressions and then dries up in the summer. It seems to leave a salty residue behind, so these patches that are left are white. (see photo 48) They are all over the place and there seems to be no obvious answer as to why they occur where they do. Some are small and some quite large in area. Then about 60K's north of Robe you start to pass on your left side, which is on the ocean side, a very long strip of water. Like a river but it's not a river. They call it a lagoon but strictly speaking it's not a lagoon either. Between it and the sea is a narrow strip of land which is called the Younghusband Peninsular and is made up entirely of quite high sand dunes. If your familiar with Dorset it is a larger replica of the

Chesil Bank but that is a shingle bank, otherwise it's the same thing.

They say that this lagoon waterway is the longest in Oz, and I can believe that as it stretches for some 225 Klms. (see photo 49) It eventually meets the mouth of the great Murray River which exits to the Ocean, South of Adelaide. Just in from the coast there are two largish lakes one is called Lake Albert (no doubt after Victoria's Albert) (see photo 50) and one called Lake Alexandria. (probably after one of her daughters). Both these lakes are shallow. Alexandria is 5 to 6 metres deep and Albert only around 1.5 to 2 metres. This means they can be choppy on a windy day. They are fresh water as they have damned the entrance to all these waterways at the sea entrances, in order to keep them fresh. Although I read in the paper that due to the prolonged drought and lack of water into the Murray, these lakes were showing a much higher level of salinity and are decreasing in size. I guess they can't damn the river 100% otherwise the outflow would never get out to the ocean at all.

Eventually I came to the town of Murray Bridge, (see photo 50) which is an apt name as there is a bridge across the Murray at this town. So some bright spark in the old days knew just what to call the town. In actual fact there are two bridges next to each other, one the road bridge which was built at the end of the 1800's and in 1925 they put up the rail bridge. Driving in I passed a petrol station and there parked was a Cobra Replica sportscar. This being the model of car I spent 20 years building in the UK, which meant I just had to stop and talk to its owner. This I do and a guy in his late 50's from Mt Gambier is on his way to a Cobra owners club meet somewhere in Adelaide. We chat about cars for about half an hour. Seems that getting specialist cars registered in Oz is easier now than when I had plans to build them back in 85, and deciding it was too bureaucratic and returned to the UK to do it.

The Murray is say 500 metres across at this spot and that is quite wide. This river is Aussies longest river and runs all the way into NSW and into the Snowy mountains. (see photo 52) It is also navigable for a very long distance. How long I do not know but I've read that paddle steamers went right into NSW. They still operate along it and there are some to be seen at this town. In fact at a town called Goolwa which is situated at the entrance to the river at the sea coast, they built over the years, 31 paddle steamers. At Murray Bridge I saw them building large houseboats in a yard next to the caravan park that I booked into which was on the river side, and there is a marina there also with a number of these houseboats moored there. They are the size of a good sized bungalow, so you could say they are the river equivalent of road motorhomes. (see photo 53 & 54.)

One thing I must say about Oz caravan parks and that is that most of the ones I have been in up to now, is that they are nice and quiet. At least they are at this time of year, as most are not very full. I guess it's because of the time of year. It is not into full summer time, so the hordes have not filled them. I was not looking forward to when they will get busier as they would be full of noisy kids and barking dogs.

I decided to stay on for two nights as on the Sunday I would be better not trying to get into Adelaide and into a park there. Also I saw on my scout round that they do river cruises along the Murray, and I thought that that would make a nice diversion for the Sunday afternoon. So on the Sunday morning I took things easy and cleaned up the home inside and out, cleaned up the scooter which gets filthy on the back, especially when it has rained.

My mossy bites are itching like hell, and I resolve to get some cream on Monday to take away the itch. I found I had picked up a slow puncture along the way and the offside front tyre was flat. So that is another job for Monday morning before I set off for Adelaide.

In the afternoon I had hoped to enjoy the boat trip, however as I and a Dutch couple were the only people who turned up for the trip at 2.30pm, understandably the boat owner said it was not worth him taking just three people. So instead I mooched around on my scooter just looking around. Saw a garage that specialised on Norton motorbikes, which considering where we were seemed strange to me as you do not see many Norton bikes in the UK let alone in a place like this. Especially as he had a little museum of about a dozen different models on show. As he was open I spent some time talking bikes to him. He had raced them and raced cars on speedway tracks. Being a lover of Brit bikes I found it strange that he had never visited the UK. But then there are many, many Aussies who have never made a trip to the Mother Country.

Not much to see really, so back to the caravan site. It is next to a marina which is full of quite large houseboats with people living on them.(see photo 55) The marina is a little lake which looks like it has been dug out of land next to the river itself. There are many swallows flying around and they are obviously nesting on the tops of the twin hulls, on which the houseboat platforms sit. It always amazes me how quickly these birds fly, they are truly the spitfires of the bird world, zooming about up and down, wheeling about, banking into tight turns and skimming inches above the water. In the UK I have never seen these birds other than in flight. So to my surprise there were at this marina, many of these birds taking it easy by sitting on the boat rails. There were rows of them preening themselves on the rails and mooring cables. Then they would jump off and do some manic flying to return back to the rails, presumably when they got knackered. So this was a first.

On Monday morning, first I had to get the tyre fixed. It turned out not to be a puncture as I thought but a weld that had sprung a leak. That was fixed by inserting an inner tube and so doing away with having to rely on the integrity of the wheel itself to keep in the air. Then it was off to do some emailing, have a coffee get a paper and then get on my way, which I did about 11.30am. Just outside the town a Freeway starts and it goes all the way to Adelaide, so the 76 kilometre trip only took just over an hour. The weather was very overcast all morning and the rain started seriously falling as I got started. This plus a good thunder and lightening show made me wonder when summer was going to start.

As you get close to Adelaide you approach a large hill they call Mt Barker, so the road climbs steadily upwards. Coming down the other side it is quite steep and you quickly reach the outskirts of Adelaide. First impressions were that it was clean and there was less traffic. Also people didn't seem to be hell bent on getting to where they were going to, as in Sydney and Melbourne. I took the road to the coastal area known as Glenelg, as this was near one of the seaside caravan parks I had seen on the Adelaide road map, which I had bought back in Murray Bridge and had studied. I was quickly on the coast and after a quick look around the marina I headed to the caravan park. Very nice too.

Chapter Six

Adelaide: Sights and History

A much smaller city than either Melbourne or Sydney, both from a city centre size, to its overall size. Like all Oz cities, easy to get about because of the wide roads built on a grid pattern system. However even though it was started by a chappy called Lights who was the Surveyor general at the time and laid out the city, (see photo 56 & 57) at much the same time as other major Oz cities and that is around the early 1800's. It has less historical buildings that you would want to check out. From an historical point of view it hasn't much to look at and take in. So one need spend less time in Adelaide than in Melbourne or Sydney. Also the seaside areas are not as lengthy or as interesting as Melbourne or S.

As with M, you could if you wanted to, use it as a base to travel to nearby areas on day trips.

There are several inland areas such as the Barossa Valley wine growing area, which is 75 Klms away. Famous for it's wines and likened to the German Rhine area, especially as it was started by German immigrants in the mid 1800's. Another area worth a look at is the nearby Adelaide Hills and Mt Lofty, some 20 Klms away, so a short drive. Here you can get good views of the whole of the Adelaide area and plains below. Kangaroo Island which is off the extreme Southern end of the Fleurieu Peninsular south of Adelaide, is a destination for many. To get to it you can drive from Adelaide to Cape Jervis and get a ferry across.

The Adelaide Port area is touted as an historical area worth a look, yet here I was sorely disappointed. It is decidedly run down and scruffy, and hardly any activity going on. Most of the dock area did not look as if it were even used, with disused warehouses and empty wharves, and town streets almost devoid of commercial activity and lots of empty shops. (see photo 58, 59 & 60) You find even in Sydney and Melbourne, that port areas are not used as they were in past years, due to containerisation. However those two cities have and are still redeveloping their port areas with new shopping centres, entertainment venues, blocks of waterside flats etc. Adelaide seems to have no redevelopments going on at all. It's as if Adelaide has gone to sleep on this one. Pity.

One thing I did like about Adelaide, is the older areas of it have nice style housing and the whole city is generally very clean and tidy. Also the general quality of the road surfaces is better than Sydney or Melbourne. The average side street is quite wide and the older houses (mostly bungalows) were all different and generally in good order. Most of them were either full stone construction, or had stone facings at the front, and were on generous sized blocks as well. This was not the case in most of Sydney and Melbourne. The streets mostly had generous sized trees which tended to cover the whole road, thus shading it from the summer sun as well as affording a bit of shade to the houses as well. So overall the feeling of space, greenery and shade, was excellent.

The only seaside area that I found to have some ambiance, was the area called Glenelg, where I first came into on my arrival here. The bay that it is on is called Holdfast Bay and it is where the first settlers arrived at, back in the 1830's. There is a jetty (see photo 61) and the main road leading into Glenelg is called Jetty Rd.(see photo 64) I wonder why? It has a village feel about it with shops on either side of the road and a tram service that runs from the City that runs down the middle of the road. It is Adelaide's only tram line and it is the noisiest tram I have ever heard Worldwide. (see photo 62 & 63) The trams consist of two carriages each and they are the originals from its inception back in the 1920's. In fact they have just announced on the local TV that they are celebrating their 75th year in operation and admitting they are extremely noisy. However in 2005 they are to be replaced with nice new modern ones made in Switzerland. So if you make it to Adelaide you will be able to ride on them. Apparently they had tram routes all over Adelaide until the 60's when they decided they were too old hat and got rid of all the routes except this one and that because of the stink put up by the locals. The bay on the weekends has plenty of sailing etc going on its waters, plus lots of activity on its white sandy beaches. (see photo 65, 66 & 67)

The caravan park is nicely laid out, plenty of nice good conditioned lawns and good facilities and quite large in size. Situated right next to the beaches and about two miles North of Glenelg centre. Cost of $25 a night, but no discount for weekly stays as at other parks. Also due to its locality near the beach it is popular with young families and as we all know children can and do make noise. So if that is not your cup of tea it will not be for you. Another plus or minus depending on what you like, is that with this park it has a resident flock of parakeets. If you know what they are like you will know they are incredibly noisy. They screech and squawk incessantly and start at dawn. Along with all the other species of birds to be found, the dawn chorus can be deafening. It doesn't particularly bother me, but may bother some. You will find at all Oz parks this problem with bird noise, because generally they plant a lot of trees in them to give shade and nice parkland looks, they attract birds like crazy. Another negative point about this particular site was that it was at the end of Adelaide's airport runway. However this airport is not so busy and the flights do not go on after about 9pm. So I found it bearable.

Mind you I have always found so far, that all the parks I have stayed at to date have been generally quiet and well behaved especially after 11pm. So getting a good nights sleep so far has been good. I have booked to stay the rest of my stay in Adelaide at a park very near to the city centre, which will enable me to look around there much easier, and they give a discount for weekly bookings.

The weather has continued to be most unseasonal because we are now into Summertime. Yet all week it has been overcast with showers. This has been happening all over Oz so the drought that has been a fact of Oz life for so long, means that any rain is wanted by the natives. As a tourist it is a bit of a damper on things. Eventually the weather did pick up and it started to feel as if Summer was going to happen after all.

I managed to get out a bit more and had some good walks around the city centre. One good thing about this caravan park is that being next to the River Torrens (see photo 68, 69, 70, 71 & 72) which has a walking path alongside it which goes through to the city, means you have a nice walk that's not too long which takes you right into the heart of the city. You soon reach the parklands that are situated on both sides of the river and there are plenty of trees which means wildlife. Parakeets, cockatoos, and ducks, and today I saw in the River at least a dozen nice big fat fish. Which I later enquired about and found that they are European Carp, introduced into Oz. At least 18 inches long and dark brown. They looked a bit like the Mullet we get in abundance in the River Stour at Christchurch, and it surprised me to see them because the river looks black and dead. Especially when I saw the sign on the banks which tells you the river is polluted and there are pipes going into the river which are pouring out stuff which doesn't look too healthy. Maybe they are aerating the water. Obviously the river cannot be all that polluted if there is a healthy population of large fish in it.

Adelaide has a mixture of old style buildings alongside the modern. There are plenty of two story Victorian buildings which have balconies on the second floor, which are adorned with lace type metal working. You do not see as much of this in Sydney or Melbourne as you do here. You do on the private houses, but not on the commercial buildings in the city centres. (see photo 73 & 80)

I found a building on Flinders St which has proved a Godsend as it houses a charity concern to do with helping the aged. They have a dozen computers which are free to use, to connect to the internet and you can stay on them for as long as you wish. So I have been saving quite a lot this week.

Back to the weather, one thing that you have to put up with Oz weather is the ability for the weather to fluctuate. If it's not hot then cold then rain then hot again, it is nice temperatures in the mid 20's then suddenly a day or two of ridiculously temperatures, in the high 30's. I had two days in the 38's on last Friday and Saturday. Driving the scooter was like driving it in an oven. So I thought on the Saturday I just had to try and find somewhere cooler to go. A lot of people would say is why not go to the beach? Well my beach days are over and as for swimming in the sea, that for me is strictly out in Oz. There are just too many sharks for my liking. This was amply highlighted by a horrific incident off the beach that I had just spent a week living alongside, when I was at the last caravan park at Glenelg. Some young men in the teens were playing in the water with a small power boat, pulling their friends along behind it on a small board. The lad they were pulling fell off as they do, and was immediately set upon by two of the most fearsome sharks known to man....great whites. They tore him in half and ate him in front of his frantic mates. He was 18. They found virtually nothing of him, just some bits and pieces. It was so horrific it made the headlines even in the UK. Couple this with the fact that recently another man was eaten off the Queensland Barrier Reef whilst spear fishing and another off Perth and both these incidents since I have been here, is why I do not swim in the sea. Of course the most popular beaches off NSW and Qld have nets around them so your safe. S.A doesn't have shark nets nor does W.A. So be careful where you swim. Most caravan parks have swimming pools and many beach areas have them as well. So if you are into swimming, you do not have to go into the sea at all.

Actually the chances of being gobbled up by a shark is lower than being knocked over crossing the road, or even by being killed by boozed up aggressive Oz drivers. To illustrate this, a fisherman out in a large commercial fishing boat, fishing with his father off Brisbane, was unlucky to have the Seine nets get tangled up on something under the boat, and the boat was flipped over with his Dad still in the wheelhouse. His Dad was gone with the boat when it sank, and as he was on deck, he got thrown over board. He had no time to grab a life jacket or an EPIRB (positioning beacon) He drifted for two days a total of 100 kilometres down the coast, being swept in and out from the coast and to as much as 20 kilometres out to sea. All he had to cling onto was a 12 metre bamboo thin pole, and his will to survive. On the beginning of his third day, a Sunday fisher coming back from a night out, almost ran him down, and he was saved. The point here is that he spent over 48 hours in a sea infested with sharks… didn't get eaten. It's the luck of the draw, but I am a coward.

Back to keeping cool. I plumbed to take a run into the nearby Adelaide Hills. I knew it would be a bit cooler up there, and there is a vantage point they call Mt Lofty (see photo 81) which was discovered by Mathew Flinders, the great British explorer of the 1800's. So it was back onto the main highway going back towards Murray Bridge and five miles down it taking the turn off to Mt Lofty. What a view you get from the observation deck they have built around the tall tower that was built in 1901 to commemorate Flinders find. There is also a modern building housing a cafe and restaurant, toilets and shop. From the observation point you get the full panoramic view of the whole of the plain and coastline, upon which sits Adelaide.

After this I had a coffee and cake and set off back down again but via the back roads rather than back to the main highway. The hills around Mt Lofty are a national park and covered in Oz trees. So the road twists and turns all the way down and back into the suburbs of the city.

Sunday was a scorcher too. So I resolved to again get back up into them thar hills. This time to visit the Car Museum at a village deep into the Adelaide Hills. (see photo 82) Some 40 K's away. A good chance to view the whole of this area. The history of this area is one that never ceases to amaze me about the early history of settlement in OZ in the early 1800's. As I have said the area of Adelaide first had settlers settling it in about 1830 and within a year they had found this area of the hills and realised that there was good soil, plenty of water, lower temperatures than the plain and the woods were not dense. They could be easily cleared to give pastures for grazing and the growing of fruits and vegetables. Within a few years the whole area was getting well settled and farms and villages were springing up. They didn't mess about those early settlers and it must have been dammed hard as they did not have the means of nowadays, like mechanised tools etc or transport to quickly transport up there what they need to build. On top of this no roads either, they had to make the tracks to get anywhere, and they were not the roads like you have today.

Multiply this activity to all over Australia, new Zealand and the USA and those folk of the early 1800's and onwards, were hardy folk, and I wonder if the soft people of today could do what they did, opening out all these great and new lands.

Anyway, the result is that the Adelaide Hills is a beautiful place to explore and anyone coming to Adelaide must go and visit the area. The hills are no more than a 1,000 metres at the highest, so what you get are lowish rolling hills. There is a mixture of hillsides that have been cleared for grazing or for growing vegetables or vineyards or orchards. It is an ever changing scenery as you drive along. The road twists and turns constantly, and you going up or down these hills, and mixed among the farmed areas are small forests of local trees together with the lighter greens of imported types of tree. An ever changing vista which I found delightful and the small villages that support the farming community were different too.

I got a booklet from the large Tourist Info shop in King William St which highlights 40 great walks in SA. From this I picked out a couple of good walks near to the centre of Adelaide. Unlike Sydney or Melbourne which are such big cities, so the surrounding countryside can be more than 50 miles away, with Adelaide being relatively small, you only have to go for 10 to 15 minutes from the centre, and you are in the Hills.

The first one I took was called the Morialta Falls Gorge and this is a gorge cut out of the hills by a stream called Fourth Creek. This feeds the Torrens River. There are four different walks around this area and well worth doing. (see photo 83)

The second is called Waterfall Gully (see photo 84 & 85) and this can be walked right up to Mt Lofty summit, if you wish to go that far. Easy to say isn't it, because I walked it right to the top and it is uphill all the way. But for those who like walking it's a good work out and it gave my slack heart some exercise. The road leading to the start of the walk is called Waterfall Gully Rd and it goes on for quite a way before you get to the end and the car park where you start the serious stuff. This road leads up the gully which is at this point about 100 to 150 metres wide. So you have the narrow road, a stream alongside it and nice houses on mostly one side only. The sides of the gully are steep and high and thickly wooded, so these houses, most of which look expensive, are in a superb location. Lots of greenery and shade around them, but houses built anywhere in Oz that are near thickly wooded areas are vulnerable to forest fires.

The walk is I guess about two kilometres long to the top, (see photo 86 & 87) but as I have previously explained there is a cafe at Mt Lofty and boy did I need it. I slaked my dry mouth on a nice ice cold iced tea. The only downer was the price, which was a dollar more than I pay down in civilisation. The walk back is all downhill, which funnily enough is almost as hard going as going up, as it is so steep and is a loose rubble track. So you are using your leg muscles to try to stop yourself slithering down out of control. I would advise anyone who walks anywhere in Oz to be fit and take a bottle of water with you and a mobile phone. At the top I could see a fire that had started on the hillside below us. Good job it was away from the area I was going to be in, on my way down. But anything can happen in Oz bush and if you can get a signal you may need the phone.

Another place that I found was great, are the Botanical gardens near the city centre and off the North Terrace. (see photo 88 & 91.) Both Sydney and Melbourne have botanical gardens but I have to say that I thought that Adelaide's garden beats them both. Very well laid out and very pretty and obviously a favourite with people as the day I visited was Boxing Day and it was full of people picnicking and just lying around in the shade of the many large trees from all over the World.

I was running out of places to visit so on the Friday after Xmas I decided to take a look at the old Adelaide Goal just outside the town centre. Built not long after the start of Adelaide. Not so large but worth a visit and I found it quite interesting. They give you a tape player and you take yourself around whilst listening to a commentary. I found it better than the old Melbourne Goal with more to look at.

After Xmas I took the Transit Home to the local Ford dealer to investigate the whistle coming from the engine. Knowing it had something to do with the turbo I felt it needed to be investigated as if it packed up in the middle of nowhere and my next phase of the trip, which will head me out to and over the Nullabour. It turned out that the turbo has now packed in, which didn't surprise me as it always felt as if it were not working at all. Quite why they didn't work this out when I had it in at Melbourne, I don't know. It messes up my plans though, as I had planned to leave Adelaide on the Monday after the New Year weekend. Now I will have to take it in on the Tuesday, the first day they are back at work, and then keep myself occupied for up to three days. As I have seen all I can in Adelaide I have decided to go on my scooter to the South and cross over to Kangaroo Island and spend two or three days there.

So after depositing the Transit at Jarvis Ford I made sure that I had enough gear to see me through a few days and loaded them onto the scooter. I had bought a scooter box whilst in Adelaide which fits to the small bracket rear of the seat, and this enabled me to carry a spare 5 litre can of petrol and other bits. I took my wet weather gear and was glad I did, and that went into the box compartment under the seat. Change of clothing, washing gear, shaving gear etc all went in my small back pack. The weather was dodgy being overcast and not too warm. So I soon had to stick on my waterproof sailing jacket and I was glad I was wearing my heavy duty hiking boots as it looked like it was going to rain. So I first went to Glenelg and caught up on my emails, had a coffee and set off down the Main South Road which runs down the Fleurieu Peninsular towards Cape Jervis, where I would catch the ferry to Kangeroo Island. The road is very good all the way to the quaintly named 'Spongy' township, it being a dual carriageway. Then it goes into a twin carriageway with mainly tarmacked hard shoulders. Now driving a scooter on such a road without a tarmac hard shoulder is decidedly dodgy. With it you can drive on it and that leaves the lane, which usually isn't too wide, on which the mad car drivers can drive on. No tarmac hard shoulder and your scooting along as far over to the left as you can get, without falling off onto the loose gravel hard shoulder. So far I have found 95% of drivers are great and give you a wide berth no matter where your scooter is positioned. They go over right onto the other lane as if they were overtaking a car. But you always get the dickheads who sneak up on you and it's usually when you have not been regularly checking the rear view mirrors. Suddenly out of the blue here's this car front wing a foot away from you and going past you. Really scary especially if there is a strong side wind, which there was on this day, as this tends to make you weave a bit. You simply cannot help it, so it could easily be that just as they pass close to you, that you get blown over to your right and into them. So for those of you who may do as I have and have a motorbike or scooter, this is what some Oz drivers are like.

I had not gone more than 20 K's and it started to rain and it did so on and off all the way to Jervis. So really glad I was fully togged up. It was just like being in the UK and very unseasonal weather too. It is quite a long run of 105 kilometres and I was able to make it easy on my one tank full of 5 litres with some left. I got to Cape Jervis about 4pm and could have caught the 4.30 ferry. However the ferry company who will also check the hotels for vacancies, could not come up with a vacancy at a price I thought reasonable. My limit was $80 or £32 and even that I thought too expensive. So I opted to stay at Cape Jervis overnight and take the 9.30 morning ferry and I could have a room for two nights at $65 per night at a pub/hotel at the main town on the Island, of Kingscote. I booked into the Cape Jervis Inn and had a meal in their bar, before retiring.

Being as I can cook for myself when I have the motorhome, the whole area of Oz food and eating out, is not something that one will generally have to deal with. However some of you will at some stage, want to eat out and try the local cuisine and like in the UK, pub meals are generally cheaper. On this enforced trip without the home I would have to rely on living in hotels and eating out. I personally think that both are very often more expensive than you can pay in the UK. For instance it is still possible to get a perfectly good B&B even on the South coast for £25 a night. Here even though they use the same term it doesn't mean that this is a cheaper alternative to a hotel. I was later on in the week offered a B&B in a family home for $110 (something like £45).

The ferry (see photo 92) was quite large, being a catamaran, which is favoured by the Aussies. You will find that the big cats on the English Channel are built in Oz. This wasn't as big as those, but big enough to hold 30/40 cars and some trucks. The crossing is only about 12/15 miles and so only takes 45 minutes. The sea was OK, bit of a swell but nowhere near as choppy as the day before. Penneshaw where it lands is directly opposite Cape Jervis, and is only a very small hamlet. I got me a paper and had a cup of coffee and filled up with petrol, then set off for Kingscote which is on the opposite side of a large bay and inlet called Neapean Bay and Eastern Cove. A 60 K's trip. The weather was much better than the previous day which was a blessing, but it was still overcast and chilly. (see photo 93)

About halfway I came across sign pointing off to the right to a place called American River. Didn't know why, so set off to find out. After a 19 K's stretch of road I got to the place. (see photo 94) Nothing much to write about, obviously a holiday home type of place. However the inlet it is on, on the northern shore, it has many black swans on it. Dozens and dozens of them, so the shallow waters which they all had they heads into, must contains good tucker for them. Some Pelicans too could be seen. At the jetty area there were about a dozen moored sailing boats, so this must be a favourite place to either sail to or to keep your boat at. Certainly well sheltered. I found from reading an info board, that the place got its name from the fact that in the very early 1800's American whalers used this Bay as a base to operate out of. Quite why the River bit got into it I do not know as it isn't a river at all but merely an inlet.

So after looking around it was back to the highway and on my way to Kingscote. The land out of Penneshaw is initially hilly then it flattens out and the rest of the Island is mainly quite flat. No big hills to talk of. Kingscote was a fairly large little township, if you know what I mean. Certainly the largest on the Island and it was here that the first settlers in South Australia settled on. That is to say the first official settlers. People had been visiting the area since the very early 1800's. The whole of the South Eastern corner of Oz was used by sealers and they would make camp at various places, and they certainly used Kangaroo Island. In 1802 Captain Mathew Flinders who explored a lot of South Australia, explored parts of K.I and named it thus. He found a hill near American River and named it Prospect Hill, and commented on a particular spot on the nearby coastline, because it had many Pelicans who appeared to go to that spot just to die. In 1803 a Frenchman called Nicolas Baudin circumnavigated the island and visited a spot now called Frenchmans Rock, which is near the ferry terminal at Penneshaw.

In 1804 an American brig, 'Union', met Baudin at a spot called King George Sound near Albany in Western Australia, while in the area on a sealing expedition, and K.I was recommended as a place to seal from. In 1819 a Capt George Sutherland visited the Island to obtain salt and seal skins and stayed for seven months. At a small cemetery I saw a description which described him as the first farmer on the Island. Also it is certainly the case that private settlers from the UK did settle on the Island before official settlement.

In 1831 whaling started from the Island and Capt Sutherland wrote a glowing report on the Island which persuaded a company which had been set up in the UK to oversee the official settlement of S.A, to start the settlement of S.A on K.I.

So it was in July 1836 that the first official settlers, through the South Australian Company arrived in Nepean Bay on the vessel Duke of York. They made settlement at a spot on the coast which is now part of the outskirts of Kingscote,(renamed in 1940) but which they originally called Queenscliff. However they quickly found that K.I was not to the companies liking. They had hoped to supply passing ships engaged in sealing and whaling, with supplies some of which they intended to grow on the Island. They found that there was poor soil where they were, and not enough rain, thus a lack of water. So in 1837 they moved to Adelaide. However in later years private settlers came to the island and it did grow and become a farming area.

My hotel is one of the original old hotels of the township and the room I am given is OK but a little scruffy with dirty windows and cobwebs hanging down from the ceiling. All the floorboards in the room and along the corridor to the room, creak like crazy. Maybe all the original nails have rusted away and not been replaced! I have a meal that first night in their restaurant, which was OK but not brilliant and the desert is a total rip off as it was so small I needed a magnifying glass to be able to find it on the plate, yet they charged me $5.50 for this. I was not best pleased and decided to find another place to eat the next night.

I pottered around that first afternoon getting my bearings and looking at the first settlement site. (see photo 95, 96, 97 & 98) This has a mulberry tree which was planted by those first settlers and still bears fruit. In fact I had a good eat of some of those berries, and they were the first mulberries I had ever eaten. I assume they must grow in England otherwise why the kids nursery rhyme, but I cannot say I have ever seen them for sale in supermarkets. Nearby is a little cemetery in which some early settlers are buried, and like many historical sites in Oz, I found it rather sadly neglected. Here they have a very important site which although in European terms is not very old, in Oz terms it is and yet they cannot do it right, or do service to the memory of those first settlers who came all that way in hardship to an unknown alien land, many only to die young. The whole area is fenced in and that was done OK, but the land was almost bare of any grass and full of dead leaves and pine needles, thus giving it that neglected uncared for air. There were not that many graves and yet they were all in a sorry state, needing restoring. The whole cemetery should have been well grassed and kept watered, like their lawns in their houses, and the graves restored. I was to see other such sites in similar condition to this.

So on my second day after perusing my map and guide to K.I, I decided that as there did not appear that much to actually look at, I would only give it another full day for looking around and then depart on the morning of the third day. There is a road running along the south side of the Island and one across the top. I decided to do the loop of the Island along these two roads, and set off fairly early (for me).

My first stop was for morning coffee was at a place called Vivonne Bay and here there was one of those stores that sells and does everything. After my refreshment I took the unsealed track which went from the highway to Point Ellen which is at the West end of the bay. I found my scooter didn't like loose unsealed tracks as the small wheels were hard to stop sliding around, but I made it in one piece. Here the coast was rocky with volcanic rock and as with all this coast of southern Oz, it receives the uninterrupted force of wind and swells of the Southern Ocean, so was pretty wild and desolate. (see photo 99) There is a jetty and some commercial fishing boats moored there and a few fisherman's cottages, all surrounded by scrub bush.

Riding further on for another 21 kilometres I arrived at the destination on the Southern side that I wanted to have a look at, and that was Kelly Hill Cave. (see photo 100) The area that this cave entrance is in is heavily wooded and there is a car park and visitors reception building, where you pay your entrance fee. A track for a couple of hundred metres leads to the entrance and a guide takes you down into the cave. Steep steel steps take you down to quite a depth and it becomes clear that the cave is a system of passages, but we would see only a portion of this system. What we did see was good and well presented in all ways. Good stalactites and stalagmites. The whole tour took about half an hour and what I learnt from it was that this cave was formed hundreds of thousands of years ago when there was more rain in the area. Water seeping down through the soft limestone ate it away and the acidic water resulted in the stalactites etc. But now it was termed a dry cave as very little water now got into the cave, so there was no longer any growth. The cave was supposed to have been found by a local farmer whose horse fell into the entrance hole and this horse was called 'Kelly'.

Most of the West end of the Island is a conservation park and as there wasn't that much to see and in any case the distances involved meant I did not have enough time to do that and drive the 100 plus K's to get back, so I took the connecting road running North to join the Northern cross road. Halfway up this I stopped at the side of a paddock with sheep in it and parked under a pine tree to eat my lunch. (see photo 101) After which I continued along the rest of my journey with nothing exciting to see. The whole of this trip was through flattish country with a mixture of scrub, forest, grazing land and crop land. The crops I saw looked like barley or oats, but not being a farmer I couldn't quite make my mind up what it was. (see photo 102) All the time I was on the Island, the weather was overcast and it was quite chilly riding my scooter.

I got back to Kingscote mid afternoon and took some photos of the first settlement landing site, and then I had a coffee. I rang the Ford dealer to find what was going on as I had not heard from them. Found that it needed a new shaft and these were extremely hard to come by as they were made by Mercedes in Germany and they were out of them. I had visions of never getting this fixed and my estimation of Ford was fast losing any credibility with me. I was assured that they thought they would come up with one.

I visited a cottage which was one of three cottages built by the brothers James and Michael Calnan. They were the first proper homes built on K.I and were built all next to each other, in 1859. They were named Faith, Hope and Charity. Faith has been demolished and Hope is now a museum to that era. Next door Charity is still lived in by a private party.

After, I wandered over to the jetty area where I knew that at 5pm Pelicans would be fed. When I arrived there was a group of Pelicans on a hillside of rocks by the waterside and another group on a beach a little way off. I was one of the first to arrive and I sat down on one of the rocks and people were arriving in a steady stream and all sitting down on the wall of rocks with Pelicans also sitting on the lower rocks but in close proximity to all the people. They didn't seem fazed by all these people, and the Pelicans over on the beach would one by one take off and fly over to the rocks. Some landing on the water and some winging in and onto the rocks which were already crowded. So a lot of Pelican squabbling broke out as they jostled each other to get a foothold. It was quite a surreal atmosphere with this large crowd of murmuring people and large crowd of squawking Pelicans, all expectant of some sort of action about to start anytime now. (see photo 103 & 104)

Dead on the dot of 5 a ute pulls up and a bloke gets out carrying a plastic bucket full of bits of fish.

The Pelicans on seeing him obviously know who he was and they are going quiet and all looking at him. He walks down and into their midst and starts to give his spiel, which I have to say was quite informative on pelicans and their habits and quite funny. Eventually he starts giving out bits of fish and some of these are quite big. It was very strange to see these large pieces of fish trying to get down the narrow necks of the bird. Some birds have two large pieces of fish stuck in their throats. I suppose eventually they get down into their stomachs. He then waded into the shallow water to throw fish into the water so we can see how they scoop up fish that are in water, with their lower jaw, with a flesh like bag attached. Amazing birds, so large and looking incapable of flight, and yet obviously very adept at flight. They apparently can fly to heights over 20,000 feet, and in flight they remind me of the old 'V' bombers of the RAF.

That last evening, bearing in mind the unsatisfactory meal I had in my hotel, I decide to give its competitor, the Ozone Hotel a go. They had a much bigger restaurant, and I plumped for a Lamb Roast. Very good too with two massive pieces of lamb and plenty of veg and gravy. So that night my stomach was well fed and my mind was contented at not being ripped off. I just hate going into a restaurant, looking forward to a nice meal, only to get a badly cooked mess that does not represent good value.

The next morning it is an early start so I can ride the sixty odd K's to Penneshaw to catch the 10.30 ferry. Now I am leaving the Island the weather picks up and it is nice and clear and warmish. Murphy's Law will always dictate this I suppose.

My ride back up to Adelaide was uneventful and I ride straight to the Ford dealer. I find that the company rebuilding the turbo have all the parts including a shaft they had got for someone else and it was the last one in Oz, but he had not turned up the day before to pick it up. So tough luck man and I got it instead… luckily. However by the time they get it rebuilt it then has to go Interstate to get balanced and it will take a few days. So I have to keep myself occupied for another three days at least. Such is life and I warn you that in Oz this is a fact of life, in that if you are in the country or bush, if things like this happen you will end up waiting days or weeks as all unusual parts or services are only held or carried out in the main cities. In this case Adelaide is not even big enough for coping with this, and only Melbourne and Sydney have parts or can carry out the balancing.

It reminds me of when I was bombing over the Nullabour in 1967 in my Mini and the head gasket went. I was near Madura, and managed to get there. I had to order a gasket set from Perth and it took nearly a week to get out to me on a passing truck. The Motel owner gave me a job in the kitchen and free food and bed. But boy was I bored having to spend a full week stuck in the middle of Oz with nothing to do at all. The Swiss couple I met in the caravan park hit a Kangaroo on Kangaroo Island (where else to hit a Kangar, I ask you?) and they had to wait TWO WEEKS to get a wing and headlight and get it all done. So I guess I am not so badly off as that!

I ride into Adelaide to check on my emails and after that and a lunch, I have to find a hotel to stay the night at. I decide that I will go to the Barossa Valley and look around there. I hadn't bothered before as it is a wine growing area and I am not a wine buff. However I read that it is quite nice visually. So I stayed at a motel on the main road North, out of Adelaide and on the way to the Barossa. Nice motel, but the noise from the main road is horrendous and goes on right up to midnight before it slacks off. The problem I am finding with Oz is that they simply do not seem to have heard of double glazing. None of the houses I have looked at or even the hotels have got double glazed windows. In fact I think the UK window companies would do well to set up business there as I haven't seen decent modern windows at all on the same pattern as in the UK. In fact this motel would have needed triple glazed windows. Also traffic on main Oz roads especially in big cities is heavy and I have noticed that here in Oz the percentage of cars with noisy exhausts is very high. It is obvious that either they do not have any laws to outlaw the noisy sporty type exhaust systems the young fast lads are fitting or the Police do not bother enforcing them if they do. Plus these fast lads are doing wheelies and fast take offs with added noise as a result. So that means that living near any highway means much noise over and above what you would normally get. So be warned when taking hotel rooms or even caravan sites, KEEP WELL AWAY FROM BUSY ROADS.

Anyway the next day I got off on my way to the Valley and after an uneventful ride along a busy highway and along very flat land, I start to approach a ridge of low hills off to my right, then the road swung to my right so I ended up going towards them. Now I started to come across fields planted with rows and rows of vines. Whereas the land had been parched and yellow looking, now it was nice and green with lots of greener looking trees as well. (see photo 105) The actual area of the Barossa valley does not cover such a great area, and it is mainly flattish and obviously covered in vines that belong to a multitude of different vineyards, together with their sheds and factory type buildings where the grapes are turned into wine. Now if you are a wine buff you could easily spend a week going from vineyard to vineyard, tasting the various wines. They all have visitor facilities and outlets for the Public to be able to taste and buy. As I am not a drinker and do not even like the taste of most wines, I was not going to indulge myself in this area.

As this whole area was settled very early on in S.A's history, I was more interested in exploring the various little towns from their historic viewpoint, and so that is what I did and my reporting will cover just that.

I drove to a town called Tanunda which I had been told back in Adelaide Tourist Office was the main town with the most hotels etc. A nice little town very clean and tidy with lots of original stone cottages dating back to their early beginnings. I booked into the main hotel and their motel style chalets, rear of the hotel were very good and very reasonable value for money at $60 per night. So booked for two nights. I had my evening meal in their restaurant and that wasn't too bad either.

The weather this first day had been much better being nice and sunny and not too warm, and on the second day it was the same, so after a quick breakfast I got going to explore the area. (see photo 106 to 111)

First let me fill you in on the historic facts of how this area was started. After the Adelaide area was started in December 1836, and do not forget that this state was a free state so all the people here wanted to make a go of things so could be said to be the entrepreneurs of those times. A George Angus, one such person, who was the founder of the South Australian Company, asked a German mineralogist one Johann Menge, to survey the ranges North of Adelaide. He reported that he thought the area very suitable for the growing of fruits and vines and corn. So Angus selected land in this area and so the area started off in the agricultural fields thus mentioned by Menge. It was named Barossa by the Surveyor General Light after a site of a victory over the French in the Spanish Peninsular War.

The very first farmers into the area were English, but within a couple of years they were joined by many thousands of German Prussian emigrants who being Protestant Lutherans, were discriminated against by the Catholic majority. They came to Australia to be able pursue their religious beliefs. So this whole area has a mix of English and German about it, some towns are more Germanic than others.

My first day I set off for Angaston a town more English than others and named after George Angus, and after leaving Tununda I went through the nearby village of Bethany and towards Mengeler Hill, (see photo 112) named after the early German pioneer settler. Before I got there I passed a very small cemetery that was not even marked as such. No more than about 20 graves, they were mainly of two families the Mengelers and one other. So the nearby hill is also connected to this man, and affords a good view of the valley. To my mind the area is not a true valley as a valley is usually a narrow strip of land bounded on both sides by hill or mountains. Very often with a river running through it. This area is really just a flat plain to the West of a low range of hills.

Angaston was mainly settled by the English and not all that remarkable. However I found a fascinating little gem of history, namely the original town Blacksmith called Doddridge. (see photo 113) Housed in shed made of corrugated iron and looking totally original, even to the cobwebs. They once did everything here including making carriage wheels and had a lathe to turn wood. An original Petter 3HP engine was puttering away dated from 1901 and had never been rebuilt. It was turning a shaft via a belt and this shaft would have originally a number of other machines also belt driven. I was approached by a quite old man of around 90 who introduced himself a Doddridge and used to work himself, in this family run business up to the time it stopped in 1988 when he retired. Now it is just run as a museum and was saved by the town from developers, for this purpose. Outside in a large cage was 'Bruce' a magnificent Cocky. I tried but couldn't get him to talk or say his name. Maybe he only spoke German?

Then I rode to the nearby town of Nuriootpa an Aboriginal name meaning meeting place, which was apt as I parked in the local supermarket car park so I could get a few items I needed, and I met a very interesting character. Nearby to my scooter I spied a VW Kubelwagen which were used in WW2 by the Germans. (see photo 114) It was their version of the Jeep, and you still see them around as VW still made them for some time after the war. This one was in khaki and quite old and battered looking. I walked up to it to have a close look and was approached by a chap about my own age who spoke to me. He looked well eccentric, thin and fit looking with long hair and goatee beard and dressed in khaki trousers with quite a thick lumberjack's shirt, which considering it was quite hot that day, was out of place. It transpired through a long conversation with him that he lived out in the Streslecki Desert and owns a string of camels with which he made a living from, by taking tourists on camel drives. He said he was Austrian and had changed his name to Omar and had taken up the Muslim religion. He had been to Afghanistan and he wore their clothes, including the head dress, when he was out in the desert. Great for keeping cool, he proclaimed. I felt like agreeing but adding that may be so, but in this day and age wouldn't one want to disassociate oneself from Afghans and being a Muslim? But I decided to hold my tongue. He went on and said that if you wet the head dress it made a great way of keeping cool in the heat. He had even married a Nubian desert girl, 20 years his junior and she looked after the camels when he had to come down to the Adelaide area for parts for his wagon etc. Wonderful I thought, maybe that's what I should do, marry a Nubian nubile girl and start a camel business exporting them to Saudi Arabia where they are apparently short of good camels.

My second day I would do a large circuit drive around the Northern half of the valley, so first thing I set off and drove north up to the Sturt Highway and along it to a place called Truro. (nothing like the original either) Nothing there so back down the highway and then turn off to take the road to Kapunda. Pleasant drive past pasture lands and vineyards and it was along this stretch that I came across my first Alpacas. I found two sitting in the shade of a large tree next to the road. (see photo 115) It transpires that several farms are specialising in these animals which look like a large sheep with a long neck. Similar to a Llama but what the difference is I can't make out.

Kapunda looked like an archetypal Oz town but on inspection it turned out to have an interesting history. From the information shop I got various pamphlets on the place, so I can tell you that it started off life in 1839 by a couple of pastoralists called Bagot and Dutton, but in 1842 copper was found in the town area. This was to become the first Oz mineral or metal mining venture, and of course in the last century Oz has been a major player in the mining of minerals and this has contributed much to it's wealth as a country. So this is where it all began. On the discovery Cornish and Welsh miners flocked to the place as they were considered the best miners in the World. Especially the Cornishmen, who also mined copper in Cornwall. It produced the purest cooper ore in the World and fetched a premium. However all the ore was fully mined out by 1879. It did help to put Kapunda on the map and it grew quickly because of it and it actually saved the new State of S.A which got off to a rocky financial start.

So during this growth many fine buildings where put up and it became the most important town North of Adelaide. Much of the iron lacework found on Victorian buildings found in S.A was produced here in the many foundries that were set up in the town. One of these fine buildings, formerly a Baptist Church is now the town museum. So this was the first place I visited, and was very impressed. Crammed full of examples of all sorts of items to do with Oz life from household items, shop items, business, school, the army, hospitals, dentists, doctors… you name it it's here. The ground floor is full of display cabinets and there's more in the large cool basement. Then there is even more out in a large purpose built shed at the back. Here they have farm machinery, trucks, engines, and exhibits to do with a large machine makers business that used to be based here. Called Hawke and Co it made an impressive range of machines of all sorts and they had their own pattern making shop and foundry. However it closed down in the 1980's.

A chap called Sidney Kidman who was born in Adelaide in 1857 and in 1880 he settled in the town and went on to become the largest land owner in Oz. He got into the cattle business and at one stage owned or leased 100,000 square miles of land, the largest ever owned by anyone then or since. At any one time he would own up to 32,000 sheep. He also bred horses and at one sale submitted 1300 horses for sale. He bought a large house around 1900, that had been originally built in 1876 by a Scotsman, one Mr Greenshields. You can visit this house as it is now owned by the town having been a school for many years after Kidman left it to the Education Dpt.

Next to have a look at was the old mine itself. This was opencast with some shafts. Although it closed in 1879 the whole site is still there, or what's left of it. Even though it is on the edge of the small town, it hasn't been levelled or redeveloped. However this is another example of how the Aussies just do not seem to be able to recognise their own important historical sites. The place is a literal tip. In fact I am surprised that it wasn't actually used as one. The condition of all the land, the remains of buildings, the remains of shafts etc etc, are a disgrace. Nothing seems to ever have been done to stabilise the site after it stopped working. You have to take into account the facts that (a) it was the first mineral mine in OZ and (b) it saved S.A as a State with the money it brought in and (c) the expertise in mining that was brought into Oz from the UK to operate it, went also into other subsequent mining ventures around Oz. So I was sorely disappointed here.

On my way out of town to the South I came across a large statue of a miner. Turns out it is a statue of a Cornish miner no less, and in the typical clothes and gear they wore to mine in. (p112.) It is in recognition of the part they played in the mine. I carried on south and eventually came across the Seppelt Vineyards, and very imposing they are. Even a wine peasant like me had heard of this wine. Nearby is a large mausoleum which was built to take the mortal remains of the Seppelt founder one Joseph E Seppelt and his family. All the roads around this vast vineyard are lined by palm trees, which enhances the look of the area. (see photo 118 & 119)

After my second night at Tununda it was time to move on (see photo 117) and I determined I would take a leisurely potter South through to the old and locally well known German immigrant town of Hahndorff. This lies on the motorway into Adelaide from Murray Bridge and to get there I have to go through the southernmost parts of the Barossa Valley area and into the Mount Lofty ranges again. I visit a little town called Springton where I want to see the Herbig Family Tree. This is a large old gumtree where a German immigrant, Frederick Herbig, set up home in the hollow base of the tree in 1855. Believe it or not he used it for no less than five years, before he moved into a pine and pug cottage he built nearby, then later to a stone cottage. (see photo 120) His wife gave birth to no less than 16 children all of whom survived and went on to form one of the well known first families of the area.

Hahndorff even nowadays pushes its German beginnings. Pubs and Hotels with German names and cafes selling typical German meals, and so on. As it was getting on by the time I got there, I decided to stay overnight, and booked into a large hotel. That night I ate in its restaurant and had the cheapest meal ever. For only $14.95 (£4) you could help yourself to whatever you wanted. There was a full array of soups and other starters, hot meals and full range of salads and deserts. All this topped off with tea or coffee. You could pig out, have seconds, as much as you liked. I had a load of salad, two deserts and a coffee and felt well full and satisfied. It had been a damn hot day and I was well knackered, so a good shower, watch the TV and a good nights rest.

The next day it was time to get back into Adelaide and see if they had done my vehicle, so it was a quick nip down the freeway and to find out the good or bad news. Of course it still wasn't done, but I was assured it would be the next day. So yet another evening to kill.

I caught up on my emails and booked this time into a city centre hotel. My thinking was that it was nearer the dealer and I may get a better sleep than being on a major highway. What misplaced thinking! I had the worst night ever. If you think the UK is full of noisy yobbos, they are also alive and well here in Oz. Even though it was only a Wednesday the noise from shouting yobs went on until 4 am and when they finished at last. I couldn't believe it when refuse trucks spent a full half hour or more emptying what seemed like a thousand bins and when they buggered off it was a couple of delivery trucks. Even after that it didn't stop because along came a noisy street cleaning machine. This road was only 100 yards long and a back street. Of course the fact that the Aussies haven't heard of double glazing doesn't help in these in these cases. I told the owner on my way out that he ought to pay his customers to stay in such a noisy place or get double glazed windows. The only thing he knew about glazing was when his eyes glazed over at my suggestions. Needless to say I did not get any refund or even an apology. So again beware when you stay in an Oz hotel. Make sure you get a room not only away from a road because of the noise of cars, but the possible noise of drunken yobs. Of course if you are miles from pubs and the like you may be OK.

I went to catch up again on emails and I was eating my lunch sandwich, when I got the news at last that it was ready. So it was that I was able to get back into action at about 3pm and on the road out of Adelaide and to the North towards Port Augusta. However I had to get a good supply of petrol at city prices before I left and a supply of food as I was right out of the stuff, having used up everything before I put the home into the dealer, so I could switch off the fridge and freezer.

Chapter Seven

Adelaide to Norseman

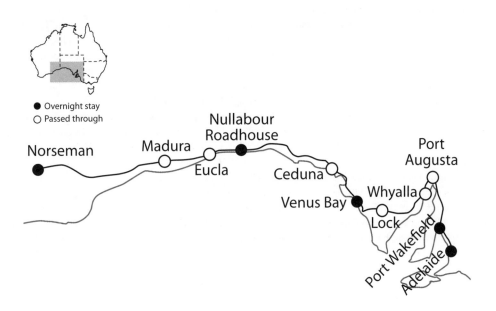

So it was that on my way out of Adelaide, I stopped at a shopping centre to replenish my non existent food supplies. I bought enough for 10 days of meals. This done it was back onto the high road to see how far I could go before it was time to pull in for the night.

As it was I got easily to the town of Port Wakefield, a nondescript town and why it is called a port as it is on a narrow river some way from the Gulf of St Vincent. The caravan park was OK just about, but they allowed animals which is the first time I have seen this allowed. As is always the case with dog owners, many are totally uninterested in thinking about others, so you will always get barking.

So it was here with a mutt tied up to the front bumper of a 4wd vehicle, naturally he barked his head off. This necessitated a bit of Pommy whingeing to the owner of the park, but at least it got stopped and the spectre of being kept awake by a whining, barking dog, receded. Lesson here is you may encounter similar problems, but then you can encounter these with barking dogs, just about anywhere these days.

Next day I drove uneventfully up to Port Augusta which is right at the head of the Spencer Gulf. I say uneventful, because since leaving Adelaide the land has been very flat and apart from the low ranges of the South Flinders on the right, there hasn't been anything of interest to see. The land is all farmed mostly for grain with a few sheep. I called into Port Pirie, but that wasn't up to much either.

(see photo 121) However it is on a wide river and has a wharfside along which you could get a couple of decent sized boats. It had a large smelting plant which I later learnt when in Whyalla, that it took iron ore from Iron Nob mine for smelting. More about that in bits about Whyalla.

Port Augusta was an in/out job too, but here I got a few more provisions which I had forgotten before. I pushed on, and down the line to Whyalla. I had been to this area back in my first years in Oz, when I decided to 'Go west Son and make your fortune' when I was living and working in Sydney. Perth in those days was a rapidly expanding town with the finding of new iron ore mountains and much money was being made. So I thought I will see if I can get a bit of that too, and jumped into my Mini Cooper in which I taught driving, and sped across to Perth via Port Augusta and intending to get straight onto the Eyre Highway. However the Mini was getting on and had done some miles and on the early Minis they had rubber driveshaft couplings, and one of these was slowly disintegrating. I was nearer to Whyalla, which is South of the Eyre Highway, so I got down there and got it fixed.

I cannot say I remember much about the place, although I remember it had a big steel works and a shipyard. Which is a decidedly odd place to have two such industries in such an out of the way place. Before, when I was there I did not have time to find out, and this time I decided that instead of going along the Eyre Hwy I would deviate South and follow the coast road right around the Eyre Peninsular. This because I had been across the Nullabour twice before, once in 67 on that trip to Perth and once in 69 on my way back to Sydney to catch a boat back to Blighty.

So once again I am in Whyalla. It is a typical nondescript Oz country town with no history to talk of. This because the town was not started until 1901 by the company Broken Hill Propriety (BHP) which is a large mining company based at Broken Hill, NSW. The earlier history of the general area is that Mathew Flinders on his circumnavigation of Oz in 1802, followed and explored the whole coast of the South of Australia, and so it is that many of the place names are names given to areas, by him. Some additional names have been given by the French explorers Baudin, and de Freycinet, at about the same time. Later on in 1839 and 1840 the explorer Eyre crossed from Adelaide to Albany and he crossed the Nullabour along its South side and following the coast. He noted that there was iron ore in the Middleback Range of hills to the West of where Whyalla is now. So eventually in 1889, by which BHP had come into being, they looked at the whole area. They found a huge deposit at a large hill which became known as Iron Nob, and this ore was used at the smelting plant at Port Pirie and at the smelter at Newcastle in NSW. Later on other local iron ore deposits were also opened up.

It was to use the nearby deposits at Iron Nob that Whyalla came into being. A steel works was born and later on in 1940 a shipyard was started using this steel. (see photo 122) The shipyards built some 66 ships up to the closure of the yard in 1978 including four minesweepers which saw action in WW2. The first minesweeper built was called Whyalla (funny that) and can be seen alongside the highway as you come into the town. Which is I can tell you, a strange sight to behold as it is quite a big ship and high and dry on land some way from water. It forms part of the Maritime Museum. (see photo 123)

I stayed at the Foreshore Caravan Park and had a pitch right on the beach edge. (see photo 124) I was surprised to see that it was obvious that there was a considerable tide rise and fall. I say this because along the East coast there is not much of a tidal rise and fall. The water here at the park is quite shallow, so when the tide went out it went out quite a way, and people were walking out to the water line and others were digging for shell fish. There is only one tide a day, whereas in the UK it is twice a day. As I had been on the go for over a week, I decided to stay at this park for two nights and catch up with my writing this written account, which goes into my laptop. As the home had been off the road and I could not carry the laptop on my scooter, I was well behind. So that late afternoon I got out my collapsible table and chair and put them out next to the sea wall. The weather since leaving Adelaide, where it had been hot for days, had been overcast and bearable and this day it too was too hot.

However there was a nice soft breeze coming off the sea, but in the late afternoon this quickly blew up into a very strong gale like wind of about 60 to 70 K's. So I had a nice sleep that night, as when it is too hot, my sleep is not as restful and deep.

In fact those very hot days we had had, when I was in the Barossa and Adelaide, had meant some bad bush fires had blown up both in the Adelaide Hills and on the Eyre Peninsular. The one in the Adelaide Hills had started not long after I had ridden my scooter down the freeway from Hahndorff and was adjacent to the freeway, and had closed it for some time. I was lucky I went through before it started. However the fires on the Eyre Peninsular were more serious as they had been allowed to get out of control and because of high winds, had raced across the whole of the bottom of the Peninsular around Port Lincoln. Nine people lost their lives and much land and farms were destroyed. So my intended trip down into that area went out of the window, as it would not have been a nice experience driving through blackened landscape. In any case the fire service guys were still all over the place damping down. In fact when I was driving out of Adelaide towards Port August there had been columns of their vehicle driving towards the Peninsular from all over S.A. It made the news in a big way and discriminations were hurling around as to why it had taken too long to order the aerial bombers in to fight these fires. The Aussies are good at hurling loads of muck at each other in a very vehement way, I have noticed!

In the morning after my first night at Whyalla I decided to get some exercise in and walk into town which was some distance away. I wanted to get a few things and look around. Funny old place the town centre, which the locals call 'the old centre' There isn't one shop that sells food in the high street nor a hardware shop. So I did not get what I wanted and as the new shopping centre is about 8 K's away on the outskirts, I decided to go there on my way out the next day.

Instead I walked up Hummock Hill (named by my old buddy Flinders). A smallish hill but one which gives you a view over the whole area. (see photo 125) In the afternoon I did a lot of writing and in the evening a lot of TV watching (BBC of course).

The next day, which was a Saturday it was a 9 am start and off to the supermarket and then onto the road down the coast to Cowell. Here I would turn inland and cross the Peninsular until I hit the South Coast at a place called Elliston. Thus cutting out the fire damaged bottom of the Peninsular. The landscape was still flat but on my right there were the Middleback range of hills that continued on for some time. A mixture of scrub and farmland all the way to Cowell. Nothing to report of this place so I quickly got onto the inland road to Lock. A series of undulating low hills and again mixed landscape of scrub and farmlands. In fact the whole of this peninsular is extensively farmed, so where there wasn't scrub and bush it was rolling farmland for grain growing mixed with some sheep. The first small town I came to was Cleve and then Lock. Both farm type towns and completely dead, not a soul to be seen

I started to see something on the roads that I had not seen before, and that was small extremely fat lizard type animals slowly waddling across the road. (see photo 126) I saw some that had not made it, so I stopped and had a close look at one. I looked up in my book on Oz and found they are called the Blue Tongued Skink. A stumpy tailed animal that eats insects and some plants. I was to see many of these creatures crossing the roads of the Nullabour and had to drive round them all to miss them.

I have noticed that since leaving the Spencer Gulf there has hardly been any traffic and I have driven for hundreds of miles and hardly come across any fellow travellers going in either direction. I have begun to see the odd very bright green small parakeet much brighter than other parakeets and also large flocks of what I am sure are starlings. They are feeding on the grain growing in the fields. I also come across something I have not seen for some time and that was an orchard which looked like either some sort of nuts or a small plum like fruit. Some lush big gum trees along this stretch as well. Another odd thing I had not seen elsewhere, are the numbers of farms that have built drystone walls. The land towards Elliston is exceedingly stony, so I guess the farmers had cleared many stones over the years. I had not seen stone walls anywhere in NSW, Victoria or S.A. I was reminded of the UK by these familiar style walls. (see photo 127)

On reaching the coast at Elliston I turn right and take what is now called the Flinders Highway (me old mate yet again… ooh he was a busy guy, this one!) It is nice to see the sea again and I follow the coast up to a place called Venus Bay. (The second such named place I have stayed at.) From Elliston past Ceduna the coastline is full of bays and inlets, some of considerable size, as is this Venus Bay. It is just a collection of holiday homes/shacks at the entrance to the bay. I book into the caravan park which isn't up to much, being really just a collection of parking sites on the beach, and for what they are, are not cheap at $17, either.

Anyway after Elliston I find that the radio station I have been listening to exclusively, namely ABC 24 hour news, has gone, faded out of range. What will I do as now I can only get rubbish, so my small collection of freeby CD's from UK newspapers, that I have collected over the years, come out and I start listening to those. They are mostly Golden Oldies from my younger days… great stuff!

There are some huge sand dunes appearing on the coastline and in one area, a large long lake is in front of these dunes, on the land side of them. Then it is into Venus Bay for the night and here I find that I am now getting difficulty in getting TV reception. I did manage to get Channel 7 and watch the last two episodes of William and Mary, which I never watched in the UK. ABC I could not get at all. So welcome to outback Oz, no good radio stations or TV at all. I had debated as to whether to buy a satellite dish which would have enabled me to get TV anywhere. However they were a rip off $1200 and that just was not worth it just to watch basically one channel, that being ABC. The others being mainly unwatchable. So it will be back to basics for a while, which will not do me any harm I suppose. I have become too dependent on TV for my evenings entertainment.

Next day, which is Sunday, and I am off again to see how far I go this day. First stop, a strangely named place called Streaky Bay. The landscape up to there is thick with scrub and bush. So much so that driving is like driving down a tunnel of bush. You cannot see anything else but trees and bush, and you can get this in many areas of Oz. Thankfully it is not like that all the time, otherwise you would get severely bored, and jack it in.

Streaky Bay was host to a Dutchman called Pieter Nuyts who explored this part of Oz in the 1620's. This is long before the Brits turned up and I am amazed the Dutch did not claim Oz for themselves as they were in a few places around the west coast. He moored at were it is now this Streaky Bay. Another large bay and a fairly reasonable place with many obviously second home holiday homes. I should think that all these coastal places are a boon to the people who farm inland and their workers. They would love to get away from the isolation and to the seaside at weekends for fishing etc. There are many power boats in evidence and much fishing goes on.

After stopping at S.B for a coffee, it is then on to another town called Smokey Bay. Me old cobber mate Flinders is responsible again for this name. He saw much smoke rising up along the shores of this bay, obviously the Aborigines were back burning, as they did. Again the countryside is undulating scrub and farmland with some sheep, all the way to a larger country and farming town called Ceduna. Just before I get there I came across a well called Eyres Well. When he was on his Nullabour trek, he stopped here when short of water having been told by an Aborigine that he would find plentiful water at this spot. It only had a few inches of water in the hole but he reported that no matter how much you took out water, it always filled right back up again. It was indeed so plentiful and pure, that from then on it was widely used by all the white men when they came into the area, and it also supplied the new town of Ceduna until in the 30's.

As with a lot of these farming towns it has a large granary storage or grain silo. It has a deep water port facility at a place called Thevenard, which is part of Ceduna, and larger ships stop here to load this grain. Also a lot of salt is produced in the area on salt flats. Gypsum also, is mined nearby at Lake McDonnel near Penong. All are exported out of the port.

I stop at the waterfront car park, as Ceduna is also at one end of a large bay. The town has many people in the oyster trade, and there are large areas where there are oyster beds. So if your an oyster fan this is the place to eat this delicacy, and there are plenty of restaurants where you can do so. I myself can't even think about eating such a thing as an oyster. I have a quick look round and get off again towards the distant W.A border.

Coming out of Ceduna the road goes inland a bit and then turns to follow the coast a few miles inland. The farmed land slowly disappears and dense bush lines the road and we go past an Aborigine Land Reserve called Yalata. At the entrance I note to this area is forbidden to the white man, and a large sign tells you if you are allowed in there are many things you cannot take in or do. Grog is one of them.

Anyway it is obvious that these Aborigines do not clear the bush to make farmland, as the bush is thickest in their reserve. I pass a Motel and petrol station called Nundroo and not long after all the bush just disappears as if someone had waived a magic wand. You are then confronted with a vast flat plain in front of you, for as far as the eye can see. THIS IS THE NULLABOUR PROPER or the start of it. (see photo 128) Soon a large road sign tells you it is the Nullabour. (see photo 129) It hasn't at this stage, a tree on it, just small bushes and it could be said to be an Oz heath. The weather has been great and today has been cool because there has been a nice cool southerly coming off the sea, keeping it cool.

After about a 100K's of this you arrive at a Motel/Caravan park/Petrol Station, called The Nullabour (very original I thought), which is all the habitation you will see on the Null. You get these places at regular intervals all across the plain, so your not going to run out of petrol unless your an idiot and do not keep an eye on the gauge, because if you do and then suddenly realise that you have only 50 K's worth left in the tank, you could be in for an extremely long walk, as they can be up to 300 K's apart. Anyway I am sorely disappointed with this place. It looks a bit of a dump and the caravan so call PARK is just a scruffy patch of sandy land with a few electric supply poles dotted around.

I go into the office reception which is in the general shop area. No one there. Eventually a disinterested bloke wanders in, doesn't even ask if he can help me or greet me in the usual Oz way. 'how yer going mate?' is the usual greeting. This bloke deigns to tell me when I ask, that he can book me in and it is $17. Bear in mind that I have had BEAUTIFUL caravan parks with landscaped gardens etc etc, for less than this. I ask him if this high figure includes shower facilities as it is not clear if there is a washing block with the caravan spaces. Then he tells me that a shower will cost me an extra $1. After I had finished spluttering he tells me that further west on the Null I will be charged $2 or $3 a shower. I ask if the sign saying TV reception means that I can actually get it out here as I had fully reconciled myself to a TV free night. He airily tells me that out in the park, I may or may not get it as it comes and goes, but they can get it within the motel building. I find this explanation a bit bizarre and not at all helpful. So I ask what is the reason why he can get it inside but not outside and I am told curtly that he has no idea. I ask if it is because he has a good aerial, and again I am curtly told he doesn't know that either. What you call a real helpful guy, so I give up. Anyway it is late and I need to stop and get a shower, so in for a Pound.

After eating I spend my TV less time watching the local bird life (feathered variety). On the Null there are certainly more crows than usual and this park has a small flock and a family of four Magpies. These two species are constantly having a go at each. A particular big crow keeps chasing the maggies. However even though they are a smaller bird, the maggies are not scared and will have a go back, and so it goes on. Later they all stand around near my home, looking expectantly, so I decide to see just how tame these birds can be. I know that maggies are reputed to be extremely tame. So I get a piece of bread and throw a few small pieces about to get them all interested and to concentrate their thoughts. When I have got all their attention, and they have moved in closer to me, especially the maggies, I get a largish piece of crust and hold it in my out stretched hand towards the maggies. Quick as a flash the biggest and boldest maggie rushes up to me, no problem, and snatches it out of my hand, and off he goes with his prize. The other maggies haven't the bottle and the crows are much more daring to come close and snatch the pieces of bread I am throwing before the maggies react, and they seem slow off the mark. Thus I was entertained and this is what you can call 'home entertainment' or better still 'Communing with Crows'. I get to bed early after spending the rest of the evening catching up with my writing up this journal.

First thing in the morning it was off to get a shower, and it is here I get to see what a tip the Mens room is. Very scruffy and in poor condition all round. The toilet bowls were all dirty and that is inexcusable. The shower taps in the cubicle I picked did not work very well and seemed about to drop off. I would advise you to keep away from this place, except to get fuels.

I am off and on the road, after filling up, and after a while the road starts to run quite close to what are obviously cliffs. I stop at a look out point and the view along the coast was awesome. (see photo 130 & 131) These sandstone cliffs must be well over 300 feet high, and rise out of the sea perpendicularly. They can be seen both to the East and the West for as far as you could see. As you travel towards the W.A border the road is running close to these cliffs and there are many stopping off places were you can marvel at the scenery. However I have to say that the general scenery alongside the road is never endingly the same, and so it can be said to be a totally boring drive.

I knew from what I had read, that at this border, there was a Quarantine check. This Oz obsession with fruit fly. (Bear in mind we are miles from anywhere where this border is.) You are supposed to declare all fruit, veg's, even jars of honey. How fruit flies can have any connection with honey I do not know. What I cannot get round my head, with all this is that no matter what State you are in, if you go into a supermarket you are confronted with fruit and vegetables that have been grown in all parts of Oz, and they have been transported about in trucks. How do these trucks manage to get through all this checking and confiscating of all the fruit and veg's. (I have already ranted on this but cannot resist another go as I find it mind boggling.) Anyway I thought 'sod you I am not throwing out my remaining 3 apples, an onion, or my 4 spuds, so there!' Where was I supposed to replenish them immediately when I am in the middle of nowhere and hundreds of miles from any shops. So I hid them on my scooter under the seat. I determined a frontier quarantine guy probably knew nothing about scooters, and would no doubt not even know a scooter could have a box under the seat. So when I got to the border, there is this massive building straddling it with signs saying everyone has to stop, and there are barriers. Bit like entering Russia, I thought. Charlie Crossing in Berlin and all that. I had visions of being thrown into goal, when a devious guard rumbles my trick and triumphantly holds up my bag of apples, spuds and an onion. I visualise a huge fine of $50,000, not being able to pay, and being banged up and lost forever, never to be heard from again.

Well back in the World of reality, I stop and an oldish guy in brown uniform with a red florid face, beams at me and asks me if I have any of the offending items. I reply in the negative. He asks if he can look in my home. I have my visions again that it will be like a Brit customs search were it has taken hours and my car is practically dismantled. Anyway this is Oz and all he does is look in my fridge and my freezer. All the cupboards I have in which could be hiding tons of elicit food, are ignored. He wishes me a good day and off he hops. Phew! All is successful and I roar off towards Perth. But it does make you wonder about the sanity of all of it. All that taxpayers money wasted on a system that obviously doesn't work. For it to work you would have to search EVERY Vehicle, and properly, and they are not going to do that by the looks of it.

Just 12K down the road is Eucla and a motel, of course. So I stop for a coffee. It is at Eucla that the blessed Eyres, on his tramp, spent 3 weeks getting his strength back eating up on roo meat and other food. Eucla had a plentiful supply of fresh water. Later on when he resumed his trek, with his three Aborigine helpers and his right hand man Baxter. Two of the Aborigines shot Baxter at a place called Cocklebiddy, saying they caught him rifling the stores. This led him to flee with the remaining Aborigine call Wye, for fear they would shoot him as well. A section of the nearby cliffs are named after Baxter. At Eucla there is a memorial plaque to Eyre. I think one has to have the greatest admiration for this guy Eyre. After you have traversed this long and arid plain in the comfort of your vehicle, with regularly stops were you can get refreshments etc, you may be able to go back in your mind to 1840 when Eyre was crossing. What did they have? A few horses, only the water they could carry, no idea what to expect or for how long this plain and its heat, which is normally in the 40's, would last for. Whether they would be able to find enough water to survive on as they could not carry enough for the whole journey. No one to that stage had been successful at this crossing. True heroes in my book.

Eucla stands at a point where the cliffs, which further back had been vertical, now run down to the sea on a gentle slope, and at this point a great wide plain opens out from the sea and the plateau which we have been travelling along slips further inland. So the road dips down through a pass and onto the plain below, namely the Eucla Pass. (see photo 132, 133 & 134) If you stand at the motel lands edge looking out to the shoreline a mile or two away, you can see huge white sand hills, and it was here that in 1877 a telegraph repeater station was built. This enabled Perth to be joined via a telegraph link to the Eastern States and ultimately with the rest of the World. It went on to being extremely, busy handling 11,000 messages a year. But of course later the telegraph was superseded by the telephone, and so the telegraph station closed down and is now just a pile of ruins and stone walls surrounded by sand dunes.

So the road is now running along the lower plain and to the right runs the plateau, which is now called the Hampton Tablelands, and this just runs on and on for nearly 200 kilometres. (see photo 135) I must say that at this stage you do see some trees on the Null, true there is a great long section without them, but after a while you start to see the odd ones and by the time your at Madura there are many dotted around. This plain, comes to an end as you approach a motel complex, called Madura. The road now starts to rise and into a pass called… yes you have guessed it… 'The Madura Pass'. The complex is halfway up the pass, to the left.

Now I have a connection in history with this place. Whilst doing my impersonation of Eyre, in early 1967, crossing the Null to get to Perth to make my fortune, I was not interested at that age in the landscape and history, just in getting to Pert as quickly as I could. Time was money, which I did not have in abundance. So I was pushing that Mini Cooper as much as I could, and boy did it go. However it overheated and blew a head gasket about 20 miles East of Madura. I got a tow into Madura by a passing motorist and had to stay there for a week while a gasket set was procured from Perth and sent out via a passing truck. Whilst I was there as the then owner was short staffed and no wonder as who would want to work out here in the middle of the Null?… (Madura is halfway between Adelaide and Perth) I got free accommodation and food for doing all the washing up three times a day.

As I was bombing along approaching Madura, I am trying to remember those days. You would think that such a memorable journey would be etched on my mind. However I simply could not remember the Eucla Pass, nor the plain by the sea and the Plateau to the right or even that Madura was halfway up that Pass. The complex looked new and in brick and had been built in 1968, so the old building was gone. But the cabins were still there and as I remembered them, built on an angle to the road. I had some lunch here and marvelled in the fact that so far the feared mid 40's temperatures I had feared for, on this trip across the Null, were much cooler, so this part of the trip was less of a bind.

From Madura it was just more of the same endless flat plain with or without bush (see photo 137a & 137b.) One thing I have really noticed is the amount of dead wildlife at the road sides. On the Eyre Peninsular there started to be dead roos every now and then, but nothing to set you thinking. But on the Null it is every few yards. Funny thing is I never saw evidence of car damage like bits of glass from headlights or even bits of wing or light units. Whatever was hitting these roos and it was mainly roos, it did not seem to suffer damage. Maybe it was only the huge road trains that were doing this. More about these monsters in a bit. Also surprising me was the fact that for hundreds of kilometres I was not being passed. Plenty of cars and trucks coming the other way and as I was generally only doing 80 to 100 K's which is less than the 100 to 120 nearly all other drivers seem to do, including these monster trucks, why wasn't I getting passed more often?

After a place called Caiguna there was a so called blowhole at the side of the road. (see photo 136) Mostly blowholes are found at cliffs right next to the sea. I stopped and all it was, was a hole about four feet in diameter and about 5 feet deep and disappearing to somewhere. A sign said that this was connected to the underground fissures system which can be found all over the Null. Being sandstone and soft there are many caves and tunnels eaten out by rain water, just like on K.I and elsewhere. This hole was supposed to breathe either in or out depending on the atmospheric conditions and had been measured at its highest flow to have wind passing through at 70 KPH. I listened and pronounced this patient dead on this day, so I quickly moved on.

From Caiguna the road is dead straight and is the longest straight stretch of road in Oz. Mind you it seems to me that most of the road so far has been straight too. It runs for 146.6 K's or about 95 miles. That is like me going from home (Bournemouth) to London along an unbroken straight stretch. At the other end is Balladonia station and then the road runs North West to Norseman, my next overnight stop. I was now pushing it to get there as soon as possible as it would be a town and have provisions as I needed some fruit etc and I did not want to stay overnight on the Null. The landscape now is heavy bush but still no sign of farming, and it is not until we get close to Norseman I see farming starting again.

Now to these wretched Road Trains. In Oz for some years the trucking companies in the outback, because of the distances and the lighter traffic, have gone to making semi trailers with two and three trailers not just the one. This is done in the interest I suppose, of hauling the maximum amount on one trip. The prime movers are mostly huge Yank tanks and you know how the Yanks just have to make everything bigger than anyone else. The problem is that they are so huge that they take up the full width of the lanes, unless it is a stretch of road were the lanes are wider than normal.

That means as you pass them, you have to go right over as far as you can in the lane you are in, so as to give you space between you and them. The amount of wind suction and blowing is enormous. If your passing each other in opposite directions, when their airwave hits you, it is like a brick wall hitting you. You get buffeted all over the place. Lastly the drivers seem all to be Neantherdals and travel at 100 plus and usually at about 120, which for their size is far too fast. OK if nothing happens but if they have to stop quick… what then I ask? Now as I got close to Norseman I meet one of the cavemen and we didn't shake hands either. We are on a bendy section and he is doing at least 100. The road lanes are the narrow type with no tarmacked hard shoulder, only loose gravel. As he is on a bend and I am wider than a car, he drifts onto the soft hard shoulder. There is an almighty clatter and I am enveloped in dust and stones banging onto my windscreen. Some sound like house bricks and the result is when all clears, a semi circle crack in the screen plus two small star cracks. I am spitting bricks at this nutcase but what can you do? (see photo 138a)

On entering Norseman I get straight into the caravan park. It is just about OK but I am knackered because I have driven from 8.30 to about 8pm and I am ready for food. I must mention that as you cross into WA you are now entering a new time zone and you have to turn back the clock 2.5 hours, so I arrive at 5.30 local time. So I basically do not get to bed until 2.30 am and as the temperature has crept up to into the 30's it is an uncomfortable night and I wake early at 7am, which is unusual for me.

Chapter Eight

Norseman to Perth

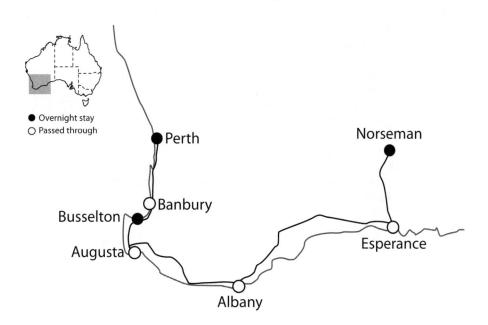

After my poor sleep I got up about 7.30. Did all my ablutions and had breakfast and spent some time working on my laptop cleaning up my last nights writings. It was no use my going into the town before 9am as nothing would be open. I was surprised when I got up that most of the caravans and mobile homes that were all around me had already disappeared. I suppose as this place is at the beginning of the Null, for those going East, they would want to get an early start.

Just before 9am, I organised the van and then left to drive the short way into town to get some provisions and a paper. Boy was I surprised with what I found. What an absolute dump this place is. It looked like it was in a time warp going back fifty years. Broken down scruffy housing, (see photo 138a) a very small commercial centre and the shops in the main street were in atrocious condition. The streets were of poor quality and unkempt. Now you have to remember that this town has a gold mining company operating the second most lucrative gold mine after Kalgoorlie, which is just up the road, and it has been going since the 1890's. Something wrong here, Even the supermarket which was run by a well known company who have supermarkets all over Oz, was a disgrace too.

I went to the newsagents and that was an odd shop, as were all those shops. They all looked like they were owned by amateurs as none of them were professionally fitted out. They had one 'Australian' newspaper only, and the shop had only just opened. Obviously quality newspapers were not the order of the day in Norseman. I took it and the owner said 'good newspaper that' I replied that it was the only one worth reading. He replied that he had to say that as his niece was a reporter on it. That obviously was his claim to fame and he just had to tell everybody! Then I went to the cafe a few doors away for a coffee, another oddly fitted out business. They didn't supply sweetener instead of sugar, either. I mentally thought to myself that they probably didn't even know what sweetener was as it hadn't arrived in this neck of the woods yet. I dreaded to ask for a Latte, but I was OK, she knew what it was and asked if I wanted a cup or a mug. I opted for the mug, which when I got it was so large it was almost as big as a bucket. Obviously they do things big in a mining town! It was alright though, so I'll give them a bonus point for that.

Then I visited the Tourist Information shop. A bit better, but still not as it should be from a professional angle. I wanted to get a leaflet in which they gave the history of the town and how and when it started. I looked all around and could not find one at all. I asked the woman serving and was told that they did not have one as so far no one has written a pamphlet on the town. She gave me a glossy leaflet which outlined some of the places to go and see in the general area, and this was very professionally made. The condition of the town was not in keeping with the quality of its commercial brochure on the town. I thought that just about summed everything up about this place. I read what I could see and cobbled the following together.

A group of people from Esperance came up to this area in 1892, to see if they could find any minerals in the area. They camped next to a small lake they called Dundas Lake (see photo 139a) after a well known personality of the time. They found ore that they thought was gold. I think that Kalgoorlie had already found gold by then. Shortly after this in 1894, another seeker of minerals, a Laurie Sinclair found gold at what is now Norseman. He was also from Esperance and was visiting the Coolgardie Goldfields to try his luck, but was unsuccessful. He heard his brother was in the Dundas area and decided to look him up. He found him in the vicinity of what is now Norseman. They were investigating a few specs of gold on a ridge. His horse which he had named Norseman, as he was from the Shetlands and of Norse heritage, hence the horse's name. The horse was tethered to a tree and in his boredom, pawed the ground and unearthed a lump of gold ore. That was the start of gold mining and hence the name of the town.

On filling up at the nearby Shell station, when paying the talkative old guy serving on the till, asked me where I was off to now. It was obviously obvious to him I was not 'one of them' I replied 'to Esperance and I hope is better than here'. As he was older than me I thought I would take a chance it and stir it up a bit. There is nothing like stirring up an Aussie by slagging something Aussie, off. He replied 'what do you mean by that' I said that I thought the place was in a bit of a time warp. 'exactly what do you mean by that' he asked. I thought 'here we go, in for a penny' 'Well' I said 'It is a bit of a dump isn't it?' I thought this will really get him going now. Well it did as he then launched into a tirade against John Howard (Oz Prime Minister) I asked what did it have to do with him. I was told that all he wanted to do with small Australian towns like this was to rape them of all the wealth they made and give nothing back to them so they could make something of the place. By now another customer had walked in and looked like he wondered what he had walked into. I mumbled something and made a quick exit left. So now I knew why it was a dump!

Trying to find my way out of the place was something. Absolutely no signs telling you which was the road to Esperance. I guessed and it wasn't until I was a mile along that road that I came across a sign telling me how far it was to Esperance.

There was thick bush with tall trees on either side of the road and this was like this for about three quarters of the way to Esp. Funnily enough I saw not one dead Roo along this road. Maybe they only want to be over on the Eyre Highway so they can watch the truckies hurtle by and play chicken with them. This road is as quiet as anything. There weren't many birds either, and they were in abundance on the Eyre Hwy.

A few miles down the track I came across a sign pointing 2K's to Dundas Rocks. I had seen in the Tourist Office that there were these rocks in the area. So I thought I would look them up. Down a dirt track I first came across a dried up lake bed, with a sign telling you it was Dundas Lake. So this is were the very first trace of gold was found. Then I came across the remains of Dundas Town. Actually nothing left of it at all, only signs saying it had been on this spot. Built by the miners who came to dig the gold. As there were no building materials, all that the buildings were, were built from bits of wood and mud. Hence when the gold dried up, these so called buildings quickly fell to pieces. 'Where are these rocks?' I was wondering, so I turned round and was on my way out to the Highway and got to the lake again. Now I was pointing the other way round I could see them, on my right and through the trees. Why no signs I wondered? What these rocks are, are huge granite boulders. (see photo 139b) Must weigh many tons. How did they get here as they were actual separate boulders. Here I have to query the way the Aussies look after their tourist attractions. They promote these rocks to the tourists to come and see, and apparently even in the old days people would come to this lake and the rocks for picnics. So why no proper signs and why do they allow these lovely big boulders to be very heavily covered in graffiti. Some of the graffiti dates back to the sixties and fifties. The whole thing was obscene, the image it gave off, was not good.

Further down this 205K stretch of road I went past many lakes, some small and some huge. In fact the whole area from Kalgoorlie down to Esperance it dotted with these lakes. However like many lakes in Oz they are only full of water in the rainy season. Even then they are very shallow, so they quickly dry up and when they do they leave deposits of salt. So when dry they are all white with the salt. I wondered were this salt came from, as they fill up with sweet water (rain water which isn't salty) I came to the conclusion that as the rain falls onto the salty land it becomes salty and when it dries out again it leaves the salt behind again. That is my theory and I am sticking to it! The only problem I can think of is that if the land is salty then how come they can grow crops on it?

As I got close to Esperance the land suddenly starts to be farmed. However I notice that some of the fields seem to have soil that is almost like sand and as it is an exceedingly windy day, this is lifting the sand and there are clouds of the stuff blowing across the road. Some of these farms have cattle on them in quite large numbers and this is something I haven't seen since Victoria.

I reach the outskirts of Esperance and as I drive in I am struck straight away by the total difference between this place and Norseman. It has nice dual carriageways and roads all in top condition and clean and tidy and many, many businesses lining both sides of the road supplying all manner of trades and goods. Many were farming supplies and farm machinery businesses. It is obviously a rich little town that seems to be doing well. It is also obviously a holiday town too. However it still does not account for why this place can do well and yet a town like Norseman with its gold mining which is doing well), is a basket case.

The caravan park is on the seafront and is very large and absolutely full of people. I know it is the peak season and the schools are on holiday, but then when I was on the Eyre Peninsular it too is on the sea and it wasn't full. However Esperance Bay is in a very pretty area with many inlets and bays and lakes with hundreds of Islands just off shore. So I guess that many people from all over WA will come down here for that, and it is cooler down here, than further North in the State.

I got a booklet off the caravan park office on the area and in it there are some things I know you will want to know. So here goes. The first people from Europe to visit the area were those adventurous Dutchmen, but they did not even stop. Then came the pesky French in 1792, but they were too late. Captain Cook had grabbed it all for the Brits by then. A Rear Admiral De Entrecasteaux in the ships Esperance and Recherche. Hence the name of the place and the Islands, just offshore. Several whalers and sealers came here during the 19th century. Me old mate John Eyre went through here on his way to Albany.

In 1863 the brothers Dempster drove cattle down to here from near Perth and took up 100,000 acres. The discovery of gold in the Norseman, Kalgoorlie and Coolgardie areas brought all the fortune seekers coming through the port on their way up there. Then the area started to develop the farming side of things, however it was hard because as I have surmised above, the land is sandy and salty. In the 20's more country was opened out for farming, but the great depression of the 30's saw off 75% of the farmers. So farming the area seemed to have been a failure. However in 1949 a research station opened to look into the problems of making the poor soil work. Research eventually found that by adding super phosphates and trace elements like copper and zinc, it could all work. Hence now it has all these farms growing wheat etc.

On my first full day I took the opportunity to get some exercise in and walked the 3 K's into town. The weather was lovely and sunny, but a stiff South westerly meant it was coolish. I walked along the foreshore until I came to the Tanker Jetty and made to go for a walk along it to take some photo's. I could see that in the water there was a large seal. On that spot on the jetty, there was a long gutting table for the fishermen. The seal obviously got fed the entrails, by them and he was waiting there. So I got some shots of him. When I got back to that spot after doing my jetty walk, he was now lying nonchalantly on the beach, surrounded by adoring people taking photos. I joined them to do likewise. You could walk up to him no problem. He was obviously very used to all this. It is incidents like this that make this trip worthwhile. They may not happen all the time, but when they do it is magic. I mean where else could you have such a close encounter with a WILD creature like this? (see photo 140, 141 & 142.)

I went to the library for my free session on the Internet. Then get my dose of Brit news by getting the latest International Express to read how the UK is getting more messed up than ever. A sit down on a bench to quickly scan the paper, then a coffee, visit the Info shop, then a wander over to the foreshore right near the end of the bay, to look over the Marina and sailing boats. Then it is time for lunch. I normally have lunch in the home, but it is too far to walk to it and then back again. So have to undergo a 'fleece the tourists' bit in a cafe, paying over the odds for a lousy sandwich and a pot of tea. (see photo 143)

Now it is time to visit the large local Museum which is housed on the seafront in a big complex of sheds that used to be the Old Customs sheds and the rail sheds. It has all the usual exhibits of general Oz life, with some exhibits that deal with the history of the town's growth. Probably the most interesting exhibits is a case with lots of bits of 'Sky Lab' which on its re-entry into the atmosphere, over Esperance in 1979, broke up and showered the area with debris. Some very large pieces too. After this I head back to the Park for a decent cup of tea after a nice day of exercise and rest, all at the same time.

After a better nights sleep than I have had for the past two nights, as I think my body clock has adjusted to the two and a half hour difference. There is not as much wind this next day so the ocean

waters are a lot calmer and I set off on the westerly road towards Albany which will be my next stop. I have to say that the sign posts out of Esperance are non existent and I end up slightly off track and have to stop at a factory to ask if I am on the right road to Albany. Believe it or not the young lad does not know! I wonder, 'where does he come from?' One of the older blokes points me in the right direction, but without clear and precise directions. So this reminds me to warn you when asking directions from Aussies. Some are not very good at it at all. Even the blokes who you would think should know, 'no worries!' can be vague. Maybe it is just their laid back way?

The Highway No 1 to Albany is an uneventful stretch of road. It passes through mainly flat land, mostly farmland given to crop growing but with some sheep. The quality of the road varies, some very good and some of indifferent surface quality and a bit narrower, with poor hard shoulders.

Nearer to Albany you start to pass many man made forests of indigenous gumtrees, which I have never seen commercially grown up to now. As the tree trunks are a bit skinny I wonder is they are used for their wood or something to do with eucalyptus oils. I will try and find out when I get to Albany. Also I start to see herds of cattle and even a field of vines. I do pass the occasional mallee scrub, which is bush without the gum trees, and I pass a whole big area where it has all died. It looks eerie with all the dead bushes for as far as the eye can see. I wonder what caused them to die off like this as I cannot see any evidence of there having been a fire.

I see off to my left a quite high range of mountains. Not very extensive and I work out that these are the Stirling

Ranges and part of a National Park. They are off the main road from Albany to Perth and Katanning. When I get very near I can see that around Albany are a few hills.

As I am going through the outskirts and past various trading estates and businesses, I can see that like Esperance it appears to be a neat and tidy town with newish buildings. I get into the beginning of the main high street (see photo 144 & 145.) which drops down a slight hill and towards the big bay and port area, that Albany sits on.

I pull into a parking bay as it is coffee time, and I need to stretch my legs. After this I take a walk down the street to see if I can spy an Information shop. I come across an info board and get what I want off that, namely where the Caravan Parks are situated. Having done that I drive to one at a suburb on the coast, a couple of K's away, and called Middleton Beach. (see photo 146)

When I get there it looks very nice but is full, so I have to drive further on round the coast to Emu Beach, where I do get in. Both these parks are chockablock full with holiday makers mostly with families, as was the Esperance park. Well it is the Oz summer holiday period and all the kids are off for weeks and I expect that most of these people will be from Perth. However they are usually OK in the evening and quiet enough. It is just during the days when they are bombing around the park on their scooters and bikes and making the hullabaloo that kids love to make. As I am out all the day, if I stop for more than one night, it will not effect me and I have booked for two nights so I can spend the next day (Friday) looking around at the local sights.

I just couldn't get off to a quick start, everything I did took ages. I had to clean up the scooter which was covered heavily in dust from my recent trips down unsealed roads. That took ages. I also needed to check out the state of the front brake pads, as they are only tiny things and I had now done 4600 K's. I had to mess about for ages to figure out how to take out the pads. The owners manual is hopeless and doesn't even touch on stuff like servicing and checking brakes etc. Anyway I eventually got them off and was surprised to see they still had enough meat on them as the disc was showing signs of uneven wear indicative of metal to metal. Probably poor quality steel as the bike is made in Taiwan.

So eventually I got away and into town and to the library to see if they had Internet access. They had several computers but gave me a load of guff that they were not connected to the Internet for emails. So this is the first town that doesn't want visitors using their Internet access, even though your spending money in their town. So had to resort to a private Internet Cafe, which was full of noisy kids playing games. Such is life!! Then I found that I had travelled about 3 K's into town without my wallet. I am always doing that, it makes me mad. So had to travel all the way back to the park, so I ended up having my lunch there instead of having it on the hoof as planned. Would I have enough time in the afternoon to see all I wanted?

First place I went to was to one of the three hills that overlook the town, called Mt Adelaide. I found that there was an old Fort and barracks on it. (see photo 147) Back in 1893 they had decided to fortify it with gun emplacements in the same way as they had done in Port Philip Bay and the Heads at Sydney. (see photo 148) This to protect these natural harbours from unwanted enemy actions. Albany is such a natural safe harbour due to its shape. It has a series of large horseshoe bays and Islands at the head of the bays.

The bay and the general area was discovered by a Brit Navy Captain called George Vancouver, in 1791 and he named it King George Sound, after George III. They stopped using the fort in the fifties, which is not in the strict sense a fort at all as all it is four gun emplacements on the hill, all facing to the sea and the Bay, and barracks to house the artillery soldiers. The guns were made in the UK and paid for by the British government (Oz was still in the Empire then) It is now a museum and contains information mainly about the connection with Albany and the Oz Forces. I learnt that in 1914 when Oz joined Britain in the First World War the Australian contingent and fleet that was to go to Gallipoli, was assembled in the Bay. Some 36 boats of the Oz and NZ Navies assembled in the Bay and troops and equipment came from all over Oz.

Very close by is Mt Clarence and here you can get some magnificent views of the bay and islands. I then made the short trip down into town and called at the info shop which is at the railway station. I get several leaflets on things to see and do and on the history of the town. (see photo 149)

Just close by are some historical building in a cluster, and a replica of a brig called Amity. (see photo 150) This small boat brought the first official settlers from Sydney to Albany to start the settlement of WA. The boat was made in Canada in 1817 and saw service across the Atlantic and in the Irish Sea, and which ended up being bought by a family of farmers from Wigtown. It then made its way to Oz. When you look at its size you can but marvel how it ever got there, yet apparently this sized vessel was common to the voyage in those days. It was bought by the government in Sydney and brought 23 convicts 18 soldiers plus crew and various others. How they all got into the small boat God only knows, but on December 26 1826 it arrived at what is now Albany.

Nearby is a house built in the 1850 for the purpose of hiring out convicts, and then used as a government residency. Now it is a museum. An old school house and goal (see photo 151) are also restored and in the same cluster of buildings. One of the leaflets I got lists and gives information on all the older buildings in the town and when they were built. The earliest date from not long after settlement and right up to the later 1800's.

Lastly I went up the third hill, Mt Melville, and on top of this hill they have built a modern communications tower, which has an observation deck you can go up. This affords you some fantastic panoramic views of the whole bay area. (see photo 152, 153 & 154) and after this, some shopping in the local Coles Supermarket and back to the caravan park for dinner.

On the next day which is a Saturday I go back to the Internet cafe to pay him what I owe him, and to catch any emails, then I plan to go with the home, to see some sights in the Torndirrup National Park which is on the Westerly peninsular of the bay and King George Sound.

After a not too long a drive I arrive at the first sight which is The Bridge and The Gap. (see photo 155 & 156.) The cliffs being limestone had been eaten away by wave action and this resulted in the bridge of rock going over to a solitary rock, and a large rectangular and deep cutting into the cliff, which they call the Gap. The power of the swell rolling into this cutting was frightening in its power. You wouldn't want to fall into it.

Further on, on the cliff tops is a fissure near the water, which is obviously connected to the sea as each time a big swell comes in, it pushes air through it with a huge roar. As the swell on this day was not excessive, no water came through, which apparently it will do, sending huge amounts of water up in the air under great pressure.

I get onto the back road to Denmark as it is supposed to be more scenic. It passes mostly farm land, and eventually I arrive in Denmark which is claimed to be the prettiest town in WA. It was OK but not so pretty in my book. The river it sits on gave something to the place I suppose. (see photo 157) The drive to Walpole, the next town is uneventful and after this the land passes through heavy forests of tall Karri and Jarrah trees. I stop at a spot where you can walk through a section on elevated walkways at almost tree top height. This I can assure you is quite something, especially as these steel walkways sway sideways and up and down as you walk on them. You do not exactly feel completely safe. These Karri trees area left over from when the Oz continent was part of the huge continent of Godwanna, before it broke away and drifted to its present position. It was joined to what is now Antarctic and the rocks on that continents Northern shores match those around Albany.

The trees are about 80 metres high and quite straight, so present a majestic sight compared to straggly gumtrees once usually sees in Oz. These trees and the almost as tall Jarrah trees are only found in this small area in South Western WA. (see photo 158, 159, 160 & 161.)

The next town that I head for is Manjimup and the forests gradually disappear and it is back to farmland again. The road from Manjimup to Pemberton is heavily farmed and vineyards start to appear, whose owners have all put in lakes to provide water supplies for those vines. So the vista is quite pleasant.

Pemberton is a small farming town which also has an old established saw mill. I stay in the local caravan park which is situated within a forest. I hear that night, my first Kookaburras laughing/screeching call, away in those trees. If you have never heard their calls, they are quite unlike the calls of any other birds. No wonder they are also called the 'Laughing Jackasses' That's fine but not at 4am when I was serenaded by two of them really close by and doing a screaming duet which seemed to last forever. I love birds but not at that time of the morning.

After Pemberton the land is mainly heavy bush and scrub which doesn't have any taller trees. They call this Mallee scrub and it is not so attractive. I passed mile upon mile of this Mallee scrub. As I got nearer to my next destination of Augusta, farms started to appear again and a lot of vineyards were evident.

Augusta is at the bottom left hand corner of WA, first settled in 1830, and the nearby Cape Leeuwin has a lighthouse on it that is said to be the most Southerly in WA. Nearby there are the remains of a wooden waterwheel that had been built when the lighthouse was being built at the end of the 1800's. It supplied water to the builders from a nearby spring. This water turned the wheel which in turn operated a pump, to pump it onto the light house some half a mile away. This wooden waterwheel had calcified and now looked like it was made of rock. (see photo 162 & 163.)

The road I next took, heads off Northwards towards Busselton and is called The Caves Road. This is because this road passes a number of caves. The area from Cape Leeuwin to Cape Naturaliste, which is a piece of WA which juts out into the Indian Ocean, is made up of limestone (again) and as I have described before, limestone being soft means you will get many caves. So it is in this area too and some 200 odd have been found in the area. Six have been developed for tourists to look around.

The first you come across just North of Augusta, is Jewel Cave. (see photo 164) I have been in a number of caves around Europe and Oz and this one was very good and you have to see it if your in this area. After going down some steps you come into a deep cavern of some size and off this there are a number of passages some opening out into smaller caverns. So the overall size of the complex is quite large and it has the most number of stalactites and stalagmites that I have seen. The tour is by guide and lasts a good hour. Some of the other caves like Lake Cave and Mammouth cave are also supposed to be very good, but at $16 a go I could not afford to visit all of them, even at their discounted price of $40 for three caves.

This whole area between the two Capes is called the Margaret River area, after that town, which is about halfway between the Capes. It has become an Internationally well known wine growing area, as well as for the Karri Forests.

Cape Naturaliste has a lighthouse on it and I wanted to walk to the cliff tops nearby, around a mile away. I would not bother if I were you, trying as I did. Around the lighthouse they have maps which tell you that there are paths to the cliffs. What they do not tell you is that they are very poorly kept and they do not come within sight of the cliffs or the ocean. The whole area is heavy scrub, the so called paths are narrow and hard going, as they are made with sand, of all stuff. It was like trying to hike on a beach, getting sand in your shoes and hard going. On top of this you saw nothing and I was plagued by hoards of bush flies. A bit of a disappointment all round and a waste of time.

I was glad to then make my way to the nearby town/village of Dunsborough, which was a delight. The whole town centre looked like it was brand new, all clean and tidy. It was a pity that the towns caravan park wasn't up to the same standards as the town. Here I met Australia's answer to Basil Fawlty, and his site was a tip. The only good thing about it was the name of it… 'Dunsborough Lakes Caravan Park'! I wish I'd had someone filming my booking in ceremony.

I walked into the Reception office and this typical Oz type male of about late fifties in age, was behind a counter writing in a large accounts book. He did not even look up and greet me as most owners do. I stood there for a good three to four minutes thinking to myself 'I've got a right ignoramus here' When he eventually put the book away, he still did not greet me and I asked him if he had a overnight site. He did and when I asked to pay by my debit card I was very brusquely told that he only accepted cash. This annoyed me as in this day and age EVERYONE accepts debit and credit cards as when people are travelling they do not want to have to carry large amounts of cash, and I was short of cash. So I said to him that it was odd that in this day and age he did not accept cards. He became even more brusque and his eyes started to bulge. I was curtly told that as it was his business he could do what he wanted and he did not accept credit cards. I told him it wasn't a credit card but a DEBIT card which meant that money went direct from my account and straight into his. I was told if I did not like it I knew what I could do… I did not need to stay there. I tried to reason with him that by accepting a debit card he was looking after his customers. I was told that it didn't help him at all. And he'd just visited Europe and they had plenty of places there that did not accept cards and when they did they made a hefty charge for them. So it became apparent that HE wanted to travel using cards himself, but his customers could go to hell. Maybe he was using this as an excuse to get back at others for perceived problems he may have had travelling. Anyway I didn't argue further, as I could see I was wasting my breath. I was not given a receipt and I think he was no doubt on a tax fiddle? Nor was I advised where I could camp as ALL owners do, so I picked my own spot, in his practically empty park. You will no doubt come across such Aussie males like this. Either they are extremely good and friendly, but they still have a percentage of absolute throw backs to the stone age, and I am not referring to the indigenous Aussies!

The next day after doing some shopping I got on my way to the next and bigger town of Busselton some 30 K's away. On coming to outskirts I could see that this area is very heavily a holiday area. The highway was thick with hotels, motels, caravan sites, holiday resorts, holiday homes etc etc.

The town was bustling with shoppers and very busy. It was clean and well laid out and obviously is a town doing well on tourism. Down at the seafront I could see why it would be popular. As the beaches are Northerly facing, on a bay called Geographe Bay, they are sheltered from the predominant South Westerly winds. The water was as calm as millpond and shallow for some way out. So it is ideal for families and children to paddle.

It boasted an extremely long wooden jetty reputed to be the longest in the Southern Hemisphere at almost two Kilometres long (which is over one mile). Built 138 years ago to enable timber from all those forests I passed, to be exported, until it closed in 1974. (see photo 165)

The town was started by settlers in 1832 which for WA is right at the beginning of things. It was named after one of those families the Bussells. The French names that apply locally are because in 1802 a French sailor named Vasse from a French shipping expedition in the area, was lost in a storm in the bay, so the river which Busselton sits on, was named after him. The others were named by this expedition. The town is expanding quickly, by the look of it, with many new homes evident and a nice new marina at its Western end.

I now made my way to Bunbury 55 K's North. The road is very good being a dual carriageway all the way. No doubt built to take all the holiday makers who use it. It sits at the Southern end of a large inlet called Leschenault Inlet, Again named by those pesky Frenchies who were at Busselton. Originally the town was called Port Leschenault, but later on renamed Bunbury after a Lt Bunbury who went there in 1836 with the Governor Stirling on an expedition to look over the area. Quite right too! (see photo 166)

There is also a large bay and another inlet, around the town site. So it is very much a water place and ideal for water sports and pastimes, and because of this, is also a holiday town. It also exports grains and has a large grain silo and port facilities for grain tankers. The town it self is another nicely laid out and up to date place. I must say it is much improved from the 60's when I was last there. Then it was a typical dowdy flyblown Oz town with not much to recommend it. It has to be said that in the last 40 years the Aussies have made a lot of these types of places, up to date and they are now brightly painted, with pedestrianised streets and malls, and many pavement eating places. The change is amazing from what they used to be and has to be applauded.

Also they all have very good parking available. Either purpose built car parks of all sorts or on street parking. Most of it is FREE, and on this point I have to say that I always thought that seaside holiday towns in the UK, could well take note. My own home town of Bournemouth always made me mad with the rip off parking charges everywhere and every inch of street car parking space, off bounds with miles of yellow lines. Don't these idiots (councillors) realise that they chase off many people because like me they simply will not pay to park especially when they are on holiday. So these Oz towns are again to be congratulated on their common (business) sense, welcoming car owners to come and spend their money there.

I saw a little hill and after driving around and around, found my way up there so I could take some good photos of the town panorama. After this I decided not to tarry as I could always come back on my scooter from Perth and explore some more. So it was back onto the road along the coast and towards Mandurah. As you approach this place you suddenly are faced with a fantastic site as you come over the brow of a hill, because there in front of you is a large inlet and a very large body of water. Eventually when you get into the town, which sits at the entrance of this inlet, on the Mandurah Estuary. It too is a grain port with silos etc and is ideal for all water activities and picturesque. Again I do not spend too much time looking round as the caravan park I have decided to stay at is in South Freemantle, only 20 odd K's away, and so I can always come back to revisit this place.

I am quickly at Freemantle Village and book into a site for a month. It is only 10 minutes south of the town centre and is quite a large and well run site with many people living here full time. It is about 21 K's from Perth town centre, so I am ideally situated to explore the whole area

Chapter Nine

Perth: Sights and History

Captain James Stirling came to explore the Swan River (see photo 167) which was already known about by previous explorers, to see its suitability for a settlement, in 1827. He thought it a great place and wrote a glowing report on it and so in 1829 a Capt Charles Freemantle arrived at the mouth of the Swan River and brought a number of convict settlers from Sydney in a small fleet of boats and they chose to start the settlement here. This place was then named after Capt Freemantle. Capt Stirling who came with them went on up the river to start the proper settlement at the spot which is now Perth. It was named so after Sir George Murray who was then the Secretary of the Colonies, back in Britain and he hailed from Perthshire. (see photo 168, 169, 170 & 171.)

The British Navy had wanted to use Perth as base for its navy ships which would guard Australia on its Western shores, from the French who were exploring and sniffing around all of Australia. One cheeky Frog had gone ashore at Shark Bay and planted the flag and proclaimed this part of Australia for the French. Luckily for us other reports of the west coast of Oz which were all negative, so did not excite the Frogs back in France, at the time as they were preoccupied with Napoleon and so they never followed it up. So it was imperative that the Brits got in and grabbed it, no matter that generally it was viewed as a basket case, not worth bothering with.

The land at Freemantle was at that time little more than a collection of sand dunes and the area around the entrance to the River Swan was full of treacherous reefs. So at first all the settlement amounted to was a motley collection of tents. In Aug 1829 Capt Stirling now made Lt Governor of WA laid the first foundation stone of the city.

The whole settlement got off to what seems the customary poor start as with all these state city sites. It took many years to get going and settlers gradually spread out into the hinterland and to the North and South. The Gold strikes in Kalgoorlie and Coolgardie in 1892, really helped to give the whole of WA a big push forwards, as was the case in Victoria.

The place to specifically visit whilst in Perth, is Kings Park. As parts of this huge park are elevated, they afford you a spectacular view of the Swan River and the skyline of Perth city centre. Most of the park is virgin bush but those parts that are developed are very pleasing to the eye. A good afternoon out. (see photo 172, 173 & 174.)

Freemantle is a must for a visit. This old port is largely original around its commercial city centre with many fine ornate old Victorian buildings still left, and they were all done up for the Admirals Cup races a few years back, and look great. Many pavement cafes and restaurants abound and they are well frequented. The streets are heaving with people on Saturdays and Sundays. A lovely old indoor market that is open on Fridays, Saturdays and Sundays. Pavement artists abound, juggling, playing instruments, card tricks and the like. Another indoor market is to be found at weekends at the dockside area. (see photo 175, 176, 177 & 178.) Visit the Maritime Museum, the roundhouse which is the oldest building in WA (1831) and was WA's first goal. The old Prison built by convict labour in the 1850's and opened in 1855, has conducted tours which are well worth going on. A large goal that was in continual use up to 1991. (see photo 179 to 184.) Freemantle is home for a large fishing fleet and for sailing clubs and the like. A very busy commercial port with large liners calling and a constant flow of large merchant ships loading and unloading or waiting out in the nearby roads to get into the port. Whilst I was staying in the area the Queen Elizabeth 2 called for two days whilst on a World tour, along with a quite large German cruise ship.

Just up the coast from Freemantle is the best known beach of Cottesloe. Worth a look, too and when I lived in Perth from 1967 to 69 I spent many an hour on this beach. (see photo 185)

Take a trip even further up the coast to Hillaries Harbour which is a fairly new private port for small craft, and has a shopping precinct with many pubs and eating places. It also boasts a sheltered swimming beach which is ideal for those who do not like the waves and wind that you get on the exposed coast. As all this is behind the shelter of a massive breakwater this beach is like a mill pond. Plenty of parking is available and it is FREE. On the way up to Hillary you will go past Scarborough Beach which is another well known holiday beach.

Just 12 miles off the coast is a small low lying Island called Rottnest, named by early Dutch boats that regularly went up this coast to get to their spice trade areas of Indonesia. It means rats nest island because they confused the quokka, which is a largish marsupial, with being a rat. These animals are a feature of the Island to this day and are quite tame. The Island has a regularly ferry service, albeit an expensive one I thought, costing $48 return for what is a 30 minute trip. Hoards of people go over there for the calm beaches and excellent snorkelling and diving on the reef which is all around the Island, and hosts a lot of tropical fish. The early boat callers used the Island to rest on, and after the early settlers arrived it was used as an Island jail in early days for only Aborigine men, who they deemed had transgressed white laws. Later on they stopped using it for Aborigines and put juveniles there instead. The Island is really not much more than a large sand dune. The vegetation is extremely poor because of this and the salty air and strong winds. Although early on grain was grown. (see photo 186 to 189)

In 1848 Governor Fitzgerald, had a house built on the Island. It was used for three weeks each year as a Summer retreat, and many guests were also invited. The Public in general were not allowed.

They spent their time fishing, swimming and hunting. (see photo 190) They introduced pheasants for the hunting and their descendant's can still be seen pottering around. (see photo 191) In 1903 they allowed the peasants to visit the Island, and it is no surprise that after this the Governor went off using the place in the summer. No doubt hob knobbing with the peasants became just too much. His residence was then turned into holiday homes, and in the 50's it was turned into a Hotel/Pub, which it still is now. Although the Island obviously has many quokkas as their droppings are everywhere, they like many marsupials are only really highly active in the evening. (see photo 192) The day I visited the Island I did see two of them and they were incredibly tame and not at all fazed by humans, and they will eat out of your hands. There are a number of people who live on the Island all the year round. No vehicles are allowed, so to get around the Island which is 11K's long by 4.5 wide, one has to hire a push bike and one should expect a quite hard ride as even though it seems flat, there are lots of ups and downs. Sand dunes by their very nature are not exactly flat. There is even a small railway on the Island, and an airport. (see photo 193)

There are quite a few buildings that were put up in the 1840/50's. However they are not architecturally magnificent. They are very plain little buildings, built by Aborigine convicts and are now used for a variety of uses, like holiday homes that are rented out, and various commercial needs. The Islands only general store/supermarket is an old grain stores building. (see photo 194)

The lakes that dot the Island have two of them that dry out in the summer and as they are four times more saline than the sea, a residue of salt is then left. So from very early days this island supplied all the salt for Perth. However as there was no wood on the island with which to heat up the salt to refine it, it became uneconomical to carry on this trade and it closed down. Unrefined salt crystals, however were still sent over to Perth in Hessian bags, for some time after.

In the late afternoon while I was waiting for the 4pm ferry, I was in the vicinity of the only church on the Island, Holy Trinity. The bells started a somewhat tuneless clanking and tinkling. I thought I would investigate what this little church looked like, and found that just inside the entrance there was a small keyboard with a notice saying that any visitors could have a tinkle on the keys, but only between 3pm and 4.30pm. The little boy who was doing what little boys do, and very tuneless at that, was probably the reason you had a limited time to play around. I thought it quite unique that the Public could play tunes on a church's bells. I had never come across this anywhere else on my travels. So if you have a mad desire to play church bells, then you just get over to Rottnest Island WA, and you can have an hour and a half to yourself. (see photo 195)

On the ferry back we were just entering the harbour roads as the QE 2 was leaving, so that was some sight, and the two moles were absolutely chokka with cars and people seeing the sight of the Worlds best known liner leaving port. Brought a lump to my throat until I remembered that Cunard is now an American company. (see photo 196)

Further South to Rottnest is the larger Island of Garden Island which is used by the Australian Navy as a base. After the first settlers arrived the British Navy started to explore the coast more thoroughly and at first they thought that because of the many treacherous reefs off the Freemantle coast, there would be no really safe area for ships to anchor. However they soon found the waters between Garden Island and the coast, were very deep and well sheltered, so it then became the main Navy harbour and a naval base was built on the island and eventually a causeway to the southern end of the island was built, which connected it to a spit of land off the mainland. This also made the waters more sheltered still. During World War II, Freemantle and Garden Island and Albany were very big bases for the Allied effort against the Japs, and the American navy were based here in force. Freemantle was the largest submarine base outside Pearl Harbour at Hawaii. The remains of the sub pens can still be seen next to the Maritime Museum and you can tour an Oberon class submarine. (see photo 197)

The museum and the nearby wrecks museum, deals mainly with the early mariners who passed by this WA coast starting in the 1600's, and the early development of Freemantle as a port, and the fishing activities. Both are worth a visit. Early mariners as I have said before, viewed WA as a very inhospitable place and not worthy of stopping at, for long, let alone claiming the worthless place for their own country. In the Round House there are a series of letters from a British sailing clipper Captain who had to offload some cargo in Freemantle in the late 1800's and he is writing to the American ship owners bemoaning his absolute hate of the place as a port, and cannot wait to get out of the place, and never wishes to ever return. It must have been a hole of a place in the very early days. Treacherous reefs, constant hard Southerly gales and an inadequate port with poor facilities and dock labour that thieved and was constantly drunk. (They sound like the dockers of my home town of Liverpool) (see photo 198, 199 & 200)

The city of Perth is some way up the River at a point where the river widens out considerably. It is laid out on the Northern shores. The streets run parallel to the river bank and nowadays it has the customary number of tall skyscraper office blocks. Not a tremendously large city centre, very compact with only four main streets parallel to each other. Not many older buildings of note are left to be seen. One is the Old Court House in Barrack St. Built in 1836, and is a nondescript building with nothing to commend it. The Governors House is nearby, but you cannot get too near it or see inside it. The WA Parliament House is a modern affair and has a freeway running across the front of it. On the other side of the freeway is a brick arch building which is all that is left of the original Perth Barracks that used to be on that site and built in the 1860's. Demolished to make way for the freeway in 1966, so you can see that in WA history is not too high on the list. In fact much of the city has been levelled in the last 40 years and new buildings erected. So it is a bit of an historical desert, I'm afraid. However it is a pleasant city, made more pleasant by the fact of its location on the river. (see photo 201 to 208.)

Close by the city on its Western side is Kings Park. The land it occupies is higher than that of the city, rising to a small hill that the early explorers who first came here, called Mount Eliza. When I was here in the 60's the park was mostly virgin bush, but now there are some nicely laid out grasslands, walkways and flower beds, with a cafe/restaurant and plenty of parking. However it is still mainly bush with walkways through it. These developments are on the Southern edge of the park which overlook the river, so you can get many marvellous views of the Swan and the city, below you. When I was living in Perth in the 60's, I used to take my girl friend up to a car park with a view over the Swan river at The Narrows, for a canoodle. So this park has some nice memories for me. At weekends the park is very well attended with many picnicking on the lawns.

There is a museum, but I decided not to sample it as I was finding Oz Museums a bit of a let down, as I have already pointed out. It may have been great, but I ran out of time. There is also an Art Gallery of WA, but as I am not into art, I gave that a miss too. So there you have it, a pretty city, but lacking historical things to see. You will have to be content with the physical side of the city, but this is fair enough, as all the big cities in Oz lack the type of history you get in European cities and that is only to be expected.

On my last Saturday I visited the city centre again and Kings Park to take some photos. The town was packed with shoppers and in the plaza around the large Bank of Australasia building, in the centre of Perth, there were many buskers and performers strutting their stuff. A bloke about 30 odd was dressed as a pirate and was loudly proclaiming that he was in the Guinness Book of Records as the only bloke in the World who could swallow 14 swords in one go. He kept shouting this fact over and over so much so that I just had to get away, and I didn't fancy watching 14 swords go down someone's throat as I hadn't yet had my lunch. Elsewhere a young lad was taking off Michael Jackson and how he strutted around doing his peculiar walks and to his music. He was so over the top that I felt embarrassed for him, real X factor stuff, yet the mostly young crowd were lapping it up and cheering him on. I must be getting old, I thought because I would have definitely not have taken someone like Jackson off, considering he was just about to get done over in the USA over naughties with young lads, but as I said I am just getting on.

On my way back I stopped off at a small riverside park in the Nedlands area. It had a cafe and I decided to partake of an ice cream. I sat on an outside table which was up against the cafe building, and it was here that I had one of those golden moments that make journeys like this worthwhile. It was quite a large ice cream and so took me many minutes of licking and enjoyment. When I got down to the end of the cone I had about half an inch of the biscuit in my fingers, when I noticed a Willy Wagtail bird had inched his way to within a few feet of my legs, and was looking at me. So I broke off some of the biscuit and threw it gently towards the bird. He saw it and approached it gingerly but he did not partake of my generosity and moved away. In a flash a Honey Eater bird, which is quite a largish bird, a bit bigger than a Blackbird, but slimmer and has a mottled breast like a thrush, and with a long curved beak, had swooped down onto the piece of cone lying near my feet on the grass. It had obviously been perched very nearby on the tree that was next to the wall of the cafe, and had been observing my actions. When the Wagtail didn't take it, down he came to claim it. It was what he did next that was magic, because this is a wild bird and I had seen many of these birds in all the caravan parks I had been in up to now, as they are quite common in these places due to many parks having many trees in them for shade. I had not seen any displays of them being unafraid of humans that you get with other types of birds like Blackbirds and sparrows. After he had gobbled up the piece of cone, he obviously knew I still had some in the fingers of my left hand, which was resting on the thigh of my left leg. It flew up onto my leg and looked at me. I naturally offered him the remaining morsel of cone which was between the thumb and forefinger. It eagerly tried to take it but in its haste it only knocked it out of my hand and onto the grass. It calmly hopped down, devoured it and hopped back up and onto the table looking at me as if to say 'any more of that mate?' when it saw I did not offer any more, off it flew. It is not often that a wild bird will so casually hop onto your leg in its efforts to get what it has seen your holding. Very tame behaviour, and probably this bird lived in this area and had learnt that people at tables equalled opportunities to get food, and had overcome the fear of humans.

On my last full day, which was the following day, I again decided to spend some of it in the city getting a few bits I needed for my next leg. Riding my scooter on the way there I took the road along the South bank of the river and away from Freemantle. I had not gone far and as I was riding I was watching the river to see if I could see any photo opportunities as the river here is quite scenic. I was looking at a man in a kayak paddling along, when I saw the unmistakeable fin of a dolphin breaking the surface. I screeched to a halt and grabbed my camera, and watched the waters intently for the next breaking of the fin. Sure enough the dolphin broke surface again, and eventually I was able to get some shots of not just one dolphin but three. Now they were only 50 yards away from the bank and in quite shallow water. The guy in the kayak had stopped and was as intent on them as me, and I guess he was as thrilled as I was at this display of nature going on so close to us both. So two days on the trot I experienced unique displays of nature that seems you can only experience in Oz. (see photo 209)

After a month here I was ready to get on, but before I did I resolved to visit two towns to the east, namely Kelmscott and Armadale, and a bit more to the North, the area they call the Swan Valley. I would do this in the motorhome rather than on my scooter. I would then stay overnight in the Swan Valley before heading out up the Northern Highway and towards Geraldton. Armadale which nestles at the foothills of the Darling Range of hill, has nothing to commend it, a standard type Oz small town. So didn't stop longer than it took to have lunch and then I was off and up into the hills.

Heavily wooded but many houses nestling amongst the trees. Always a dangerous thing I think in Oz with all the fires they have. However they just like to take risks.

The road I took was to take me to the Mundaring Dam which catches water which is then piped to the goldfields towns, over in the dry Eastern part of WA. (see photo 210) After a while the houses cease and it is just typical Oz gum tree woods, but for some time there were many orchards in evidence growing apples and other fruits. After the dam I hit the West East highway which runs from Perth to Kalgoorlie, and I took that heading back towards Perth. After a while it dips back down to the coastal plain that Perth sits on and you can see the city away in the distance with its tall buildings sticking up like tall trees. Very similar scenery to that I encountered coming down off the Adelaide Hills. You then hit the towns of Guildford and Midland, both rather scruffy and flyblown, but they are both old towns having been started within a year of the start of Perth (1830). They could do with a good tarting up. North of Midland and following the course of the Swan River is the Swan Valley where like North of Adelaide, they grow vines and there is a thriving wine industry. It was amongst this type of landscape that I found the Swan Valley Caravan Park for an overnight stop prior to leaving the next day for the next town of Geraldton.

My route out of the Perth area, the next morning took me across the Northern suburbs and back towards the coast, where I would pick up the coastal road that would take me North and towards my eventual destination some thousands of miles away, of Darwin.

Chapter Ten

Perth to Darwin

My trip out of Perth was not without incident and did not do my blood pressure any good at all. I think I have already mentioned that the Aussies can be hopeless on the road sign front. Some places are absolutely the pits. Coming through the Northern suburbs of Perth wasn't too bad as I only had to stick to two major highways and they saw me right up to one of the furthermost northern suburbs called Joondalup, a newish outer suburb. It was here that things deteriorated signwise. I got to a major, major junction and because they will insist in not putting the names of the roads on the junction so you can check on a map just where you are, I had to guess and went straight across. After a mile I realised that this road was no longer a main highway, so I turned back to the junction where I turned left thinking that I was heading North up the coastal Highway. Well I was on the right road but now I was heading back to Perth and I did not realise for quite some time until I reached one of the major highways I had used to get out of Perth. Was I mad, as I had gone some 15 K's and wasted at least half an hour. So had to turn round and retrace my steps.

The problem with navigating on your own is when your on a very busy road and trying to read the street map for the city your in. Oz city maps are large book size, but each page actually only covers a relatively small area so you have to keep turning to the next page you need, which may be pages away. So your trying to work out which page to turn to, get to it and drive at the same time. You can't stop because it is chockablock traffic and nowhere to stop. Even when you know the name of the street you have to turn at, because they do not clearly show the street names, you often miss them in heavy traffic. Many times even on major routes and at major junctions they do not sign the junction as they do in the UK with where each road goes to, from that junction. So I hope you have a good navigator with you.

Anyway, eventually I got out of Perth and heading towards my first stop, Lancelin. Just out of Perth there are two roads that you can use to head up the coast. One is inland and is called the Brand Highway, but as I like to follow coasts I wanted the coast highway, which is Highway 3, but according to my map it seemed to finish at this place Lancelin. My next port of call was 75 K's further on and called Cervantes and also on the coast. According to the map there was a linking road between the two, but it was listed as a gravel road. I thought I would at least get to Lancelin and ask if it were good enough for my vehicle. I went to the local cop shop and asked there only to be told that it did not go all the way to Cervantes and anyway it was 4WD only. Wouldn't you think they would have joined the two places, especially as Cervantes has the nearby Pinnacles which everyone wants to visit. No they make you head inland for 45 K's to hit the inland Brand Highway, then 75K's along that only to turn back to the coast for another 53 K's. So you have to do a detour for about 100 K's for your troubles, More Blood Pressure!

I must say I have found that the Aussies have a strange way of doing things, always have thought this. With their so called coastal highways, most of the time they are not coastal at all, and can be inland by as much as up to 30 miles away from the coast. I don't know about you but I would rather follow a coast than drive through boring endless bush on an inland road. It is not as bad on the East coast as at least there you can get some nice rural landscapes to drive through. In WA forget it, your going to go through non stop dry and boring mixtures of farming land and or bush, and very little green to be seen.

So the drive to get to Cervantes had nothing to comment on, except that Lancelin is a small lobster fishing village with a wicked wind that apparently never abates. So much so it has also become a Mecca for wind surfers and kite surfers, and they were in much evidence. It is also surrounded by high white sand dunes.

Just outside Cervantes is this place called the Pinnacles. If you saw that Scottish twit Connolly when he did his travel show on TV, from Oz, he stopped at the Pinnacles. There are hundreds of stone objects sticking up in a desert of sand not far from the coast. Most of them come to a point, hence the name Pinnacles. As I got close to the entrance to this place I could see I was going to be subject to yet another rip off from the Aussies, namely a booth and a warden taking money off you. $9 to be exact, which I thought was rich. This was a naturally occurring phenomena and the Government had done absolutely nothing to produce it, yet here they were making you pay just to see this. To add insult to injury after having driven over 250 miles just to look at a bunch of stones, you have to pay $9. On top of this although they had a track which went 3K's through the area. As I was in a motorhome I couldn't use it and had to park at the entrance and walk round. More high blood pressure. I could see that all the area looked exactly the same, so I was sure I was not going to walk for three K's through scenery exactly the same as everywhere else. I just walked into the area for say half a mile, took my pictures and got out. So I ended up paying $9 for 15 minutes of looking and three photos. They certainly know how to extract the money off you these Aussies. More on this later, no doubt. (see photo 211 & 212)

Cervantes itself is also just a small holiday beach area with mainly holiday type homes and a few service businesses and a caravan park at which I stayed at for that night. On the way up from Perth the land was the usual mixture of bush and farmland, and the land between the Brand Highway and Cervantes was the most heavily farmed. How they grow anything on this WA coast beats me as the land is so sandy and of course the place doesn't get a lot of rain at the best of times, and they have had not enough rain for sometime now. It wasn't until I got into the higher grounds of the Darling Ranges (at the back of Perth) that the soils started to look good and that was probably why they had lots of fruit and vine growing up there. I also went past some lakes that were thick with fowl. One small lake had so many ducks sitting around the edge I wondered what the attraction of that lake was. The ducks I have seen in WA are all the same breed, same size as a Mallard but with boring brown plumage.

The wind here in Cervantes is like that at Lancelin, very strong. I recorded on my wind meter a top force of 26 mph which is quite blowy and good for sailing.

Got away to a reasonable quick start at 8.30am and headed down the road to Jurien Bay. A supposed coastal road that you hardly saw the coast from. Mainly because on your left, the seaward side, there were large dunes. The land was mostly bush scrub and the soil was basically just sand. A couple of small coastal settlements, but not worth stopping for. They are mainly holiday and fishing places. They catch a lot of lobsters in this area, so there are many large powered boats for that purpose to be seen in these small harbours and out at sea. Eventually this road joins the Brand Highway and on doing so I turn left and head for Geraldton. The closer I get to G the more the land becomes farmed, and the scrub is sparse, and the soil begins to look like soil and not white sand.

Further along the way I come to a historical village and my guide book tells me that Greenough had been a busy mining town, with several older buildings from the 1860/90 era worth looking at, so I turn it into the place. These buildings are all on what was obviously the old main street, but that has a gate across it and a sign which says that to get to see these buildings you have to enter the site through the shop which is in a building on your right, and the charge is $5. I gave it a miss as I can see the buildings quite easily from the main road, and whilst they may be old for Oz there was no way I was going to pay to walk past them. For some time now there has been a range of hills to my right and these continue right into Geraldton.

Now this town has a very special connection for me, because when I was in Perth in my 20's I went out with an Oz nurse called Elaine who was from Geraldton (she of the Kings Park canoodling!) A very sexy good looking blonde, who I fell for. Well it didn't last as I realised she didn't feel the same for me, so I split. Over a year later when I went back to Sydney to catch the Oriana back to the UK, I went to a nightclub and bumped into her. I got back with her and we went out together for about three months until it came time for me to get on my ship. She was going to also come to the UK to do a midwifery course in a London hospital. Of course as soon as I was out of sight... out of mind as well, and letters were few and far between. I thought that this did not show commitment on her part, and that as London was full of birds for me to pick from, I gave her the heave ho. I was rash like that in those days especially with women that messed me about. I always regretted it and wonder what happened to her. So here I am in the very place where she was born and brought up. She's probably married to some rich Doctor now, maybe even an English one.

Well apart from the connection, I found it to be an agreeable place. The centre is built on a series of little hills, so it gives it something most Oz towns don't have, as they are mostly dead flat. The shops in the centre are all original and bustling. Although they do have the obligatory new shopping malls as well. There is quite a large deep sea port, but not busy by the looks of it. One of the hills has a memorial to the Aussie Navy ship HMAS Sydney a cruiser, I think, that was sunk off this coast in WW11 in 1941, by an armed German merchant raider boat called the Kormaron. When this ship came across the Sydney, which was trying to stop it to investigate it, it opened fire and some lucky shots hit it in the right places and the Sydney was sunk with all 650 hands. Mind you the Aussies managed to get some shots in, enough to eventually to cripple it for good. The crew were picked up by the Aussies and interned. (see photo 213)

After a walk around I came across the Geraldton Cathedral, which I must say I thought it odd that such a place has a Cathedral. It is larger than a normal church but not as large as most cathedrals are. (see photo 214) I thought whilst attractive it seemed to me more like a Greek church in its style, rather than the Roman Catholic that it is. However it is the story behind it that is most interesting. Apparently it was designed by an Englishman called John Hawes who was born in Richmond, London, in 1876. That immediately pricked up my ears as I used to live in

Richmond and it is my favourite London borough. Anyway he trained in London as an architect, but then swopped to train as an Anglican priest. After his ordination he worked as a missionary in the slums of London. Then he went to the Bahamas and helped to build some churches there. He then converted to Catholicism and went to study in Rome and after this he came to Oz in 1915. He certainly changed his mind a lot this one.

He was invited here by the bishop of Geraldton and he worked for some 24 years in the area as a parish priest including Greenough the $5 village I mentioned. He designed some 24 churches of which 16 were built including this Cathedral. However just after it was completed he got itchy feet again or maybe after 24 years in the hot sun of WA his brains got fried, because he then went back to the Bahamas and lived out the rest of his life on Cat Island. (Wherever that is.) He lived as a hermit in a small stone building until he died in 1956 in Miami. Well I never, real eccentric these Englishmen can be. So his body now resides in a tomb he built for himself on Cat Island, so if you are ever there you can look him up?

Well after all this excitement in Geraldton, especially as I managed to find a place in WA, at last, that does not charge for emailing. I went to the library thinking I may strike lucky, but they wanted $12 an HOUR I ask you. I think these WA Aussies must all be of Scottish stock. They directed me to a building nearby that allowed old geezers like me, FREE ACCESS. So it was now time to move on, I had thought that I may stay here overnight, thinking I would arrive later in the afternoon, but I was ahead of myself and arrived before lunch. The only thing I thought I could do while here was to take a boat trip to the Abrolhos Islands which are just off Geraldton. I found that this was not possible as they are protected and no visitors allowed. So that was out.

However before I move on 'let me tell you a story' (Max Bygraves who used this catch phrase on the UK TV, sold his mansion in Sandbanks and moved to Sydney) As I have previously recounted, the Dutch in the 1600's, used to use the Southerlies in the Southern Ocean to whip across to the WA coast then swing up it to get to Java for the spice trades. It was quicker than plodding directly across the Indian Ocean to Java. This coast has many reefs off it which you can clearly see when the supposed coastal roads come close enough to see the sea. The winds are predominately SW coming off the Southern Ocean and as I said they can be quite stiff winds. So stiff that many of the trees I have passed today are bent at all sorts of crazy angles including ending up parallel to the ground. So you can see how hairy it must have been trying to sail these older type ships which are not the best at going where you want them to. As a result many foundered at various places along WA's coast. One, the Batavia commanded by Francisco Pelsaert founded in 1629, on what is now Abrolhos Islands, just off Geraldton.

Most of the crew and passengers got safely off and onto an island. The captain took most of his officers off the island to the mainland to look for water, leaving 268 people behind on the island and this included some soldiers he had on board. A merchant nutter named Jeronimus Cornelisz tricked the soldiers out of their arms and set about a reign of terror killing some 125 women and children during the three months that the Captain was away. Capt Pelsaert did not find water on the mainland and had to sail in one of the small ships boat, all the way to Batavia (Java) to get help. He came back with troops and set about killing all the rogues who had done all this murdering and mayhem. But he dumped some of his men on the mainland and left them there at a place near what is now Kalbarri, North of Geraldton and on the coast. They would have been the first white men ever to have landed and stayed on Oz.

It is interesting that in recent years it has been found that a very rare syndrome has been found in Aborigine children, called 'Ellis van Creveld syndrome' This syndrome was very common in Holland at the time of the Batavia being wrecked. This suggests that some of these men left here had liaisons with the natives and introduced this syndrome which still exists to this day. What happened to the men has never been known.

Well after leaving Geraldton the first town I came to is called Northampton. I felt like stopping someone and asking where the shoe factory was. You may not get that one? Anyway my guide book tells me that this little place was started in the 1840's as lead and copper were discovered nearby, and it became a mining town. So there were a few older buildings to be seen and one surprised me as it had on the front, the fact that it was a convent. (see photo 216) I thought that this place was a strange place to have a convent. Next to it was a nice church which I thought was different from most of the plain old churches they seemed to build back in the 1800's.

The land from Geraldton to the Murchison River area was quite well farmed with much less scrub evident, but after the river it gradually fell back to heavy scrub and bush and for at least 200 K's all you saw was bush....very boring.

However it was obvious that something was going on with this land as there were fences evident all over the place. I saw no sheep but kept seeing goats of all things wandering about the roadsides. I did see my first snakes in Oz (on this trip) two of them coiled up and on the road. As they did not look flattened I presume they were live ones. Only small and thin though, nothing spectacular. Eventually at about 6pm I arrived at the Overlander Roadhouse. This is a typical bush service station with cafe and motel and caravan park (of sorts).

I am making for Monkey Mia on the Peron Peninsular and have to turn left here. (see photo 217 & 218) I had wanted to make it there for this night, but I had had enough, so decided to stop here. It only cost me $5 for the night, which is the cheapest so far. Maybe I will find a place for nowt, because on $5 they cannot make any money on that. For that I get electricity, a shower and toilets. Even though everything was very rudimentary, it was still cheap. About 50K's out of G, I lost the mobile phone signal, then I lost the radio and ABC and at this place no TV. It was like being on the Moon. So I passed the evening away writing and turned in early so I could get away early in the morning.

One thing I was not pleased about is that all the way up to G, the weather was great, around mid 20's and kept like that with the coastal breeze. The Highway North of G is now called the North West Coastal Highway, Very grand, especially as it miles away from the coast and so the further it has got away from the coast, the dam hotter it has got. Eventually I had to turn on the aircon whilst driving, and that is the first time I have had to do that since leaving Sydney. I had been watching the weather forecasts on the TV, and the temperatures up in the Northern coastal areas had been in the 40's. Of course it was still summer but I could not stay any longer in Perth, until end of March when the temperatures would start to come down. So I guessed I was going to have to put up with it, and I guess I may get used to it.

I had a talk with the owner of the roadhouse and picked his brain about what the land is being used for around his area. All the lands I have passed with thick bush are owned by pastoralists. That is to say farmers who have cattle and sheep on their land. Even though it is bush they still keep sheep on them. I asked him how they managed to find the sheep when they wanted to round them all up, but I got no satisfactory answer. Apparently these farms are enormous covering hundreds of thousands of acres and carrying hundreds of thousands of sheep. Some of them are carrying goats and the ones I saw are ones that got away and are running around loose. Also despite the dry appearance of the land there is plenty of water albeit salty water, in aquifers underground. He got his water for the roadhouse by drilling and then desalinating it for use.

Didn't get up as early as I would have liked, so only got away at 8.30am. I drove along the branch road to Denham which is on the peninsular to the West of Shark Bay. I drove for some 100 miles and although I saw a reasonable number of cars approaching me, not one passed me. As I only travel at 60mph I usually have many who zip past. This just goes to show how big Oz is and how little traffic there can be. This distance is equal to me travelling from my home town of Bournemouth to London and not having any traffic passing me, and not going through ONE town all the way.

There was also no sign of any civilisation. Denham had a sign at its entrance saying it was twinned with Denham in the UK (Bucks). (see photo 219) This is the first time I have seen such a sign since starting this trip. Unlike in the UK where they are everywhere, the Aussies must be more sensible on this one and don't allow their councillors all the freebie trips around the World to towns they are twinned with. A pleasant enough place, and like many of these coastal settlements in Oz , a mixture of holiday establishments and a fishing industrial place. Had a coffee and picked the brains of a gnarled local oldie. On the way up the peninsular I could see two what seemed to be white islands way off the coast and to my left. They looked almost like two icebergs. I found out that they were two enormous mounds of salt waiting on the banks of the opposite peninsular called 'useless loop' thus named by some Froggies exploring the area eons ago. A ship would come in and take it away every so often.

Denham apparently was named after a British Captain called by that name and who charted all of Shark Bay in 1858. Off the Peron Peninsular is a large Island now called Dirk Hartog Island after the Dutch mariner who set foot on the island back in 1616 and therefore was the first white man to set foot on the Oz Continent, some 152 years before Cook.

On the last leg of this road to Monkey Mia I noticed many saucer shaped depressions in the land. Almost as if meteors had smashed in numbers all around here. Most of them were round in shape, and obviously they collected water in them, but all were dry as a bone. This I had noticed greatly, all over WA, that wherever there were depressions that normally would have collected water, they were all dry. It only emphasised that Oz was really suffering a bad prolonged drought. (see photo 220)

Another 32 K's and I was at the resort and paying my usual Oz ransom to get into the place. I mean you pay to get in then they charge you another fee to stay overnight. Double whammie!

Anyway it was a nice place well laid out with many facilities and I suppose they had to pay the girls to pop the fish into the dolphins gullets. What was puzzling me was why was it called Monkey Mia. I asked the young girls in reception but only got blank looks. Luckily at the time the Captain of one of the tour catamarans was present and he knew of several possible answer, as there seemed to be no definitive answer. One answer was that in the early days of settlement in this area there were hundreds of Malays who were here camping and involved in pearl fishing. (Now fished out.) The Aussies took to calling them Monkeys. Another slant on that theme was that it was believed that some of the Malays kept Monkeys as pets. A third answer is that a ship sent to the Bay with the government surveyor to look it over, was called The Monkey, and a small island in the Bay was named after it. Yet another story is that an early settlers daughter was nicknamed monkey, as she was a little Monkey. She died at an early age here. Mia apparently is Aboriginal for home, but I always thought it was Italian as in Mama Mia. So you takes your pick, but whatever the name has absolutely nothing to do with fish or marine life which is what the area is World renowned for.

Some facts about Shark Bay include the fact that it hosts 12,000 Dugongs which is about a third of the Worlds population, and they have a bay which is the largest in Oz. It has about 900 Bottle nosed Dolphins (Indian Ocean variety) and it has an ecosystem unequalled in the World. It has calm shallow waters with abundant sea grass growing, which in turn attracts many species of fish, who in turn attract the dolphins and other fish stock predators. It has many turtles and stingrays and of course the sea cows or dugongs, who feed off the sea grass. Scientists come here from all over the World in great numbers to study the dolphins and this is only one of two places in the world where they do this. The other being in the USA (probably California). So that is why it has been awarded to be a World heritage Site. Good on Ya Mate!

I got to the resort about 11am and as soon as I got the home parked I walked to the spot on the nearby beach where I knew they interacted with the dolphins. The wardens told me that they fed them three times a day, but ultimately it was up to the dolphins as to whether they actually turned up. However they said that for the last three days they had come three times. So it was a matter of waiting around, but they never fed them after 1pm. I also booked for a catamaran trip round the bay which started at 1. So first I made myself some sandwiches and packed them and some fruit into a bag and went back to wait. There were several people swimming in the shallow water and I sat on a bench on the beach. Sure enough there was a hubbub amongst those in the water, and looking up I could see two fins in the water amongst them. They were here and on time too.

I went to join the others and to get close to these wonderful creatures. Here they were cool as cucumbers in just a few feet of water and I like all the others was furiously snapping away with my camera. The warden had heard the noise and came down to the waters edge and got us all to stand in a line so as not to crowd the creatures out and frighten them. One dolphin was called Nicky and she was the mother and the smaller one was her two year old calf. Well Nicky knew who the warden was and she spent most of the time around her feet waiting no doubt for her fish. We were told that touching the dolphins was out so as not to transmit any human viruses etc or get them too familiar and dependent on humans. Well we were given many facts about these fish and the area, and her talk went on for over half an hour. I was surprised the mother dolphin was so patient and waited all that time. Eventually my patience and more to the point my time ran out as I could see the catamaran was filling up at the nearby jetty. So I had to scoot and so missed the actual feeding. Maybe I will catch it tomorrow at the 8am feed time. (see photo 221)

The catamaran took us slowly under sail out into the bay and we hadn't gone far when we saw the first Dugong. We tried to get close to it so we could take photos, but they are shy creatures and on this occasion we never got that close. Well we spent two and a half hours and a fantastically sunny day slowly going from one sighting of dolphin fins, to Dugong sightings to turtle sightings, the whole area was teaming with fish of all types and so many dolphins with calves, plus Dugongs many also with calves. An absolute marine paradise. During the last ten minutes as we headed back to the jetty, we went through a school of about ten dugongs. We were told that this was unusual as they are usually solitary creatures and the most you see in numbers at one time is two when you get a Mother and her calf. So a very memorable afternoon and very special. Well worth the $60 it cost. They even threw in free cold water. God they're so considerate these Aussies. (see photo 222 to 224)

After getting back onshore I was so hot as the day had gone from very cloudy in the morning to at least mid thirties, I needed a swim. So soon I was in the lovely calm and really quite warm waters, for my very first Oz swim since I landed. Very nice too. Then I capped all that off with a nice Latte at the waterside cafe, and I was feeling so elated that I even shared my large biscuit with a scavenging seagull who stood next to me in that seagull begging mode that they do. But I would only let him have a piece or two if he actually took it out of my hand. He did too the greedy blighter. (see photo 225 & 226.)

Next morning at 8am I was packed and ready to move on, but had a look to see if any dolphins had arrived at the beach. Wow! I was amazed at just how many where there, over a dozen, many right up to the waters edge. What a sight. But also so many people, hard to get decent photos. Anyway I found out that even though there were this many, they only feed just four of the females. So that is what I did for a few minutes, watching various people being picked to feed them. Then on my way. (see photo 227, 228 & 229.)

As it was fairly early and still cool I saw a little wild life on the road South of Denham. Two quite large lizards, probably Goannas, scuttled across the road in front of me, but were too quick for me to photograph. Then I saw my first live Roo. All I have seen have been dead ones, so far. This was a small one, probably a wallaby, and was lying under a thick bush in the shade and right next to the road.

Travelling down the peninsular I was getting a nice cool breeze coming off the sea, but this was to quickly change when the road went away from the coast. I came to a beach called Shell Beach which I had passed on my way up, and so pulled into there for a butchers. (see photo 230) Very wide beach absolutely brilliant white and made up entirely of millions upon millions of tiny cockle shells.

The bay as it is very shallow and warm is ideal for small cockles to grow in great numbers and over hundreds of thousands of year, when they have died their shells eventually get washed up onto this particular beach. Then they get blown inland to thus make this very wide beach, which is 5 metres deep with shells. They mine them and use to put on paths in gardens, and car parks etc, so as to keep the dust down. Funny though I never saw any Chinese cockle pickers, maybe it was too hot for them here.

A little way down the road was the Hamelin Old Telegraph Station and Stromolite beds. The telegraph station is supposed to be the only one still standing intact in Oz. Now these stromolites which I must say I had never heard of before, are where we all originate from, you could say. They call them living rocks, and they were the first living organisms on Earth. They are single cell organisms and grow in shallow warm saline water and about 3.5 million years ago they kickstarted off, on Earth. As they produced oxygen during their growth this actually put a lot of oxygen into the Earths atmosphere and eventually led to forms of life that breathed it to live. Then of course eventually man came into being. So without the Stromolites we would not be here. Ahhh!

They look just like rocks and you would not know they were living creatures, and this location was not discovered until 1954 by some geologists who realised just what they are. Only one other place on Earth still has them and that is in the Bahamas. (see photo 231 & 232)

As I came out of this site two youngsters were hitchhiking and I had seen them back at Monkey Mia, so I gave them a lift. These were the first hikers I had seen on the roads. They were German, a bloke and his girlfriend both from Munster. So they made the next step of my journey pass a bit quicker as they both spoke good English and we chatted away. They had come from Melbourne and were making their way to Coral Bay, up from Carnarvon, where I intended to stop overnight. The main highway which we rejoined at where I had stopped over at the Overlander Roadhouse, to Carnarvon was uneventful apart from the fact that it was a dam hot day again. We pulled into the place about 3pm and I dropped them off at the road out of town.

Carnarvon is nothing to write home about, and as I had arrived on a Saturday afternoon, it was DEAD. In WA from Saturday lunch, everything shuts. Actually in Perth a lot of places now stay open until 5pm. This Saturday they were holding an election for a new State Government and included was a referendum on should they allow opening all Saturday everywhere and on Sundays and in the evenings on weekdays. Of course in all the Eastern States this is the Status Quo and has been for ages. WA it seems is still as behind as it was in the 60's when I lived there.

Nothing to report about this place. Even the guide book says it is a sleepy place. I would rather say dead, and so it was and is. The only feature of slight note is the One Mile Pier. A dilapidated structure built in the late 1880's to allow the export of livestock and wool and grain out of the area., which nowadays is all done by road. The town is situated on the Gascoyne River. I booked into the first caravan park I could find but actually the town had five more parks which was odd for such a sleepy place with nothing of note to see or do.

At 8.30 next morning I was back on the road and out of Carnarvon towards my next destination of Coral Bay where I had read that it had one of the best reefs in the World and was a Mecca for those who want to do some diving and snorkelling. I am actually going to head for Exmouth which is up at the end of a peninsular and I have to go past Coral Bay, so I thought I may as well take a look. It is Sunday anyway and Exmouth will be closed. On the way out I passed a number of banana plantations which I did not know they grew here, as I thought all Oz bananas were grown in Queensland, hence why Queenslanders are called Banana Benders. Soon the road goes over the wide inlet of the Gascoyne River and I was very surprised to see that it was completely dry! An amazing sight to see such a wide river with not a drop of water in it, which just goes to show how little rain has fallen in Oz in recent years. (see photo 233)

The landscape is much the same as usual, but I did see and magnificent Wedge Tailed Eagle which they say can have a wing span up to 6 feet. This one I guess was at about 4 feet, so still quite big. I was approaching the usual road kill in the middle of the road and I could see a group of birds having a feed. However one bird seemed much bigger than the usual crows who feed off road kill. They all scarpered quickly when they saw me approaching but this big bird just stayed where he was I could then see he was an eagle, and he almost managed to stay the distance but chickened out when I was almost on top of him. I wouldn't have hit him as the kill was on the other side of the road, but his nerve gave way. So I had a great view of this bird taking off, to fly to a nearby tree. Had I thought a bit quicker I could have taken a shot of him out my window as I passed, but alas although my camera was right next to me and ready to go, my brain isn't so quick these days.

Talking about the lack of rain, it has been puzzling me how the farmers who carry all these sheep on these massive farms, manage to get water to them. The bush in which they are grazing looks so dry and I have seen no sign of water at all, yet I have seen some cattle and plenty of goats, and of course the wildlife like kangaroos and birds have to have water. It is a question I must find someone who can answer it for me. Especially as today I passed three dead cows at the side of the road and they started me thinking about this question.

Since leaving the highway and coming onto this Exmouth road I had started to see termite mounds which begs the question, why right now? The tallest were about 4 to 5 feet and in some places they got to be quite thick on the ground. Then they stopped and started again so some areas obviously don't agree with termite buildings. Of course one could ask why don't the ants in the Southern part of WA build houses?

Eventually after a mornings driving I got to Coral Bay. You can see the reef just offshore and I read that this is one of the few coral reefs that has formed on the West coast of anywhere. Apparently they usually form only on East coasts. It is as close as 100 metres to the shoreline and the bay really only started to take off as a holiday place in the fifties but got really going in the 80's when they built more decent infrastructure for people to stay at. So now there is a hotel and motel and camping and caravan parks etc. It is quite small but the reef is only reason why people come here and there are boats that take you out onto the reef proper. They are glass bottomed and you can also snorkel off them.

However they only do one trip a day starting at 9am and 10 am so I was too late. I guess the afternoon wind gets too much and it is calm in the morning. I thought I may just hire snorkelling gear and take a swim off the beach and out over the reef. After I had had lunch I thought, 'no hurry I will have a little rest' When I awoke it was 3 and I just didn't feel like swimming. I thought 'To hell with it it's Sunday and I have spent the week driving all the days, and have now done almost 2,000 K's, so as it's the day of rest I am going to laze' So that is what I did. I booked for the 10am, 2 hour trip for Monday and took a walk along the beach. Just paddling in 6 inches of water, there are fish everywhere, even a decent sized stingray. At the tour booking office they had books with pictures of the reef and the fish that you can expect to see. All very tropical and bright, so I am looking forward to the trip tomorrow.

Then I am sat out side my home on the grass with a lovely cool breeze blowing, overlooking the bay and you couldn't get a more idyllic location to be in. Just the noise of the wind in the palm trees and the trilling of the birds. Then I would cook my ready made roast beef dinner and watch ABC all evening, showing Foyles War and a few other BBC programmes. Beats being in England in February where I heard the weather is foul and snow everywhere.

I was dutifully waiting on the beach for the boat to pull up, which it did right on time at 10. However I was out of luck as I was told that I was the only one to have booked for that tour. Damn!

I got talking to the two guys whilst I waited to see if there may be a late booking, and although the boat was in shallow water, there were a lot of quite big fish under the boat. I was told they were snapper and were with the boat because they knew they would get a feed. The operator took out some feed and threw it off the back of the boat. What a site, the water thrashing with the bodies of fish desperate to get the feed. They were like dogs coming up to the back of the boat, half out the water with mouths open almost saying 'give us a feed then' Apparently these large snapper are the fish often used to go with the chips in your fish and chip shops. They look a bit like Cod. (see photo 234 & 235)

I would now have to hire some snorkelling gear and DIY it instead. But the only thing is that the coral nearer to the beach is dead and you have to go 2K's right out to the outer reef to get the best coral and therefore the best concentrations of fish. I do not fancy swimming out that far on my own.

Anyway I got the gear and spent an enjoyable hour swimming around up to 300 metres offshore. There were still quite a number of fish to watch some very colourful but not too many good sized fish. I did see a small reef shark, but it was the big buggers I didn't want to see at all. After an hours swimming I started to get a bit tired as it was exercise that I wasn't used to but doing me some good. There was a strong current which kept pushing me up the beach and that made the going harder. But a very good experience and when I eventually get to the Gt Barrier Reef I may get an even better experience.

After leaving Coral Bay I drove the rest of the way up the peninsular to Exmouth, reaching there just after lunch. I passed the RAAF station which looked dead, not one plane to be seen anywhere. Maybe it is in mothballs for future use in case of trouble. Exmouth itself was only built in the 60's for the Services and there is still a navy communications station in use, so the area is dotted with masts. As there doesn't seem anything else going on in the area apart from tourists, and those not in huge numbers, one wonders just how the place survives. Certainly not much going on the small town, so after catching up on my emails, I headed out of town to visit the end of the peninsular.

Here there is a wreck of a largish boat that got wrecked in 1904 and a lighthouse. The boat has hardly any of it left, just a bit of the bottom of the hull and two large boilers which would have originally been well inside the boat. So no excitement there. The lighthouse is on a bluff so it afforded good views of the whole peninsular. (see photo 236, 237 & 238)

Just near the lighthouse was one of four caravan parks in the area and it was completely empty. Quite how these places survive beats me because every one I have stayed in since leaving Perth has been practically empty. I was told that it starts to get busy again after April as right now it is still what is called the wet season. This stops people visiting the inland Kimberleys Mountain Range, further up the track, as now the non tarmacked roads are closed due to all the rain they are getting.

So if your visiting the North of WA or NT, remember that in the Summer months they get their summer storms and rain in the afternoons with plenty of lightning etc. If you are like me and keeping to the blacktops, then it doesn't matter. If you want to go off road then you need to do it out of the Dec to end March season.

I booked into a caravan park which was also practically deserted and picked a site well away from the nearest other motorhome. Shortly after another motorhome came and parked right next to me. I don't know about you but I call this the 'supermarket car park syndrome' I have a car in the UK that I do not want idiots who don't care, banging their car doors against mine and putting loads of small dents in my doors. So whenever I park in a super market car park I always park in 'empty' areas with no cars near me. Guess what? You can bet your life someone will come along and park their grotbox right next to mine. It is almost as if they can't bear to have their car sitting all alone, so they just have to park right next to someone else's car. Then they repay you by damaging your car door!! So the syndrome is alive and well and living in WA. These two characters parked next to me sound like Spaniards, so I hope they don't keep me awake playing their guitars and castanets all night.

If I survive my close encounter, tomorrow I will head for Port Dampier. Today the temperature was 42, and more of the same forecast for tomorrow. At 8 pm it must have been still 35. So these are the temperatures that you can expect up here, if like me you travel at the summer period.

In the morning when I get up early the two next to me are feeding bread to the birds and a large white cockatoo. He is very tame and will take the bread out of his hand. They are Italians and not Spanish as I first thought. Not at all friendly as I pass them several times within feet of them, and try to get eye contact, but not a peep out of them. Maybe they were Mafia and on a contract job and didn't want to be friendly. Mostly people in parks are only to glad to talk and swap experiences etc. The one doing the bird thing looked a bit like a Calabrian, short, very dark and podgy. The other was much younger and equally unfriendly. I think this sun is beginning to play on my imagination!

On my way out of Exmouth at 8am (early for me) I spied an Emu happily munching away on a tree at the roadside in mid town, and another one a few hundred yards away partaking of the grass on the cricket pitch. Where else could you get such exotic animals happily ensconced in the middle of a town. Wouldn't do to be an avid rose grower around this place. (see photo 239)

It was a long 164 K's to get back onto the main highway which at this point where you rejoin it, it well inland from the coast. I just don't know why they routed it so far inland, especially as up the road you will have to drive 80 K's to get to Onslow, which is on the coast. There are absolutely no towns along the stretch that they take it, so far inland. I just do not understand the Aussie road makers way of thinking at all. Before I rejoined the highway I passed some interesting wildlife in the form of three camels, which surprised me as I did not think they were to be found in WA in the wild. Then I saw two more Emus and a load of sheep running around on the road. They must have got out of their usually enclosed pastures. But it shows just how careful you have to be on Oz roads, in addition to Roos, you are likely to meet anything.

I had not been on the highway long when I had a right scare. I was finding this particular highway to be hard to stop the home from wandering to the left all the time. They have built this road with quite a steep camber from the crown of the road. No doubt to drain away rain water to the edges more quickly, as now I was getting into the rainy area of North WA. I had just finished a drink and was putting the plastic cup on the floor, and my seconds of inattention allowed the vehicle to wander off the tarmac and onto the shoulder which is loose gravel. Before I knew what was happening, I looked at the road again and we were half off and going sideways. We hit one of the nuisance plastic sticks they have along each side with a reflector on, with a bang. I got it back straight and managed to get back onto the road. Luckily being plastic it did little damage. Since being in Oz I have been thinking to myself that these sticks are a bloody stupid because they position them a foot or so off the tarmac edge, so when you drift off the tarmac which happens all the time, sooner or later you are going to collect one. They are meant to show drivers where the edge of the road is at night, as if you couldn't see it in your headlights. I think they are a complete waste of time and money. Or they could position them further away from the tarmac.

The land I am passing through has little vegetation, no typical bush or scrub, as further South. There are clusters of bushes and occasional trees, and the soil is very red in colour. I am beginning to see evidence that there has been rain because I am seeing puddles in ditches and depressions, and some of the creeks have patches of water in them. The land looks a bit wet too. It is obviously a part of WA that has more rain, as the creeks and rivers I am passing over have plenty of gum trees growing along their banks, showing residual water is there. Soon I start to see hills on both sides of the road, and it reminds me that it has been sometime since the land has been hilly. (see photo 240)

I pass over one quite large river with a lot of water in a large pool, and there is a lot of birdlife going on there. I just got over the bridge and a large flock of light green budgies were manically flying over the road from my left to right side. Obviously going towards the river, and they nearly collided with the front of my home as they passed over. Talk about not concentrating drivers of motorhomes, these birds were just as bad. (see photo 241)

Around lunch time I came to a rest area at another one of these large rivers with water in it, so it was a nice stop alongside the river which had Coots, Black Swans, and Ducks and loads of other small birds. However today is so hot I have had to have the aircon on and at this stop had to leave the engine running and the aircon on still, whilst I had my lunch in the cab. Whilst I was there a tanker truck backed up to the river, stuck a hose into it and started to suck out water into the tank. I wondered if this was an illegal theft of water as there were no markings on the truck sides. Water being so scarce anything could happen. (see photo 242)

Soon after lunch I drift off the road yet again and collect another damn stick. This road is so hard to keep a straight line on, and it is not exactly level or smooth. You find the contours of the road push you this way and that. I am not surprised that one sees so many roadside shrines, where people have had accidents and been killed. They are nearly always on highways that are in the middle of nowhere and reasonably straight and I have wondered how accidents can happen on such traffic free roads that are quite straight. I am beginning to think that many will have done as I have and drifted off and lost control, turned over or maybe hit oncoming traffic. It is also so easy to get too tired and drift off. I passed today a number of spots were the Police had marked out the skid marks, which is what they do when surveying an accident, where life has been lost. At one large bridge where I stopped to take a photo there was one poignant shrine. A large white cross with the inscription 'Perry Shriers died 2001 fulfilling his dream' Obviously someone who was only 41 had died at this spot somehow, whilst travelling around Australia. Didn't say if he was a tourist or an Aussie. But what all this means is that travelling around Oz can and is a dangerous thing. It is not like driving in Europe or the UK, where the roads are chocablock with traffic, which keeps you on your toes. Here you can drive for 8 hours and not see a town or much traffic. Today I have passed a number of vehicles going the other way and quite a number have passed me, but for the past three days not one car had passed me. (see photo 243)

All morning I have been seeing 'Willy Willies'. These are mini tornadoes and at one stage there were 8 of them on the horizon in front of me. Eventually one small one started up just in front of me and to my right. I had my camera ready and tried a shot of it as it passed across the road just in front of me. Not as big as some of the ones I can see in the distance. On hot days they are a feature of Oz bush life.

Eventually I can see the sea as the road gets close to the coast as I near my next destination of Karratha and Dampier towns which are both next to each other. On entering Karratha I come across this Oz reluctance to properly signpost towns. Couldn't see many signs telling you where the Town centre was until I got right there and could then see it without the need for a signpost. I was looking for their shopping centre so I could get a paper and a coffee. I was very surprised at how big the place was and the big variety of shops there. It was on par with the big city type centres not at all like the usual small town places I had been seeing. Obviously this area has some serious brass around I thought. When I found the local caravan park and booked in, I inquired and found that most of the people around these two towns, worked for the iron ore industry and the natural gas industry and were all well paid. It showed in their shopping centre with all its swanky shops.

The day has been very hot and on the evening news they said the temperature today reached 46.3 in this area. The temperature was still at 35 at 9pm and I am blessed that I have the aircon. However it is too noisy to have on all night and so I had to suffer a hot and sweaty night. It did get a bit cooler, and in the early hours of the morning a wind did blow up.

So a new day and a bit cooler, which saw me off to have a look at Dampier which is nearby. When you are approaching the place all you see is a hill range and the town sits on top of this line of hills. Strange place, it is purely commercial and given only to the loading of iron ore onto ships which carry it to Japan and China. The whole of the hill is covered in granite rocks. Not round ones but nearly all are rectangular and different sizes. Every spare piece of land that does not have a building on it, is covered in these dark brown rocks. It makes the place look terribly untidy, everything is brown even the soil is a dark reddish brown. Everything is covered in a red brown dust. People's houses generally were scruffy and many seemed not to bother with trying to make any sort of garden. So all in all, not a touristy place. Even the beach is lettered with boulders. So had a quick drive round (5 minutes) and back to Karratha to the mall to get a paper and some fruit. (see photo 244 & 245)

Back on the road and heading towards the next town of Port Headland. Not that I will want to look around as this place is also an iron ore loading town. Whereas the iron ore going through Dampier comes from Mt Tom Price, that going through Headland comes from Mt Newman. In both cases the ore is transported to the docks by enormously long freight trains. I had gone about a third of the way towards headland when there was a thump from the back of the home and I had to stop to see what it was. The Transit has dual rear wheels and one of them was starting to disintegrate. Well it was just too hot to go through all the hassle of changing it for the spare, so I continued on. Having dual rear wheels means that it will still be OK to carry on with one taking the load. I got into Headland and made my way to the centre and found a tyre place as I did not fancy to do it myself with the heat. I was sweating like a pig as soon as I got out of the aircon cab. The spare was put on as they did not have a new tyre to put on . This is typical Oz as this tyre would in the UK be quite a normal tyre to be found in stock ANYWHERE. Here they say it is an unusual size. So now I am without a spare, hence why I wanted to carry two spares, but found that the bullbar at the front wasn't solid enough to weld a bracket onto it to take a spare. I should have made two brackets at the back end, at the ends of the large toolbox I had put on the back. Well you know what they say about hindsight. I will have to look around at the next town of Broome, where they say there are four tyre places.

Headland is an absolute dump. Worse than even Dampier to look at, very untidy and dusty and almost every house I passed looked a dump. So after the tyre work it was 'Heh Ho and off we go'. It was 3.30 and I wanted to get to a caravan park about 160 k's away called Eighty Mile Beach Caravan Park. Getting to there would give me a nice easy run to Broome the next day of about 300 K's.

The landscape all day has been basically very flat with occasional small hill ranges around. Out of Karratha the land was very dry and little grass or bushes and hardly any trees. The only trees I saw all day where whenever we got to a creek or river, where they would grow on the banks as there was water or residual water underground, in these places. After Headland it was a bit greener and there was evidence that rain had also visited here as a lot of the land looked wet and there were small lakes left in the river beds under the bridges, as I passed over the rivers. A type of grass was much in evidence, it grows in clumps and is dotted all about and in places very thick so it gives the impression of richly grassed lands. Later on I was to pass fields holding many cattle of the Brahmin type. Up to now I have never seen more than 20 to 30 cattle in any field. These fields had hundreds in and I guess it is because there was plenty of grass for them. Many started to appear loose on the roads so I had to be careful and vigilant. (see photo 246)

I eventually got to the turn off to the coast, a 9 K section of dirt road that would take me to the beach and park. Boy was it corrugated. Every inch of it was badly corrugated so I had an unpleasant bit of driving with everything shaking and rattling. This is what many tracks in Oz are like and I don't know how even 4WD vehicles can drive all day being shaken to bits. They are OK if regularly graded, this one looked like it hadn't seen a grader in years. The only good bit about the trip down this sheet of corrugated road is that I got to see my first live Roo on the move, as it shot across the road in front of me. It was only a small one, either a baby roo or a Wallaby. It was dark by the time I got there, so couldn't see what the park really looked like, but I wasn't impressed by what I saw in the dark. I had no choice so hunkered down. At least tonight is not as hot, but still hot enough.

Didn't sleep so good as I kept waking up drenched in sweat. But when I finally staggered out of bed, the park looked a bit better than I anticipated, but still one of the scruffy Oz parks. They seem to come in two types, immaculate or scruffy. Can't see the sea, but a short walk through a sand dune brings me onto a very wide beach, with the sea some distance away. It reminded me of the Mersey estuary at Crosby and Formby which is also bounded by similar sand dunes and also the sea disappears at low tide way out. There were many shells on the beach so obviously out on the sands, as at Morecambe Bay (UK), there are cockles and the like living there, (see photo 247)

After leaving the park and another bumpy 9K trip I was back on the road and heading towards Broome some 400 K's away. No towns or settlements en route absolutely nothing and I was going to push on and get there by lunchtime. The road skirts the Gt Sandy Desert, so would I see any sand dunes I wondered? I saw some more roos on that bumpy road, four to be exact. I suppose that as it was still coolish being only 8am, they were still hopping around and hadn't gone to bed yet (being nocturnal).

The whole trip was more eventful on the wildlife side of things, I saw many geckos which are small lizards, they were stood on the road frozen and never moved as you approached. Whereas the bigger goannas would shoot away when they heard you coming. Saw loads of those too, but still couldn't get a photo of one. A lot of the usual road kills everywhere and many flat goannas and geckos which in turn has meant that this section of road had an enormous amount of falcons on it. They were everywhere. Swooping across the road or sitting in trees at the side of the road, mainly they seemed to choose dead trees. Saw a few Wedge Tailed Eagles and one of them was a massive bugger with a wing span of about 6 feet. Saw another bird that I couldn't work out what it was. It was very big and I thought at first it was a baby Emu, it was standing on the side of the road and as I got closer it took off. It had longish legs, a big body and a tall neck with a head that was black. The rest of its body was brown with some white. I think it must have been some sort of wader, but big. Then I was really surprised to see a wild cat because I thought they were all in the eastern states. So it was a wildlife day.

The landscape was very flat all the way, with alternating grassy plains with no bush, to short and tall bush. Things were much greener due to rain, evident again by full puddles at the side of the road, and this has meant I have seen many small birds due to the plentiful water. Also because of more grass I have seen many cattle, more so than at any other time. In fact when the road got near to Broome it went past an area which the map showed as boggy, but which just looked to me like luxuriously green which heavy grass growth. It stretched on both sides of the road to the horizon and on this land were thousands of grazing cattle. The farmers round here must do well with their cattle. (see photo 248)

Broome is quite a pretty place and has an air of sub tropical about it with many palm trees. The airport runway comes almost right up to the centre where all the shops are. So there were small planes roaring right over the town, on their direct path onto the runway. Seemed quite a busy little airport. I know that you can get airplane trips to see various sites around the nearby Kimberleys and some of the planes I saw where seaplanes.

I got some food and found an internet place to check up on my emails. Then it was time to see if I could get somewhere that stocked my sized tyres. I was in luck but will have to go back tomorrow morning as I reached the tyre place just at 4pm when they close. I suppose because of the heat they have had enough by then and it is beer time at the nearby Pub!

I drove to the Port area to have a look. It was some 6 K's out of town at the end of a peninsular. Pretty area and a nice deep water jetty, but I thought, 'where are all the pearl luggers?' None to be seen except one old one that I saw does tourist trips. I went to one of the local beaches and that was nicely laid out with gardens and restaurants etc. (see photo 249 & 250) Then it was time to try one of the caravan parks. I chose to check one out at the Town Beach area as it was next to the beach. Another scruffy one even more scruffy than the one last night. Not impressed at all. I wouldn't mind if these scruffy dumps did not charge top dollar, but most of them do. Last night and tonight both $19 per night. Should have been more like $12 to $15. After I have got the tyres done tomorrow I will have a look at a couple of sites they say worth looking at, and then push off for the town of Derby, which is only about 175 K's away. That is also on the coast.

Next day I get away from the park about 8.30 and I decide not to look around Broome anymore but to get my two tyres done and be off. The young lad who owns the tyre business, turns out one of his friends is a local copper over from Liverpool, my home town, and working with the local Police. Must be a glutton for heat as it is another warm one, but at least there is a cold water machine next to the waiting room, to which I am almost permanently attached to while I wait. It is so humid that your practically running rivers of sweat just thinking about it. After the tyres were on I hopped over to the supermarket to get a few things and a newspaper, then I went to the internet place to have a quick check on emails. Then back on the road towards Derby.

I was surprised at the luxurious growth of grass to be seen growing in the fields on this section, Surprising what a bit of water does, which I would later have first hand experience of. Also the number of anthills was quite staggering, there were untold thousands of them. (see photo 251) I thought of just how many ants there must be in the whole of Oz, it boggles the mind. Each mound must have millions of ants in it. On this stretch it also surprised me that I saw no road kills of any type at all, and that got me wondering why some areas have Roos and lizards who get themselves run over, and other areas that don't. Why there would not be many roos where all this lush grass was, beats me. So not may falcons to be seen either. So this little section, was quite boring for most of the way.

About 30 K's from Derby the road splits, East to Fitzroy crossing and North to Derby, where I headed for. Had I not left Broome at 11.30 and got away early I would have missed Derby out.

As I had been heading east I could see dark clouds building up in the distance and the unmistakable signs of heavy rain falling. Lightning lit up the sky and as I got within 10 K's of Derby, it started to rain. Before long it suddenly absolutely bucketed down, and the wind got seriously strong. I was thinking I may have to stop, when it quickly became so windy and the rain so dense I could not see more than a few feet in front of me. I then had to stop, hoping no one else came along like an idiot to run into me. The wind was tearing branches of the trees and smashing themselves into the home. Real scary, but luckily it lasted but a few minutes, then it was over, moving ever forwards. Said Three Hail Mary's? and got going again. Gave the home a good wash if nothing else. Both today and yesterday I have only been passed by one car all day, (going my way) so it's been a busy traffic day again.

About 7 K's south of Derby there is an interesting tree to look at. For some time it became apparent that I was in Boab tree country as there were so many everywhere. Actually these boab trees are quite amazing as they come in a variety of shapes and sizes. Some tall and slender, others short and squat and fat and some extremely fat with enormous girths. Some have single trunks, some have two, and some have a profusion of trunks and these are usually the real big trees. The only other place on Earth you get Boabs is on Madagascar off the coast of Africa. They checked the DNA of the trees found in Oz and found they had the same DNA as the African ones. So it is surmised that boab seeds have floated right across the Indian Ocean and to the Northern shores of West Australia at some stage in time. (see photo 252 & 253)

At this spot there is a magnificent specimen which had some history attached to it. In the late 1800's when pastoralists were settling the area, they needed labour which was scarce, as not enough whites were around. So gangs of white men got to raiding the Aborigines in the Kimberly region nearby. (They called it Blackbirding) They would kidnap the young men, put them into chains and force march them to Derby. When they got to this spot just out of town, this huge boab tree was completely hollow, so they used it to imprison these men overnight. It became known as 'The Boab Prison Tree.' It certainly is an amazing tree. (see photo 255 & 256)

Derby is a right hole of a place, very scruffy, and certainly not trying to be a nice tourist trap. Loads of aborigines all over, many lounging around in the parks and under trees, always in groups. I took it that these were the ones that didn't have a work ethic. Others obviously must have done work as they were driving around in flash modern cars and 4WD's. I had a drive round which didn't take long as it is a small place. Nothing to see, even the jetty were it said they loaded nickel ore from a nearby mine, was deserted. (see photo 254)

I went to the Information office to see if they did any flights up into the Kimberleys or to the North were the rugged coastline would be worth a look. But as it was out of season there were not enough visitors to make up the numbers. So lost out again. But if you come at the right time there are loads of coach trips, boat trips and flights to all the surrounding mountain areas which have gorges and pools and waterfalls etc. Most of these areas are served by tracks that are not tarmacked so in the wet as it is now, they are all closed. The woman in the info place told me when I asked why the whole peninsular to the North which has all these mountains and valleys etc, was not settled as there were absolutely no towns at all, I found that it is all land owned by the aborigines. Which says it all, I think.

I then went into the nearby pub as I fancied a coffee, and got talking to the barman, who confirmed that the Abo's I saw lounging around were the few percentage wise that were social scroungers. I then went down the road to the caravan park I had seen and booked in. Talk about deserted, I was only one of three vans there, with about six permanents in this very large camp. It abounded what looked like tidal flats. The water when in couldn't have been very deep at all and the owner confirmed this and showed me the vast area that got covered when the tide was in. Here there is a 10 metre tidal rise, which is very much higher than in the South. Tomorrow it will be onto Fitzroy Crossing and on this stretch I should see some mountains or hills, and in the meantime I will amuse myself tonight watching Dalziel & Pascoe on TV.

After another hot night and being woken up at six am by squawking birds. So I get up early at just after 7 and have a nice cold shower. Funny thing is, the cold water in northern WA is more like it's coming from the hot tap. So refreshed, I have breakfast, then I go to the visitors shop to see if I can use their email service. They do not open until 9am and I can't wait, so I go to see if I can get a newspaper. They still have yesterdays papers on show and the day before as well, so I guess that maybe they will get the Saturday one on Monday. So having got nowhere it is time to get somewhere and get back on the road.

I want to get as far as I can today as the next stretch of road to Wyndham is some distance and I would like to make Halls Creek and call into Fitzroy Crossing and see if I can get to see the Gelkie Gorge. Well cannot say that it was an eventful day with stunning and different landscapes to report on. I passed through countryside that could have been anywhere that I had passed through already. Sometimes heavy bush, sometimes lighter, sometimes cleared bush with pastures, but all much of a muchness. There has been a lack of wildlife today, and absolutely no roadkill again. Either there aren't any Roos living in this part of WA or else they are all road savvy. No goannas squashed on the road either, so very few birds having takeaways. The only bit of excitement I got was wondering if I might get caught in a wild storm again, as there were constant dark storm clouds around.

Fitzroy Crossing turned out to be bigger than I thought. (see photo 257) There were a number of houses and businesses, when I thought it would just be a roadhouse job. I took the side road that leads to this Gelkie Gorge which is on the mighty Fitzroy River, and after 9 K's arrived at the car park where your supposed to be able to see the place. I am afraid it was a bit of a waste of time again, because to actually see the Gorge you have to take a boat from the car park area up river and through the Gorge. Guess what? Because it is the rainy season… no boat service.

Back to Fitzroy metropolis and back onto the highway towards Halls Creek. As I get near to it I went through one of the storms, but not as bad as yesterday, and as I drove into the local caravan park, the heavens opened again. Luckily these summer storms do not last long. Another scruffy and practically empty park. So the message I am getting is definitely do not come up this part of WA in their summer as everything is shut or empty. Tomorrow I will see if the local air operator who does flights to and around the nearby Bungle Bungles (no its not something out of toytown) a mountain range worth looking at and as the road is closed… best by air, but don't hold your breath as I probably will be the ONLY one wanting the trip and that will be too expensive.

I was right. I spoke in the morning to one of the pilots of the local scenic flights company. He had no other people interested and if I went on my own it would be $500. I am not prepared to spend that kind of money so I reckon will try further down the line as I know that at other towns they also do flights. Even small towns and settlements have a little airport as in Oz they use airplanes like taxis, due to the distances.

After tanking up I am off by 8.30 and I feel that it is going to be a better day. First of all it's nice and cool as there is plenty of cloud. So I can drive without the aircon on and just with the window open. All this temperature changing has done my chest no good and I have a bit of a tickling cough. Not far out of town I see my first Dingo dog as it shoots across the road and into the bush. The next settlement of note is Turkey Creek, which is an Aborigine settlement. The drive there soon starts to be more interesting as there are ranges of hills coming into view all the time and by the time I get to the Creek they are quite close to the road. After the road gets up into small hill ranges and goes from mostly straight to up and down and plenty of curves, which makes driving more interesting. Also many of the creeks and rivers I cross have got water flow in them. Not a huge amount but at least some. The pilot I spoke to said that this year the amount of rain has been very poor. Last year he said that the Fitzroy River level was up to just under the bridge road level. When you look at the photo I took you will see that the water level is way down off the bridge, so you can get an idea of the huge rise last years level, is compared to this year.

Turkey Creek has a village settlement which houses only Aborigines, and a roadhouse where I fill up. (see photo 258) There I see a Dutch couple on a pair of Dutch registered motorbikes. Don't know how they can do it as they can't carry much, let alone camping gear. They must be staying at motels all the time which would turn out to be expensive. A bunch of Aboridginal kids are pestering them to give them a ride on their bikes. Kids are all the same no matter what their background is. I walk just up the road to where I noticed a couple of helicopters parked and an office but it is the same story, no one is booked to go and that's because not enough tourists right now. So miss out again.

The last stretch of road to my final destination, proves to be the most interesting for quite some time now. I am making for Kununurra which I read is the areas administrative town and was set up in the 60's when they built the nearby Ord River Dam in the 60's. This was to provide irrigation water for farming in the area. An attractive town, well laid out clean and tidy with good parks and lawns etc. As it is a Sunday everything is shut, but the town is bustling with many Aborigines walking about and sitting under shady trees. As I entered the town I had passed the airport so went back there but situation still the same, no tourists and so no one else to share a ride, to get the cost down.

I also look at the small dam which encloses a lake, which is situated on the towns western edges. (see photo 259 & 260) There are swimming spots on it and people are fishing on its banks and from boats on it. There are plenty of tours that go from here but again when the tourist season is going. (From April on.) On the way to here I passed the Argyle Diamond mine which is just south of the town and I believe it is one of the most productive diamond mines outside Africa.

I decide as it is only 3.30 that I will not stay overnight here but will push East to the Lake Argyle which was formed when the Ord River Dam was built. It is Australia's largest expanse of fresh water. The road there was very interesting, as you are now driving into a mountain range, which goes all the way there. (see photo 261) The dam is certainly very picturesque and so are the mountain ranges it is in. (see photo 262 & 263)

There is a caravan park near the lake but not on it and I intend to stay there. No one is around… a note saying they are on the lake and to find a site and see them in the morning. It is only a small site which is exceeding scruffy and unkempt, and there is only one caravan here. Knee high grass everywhere, bins that have not been emptied in weeks and a toilet block that has not been cleaned in months or longer. An absolute disgrace and I wonder what they will charge me in the morning. So I would recommend to come to see the lake, but stay in Kununurra at one of their many parks.

Tomorrow I will cross the nearby border into the Northern Territory and a hop of 500K's to Katherine and then the last leg of 300K's to Darwin.

Another hot night, but as I went to bed at 10.30, by 6.30am I was getting increasingly unsettled. It was time to get up anyway, especially as I wanted an early start so I can make Katherine and I have to contend with losing an hour and a half because as soon as I cross the border I have to put the clock forward. No one was to be seen at the park office, so I got a free nights stay. However I reckon they should have paid me to stay there.

There is not much to report on today's journey as it was much the same as usual. The first leg to the next town of Halls Creek was through landscapes like the day before. That is to say mountain ranges to the right and left of the road. (see photo 265) The next leg was to Victoria Creek which is a bit of a misnomer as there is no creek (stream) but a very big river, the Victoria. Coming towards Vic Creek you go past a sign which directs you to an historic tree. So I went down this track for 5 K's and then a couple of hundred metres walk and there before you is this wide long river. It runs right through to the Joseph Bonaparte Gulf (don't know how he got into the frame, in Oz) and starts in the hills to the South of the highway.

The walk brings you to a large old Boab tree which is just off the bank of this river. Here in 1856 an Australian by the name of Charles Gregory set up camp on an expedition where he wanted to set off south into the Gt Sandy Desert to see if the long held belief they had in those days, that there was a great inland sea in the middle of Oz .(see photo 266 & 267) He was actually a Pommie born in England who came out with his parents in the early days of settlement on the Swan River at Perth, and was brought up there. He then wanted to explore and he set out in two ships from Sydney and into the Gulf and up the Victoria River to this spot. He then, with all his men and equipment made a long trip south. Of course he found no sea and he returned to the camp and then decided to explore the north of Queensland on a trip back to Brisbane. He made it in four months, and it was on his reports on what he found as far as what the land was like in this part of northern Oz, that very quickly after, lands were sold off and farming was set up in these areas. Mainly cattle were put onto the land. The tree was inscribed with the date July 1856 and a letter was left informing anyone who found it were they had set off to (Brisbane). So the tree is at least 150 years old and probably much older, as these trees are reckoned to live to more than a thousand years.

The last leg to Katherine was uneventful and I arrived about 4.30. Seems quite a clean and tidy town, not quite what I remember it to be when I was last here. Actually by getting here means that I have now completely circumnavigated Oz. I was here in 1966 on my way to Sydney at the end of my overland trip out from the UK. So even though there is a gap of 39 years… better late than never! My memories of the place then was a scruffy typical outback town. Now it has been brought up to date and the streets are all tidied up with grass verges so the place looks all very civilised. After having a look around I found a caravan park and booked in. Wow what a difference from last night's park. This one is large well manicured with completely grassed over parking areas and many trees to give shade. Nice clean toilets and a swimming pool.

I went to the toilets in the evening and found a large group of frogs, some of them quite huge, all sitting outside the toilet block under a strip light. The light was attracting loads of insects and they were having a feast. Couldn't resist a photo of them.

Next day the road up to Darwin was pleasant enough, nothing unusual in the landscape. For a while now the gum trees have got the company of a palm type tree, so it makes it look a little tropical. I pass by many old WW11 airfield sites, there must have been at least 7 or 8 of them. Most I think are returned to farmland now as they are not listed as places you can visit for a look.

Just South of Darwin you pass a small town called Palmerston. It is all new and is like a dormitory town to Darwin. Then you start to hit the outskirts which are mainly the businesses of Darwin, lining the main highway in. You also pass the airport which is shared with the RAAF. I find a caravan/motel place just by the airport called the 'Lepracaun' so I am staying at a little bit of Ireland, even if it is a damn site hotter. Quite a small site and only costing $12 a night but well grassed and although the toilet block is a bit oldish, it is always clean and everything works. There is also a small swimming pool and plenty of trees giving shade, if only it were not so humid.

Chapter Eleven

Darwin: Sights and History

A small city especially considering it is a capital city with a population of about 71,000. Initially back in the early 1800's the area came under an expanded state of NSW. Then later on it was given to SA to administer and it wasn't until I think the seventies that it became State in its own right with its own government.

Driving into Darwin, you first go through Palmerston, so it is quite a long drive in along a dual carriageway and past the airport and RAAF station. Then you will eventually reach the city centre and can go no further. (see photo 268 & 269) The business centre is located at the end of a peninsular and is quite compact. The rest of the city is mainly suburbs and industrial areas located along the Stuart Highway that comes into the city and right into its centre. The centre is built on a raised area of land and is adjacent to a foreshore which housed the harbour area, which is now largely derelict, which doesn't give anything to the ambiance of the place. It would seem that like most modern ports they have built a new container port on the other side of Frances Bay. So I suppose it will eventually be redeveloped with high rise expensive flats.

Quite frankly there is not much to see in Darwin apart from walking around the small city area just to see what is what. There are very few old historical sites to see and I was not surprised at that. Thinking back to when I arrived in Oz in 1966, I remember suffering somewhat from a culture shock, on arriving in Darwin. To put it bluntly it was in those days a bit of a dump and a throwback to the 19th century. Very substandard buildings and full of cowboy males who ate huge 'T' bone stakes with chips, for their breakfasts. It is therefore good to see that it has come on since then and the big cyclone they had in the 70's, did the place a huge favour, because it all had to be rebuilt and I guess it pulled them into the 20th century. So now you have a newish modern town with all the modern trimmings. But no real history. Government House survived and I think this like all other such buildings, houses the territories Governor and is used for State functions. (see photo 270)

They have a new Parliament House which also doubles up for the State Library. (see photo 271) Clustered around this building are other government buildings, all newly built to modern designs. There are plenty of shops and malls and eating places as with all modern Oz cities. (see photo 272 to 275)

Only two things have ever happened in Darwin which they mention all the time and everywhere you go. The first was the attack in 1942 by the Japanese Air Force, when they did another Pearl Harbour type attack on the harbour and airdrome. A force of 188 bomber and fighters, many who saw service on the earlier US attack, operating from aircraft carriers, caught the Aussies and Americans napping. It never cease to amaze me how man is always complacent, because just like Pearl Harbour where they had advance radar warning which they ignored, here they had warning from a priest on the Japs incoming flight path. He too was ignored. 250 odd people and servicemen were killed. Then there was Cyclone Tracy and all the history and facts about that, amply covered in their museum. So these constitute the sum total of the history of Darwin. (see photo 276 to 281)

Consequently only two days are needed to adequately see all you need to see. You can of course use it as a base to take various trips to surrounding areas, and to this end there are many companies organising many types of trips. Boat trips, air flights over nearby national Parks and the rivers and gorges and mountains etc, or 4WD trips into various areas. As I could not afford any of these after my two days I was ready to move on Southwards, but first I would go east and into the Kakadoo National Park.

The weather in Darwin is as it has been since I went North of the Tropic of Capricorn, that is to say daily temperatures of mid thirties, sometimes as high as 40, but the real killer is the very high humidity, which makes you sweat with the slightest exertion. Each afternoon at the time of year I was visiting in, you get a build up of dark rain clouds, then a downpour. I was lucky or unlucky, depending what way you look at it, in that for the three afternoons I was there, the dark clouds brewed up, but no rain. A good downpour will cool things off a bit if nothing else.

Chapter Twelve

Darwin to Alice

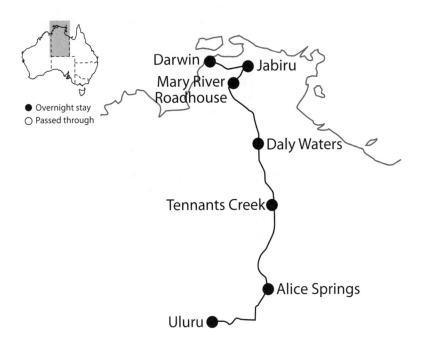

After another hot night, (it never went below 29 degrees) with the blower on all night, I first went into Darwin centre to get some photos I had had processed, and to pick up a spare water pump as the one on the home had started to slowly leak. I have put in some stop leak into the water system and that has worked, but one cannot be too careful because if it goes and I am in the middle of nowhere at least I have the item I could wait a week to get.

After a mornings leisurely drive along the Arnhem Highway towards the Kakadu Park, past pleasant green lands, after a mere 254 K's, I arrived at Jabiru. A town built to service a local mining company which mines uranium and so happens to be the largest uranium mine in the World. (see photo 282) But Jabiru is also the centre for trips into the park, 4WD tours and aircraft flights, which I am booked to go on tomorrow. The road passed a number of wetlands which this area is famous for (as well as crocodiles) There are a number of rivers and creeks which start in the Kakadu Mountains a little to the South and run into the Van Diemen Gulf. The deltas of these rivers form a number of wetlands on which all manner of wildlife lives on. The place is a bird watchers paradise.

It was only about 3pm when I arrived, so I thought I would drive a little North of Jabiru to a place called Ubirr where there are supposed to be cave paintings. I drove some 10 K's up the road, only to come across a ford across a creek which had a metre of water over the road… end of story! (see photo 283) Also much the same story I have been experiencing all along. Once again I cannot understand why the Aussies could not build a small bridge over such places so that tourists can see these famous places (for which they come all the way to Oz to see) all the year round.

So I booked into the local caravan park which turned out good value at only $15 a lovely place with a great swimming pool which I partook of. (see photo 284 & 285.) Again as it is out of season, it is practically empty. As the evening came on, we were treated to a fantastic lightning show for about two hours, but no rain. Further away from us a cyclone has built up over the Northern Queensland coast which has steadily come close to the NT northern coast, not that far North of were Jabiru is. Winds of 200KMH, so I hope we are far enough South to miss it! Also at the same time as evening fell, great flocks of large fruit bats began to wheel around, above us. A tree next to my home has lots of flowers on it, so I was treated to a display of fruit bats feeding. It is a little cooler which is good.

After a good nights sleep I went to the small airport to get on this scenic flight. It was only a small Cessna seating two pilots and six passengers. Bit like flying in a sardine can. With a propeller which I thought looked impossibly small. However it propelled us up to a rapid 150 mph take off speed in a thrice.

Up to about 4,000 feet in no time and heading towards the range of hills a little way to the South. A cliff like escarpment runs for many a mile from Arnhem Land to Katherine and it is off this escarpment that these various falls are situated. We pass over bush as far as the eye can see, and from the hills to the sea is this vast flood plain covered in this bush, with many creeks, rivers and streams and boggy wetlands. We are heading for the biggest waterfalls in the area, called Jim Jim falls. (see photo 286) On the way there we pass a huge rock called Nourlangie Rocks, which is an old Aborigine sacred site, which I will call on, on my way back out of the park and on the road to Katherine.

Whilst the falls are certainly not the Niagra falls they are quite impressive, nevertheless. The rock formations on the cliff faces and on the top of the escarpment are a mass of different shapes, fissures and splits from the weathering they get. We wheeled around the falls several times and then headed to the second falls called Twin Falls. These are not as high as the Jim Jim falls but an impressive gorge in front of them makes up for this. (see photo 287 to 291)

All the time we have been flying there have been many dark clouds and we can see that a bank of heavy rain is approaching from the East. Being a small plane we do not want to be flying through that. So the pilot, a young chap who I think is getting his hours in, in the company of the older pilot, flies in an evasive pattern to keep away from this downpour. He does well and we fly back towards Jabiru Airport and land just as the rain catches up with us. A very good flight, very worthwhile to pay the $150 it cost as this really was the only way I could see what we saw. The dirt road to the Jim Jim falls is closed due to flooding and in the non rainy season they are not allowed to overfly the area at all. Seems nonsense to me, but there you are. So if you look at it this way, coming here in the rainy season, at least you can take these flights and see what you see, which is more than going by road, plus the rivers and falls are at their fullest water wise.

I continue down the highway and head towards Pine Creek, and a little way down the road there is a turn off to the big rock Nourlangie, that we flew over. This area has been visited for 20,000 years by Aborigines and they have painted on the various walls of this huge rock. The various areas are joined up by a walkway which takes about half an hour to walk. There is also a high look out point which affords you an impressive view of the wetlands all around the rock. One picture impressed me as it was of a spirit called Nabulwinbulwin who disliked women and ate them. Man after my own heart, I thought. (only joking!) Even David Attenborough has visited the place, so it has some importance. (see photo 292 to 301)

Further down the Highway there is a spot called Cooinda, which is on the Jim Jim River and where I can get a boat trip through the wetlands. All through these wetlands, hundreds of thousands of various birds live and migrate to. Also there are untold thousands of crocodiles, and it is my wish to see one in the wild. The boat is quite large, made from aluminium with a canopy and is of shallow   After about a mile the river narrows considerably and is just wide enough for the boat to get through. In fact trees are growing out of the water and we are told that in a month this will be completely dry.

We proceed on for another mile and it widens out again. All around us are large expanses of water grass, which floats on the water. Water lilies grow here as well and we see abundant bird life in the trees and in the water. Geese, herons, darters, egrets, and then we see a pair of magnificent Sea Eagles perched in a tree next to the river. This is the first time I have seen such a bird. Their nest is in a nearby treetop. We spend an hour and a half gliding round the rivers system and near the end we see what all of us want to see, and that is a crocodile in the wild. We were told before we started that in the wet, there is so much water that it disperses crocs widely and makes it more difficult to come across them. Also their mud banks on which they like to sleep are covered with water. Anyway we do come across one smaller specimen of about 2 metres long. I will just have to wait until I get to Queensland before I will see a biggy. So a nice diversion from driving which shows you what this whole area is all about. (see photo 303 to 310)

I carry on driving on down the highway to rejoin the Stuart Highway south. I had hoped to reach it at Pine Creek but by 6pm I still had 55K's to go and was feeling tired. So pulled into the Mary River Roadhouse which had a park attached to it. Well not quite a park, but a bit of waste land, with an electric point and run by a typical rough Oz bloke. This place being practically in the bush was an absolute insect horror story. There were millions of the little buggers and they all wanted to get into my home. I shut everything and taped up a few suspicious entry points yet they were still gaining entry. I was inundated with flies, moths and all sorts of bugs. Eventually I managed to stop them but only after about two hours of battle with them and judicious use of Mortein insect spray, which you MUST take with you for such occasions. I have not had this trouble on this scale before.

Next day after a nice sleep for a change as it had been quite a cool day, due to the clouds and rain, I got going and passed through Pine Creek (see photo 311) and carried on down south to Katherine, where I wanted to stock up on provisions again. In 1966 I got a job laying rail track at Frances Creek which is about 50 K's out of Pine Creek. They had discovered that a hill was pure iron ore and wanted to mine it and ship it out of Darwin, so needed to lay some track and join the existing track that ran from Alice to Darwin. So this area had some connection to my past.

After a stop at Katherine to stock up on food in the local Woolworths supermarket, I was off again and some miles on I wanted to visit a cave system just South of Katherine called the Cutta Cutta Caves. I really would like to have gone into the Katherine Gorge but that would have entailed another boat ride and yesterdays was enough for a while. Plus the weather today is extremely overcast with lots of black rain clouds. For over a week now a cyclone has been slowly working its way across the Northern half of Oz. It started out in the Pacific, came across the North Queensland coast at Cooktown and has spent the last three days working across the top end of Queensland and the Northern Territory. So I reckon all these clouds are mixed up with that system, even though it is some way North of me right now.

Anyway this cave system turned out to be fairly mediocre. The one cave you can go through was quite long (250 metres) but not very deep and not as full of good things to see as had the others I saw earlier on. It did have some wild life living in it, like a very large colony of bats and little frogs and snakes (which we did not see) plus some cave moths. Actually more interesting, was the young Oz couple in their twenties who made up the party of three of us. They studiously ignored me, and throughout the whole journey said not one word at all. Never asked any questions or made any comments. You do get some odd people.

After I came out I made some lunch and after eating it was back on the pedal. I am afraid the landscape is just normal boring Oz bush, so nothing to report. I have been passing several WW11 airfield sites, or at least signs that say the track to the left or right leads to an old WW11 airfield site. So out of curiosity I went down one of these tracks to see exactly what would be left of such an old airfield 60 years on. Well after going some 3K's the road split into three ways, all going off in different directions, and no signs. Typical I thought and chose one of the tracks, which led nowhere. So I turned back to the main road as it would be too easy to get lost in a maze of unmarked tracks.

During the afternoon there were several heavy showers but they were great because they just help to keep the temp down nicely.

By 6pm I had reached Daly Waters, were in 1966 I had stayed overnight during my trek from Pine Creek to Sydney. (see photo 312) Then it was mainly just a pub and although the pub is still there and described as an 'historic pub' circa 1930! plus it boasts that it is the oldest holder of a liqueur licence in the NT having had one since the 1880's)) Really it is just a tin shack, but now it boasts a caravan park (just another bit of waste ground). Cost overnight, just $7 and the second cheapest rate so far! I couldn't exactly remember it, but I do remember that in 66 I was not impressed then, either. Whilst booking my spot I looked at the gathering of men there, and thought they looked like they were just like those out of that film 'Crocodile Dundee. A typical outback drinking hole together with cast.

As I parked the home I saw a group of birds mulling around a car with two women in it. They looked a bit like English female blackbirds and I certainly had not seen birds like these before, so I went over. They were two German girls who said that the birds were very tame who were taking bits of bread from their hands, but they did not know what species they were. Extraordinary!

On leaving in the morning I remembered that on leaving in 66 I had to stand on the highway waiting for a car that would be willing to give me a lift down the Highway. Hardly any cars went by and as the morning went on and the sun got hotter and hotter, my only shade was that given off by a sign post, and as the sun moved with the hours moving on, so did the shadow and I had to keep moving. Eventually a German came along in a beat up old VW Beetle, who gave me a lift all the way to Mt Isa in Queensland where I caught a train to Sydney. I did not fancy waiting for days in the blazing sun and gave up the idea of further hitchhiking. I caught the train that starts from Mt Isa and goes to the coast.

Today started off nice and cool but as the day went on, the hotter it became, as there are not as many clouds around today. Plus as I go more to the South the weather is becoming dryer and hotter. Certainly the more I moved further south away from Daly Waters, the dryer the landscape became, and the lush grass and thick bush vegetation began to disappear. It became very dry looking, brown grass, and less trees and more stunted bush. It is reckoned that by Renner Springs this will be the boundary between a tropical North and the drier Central Australia.

Some way down the track you come to a town just off the new highway, called Newcastle Waters. This collection of shacks, it cannot really be called a town, came into being in the late 1880's as a stop off point for drovers driving their flocks of sheep across this part of the NT. There are about a dozen houses, most of which are empty and not used. They are open and I went into two of them. One had been the towns pub and hotel and it was made entirely of corrugated iron sheets. Even the inner walls were in this stuff. It brought it home to me just how rough these outback places were in the old days. Nowadays there seem to be only Aborigines living here. (see photo 313.

Near Tennants Creek, where I intend to stay the night, there is are some old cottages still standing, built in 1872 to house an overland telegraph repeater station linking Adelaide to Darwin, and then onto Europe. A linesman in 1925 discovered gold nearby and that led to the building of the town of Tennants Creek and the rise in the areas population. (see photo 314) There are a couple of mines still operating in the area, and the original Gecko Mine is Australia's richest gold producing mine. The gold is found in magnetic iron rock, unlike elsewhere.

The town's visitor information shop is next door to a museum on mining so I went on a tour of a purpose built shaft which replicates what a shaft would be like underground in a mine. A nearby hill had a shaft bored some 200 odd metres into it and it was set up by an ex local miner complete with all the original equipment that they used in mining. He takes you on a walk through the tunnel and explains fully how they dig the shafts and tunnels and extract the gold from the ore. Very interesting especially if you do not know anything about mining which I don't. (see photo 315 to 318)

After this tour I had myself a nice coffee in the almost deserted main street and then booked into the caravan park on the highway. Cost $12 a night, not too bad. The town is a typical outback town with one main through highway which has all the shops on it, and roads running off it. Mind you like Katherine it has been tarted up since the 60's, as the highway is all tarmacked now with a central reservation which is all grassed and landscaped. However these towns always give off an air of desertion and almost all the people you do see are bands of Aborigines wandering around or sitting in groups under trees. Certainly if you want to see Aborigines, it is in Northern WA and in the NT that you get the greatest concentration of them. However they do not mix with whites and you will not get any inter reaction with them. They do not serve in shops very much, and it is hard to come across any of them in a working environment, so no contact there either. I personally think that the way Australia has dealt with them over the last 200 years and the missed opportunities which they could have been given, is a heavy blot on the Australians as a nation. This has resulted in what you see as a visitor, which can be very negative. (see photo 319 & 320)

Tomorrow I hope to reach Alice Springs, which is supposed to be the geographical centre of Oz. So a trip of some 530 K's is on the cards for tomorrow. I have done just under 400 today.

I was surprised on the way out of Tennants to see a farm growing vines. Whilst plenty of sun would be ticket, I thought that surely a lack of water would not help. Well I suppose that they must have access to plenty of water. Then I have to ask, why aren't other people growing grapes or other crops in this general area? Another mystery.

The road to Alice… was quite uneventful with landscapes of nothing out of the ordinary until you get to the Alice, which is surrounded by high hills. There are a few hill ranges on the way, but nothing spectacular. The whole section is served by many places where you can get fuel, more than normally, so 'no worries' on that score.

All day I saw willy willies again which I had not seen since Northern WA, so I knew that I was back in a hot, dry and dusty part of the country, again. So goodbye to the humidity. The first place of any interest on the way is about 114K's South of Tennants and that is the Devils Marbles. A whole area just off the highway where you can see many boulders of all shapes and sizes all scattered about and jumbled up on one another. They were exactly like the boulders just South of Norseman at the end of the Nullabour, whereas they were black granite, these are brown in colour. (see photo 321)

At Wycliffe Well Roadhouse the whole place is daubed with paintings proclaiming this place is the centre of UFO's in Oz as many sightings of them are claimed in this area. I am not surprised that people see little green men and the like around here, what with the heat and the amount of booze people consume to keep cool!

The next roadhouse at Barrow Creek also has yet another old telegraph repeater station. Next to this is a monument to a linesman and a police constable killed by restless, warlike, local natives in 1874 and their graves are next to the road. Further on there is yet another memorial to Stuart who was the first white man to traverse the continent of Oz from South to North and that in the 1860's I believe.

At the next watering hole is the roadhouse of Ti Tree which is also an Aborigine settlement, so many of them to be seen here and there is a large Aborigine Art Gallery here.

I did not see much wild life on this stretch at all, only two Emu's trotting away from the roadside on hearing me. Then the closer you get to Alice the more hills there are. A lot of the way from Tennants the Ghan rail line is not far from the track, but I saw no trains on it. So it must be an infrequent service. This line has only been in existence for a year or so. It replaces the old Ghan which was built before WW11 and which was badly built, narrow gauge, very slow, and only went as far as Alice. (see photo 322 & 323)

Alice is quite a large town with a population around 25,000. However the town centre is not all that large and although it has three supermarkets, there are no department stores, only a lot of small businesses. It has the famous Todd River (named after the Telegraph Manager based in Adelaide, who oversaw the building of the line from Adelaide to Darwin in the mid 1800's) He was an Englishman who migrated to Oz in the early 1800's with his wife. He later became the head of the Post Office of South Australia. First the place was called Stewart then renamed Alice after Todds wife, in the late 1800's. Of course the river is usually bone dry and it is famous for the make believe rowing races which take place in the dry! The boats are just mock boats and the so called rowers run the distance. It is funny what the sun can do to you! (see photo 324 to 327)

First I thought that I would try the library to see if they had any computers. They did not open until 10 am. The only Internet place I could find was part of a travel agency and they did not open until 10am. So it seems that some businesses in Alice do not start early. That surprises me as you would think in a hot area they would start early and finish early. So I went to a supermarket… they were open.

Then I thought I would revisit the garage I visited yesterday to fix up an appointment after I had visited Ayres Rock, to get my water pump replaced. He could not give me a quote and said if I called back first thing he would have had a word with someone he knew who knew what was entailed and then he could give me a price. He wanted to look over the engine compartment to see the layout. The first mistake he made. If he had talked to someone familiar with Transits, he would have been told how long a job it was. So why did he need to look at it? I opened the bonnet and he immediately went into a spiel just like a used car salesman. Mistake number two. Of course he did not know that I had spent over 40 years in the auto trade and had owned my own garages and had the spent the last 20 years building hand built sportscars. He said 'my mate tells me its a big job and will take 6 hours and you have to take all the front end off including the headlights' I asked why that was necessary as I had read the workshop manual on the job last night and that did not say you had to do all that. I said 'for instance the headlights are nowhere near the front of the engine where you have to work and there is even a bulkhead that divides the outer front with the middle front, so taking out the headlights would be a complete waste of time' To that, I was told that as I knew how to do the job I should do it myself as he wasn't interested. In other words he knew I wasn't going to be bullshitted and he didn't like that. I should try Ford instead and see where I got, I was told.

Which is exactly what I did when I found out where they were. They quoted without any bull, 4 hours and gave me the price which was no doubt less than he would have charged. Now the moral of this story is that in Oz the auto trade is full of rip off merchants. If you think that garages are bad in the UK, take it from me that in Oz they are twice as bad and I aught to know. Hence why I always make sure I get a hard and fast quote and if they start giving you bull that you think sounds like bull, walk away. A garage tried the same trick on in Darwin over quoting for the same job, saying what a big job it was that would take 8 hours. So be warned if you have to ever get work done on a vehicle you are using. Go to more than one place and see what they all say and pick the one you feel is telling you the truth, if you can find one that is. Often it is better in such circumstances to go to a dealer because they have set times for set jobs and if you feel they have overstated you can always demand to see the 'book time' You also always have the right to complain to the manufacturer about any rogue dealer. (that is you do in the UK, probably in Oz the manufacturers are as big a lot of bullshitters than their dealers) With an independent as this garage was, you are on your own.

Anyway I am booked in for Friday and I will take a two day trip to Ayres Rock before that. One day there, second day in the morning down the road to the Olgas and then back to Alice. I had booked into one of many caravan parks just South of Alice town centre called Heavitrees. Not fantastic, with dirt roads again and not brilliant toilets and not overly cheap at $20. One good thing about Alice is that in the evenings it really cools down nicely compared with further North and I actually have to use my duvet. The park has the usual collection of trees and these are heavily populated with bright green parrots and when the sun sets, loads of small bats which wheel about all over the place. (see photo 328)

The next day the trip down to Ayres Rock was fairly uneventful, but one thing that did make my day was that I saw a huge Goanna and even managed to get TWO photos of it. I had earlier just missed running over a nice frilled lizard that was sitting just on the road. First time I had seen one of those, but I saw it too late to stop, but managed to drive round it. Then Lo and Behold there was this huge Goanna just about to cross over in front of me from my right. I saw it in time to screech to a halt right opposite it. These bigger lizards are slower moving than the smaller ones, so it didn't shoot off and out of sight, but merely stopped in its tracks. I managed after grabbing my camera, to get one shot in through the door window. Then I was out, hoping to get a closer shot. Of course when it saw me it started to go back into the bush but I slowly followed it and got in a second shot. Wow! (see photo 333 & 334)

I had to drive South down the Stuart Highway heading as if to Adelaide. (see photo 335) Some 200 K's along, you then turn right at a roadhouse for another 200 odd K's to Ayres. I stopped at the roadhouse car park and made me some lunch. They had a large field with a load of Emus in and these were tame and they were all sitting at the fence nearest the car park. So whilst eating my apple I wandered over to have a close encounter. One who was standing up (all the others were mainly lying down under some trees) came right up to the fence in front of me and gave me the beady eye, (and they have very large eyes too) watching me chomping on the apple. So I gave him a couple of pieces to see if he would take them out of my hand. No problem and very delicately too, didn't even take my finger as well, so I gave him the core as well, in two halves. No problem, down they went in a flash. No chewing, just straight down the old long throat. I reckon if I had given him pebbles he'd have taken them. (see photo 336)

Someway down the second leg I eventually spotted a huge rock rising out of the desert floor. I say desert because by now the land was covered in high red sandy dunes. There was plenty of vegetation around but it was very poor scrub bush. I at first thought that this was my very first glimpse of the Rock. However as I got nearer I could see it was a mountain, that was huge and looked like a ship. About a 1,000 metres high and with sheer sides and a flat top. Easily the biggest rock like mountain I have seen to date. It wasn't part of a range like most of the rest, but just one isolated mountain. According to my map, it is called Mt Conner. (see photo 337)

When I was within 20 K's of the resort of Yulara near the Rock, something happened on the road which will serve as another warning to you about travel on Oz roads, and the dangers therein. A large tour bus came up behind me. Now as I was in a hurry to get to the Rock in time to look round it and catch the sunset viewing, I was not hanging about, but doing a steady 100kph. He got right up my backside and then picked the absolute worst spot to try and overtake me. This stretch of Lassiters Highway to the Rock, is not brilliant. By that I mean there are many stretches of indifferent surfaces and narrow lane widths, with very poor gravel shoulders. I have a vehicle of 2.75 metres width and the lanes are 3metres wide. The width of a modern coach is at least 3 metres, possibly more. So I am sure you get my drift, that is to say not enough room for him to safely overtake me. He came so close to me I was forced to move over onto the gravel with my two nearside wheels, but worse was to come. The idiot had chosen a short stretch before a bend to overtake and he then started to move over into my lane when he was only three quarter the way past me. Thus I had to brake and move over even more. A nervous driver could have taken sharp evasive action which could have meant losing control on the loose gravel. I will be reporting the driver to his company and maybe the Police.

Then some time later a similar sighting but this time it obviously was the Rock as that is just what it did look like, a one piece great hunk of ROCK. I was at last seeing Ayres Rock, and some 20 K's away from it, you first go past a resort then there is the entrance gate to a National Park where you have to pay $25 for a three day pass. Talk about money for old rope. You have to pay to see a big rock and a strange shaped set of mountains (the Olgas which are nearby). I drove closer and was surprised that this Ayres Rock is actually bigger than I thought it would be. The rock is HUGE, definitely one of the wonders of the World, I would say. I drove right round it taking photos from all angles. It has so many different faces to it, depending just where you are. (see photo 338 to 345)

As it was getting to be around 6pm, I thought it best to get into the parking area I had passed on the way in, at which you can view the rock at sunset. The car park is about a mile long and is next to the road. I picked a parking spot, made a cup of tea and sat down to wait for sunset which would be about 6.45. The only thing was, it was a bit cloudy. However having come all this way you have to take your chances and the cloud was not solid. The park slowly filled up with cars and vans etc and one could hear the chatter of many languages. In fact on the road down I was passed by many tour buses and other vehicles all streaming towards the Rock. A special vehicle park for buses was chocka block with them. (see photo 346 & 347)

Anyway a four wheel drive pulls in next to me and out gets a number of Germans of various ages, but all of the older age grouping. They are priceless these Germans, in a thrice out comes five collapsible chairs and a large table which they proceed to block the entire footpath that is in front of the parked cars. I caught the eye of one of the women and said to her 'having some schnappes and bratwurst then?' 'Oh nein' she said huffily. They then brought out plates, cutlery and many pans and it was obvious that it was German teatime! Where they here to see the sunset or stuff their large German tummies, I wondered. I was totally pissed off with them because they were doing the usual German thing have taking over the area for themselves and bugger everyone else. I had planned to stand at the fence that they had now commandeered for themselves. I had to move elsewhere to get a view of the Rock.

I thought that the general layout of this car park was typical Oz, that is to say not well thought out. People have paid big money to come thousands of miles to see this Rock and maybe have a unique experience. Yet the spot at which they allow you to do this is adjacent to the wild bush, which is on the other side of the fence, which itself is dividing the car park from the bush. What do they have in the Oz bush, why loads of bloody big bushes and right up against the fence. So everywhere there were these bushes you could not get a clear view of the rock. Why on earth couldn't some dimwit realise this and have the bushes closest to the fence, CUT DOWN?

So the people had to congregate in groups around spots that luckily did not have these view blocking bushes. It was the same when you were driving around the base of the rock, bushes everywhere cutting off your view of the Rock as you drove by. All you could see in many places were bushes, of which there are millions of square miles of, in every direction you can see, all full of countless billions of bushes. Also in the general area around Ayres Rock the bush is of very poor quality. Probably due to the extremely poor soil, so it is the type of bush that has little colour and is half dead looking and very straggly and unappealing. In fact the absolute worst type of bush you can get. So cutting down a few in order to enhance the views, would not go amiss. (see photo 348)

I was surprised that when paying for my ticket the office was manned by whites and yet this area is supposed to belong to the local tribe of Aborigines, so why aren't they running the show?

Sunset came but I am afraid the Rock never showed it colours and it remained mainly one colour throughout. Too cloudy, so I miss out.

I leave and make my way back to the nearby resort and on the way get a terrific shot of the Silhouette of the Olgas in the setting sun away to the west, which tomorrow I will visit. (see photo 349)

The road to the Olgas some 50 K's was a windy old affair, that instead of heading directly to the mountain range actually started to go past them and then curve back towards them. I am sure it was thus made longer than necessary, but then that's the way Aussies seem to make roads in this flat land. Maybe it is a case of 'let's make it more interesting and windy' and to hell with the extra expense and the fact people will take longer and spend more on petrol.

About three quarters of the way there you come across a viewing platform with a car park. There was no one there when I pulled up, except a large flock of Oz wild pigeons all sitting around waiting expectantly. I wondered why, and when another vehicle pulled up, I saw why. They were on the scrounge, expecting titbits of visitors, as they all deserted me (I wasn't feeding them) and flew over to this newcomer. A long path through the sandy desert floor to the view platform, which was on top of a little hill, was covered in a wire mesh walkway, which I thought entirely superfluous. The Olgas in all their finery were laid out before you, but even though you were on a hill, your view of them, especially for photo taking purposes, was again ruined by a sodding great tree slap bang in the middle of the view of the mountain range. If I had had a chain saw I would have chopped it down there and then.

Once there I parked in the first car park and took the path that takes you through the ravine which separates two of the big mountains (if you can call them mountains) From afar the Olgas look like a range of dome headed mountains. When you get close you can see that they are rocks on the same scale like Ayres, but are actually many separate rocks which look of volcanic origin, but unlike Ayres which is a smooth rock, these are rough looking because the lava contains millions of boulders or rocks, within the lava. The ravine path is mostly on a larval flow and as it contains all these rocks within in it, it is a most uneven path. (see photo 350) In parts where there are gullies eaten out by rainflows, they have put little bridges and slatted walkways. Now quite why they have not put a walkway across the whole length of the walk, which is only about 750 metres, I cannot work out.

When I got there were two coaches in the car park and I met the people from them when they were walking back. They were all older people many older than me and some quite infirm looking especially as they tried to go along this knobbly path. On my way back I passed a coach load of Yanks and they were even older and some looked positively too unfit to make the journey. Why was it that they could put a long walkway over sand, which is flattish and easy to walk on as found at the lookout, on the way in, yet here where a walkway is definitely needed, there is none. Such is the wisdom of the Aussies. Well to the walk and what I saw, the piccies show all that can be said in words. (see photo 351 to 354)

I wanted questions answered and here I have another beef. (My grumpy old man act again) There were a certain number of signs around, as there was at Ayres, and all these signs were to do with the fact that these places belong to the local Aborigines and what significance everything is to them. The pamphlet they give you when you come into the park after paying to see these rocks, all deal with their background and their thoughts on the rocks. I know all that, but what I want to know is HISTORY! Who found these rocks, and when, and how and when in time were they formed? What are they made of and what has happened to the appearance over the years. Why has Ayres rock no vegetation on it, yet there is some grass and some trees or bushes on the Olgas. I personally think that there is too much emphasis on the Aborigines, who lets face it, had nothing to do with the formation of these rocks and they belong to the whole Aussie nation and the World. Not all the World is interested in their folk lore but are interested in more intellectual matters to do with such geological wonders.

After my walk I went to the second car park from where you can take a hike taking some hours, around other parts of the rocks. As I did not have the time or inclination to do this I just took some photos and then moved on. One problem I have encountered when one gets out of your vehicle... FLIES! For some reason down this part of the country they are in plague proportions. Walking means you are covered in the horrors and it is the buzzing in your ears, and when they get on your mouth and into your eyes, that they become unbearable. So most people are sensibly wearing the head nets you can buy almost anywhere. These cover all your head to your neck, and at least keep them away from your senses. So put them on your 'must buy list'

I drove back to the Ayres Rock area with the intention of calling at the nearby airport. You get large jets coming in here with hoards of International visitors and I knew that scenic flights operated out of here. I fancied a flight over to Kings Canyon which is North of here and a long trek to get there as… you've guessed it, the road to it does not go direct, but via a circuitous route of some 303 K's which I was not willing to do as I needed to head back to Alice so I could get my water pump done on Friday. Well they did flights to there but they took in other places as well and were too expensive. So I will see if anyone is doing flights from Alice or the MacDonnel Ranges, where I will visit after I get my home back.

The road back to the Stuart Highway seems to take forever, but then it is 250K's long. It is just such a big country. I have lunch at a roadhouse just before I get back to the highway, and called Mount Ebenezer. Quite why I do not know as no mountains are anywhere to be seen. When filling up with fuel, the white Oz lady and I get talking. I ask her what are the little tennis ball sized melon type plants that are growing wild at the road sides. I have seen them on this stretch of road and in Southern WA too. I show her one I picked up. I was told they were 'Paddy's Melons' and were too yucky to eat. They apparently were of Afghan origin, the seed having fallen out of the Afghan camel drivers saddles that were used in Oz in the 1800's They are of the water melon family which they look like but much smaller. Then we get talking about Abo's as there were some who had just driven up in a battered old car towing another battered old car which was out of petrol. The back suspension was at odd angles and obviously knackered, and it had no battery as they had to push start it. Many of the cars I see them in look fit only for the knackers yard. So I ask if they have driving licences, tax their cars or have insurance. I am told that mostly not and if I ever had one hit me I would be lucky to get paid. So one law for them and one for us. So whatever you do, do not have a coming to with any Aboriginal in a car on the highway! As I was curious as to why I hardly ever saw any Aborigines actually working, I wanted to know how they managed to afford some swanky cars and be able not to have to work, but could afford the booze that many obviously drank to excess, smoke and get food. This local tribe it turns out get money from all the visitors to the Rock and the park. Last year the park took 31million dollars, which went to them. Plus they get free handouts from the Government and plenty of social security for all their children etc. Obviously the Aussie Government are as balmy as the British one and the working Australians are as apathetic as the Brits. It then turns out she was born In Lymington Hants, near where I live and came out with her parents as a child. Later on I see a hand scrawled sign on the back of a road sign, saying 'Go home Poms' Did it refer to her I wonder or just the Pom tourists that came to the park and paid for the privilege to do so?

The rest of the drive to Alice was uneventful and I had a smashing cup of coffee when I got there, and a couple of Brit papers to read in the evening to catch up on the footy results.

In the morning at 7.45 I put the home into the Ford dealers and took to my scooter to go into the town centre. I spent the morning wandering around looking at things, watching the Abo's who fascinate me, trying to work out just how educated they are or otherwise. There are certainly more of them wandering around this town, than any other I have been in. Many of them very dirtily dressed as if the word 'Wash' isn't in their vocabulary which seems to consist mainly of only their own lingo and not English. I dropped my films in to be processed had a sandwich for lunch, which cost the equivalent of £2.50 in UK money. Also they do not seem to have heard of wholemeal bread as all their sandwiches and rolls are in white bread, even though the supermarkets sell wholemeal. So if you are travelling away from your home, for a day, you save a lot of money if you make sandwiches etc yourself, and take them with you.

In the afternoon I went to the airport to see if I could get a flight that went over the Kings Canyon, which is supposed to be spectacular. Only if I chartered to flight for myself at about $700, no way.

So looks like I will have to miss that one out like all the others, as I am not going to drive there, as some of the drive is on dirt.

Then I went to have a look around the Transport Museum which deals with the Old Ghan Railway and there is also a section that deals with old cars and trucks. The Ghan Museum is a typical Oz type museum seemingly run by amateurs with little money. There was a plaque dated 1988 which commemorated the opening of this museum, dedicated to the restoration of the Ghan trains and carriages and station. Well all the three trains had had sod all done to them and there did not seem to be any work in progress either. The old station had its rooms full of train memorabilia and photos. So again one has to ask why such an important Icon of the opening up of the Northern Territory and Central Australia did not attract Federal money. A stretch of line should be open and a working train in operation.

The same went for the auto museum, which was also decidedly amateur. It was while I was walking round looking at the vehicles, that I got a call off Fords. Bad news, which is always what I seem to get. I told them to replace the cam belt as I did not know when it had been last replaced. Also to replace the cam pulley oil seal. It was this seal they messed up on by not putting it in properly. They have to get another one from Melbourne and they will not get one until Monday, so I am not at all best pleased at having to wait another three days in a place I have fully explored by now. This is Oz which you will find is too laid back and not well organised. As I have said before, the Transit is not an odd vehicle in Oz yet no one keeps parts for it. Even in Adelaide they got things from Melbourne and so on. So once more I will tell you to be prepared for delays if your vehicle has any problems and needs work doing on it. I should have taken spare seals and water pump with me. They towed the vehicle to the caravan park so that I could live in it over the weekend, which was something.

So on Saturday I went into the town centre to put more films in and to see if I could get a haircut. Couldn't find one gents hairdresser, but found one ladies one who wanted to charge me the grand sum of $25 for trimming my semi bald pate. I declined their generosity with a few choice words and will try again on Monday. Did some topping up of provisions, partook of a coffee served to me by a lady with an unmistakeable Brit accent who asked me if I wanted full milk or skimmed. This is the first time since being in Oz that I have been asked that and I have been wandering if all my coffees are doing my weight any good as I should be only drinking semi skimmed or skimmed. It is something for anyone to think about as they do make good coffee and I prefer it when out, to tea, which I think is a complete rip off because all it is a coloured cup of water.

Picked up my films and a weekend paper. If you are like me, an avid newspaper reader, be warned. I get the Australian because as in the UK, the tabloids are garbage and full of adverts. Normally this paper is $1.20 which is about the same that the 'Times' costs. However since leaving city civilisation I have had to pay up to $2.40. On the same theme, petrol has shot up and I am paying up to $1.40 a litre for Diesel, as opposed to $1.06 in Perth. When your in the middle of nowhere and just HAVE TO HAVE fuel, they have you by the curlies. I know they have to transport it to out of the way places, but when you see huge petrol tankers with FOUR bowsers being pulled, the per litre breakdown cost per litre must be very low.

After lunch I headed South intending to go to Ewaninga where there is said to be rock carvings. The road is shown as a dirt road and the scooter will take dirt roads provided they are good ones. This one was a horror and the scooter with its little wheels just would not take it. As I did not intend to put up with that for 26 K's I turned round after a couple of K's and went down another road South to a couple of spots that were supposed to be worth a look. All these ranges of hills that are in this area have spots along them where over millions of years flood waters have broken through these weak places and swept away the rocks, to allow a river to form and go through the now resultant gap. So places they call Gaps, Gorges and Valleys, have formed which can be quite spectacular. So I visited Emily's Gap and Jessie Gap. Emily was quite nice but Jessie was very ordinary. (see photo 355 & 356)

The next day, Sunday, I thought I would go along the West ridge called West MacDonnels. Nearish to town was a gap called Simpson Gap. This was better than the two the day before. In this spot they have a tribe of Rock Wallabies, but I did not see any and the evening is the best time, when they come out, as it is cooler. During the day they are hiding amongst the rocks and you cannot see them. There were many Finch like birds and dragon flies in bright blue and red. (see photo 362 to 365)

Then I wanted to go to another gap called Standleys Chasm which is supposed to be very good. But on the way there the scooter started to play up by constantly running out of power. So I turned back not wanting to konk out too far out of town, plus it was a damn hot afternoon, at least 36 degrees I reckoned. I will visit this place and others, after I get the home back on Monday afternoon, I will go on Tuesday. On Monday while I am waiting for the repair to be redone, I will visit the Desert Park also just out of town.

My home was not due to get picked up until midday, so I took a trip into the town centre to pass the time away and get a newspaper for the UK footy results which appear in Monday's Australian. No paper was available today as they come in via airplane from Melbourne and as the plane was at it's limit for weight, they throw the newspapers off! The joys of living in out of the way places in Oz! No wonder they are the most urbanised country on Earth.

Another example of this was brought up over my reading glasses. I don't know about you but I have always thought that the glasses industry is the greatest rip of you can get. Every pair of glasses I have owned since having to get reading glasses in my 50's, have broken. Usually I lose a lens because a screw falls out and allows a lens to disappear. The last pair I bought I got from Asda as they were the cheapest and fastest by far. I also bought the cheapest plastic frames as why pay for expensive ones if they fall apart. I got the hinge screws Loctited and everything seemed to be going great. Until I went on my scooter trip on this last Saturday when low and behold I lost a lens. I could not believe it. What looked like a fool proof system turned out to have tricked me AGAIN. The frame around the glass was half plastic, with the lower half a metal frame which appeared to have been bonded to the upper plastic frame. No, if you used a magnifying glass you could see a tiny screw holding it together. Guess what? Whilst in town I went to an optometrist, but of course it would take 5 days as he would have to send them to Darwin! So the moral of this story is… Bring with you a couple of spare pairs of glasses. Luckily I was able to buy a cheap $20 pair of reading glasses from a chemists which work just as good as my cheap $75 UK glasses.

Whilst waiting for my home to be picked up, I heard the whistle of the Ghan train. This caravan park is adjacent to the rail line into town from the South. I jumped on my scooter with my camera and shot off to the nearby road and rail track. I got some good shots of this famous train, which surprised me with the number of carriages it had. I reckoned there must have been about 30 of them and most seemed empty. I have read that the line, opened a few years ago is losing money. (see photo 357 & 358)

In the afternoon I scootered to the Desert Park about 3 miles west of Alice. Here I scored a rare 'one up' on life. I had taken my lunch with me and as it was 12.30 when I arrived I decided to sit outside the entrance eating it in a convenient shelter. Just as I finished three large coach loads of what looked like Yank tourists, arrived. As I walked in through the control gate where I would have had to pay, one of the wardens ushered me through an open gate thinking I was with all these Yanks, who had obviously had their entry fees paid in advance by their tour company. I love it when I can get one over in such circumstances, saving myself $15.

I must recommend this park to anyone visiting Alice as it is most informative of the desert wild life. They have many walk in enclosures with wild birds in. As I have said already Oz has a vast array of birds living in the wild. You cannot see many of these as they are only seen in the wild. Around the cities you will see many of the common ones that can survive in cities. So it was nice to see some you would never see. It was also nice to sit and listen to some of the ones that sing a lot. Some have beautiful songs that they sing. One made a noise just like a flute playing 3 or 4 notes. A bit like the bird that inhabited a lake I walked round in Melbourne that had a song that sounded just like a bell ringing. I was wondering where all these bells that were ringing away, were coming from, as the bird was unseen. Eventually I twigged on.

They had an enclosure you could enter and be with some wallabies. There were two lying under a small bush. You could walk right up to them they were obviously used to humans so at least I got some shots of a kangaroo if not actually in the wild, near enough. There was a large indoor exhibition of nocturnal animals, so here the compartments the different animals were in, were in very subdued light. However so dim that in most compartments you could not see anything. But various snakes, lizards and other small animals could be seen. So a good 3 hours of entertainment, which took me up to 3.15pm. (see photo 359 & 360)

Then I went back into town, had the much needed haircut, which cost me double what I would pay in the UK. I wandered around town a bit more and came across another building that had some history, albeit not that old. I am talking about a house they call 'The Residency' Built in the twenties it housed the territories first Governor, but only for five years. It looks just like a very ordinary Oz type house. Apparently in the intervening years the building has hosted visits by British Royalty, including the Queen and Prince Charles. On the description board outside the building it seemed to me that its biggest claim to fame was that it was here that Prince Charles caught food poisoning at a do there. Doesn't say much for Oz catering at high class functions, and what the Aussies think constitutes real fame. (see photo 361)

After this I went on to the Ford dealer as the home should now be ready. Guess what? Yes they ballsed it up yet again and they only ordered ONE seal! So they towed it back to my park for a second time. They say they have now ordered TWO from Melbourne which will be in at 8am and they will pick the home up at 8.30am tomorrow, Tuesday, and have it done in an hour. So it is 'all hold your breaths time' tomorrow. Maybe one day I will get away from this charming town?

The Ford people pick my home up at 8.45 and I go off into town, where I put in a roll of film and then spend an hour and a half trying to pass away the time. Eventually at 11 am I am back at the dealers and Wow! they managed to do the job without messing up the new oil seal. So scooter goes on the back and I am off down the track past the West MacDonnel Ranges to see the gaps, chasms and gorges I did not get to see on the scooter.

The first one I saw was the Standly Chasm (I actually got within 3 K's of the turn off on the scooter before turning back). A narrow river bed with sheer walls on either side which would in the wet, be a raging torrent. (see photo 366 & 367)

Second gorge is called The Ellery Creek Big Hole, which is what is says, a big water hole in a creek, only not so much water. Again would be much better had there been more rain this year as it would be fuller. (see photo 368)

Third gorge is called Serpentine Gorge, which is a big disappointment. All these gorges are 4 to 8 K's off the main road, which means turning off and driving that kind of distance to them. Ok if the road it hard top, not so good if it is a real bad dirt track. The track to this one was a stinker, being narrow and very poorly surfaced. So after 7 K's you get to a car park, THEN you have a 2 K walk down a very uneven track and when you eventually get there the gorge gap is nothing to write home about and the pool that is supposed to be there is very small as to be almost non existent. So a lot of effort for nowt. (see photo 369) After here you can visit a set of low cliff faces where in the past Abo's hacked away at the faces to extract various coloured mineral deposits which they used in their body painting. They are called 'the Ochre Pits' (see photo 370)

Fourth gorge is called Ormiston Gorge, which has a hardtop road to it and the car park is very close to the gap. A huge walled gorge which disappears off to the North, North West. A river bed which is dry on either side of the gap, but a good sized lake in the gap. I walk some way into the gorge, take some photos and then start walking back. The time is 4.30 and it is overcast and fairly cool. I spy as I pass the lake again, a small wallaby feeding at the lake shore on some of the green plants growing in the water. I start to take photos as I move closer. He takes no notice of me at all, and I am able to get within 10 feet of him, when I sit down. He just continued eating as if I wasn't there. So the days work becomes all worth it, all the flies on each walk to the gaps, the long 160 K drive, and the sometimes disappointment of what I see. To be able to sit so close to a wild animal is enchanting and unexpected. Then to top it two grey wading birds fly to the lake from further up the gorge. Egrets I think, they are more tricky to get a good and close photo of. (see photo 371 to 374)

Lastly a couple of K's on after the Ormiston, you come to the Glen Helen Gorge. (see photo 375) Here they also have a camping site and holiday resort of sorts. I get a nice cold beer and an ice cream and then set off for the nearby gorge. Like all the others it is a gap in the hill range through which water has forced its way through creating a gap, and at all these places the depth of the river is always the deepest at the actual gap, so when the water stops running, a lake or pond is left behind. It's at these places that all the wildlife comes to feed and drink. Mostly in the cool of the evening. However I did not want to wait until then. On this lake there where a lot of ducks and Coots and the lake did go some way off into the distance. Of course people were swimming in the larger lakes, mostly youngsters.

time to dash back to Alice so I could book into a park before it got dark, and tomorrow make an early start off towards Mt Isa and try my hand at prolonged dirt road driving. This time I try a different park to the last few nights. This one is much better quality with nice toilets and better sites. Called Stuart Park if you ever get here you may try this one. $21 per night.

Chapter Thirteen

Alice to Cairns

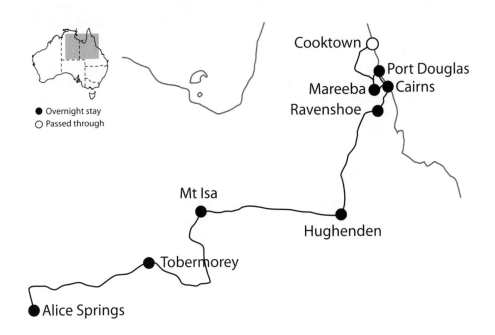

As I went to bed at 10.30 I was able to get up early at 6.45. After breakfast and ablutions, I got out and over to a supermarket to stock up on provisions. It was 8.30 by the time I was on the road North and out of Alice. After 68K's I turned off to the right and onto the Plenty Highway. This heads due East for some 450K's before it hits the Queensland border and I guessed I would either stay at a roadhouse just on the border called Tobermorey, or I would head towards a camping site at a place just to the North and just inside the border, called Urandangi. (see photo 376)

For some 69 Ks the highway is tarmac then it changes to dirt road. My guide book told me that it was a well used highway kept in good order by regular grading. Well you would not have known it, because it was rough in many places. I had asked at the Police Station in Alice as to its condition and they said it was OK and well passable, which it was. However the quality left something to be desired I thought, especially if it is supposed to be well used. The main gripe was the amount of dust, which then goes into corrugations. The only way to keep this down is by regular grading, so that obviously wasn't being done regularly. In places it was fine, with either hard packed gravel or soil with little or no corrugations or loose dust. In other places it was thick with dust. I found after a while that the best thing to cut down on the whole vehicle vibrating was to go as fast as I could over all this. This had the effect of smoothing it out somewhat. However you have to concentrate even more, looking for large stones to avoid or holes into which you can drop a wheel and damage a tyre.

After about 140K's you reach an outback Police Station at Harts Ranges, so I dropped in to recheck the road conditions. I was told much what I had been before, but it was reassuring and I found that the section from Tobermorey to Urandangi was good even though it was more minor a road than the Plenty Hwy. So it was a day of furious driving, much concentration, much vibrations and everything in the home rattling away and DUST everywhere and all the time. You raise a huge dust cloud behind you but the dust off the front wheels gets into the vehicle through every little crack it can find. So I can see that one big minus using this short cut to Mt Isa is not only the uncomfortable driving but the fact that I will have to spend a good deal of time cleaning every inch of the vehicle and the home and the scooter on the back, which I can hardly recognise. It has so much dust on it being at the very back.

I had decided to take this short cut as it saved me about 550 K's, one days driving and a tank full of diesel. Also I have so far not driven on dirt for any real length (more than 30 K's) so I thought I have to get away from the madding crowd and do some real Oz rough driving, like I did in the 60's when they were very many non tarmacked roads. I wish I had not bothered because even though the vehicle made it OK and never came close to any bother, the road surfaces are so rough it is easy to shred a tyre, get a puncture or damage your suspension. As it was when I got to Urandangi I saw that the plastic number board I have attached to the scooter rack, because the scooter now hides the lights and the number plate which was on the Transit back end, had disappeared. I would say that it got caught either as I went into one of the many vicious dips which being not long, would catch the back end, or when I went along the very last section of road leading to Urandangi which was little more than a dirt track across farmers fields, with a raised centre section. The raised centre could have caught the board and ripped it off... together with my rear number plate.

This being Oz and they having such a strange way of running the country with each of the EIGHT states having their own Parliament and rules and laws, it also means they have their own number plates. So if you are travelling and out of the state the vehicle is registered in... how do you get another replacement plate? I will just buy another plastic trailer number board and write the number on. If I get stopped I will just have to point out the stupidity of their registration ways and see how I get on. Although I may run the risk of being shipped back to the UK on the next returning convict ship!

I came across some stretches of road that were actually tarmacked, but these stretches never lasted long enough. Anyway this route did show up a lot more wild life on the way. The country through which I passed had a great deal of cattle on it and they were very visible. (see photo 377) Also they were on the actual road much more than anywhere else I have been. Had to slow down for them many times, no wonder there are so many dead ones lying at the side of the road. In some places you just wonder how they can scratch enough to eat from this dead and unfertile land, but they obviously do as none of them looked as if they were starving.

Then I actually saw my first full sized Roos in the wild. I have seen a few small wallabies as I have mentioned, but here there were two full sized male roos standing, not lying, under a tree at the side of the road. I should have stopped to see if I could get a close up, but by the time I thought of it they were too far away to go back. I saw a few of the magnificent Wedge Tailed Eagles and one sitting on a road kill, I slowly rolled up to it to see if it would stay on while I got a shot of it. It almost worked I stopped opposite it but it chickened out at the last moment and I only got a shot of it as it flew off. They are big birds. Then there were many goannas, and one I could not avoid as it crossed right in front of me, and is now probably sitting in some birds stomach having made a nice evening meal. Lastly I saw a mob of wild Camels, a bigger number than I have seen previously. (see photo 378)

My vehicle is not only covered with dust, but also the remains of many locusts which have splattered themselves on the front. After I crossed into Queensland I was amazed at how many of these creatures there were, and of course they are quite large, so when you hit one they make a sizable splodge on your bodywork. More cleaning. (see photo 379)

The countryside through which I have passed has been unremarkable, very flat with occasional low ranges of hills. Medium density bush of mainly gums and some bushes. The weather has been mostly cloudy, which helped to keep the temperature down, but it did rise in the late afternoon.

When I got to this Urandangi place it was just a collection of shacks and loads of Aboriginals, so it is obviously one of their dumps. Sorry to describe them like that but that is what anyone would describe them as. They seem to largely live in groups, in houses (built for them with Public money, of course) and they can be out in the bush proper, or on the outskirts of towns like Alice or Tennants, or even within town boundaries. However almost all of these groups of houses look like a rubbish tip, with abandoned old cars and heaps of household rubbish all strewn around the houses. This is what this place was like, and when I had to go in the Pub (Oh yes all these outback places have a pub, no shops, but always a pub.) It was also a dump, run by a white woman of dubious looks. Of course the pub was full of Aboriginals drinking, which I thought they were not allowed to do, and the noise was terrible. They are exceedingly noisy people, shouting at each other all the time. Many of them show signs of injuries obviously got from fighting amongst themselves. Anyway I asked this woman if she had a powered site (even though I could see no sign of any caravan site the map did show there was a camping site), she looked blank, so I repeated myself four times then she got what I was asking. I came to the conclusion she was so used to listening to pidgin English off the Aboriginals that some real English threw her completely off. I was directed to a grassy patch to the side of the pub where I was told there was no electric but a shower was there, and everything was free.

Well I suppose it was just about better than being in the bush but I don't know. The grassy patch had cowpats all over it, so I would not have liked to camp there. The shower was an open air job with just some corrugated sheet around the shower head, which was black with gunge and the thing dripped, so there was a pool of stagnant water on the floor. It looked like something out of a Calcutta slum. Even though I desperately need a shower to get this dust out of me (my white polo shirt is actually now brown) I will wash myself down tonight in the home with a flannel and make do until tomorrow. The noise from the Aboriginals living nearby has to be heard to be believed, screaming adults, shouting kids and barking dogs, loud music, and noisy cars being driven up and down by Aboriginal male youth. I wonder how much sleep I will get tonight?

Well by 9.30 the noise was still in full swing so I decided not to wait around to see if it would die down. I upped sticks and drove to the end of the road and down a narrow track away from all the buildings. It brought me to the settlement cemetery. Good place I thought the Aboriginals are scared of spirits, so will stay away and I can get a good sleep among the dead. I got to bed by 10.15 and so it was that I got off to sleep. I would have had an unbroken sleep but when I temporarily awoke at 2am I could not hear my generator going. I thought some enterprising Aboriginal may have sneaked up a stole it (worth $2,000 and used once) It was still there but had stopped. It had run out of petrol and I hadn't thought to check it for petrol as I thought I had kept it full. So I switched to the house battery and hoped that it would last for four hours. I got up at 6 just as the sun was rising, feeling full of the world. The battery was OK and I started the engine to get charging the battery back up, straight away. Had a nice breakfast of tea and toast which is all I ever have, but usually a bit later on than this early hour.

It is only 180 K's to Mt Isa and I shall be there fairly quickly...I hope. On my way out at 6,30 I came across the landlady of the pub and another lady walking towards the Pub with a dog. Blimey I thought they do get up early here to walk the dog. What I found funny though was each woman had a large cloud of flies hovering over the top half of their bodies. And I mean large! The pub lady sensibly had a head net on but still. How the other put up with it, but then I suppose you can get used to anything! I stopped by them just to check I was on the right road to Mt Isa. Yes I was told. 'Couldn't you stand the noise then last night?' they asked me, 'Not bloody likely' I replied 'I moved to the cemetery to get some peace and quiet' They thought this quite funny and on that I got on my way.

I took it nice and easy as I was in no hurry to get there and I wanted to keep the dust down, so I only pottered at 60K's. The road was quite good, even and not much corrugations or dust. The land I was passing was quite different to that in the NT I had just come from. Here they had obviously cleared the bush in a big way, as there were huge expanses of flat grasslands with tree lines of bush way in the distance on either side of the road. When I say grass I mean Ozzy outback grass which is in clumps of a type of grass which grows up to a foot high and has ears of seeds on the end of stalks. Each clump is on its own and there are gaps between each clump, but when you look over a large distance they all blend in and it looks like solid tight knit grass as at home. This type of landscape obviously provides cattle with good and rich feed. So much so that all along the 200 K's to Isa there were many cattle to be seen feeding on the land, and many crossing the road on frequent occasions.

They are quite funny these cattle, I have been watching them and how they behave. This morning while I was standing next to my home contemplating the lovely red sunrise, a herd of cattle started to walk past the cemetery in single file. Well not walk but a good trot, all nose to tail and they looked quite comical. I mean where were they going and why the hurry? They seemed to know were they were going OK. To make it even more human like, about the sixth bull from the front kept stopping and he would turn around to look at the others following and he would give a big bellow. I thought he was saying 'Come on you slow, dozy buggers... get a move on we've got to get there' He did this several times and after bellowing would carrying on his trotting. As with all humans at the back of this line were several youngsters all fooling around and giving to much cowplay (as opposed to horseplay). Just like all youngsters I thought. Then these cattle that you come across at the side of the road, when they hear you coming, if they are not too close to the road they will stop munching and all look up to you watching you with great interest as you slowly pass by. Their heads turn as they follow your progress. At other times when I was shifting along, there would be great alarm as they took off into the safety of the fields or bush. Intent to get away fast from this thundering big white beast and its dust cloud. Once they felt they were far enough away from the road they would stop and stare at you as you thundered by. Almost human I thought.

You see many dead cattle at the side of the road and I have wondered whether all of them had been hit by traffic. But they are such big creatures and quite quick to get out of the way unlike dozy Roos. If you are going fast, they are away from the road long before you get there. Roos tend to be dazzled by the lights and stay in the road or jump out straight into your path. I think a lot of the dead cattle I saw had died of starvation or lack of water or sickness. On my way to Uluru I passed a roadhouse with SIX dead cattle dotted around the nearby bush land within metres of the place. Some were under a nearby tree, so had obviously died there. I am sure it must be from the effects of this lack of rain they are having here.

I had wanted to fill up on diesel at Urandangi but the pumps would not be in action until 9am as the generator was kept off at night. So I did not have enough fuel in the tanks, so it was good that I had two 20 litre fuel cans of the stuff that I have been carrying in my box since Adelaide, and now will be the first time I need them. I stopped further down the road and opened the box up and extracted the two plastic jerrycans. This gave me a range of 360 K's and more than enough to get to Isa. So this episode shows the importance of carrying spare fuel, even if you do not think you will ever need it. On major routes there are plenty of sources of fuel and close enough not to have to worry. However if you ever go off the beaten track you will have to be very careful to work out where you are going, what supply will be available, and how much spare you should carry. It should not be forgotten that in these out of the way places, supplies of fuel can be by farms/stations or places like Urndangi, a pub. What happens if the tanker supply breaks down or for some reason doesn't turn up, or is late, or the pump breaks down, or the generator supplying the power for the pump breaks down? You could then arrive at a point where you will not get your intended supply. You need to know how much fuel consumption your vehicle is capable of at the best and worst, so when you get into situations where you have to work out, 'Will I get to the next supply on what I have?' So this subject is of the greatest importance.

On this stretch of dirt road I came across a large collection of trees and raised earth mounds. So I knew this was a bore hole, and as I have never seen a watering place at a bore hole I stopped to have a butchers. The bore was about 100 meters from the road and the field was dry and flat, so I drove there. There was hidden a gantry of a bore drill with a petrol engine to pump. There was a hole dug out and the earth banked around the hole, but all was bone dry. Had the bore dried up, I wondered? All these questions and no one to answer them. (see photo 380)

This road which is used very little as opposed to the highways I have been on, certainly had more wildlife on it. I saw two large water birds grey in colour with a huge wing span, long wading legs and long necks. They were near the road edge but took off flying at low level and away to the nearby trees. I wondered as I do, what were water birds doing so far from any large body of water?

Then there were many goannas of about a foot long crossing the road. Most of them do it quickly but two were slow and I am afraid ended up flat and potential hawk breakfast. So many different types of birds in the grass fields, black cockies, white cockies, galahs, green parrots, all kinds of small birds, martins I recognised, it really is a bird watchers paradise. Yesterday a hawk sat at the roadside took off late, and instead of flying away from my vehicle which was travelling at 100K's, and it flew in front of my home, and at my height. It was a little slower than me as I started to slowly catch up with it. So I had a marvellous view of a hawk in full flight just in front of me. Eventually just as I caught up with it, it wheeled up and over me.

Eventually the dirt road meets the tarmac road that will take me North to Isa. It is a one lane wide road as all Oz roads were in the 60's. That is to say tarmacked roads. On these type of roads you have to take extra care when confronted with an oncoming vehicle. The idea is that at the right time you drop your nearside wheels off the tarmac and onto the dirt hard shoulder. This has to be done gradually and not suddenly, as that can put you into a slide. This can mean you lose control. Watching the other vehicle closely to make sure he does the same. A puff of red dust means he too has dropped his wheels off. Leave enough of the middle of the tarmac strip for both vehicles to miss each other. This is OK with vehicles no bigger than yourself, but with large trucks this is another matter. If you see a road train approaching, get off the road completely and stop. So you have to slow down when you see a road train, as you have to be able to pick the right spot to do this and quickly. Much quick care has to be the order when approaching a road train on a completely dirt road, as road trains or any large truck makes a hell of a lot dust. As road trains can have up to 4 trailers, this means that the dust being kicked up by the trailers, completely hides them. If you watch the progress of such a rig, you will see that the 3rd and 4th trailers can and do weave about a lot. So if you do not get off the road, you could end up slamming into the side of a trailer. Even on a single lane hardtop, it is best to also get off the tarmac completely and maybe stop as well. A lot of truckies will not risk dropping off their trucks nearside wheels in case they lose control, so they will keep on the tarmac. You have been warned. Be also very careful of idiots who go to sleep and are not watching what your doing as you approach them. Many people have died in 'head-ons' because when you get two dozy drivers, and this can also happen on full width highways.

As I got close to Mt Isa I came across a low range of small hills with rounded tops and covered in grass and small bushes, called I believe, The Selwyn Ranges. Then as the last one went by you come out of a pass and there are the tall chimneys of the power station in front of you and to your left the tall chimneys of the mine and all the large mine buildings. (see photo 381) This town is a fairly new town started only in the 20's when a chap called John Cambell Miles who was a gold seeker on his way to the Northern Territory on his horse called 'Hard Times' The horse got thirsty and made for a river called the Leichardt River (named after the famous German explorer of the 1800's who explored the North of Oz.) Horses can smell water of course. This chap, when at the river recognised several rocky outcrops he saw in this area as having potential. It came to be that in this area there were very rich bodies of copper, silver, gold, lead and zinc. Subsequently with the mining in the area, which became known as Mt Isa, who Miles named after the Western Australia goldfield of Mt Ida. (I think he was indulging in a play on letters here!)

It is recognised that this mine has the Worlds richest bodies of these ores, so someone has made a lot of money. It therefore goes without saying that this town is a rich one and all its business are mining based. Even the Aborigines here are a cut above those I have seen so far, elsewhere. They are better dressed, cleaner and seem quite sophisticated, which makes a change. It certainly has changed since I was here in 66, when it was quite a rough cowboy type town. It is now a typical modern Oz town with all the usual modern facilities. However there is not that much to see here as a tourist, but they do have a mine tour which I will see if I can get on this Friday which is Good Friday, so they may be closed, we will see.

The caravan park I booked into on the Barkly Highway, which goes through the town, is OK but has the usual dirt parking sites. This is doubly annoying seeing as I am going to have to have a massive clean up of all the red dust that is everywhere. I make an immediate start but only get about half done by evening. So will have to finish it off tomorrow.

The evenings are still much cooler than further North which is great as it means you get a decent sleep. I spent the first two hours in the morning doing more cleaning, then I went to the Mt Isa Outback Information Centre to go on their underground mine tour, which I had heard was extremely realistic. The cost is $45 or $38 for a pensioner and is well worth it as this purpose built set of tunnels which are underground, so the whole set up is exactly as it would be in a real mine. It is fully equipped with all the machinery that has been used in the past and also the present. You have to get togged out in miners overalls with lamp and hardhat etc. The tour takes 2.1/2 hours and the guide is an ex miner. In this case he was an ex Pom from Redditch who had come out in the 60's. A very interesting tour it was. (see photo 382 to 385)

After the tour I went up the nearby little hill that serves as a town lookout. I had my lunch there and took some photos of the town and mines areas which dominate the whole town. Then it was back to the park to finish off all the cleaning of this dust which took me the rest of the afternoon. Tomorrow it will be off towards the next large town along the track, called Richmond.

On the road out of Isa and all the way to the next town, Cloncurry, you go through undulating land full of small hills. They have plenty of grass on them and a thin covering of small trees and bushes.

The road winds and bends through these hills and that makes a change from flat and mainly straight roads. The condition of the road is very good, looking as if it has recently been rebuilt. Well wide and very smooth surface and level. Plenty of good linage and barriers. Unfortunately it doesn't last and eventually it degenerates into the worst section of highway I have encountered since leaving Sydney. Some sections were OK but for the most it was too narrow, extremely uneven and far from level. Your vehicle is bouncing up and down and lurching to the left and right. In fact at times it was as rough a ride as on the dirt road I went on from Alice. It would seem that in Queensland the state of major highways doe not rate as high as other States. This highway don't forget is the only major highway linking Townsville area to Mt Isa and Darwin and ultimately WA. Good job it was Easter Saturday and heavy traffic was at a lower level. Even so when you were on a narrow section with virtually no hard shoulder, when a Road Train passed you going the opposite way, it was a bit too close for comfort. Then you get bridges over creeks that are too narrow for me to pass any truck. It would be suicide to try it, yet there are no signs to warn you not to attempt to pass an oncoming truck, but to stop. A younger tourist with a lack of experience at driving wider vehicles, as the home is, could attempt it.

I am constantly appalled at the lack of safety barriers on the many creek bridges. These are narrow small concrete underpasses for the small creeks or streams to pass under the road. They have a concrete low wall across the creek and a deep drop into it. Misjudge the width, which is narrow at this point and you could find yourself going over and into the creek. Some creeks have got crash barriers on the bridges over the creeks, but don't. Similarly there are many elevated sections with no barriers to stop you going off and making a big drop.

I am making for a town called Hughenden and from here I will head North on a short cut inland and through to Cairns. I do not want to drive to Townsville and then head North up the coast road, because I will only have to come back down it. I will drive very slowly this time as it is another dirt road and I will need to keep the dust down as much as I can. On this ride the total distance is just over 500K's and four towns Cloncurry, Julia Creek, Maxwell, and Richmond. All of them are what I call typical Oz towns from an era long gone by. They are what I also call 'one street, one horse towns', few shops, deserted streets and blink your eyes and you are through! Cloncurry I thought would be a decent little town and I was looking forward to stopping for a coffee. Didn't even see any shop let alone one that would sell drinks, so I just kept going.

It is a mining town or was, and it was here that the famed Australian Flying Doctor service was started by a Reverend John Flynn. He worked in bush towns and saw the absolute need for such a service. He is celebrated in many outback towns in the centre and North, and especially in Alice where he is buried, so you see many memorials to him in these central Oz towns.

The land since leaving the hills is very flat all the way, mostly with a rich looking carpet of grass. Few trees or bush and I think they call this part of Qld 'The Savannah.' When you do see animals it is all cattle but I see my first sheep since Southern WA, just as I approach Hughenden. For some way the grass is a dark reddish brown, which at first I thought was soil. I have never seen red grass before. The only wild life I saw was two Emus and plenty of Hawks, a distinct lack of birds even on the crow front, for some reason. (see photo 386)

For a lot of the way, the Mt Isa to Townsville rail line that I rode on in 66, runs alongside the road. I couldn't believe how uneven the track was. It was up and down following the undulations of the land in much the same way as the road was. Most railways I have seen around the civilised World, rail engineers cut through hills with cuttings, and create banks when confronted with dips and hills. No wonder the trains on this line appear to only do about 45 to 50 mph! Two trains passed me on this trip going quite slowly. On top of that, the line is a narrow track, which is out of kilter with the other States. (see photo 387)

Finally at 4 in the afternoon I arrived in Hughenden and there was a cafe open, so I got a cappuccino. However as is often in bush places, they haven't a clue how to make proper coffee. So you get one made with instant, which is simply not the same. This place is like the others I have passed through today, looking like a place frozen in a time warp from the 40's.50's or 60's. Wooden house on stilts which are common in Queensland, many looking very scruffy. A very poor shopping area with shops that look like they are out of a Wild West film set. Not a sign of a modern supermarket like Coles or Woolworths. (see photo 388 & 389) Still the caravan park was laid out like I think ALL caravan parks in OZ should be. That is to say the parking area on each site is a tarmacked lane and the land on each side is grass or concrete bounded by kerbstones. So no interminable dirt to get in your home all the time. (see photo 390) Cost $12 which is fine (£5) I ask about the dirt road which I am told is in good order and 'no worries mate' Spent the early evening watching football, Oz playing Iraq, who they beat 2.0. Then an episode of The Bill (which is supposed to be very popular in OZ, quite why I can't say) and which I never watch in the UK as I think it is rubbish. Just goes to show how you lower your standards when away from home and there is nowt else to watch!

I'm on the road by 8am the next day as I want to get an early start as I don't know what the state of this dirt road is going to be or how long it will take me. There was a certain length of tarmac road before it went to dirt. It wasn't too bad for the first 160 odd K fairly smooth, not too many dips or bumps, or corrugations or dust. So I was able to average about 70 K's. One thing I couldn't understand, but then you will find in Oz as I have said before, they do things here that do not appear to have any logic to it. Here I mean with this road, every now and then for no apparent reason, in the middle of nowhere, it suddenly goes to beautiful tarmac. This lasts for maybe up to 5 K's, then its back to dirt. You could say that very now and then they get some spare money and so spend it on a bit more tarmac on this road. Then my question is why don't they (whatever council we are talking of) gradually tarmac the road as it progresses away from Hughenden? Maybe likewise from the other end, then maybe in the 22nd century they will meet up in the middle!

It was quite a busy road, more busy than the shortcut dirt road I took from Alice to Mt Isa. Here I have to have another grouse (Oz for complaining) about Oz male drivers, especially in the country.

Most of the drivers that overtook me either way were obviously working class men with their utes. (Oz for pickup truck) So these Neantherdals, (I call them that because of the way they drove) were driving at well over 100K's. Far too fast for this road especially because of the width of it which was mainly narrow, and the fact that there was a bit of traffic. They come at you like express trains with a huge dust cloud. Do you think they slow down as they approach you, especially bearing in mind that your a lot bigger than they are and wider? They do not even move over to their left, thus making me move over, and of course they show their complete and utter ignorance, by then showering you with their unnecessary large dust cloud. When I saw someone behind me I indicated I was pulling to the left so they could overtake. The majority did not even acknowledge this, a couple did by tooting their horns. So this is one more thing you should note if you ever have to take to a dirt road. More on this road in a bit. One thing you should also know about dirt driving, and that is the possibility some idiot could try to overtake a vehicle that is coming towards you that even though the road may be straight, the vehicle in front of him will be kicking up a large dust cloud which will be blinding him. If the bloke in front of him is as big an idiot as he is, he will not slow down or move over. If he is determined to overtake he could appear towards you through this cloud of dust. So watch carefully, all approaching vehicles and see if there are any vehicles behind it, especially close behind. Defensive driving has to be the order of the day in Oz, I am afraid, and at all times.

Whilst on about roads, another thing I find annoying is the lack of lay-bys. They are great distances apart and on dirt roads, none at all. You can go for ages on a dirt road before you get a place you can safely pull completely off. The trouble with dirt roads is that you get either banks of soft dirt and dust building up at the edge of the road or you get a semi ditch which looks too soft to go across, and the last thing you want to do is get bogged down in soft dust. In fact driving on a dirt road is more demanding than driving on a tarmac road, so you need lay-bys even more.

The landscape was wholly uninteresting right the way up to a junction some 263K's away, called The Lynd Junction, where you then joined the Gregory Developmental Rd which was tarmac. It was light bush forest with trees not too close and grasses growing in-between. I would say it had been cleared of bushes to allow cattle to graze on the grasses. You certainly saw many cattle. The landscape was generally flat with a few dips into creeks and rivers. Now here I saw creeks and rivers that had some water in them, for the first time since the big rivers of the Kimberley's. Also the grasses were nice and green, so this area has had rains. (see photo 391)

I saw little wildlife, only two Wallabies early on (this is the best time early in the morning before it gets hot) and then I saw a solitary wading bird that did not fly off like the two I saw yesterday. It was standing at the right side of the road, so I slowed down some way of and gently drove up to it. It was nervous but as I say it just trotted into the grass, so I got a photo of it. (see photo 392)

Early on at the beginning of this road there were a few sites of interest, as the roadside signs said. Two burial places, one a grave at the side of the road marked by a pile of white painted stones, which the sign said could be the grave of an Aboriginal woman, or that of a wandering Chinaman Well I never! I suppose you takes your pick on that one. The other grave was more specific. In 1886 the local postman who then rode his horse up and down this track, was one day waylaid by a bunch of belligerent and angry Aborigines who leapt out on him and speared him to death. Quite why he was buried there and not taken to the nearest town and given a decent burial plot, I do not know. Then there was the whistling bore hole. They put down a bore pipe to pull up water they knew was plentiful down there, but it would not rise. What they did however hear, was that there was a whistling noise coming from the bore pipe, indicating a movement of air. This can only happen if there was a tunnel connecting their bore with an outside source of air input. So you are invited to stick your ear next to the capped pipe which has a small hole on the side of it. All very exciting, and indeed you can here the rush of air producing a whistle. I half expected it to be whistling Waltzing Matilda, so was a bit disappointed.

One thing I have noticed driving on these dirt roads and that is the complete absence of mileage signs. All roads I have encountered to date have had every ten K's, a green sign giving the number of K's to the next large town or settlement. This helps as do all signs informing you how far you have left to go. As these roads I have been on have been of long distances, it really does help to know where you are at any one time. My maps have not always shown every side road or track coming onto it, and as these can also be used to determine exactly where you are, you end up driving in the dark as it were, as to where you are. Maybe they think traffic on dirt roads do not need to know where they are?

Now this dirt road again, the last 100 K's were awful, the worst so far I have been on. It degenerated to a one lane width, with very poor hard shoulder, and in some places no hard shoulder at all. The general condition was dreadful, being bumpy, uneven, lots of dust and corrugations. The two lengths that had tarmac mysteriously inserted in the middle of nowhere, looked as if they were the original tarmac put in the 20's, because they were even more uneven that the dirt sections. They were also cracked and the tarmac had melted and shifted. At the beginning of this last 100K's they even had the temerity to erect a sign which told you that you were about to enter a 100K's length of shit and rough road. It would seem that this stretch did not warrant any grading or upkeep as it looked as if it had not been touched in years. Then inexplicably again, these brilliant Ozzy road men, put in a brilliant 3 K stretch near the end and I thought 'Oh well at least it will undoubtedly go right to the junction like this.' Not on your life, as it finished well short of the end, and the crap dirt road went right up to the junction.

Here, there was a roadhouse where I filled up and it was here that I was perplexed by the fact that it only took 21 litres and I had just done 261K's since Hughenden where I last filled up. That gave me a consumption figure of 36mpg when the best I normally do is 23mpg. Now I know that on this section I only went at 60 or 70 and sometimes 80KPH, it just doesn't work out. I had wondered why my fuel gauge wasn't moving. I had done 150 plus K's before it had started to move off full. Maybe my Transit just does much better consumption if you keep the speed down to 60/70K's. That is OK on dirt roads but on the normal Highway I like to do 80/90K's.

As I got towards the Lynd Junction I could see a large range of fairly high hills coming up, and as I drove away from the junction towards my ultimate destination of Ravenshoe, the countryside began to change rapidly. I actually came across a couple of large fields that had been planted with crops of some sort, and pine trees started to appear, which I had not seen since South of WA. The hills I was now driving in were heavily dotted with lots of healthy looking gum trees of some height. The map told me I was approaching the Atherton Highlands, which I had heard of. There were also many houses built in amongst the trees and near the roads, so this area was more populated than many of the areas I have passed through of late.

I came to a place called Innot Hot Springs. Not many houses but a caravan park, a pub and a few other buildings. Apparently the local creek runs hot, as this area in the distant past had lots of volcanic action. The caravan park had the monopoly on these springs and you had to pay to wallow in them. So gave it a miss as I wanted to get onto Ravenshoe and into a park there.

So a few K's up the road I entered Ravenshoe. A nice little town and the caravan park is set amongst a nice forest of very tall gums and pines. I drove round the town and visited the Visitor centre to read up on what the area has to offer. It is an old logging town and still is involved in the timber trade. Also it is heavily into dairy farming and milk products like butter. The local milk goes all the way to Darwin. Also this whole area was used in WW2 by the army to train its soldiers how to fight in the jungles. This just prior to them going off to New Guinea to fight the Japs as they did. A lot of the forest nearby is tropical rain forest, so ideal to train in. I went to see the local historical steam train that they run out of here. When I pulled up at the old railway station a bloke asked if he could help me. I asked if they were running any trips tomorrow, and they were, but at 1.30 start. Bit late for me as I want to move on to other sights to see, and I have been on many a steam train in my life, as I used to be a dreaded train spotter in my younger days!

Anyway this chap is yet another Brit emigrant from the sixties who came from Leicester and he helps in the running of the trains and the restoration work. I learnt from him that the woods used in the restoration of the interior of the Houses of Parliament in London, used woods that came from the forests around this town. Also a local carver made a replica chair for the Speaker and it has carved on the back 'A present from the people of Australia', well I never! He was a graphic artist and he did an oil painting which hangs in the 'Houses.' So I was in illustrious company this afternoon. We had a good old chin wag about all that is wrong with the UK and why no one in their right mind would want to live there now. All this over a good old cup of tea.

The temperature all today has been excellent it is definitely getting cooler as I near the coast, and in the evening it was really nice and cool with a good breeze blowing. Well this was no doubt helped by the fact that Ravenshoe is Queenslands highest town at just 1000 feet high and is also supposed to be the windiest, hence the big windfarm just out of town on a nearby hill. You would never get this in the UK in such a beautiful spot as all the nutters who campaign against anything and everything would have had it stopped. (see photo 393) On the bird front I see that sparrows are back in this area. I haven't seen them since Melbourne, not even in Perth. Also mynah birds which also I had last seen in Melbourne and these birds are very gregarious and noisy chirpers.

As I headed out in the next morning towards the North and Lake Tinaroo I was immediately struck at just how beautiful the landscape was around here. Large mountains heavily wooded and lovely rolling smaller hills and valleys, covered in wonderful green normal grass. Loads of dairy cows like Friesians and Jerseys everywhere. The soil looks a rich dark brown/red and lots of different things being grown, sugar cane, corn on the cob, vegetables, fruit trees, and lots I didn't recognise. Truly this part of Oz has some of the best landscape to be seen. Any Brit would feel at home here and as far as I am concerned you can keep the dry parts of Oz. OK to experience for once, but I couldn't live in the outback. (see photo 394 & 395)

Also it was a pleasure to be able to drive along windy roads that also went up and down. Much more interesting. So it was not long before I came to a site worth checking out, the Mt Hypipamee Crater. This is a volcanic hole created by a gas explosion under pressure which blew upwards and created this very big deep hole in the rocks of the hillside. Now filled up with water and all this is set inside a tropical rain forest, through which you have to walk through to get to the crater. This was pure magic, such thick growth and such tall trees and a rushing stream, falling down in a series of small waterfalls. This is the Barron River which starts off all these surrounding Hills and mountains, and makes its way down to the coast at Cairns where it becomes a wide river indeed. (see photo 396 to 398)

After this enchanting visit to my first rain forest (and it was actually raining throughout the walk) I carried onto the town of Atherton after which the Atherton Tablelands is named after. The town was named after an early farmer settler called John Atherton and he went on to find tin in the area. A nice little town all neat and tidy and businesslike. (see photo 399) I stopped for a while to get some food and a coffee and newspaper, then onto the nearby dam called Tinaroo Lake. I had lunch there on its shores, watching the low black rain clouds scudding across the surrounding mountain tops. (see photo 400)

Then it was back on the road to make the final stretch of road to Cairns on the coast. A good road which was now on the plains in between the surrounding mountains, past all the busy looking farms. Then it reaches the mountains and it is an uphill drive into the higher reaches of them. You do not notice just how high your going, and then suddenly your on the way down, and boy is it downhill, corner after tight corner and you go round one corner and before you there is the panorama of the coast, way down below you. These mountains are deceptively high and I must find out just how high they are. (see photo 401)

Eventually you are down at sea level, or thereabouts and I am heading down a three lane highway, southwards and into Cairns. Quite a large town and all looking quite modern and recently built. I park in the centre and go walkies to look around. Very much a town totally set up for tourism, and why not? This area has so much to offer the tourist so that it used as a base to go on many tours. North to Cooktown and the Daintree Tropical Forest, to the nearby Great Barrier Reef, to the tablelands I have just visited and the forest there, and so on. So all the shops and commercial buildings are geared to the almighty tourist dollar. Cafes, restaurants, hotels, backpackers hostels, souvenir shops, so many tour booking shops, and so on. But all very pleasant and well laid out and neat and clean and tidy, which I like.

Of course Cairns is on the coast, as I said, but I was very surprised to see that the tide was out and the sea was miles away. Even when it would be in, the sea off the promenade would be very shallow, and there wasn't sand, but mud, so I don't think anyone would be frolicking in the waters of Cairns. So to get over this they have built on the waterfront area, a great big swimming pool of the likes I have not seen before. They have well manicured lawns along the sea front with a board walk and set amongst the lawns at the Southern end near the port area is this pool which you can just take you gear off dump your towel etc on the grass and walk into the pool. It is not a separate entity surrounded by a fence or a wall, and at which you have to pay to get into. It is an integral part of the of the seafront layout. Lots of people mostly younger people in the water, but not much swimming going on. I think everyone was just trying to keep cool, because since I came down from the mountains and the tablelands I have immediately notice my old enemy… HUMIDITY!! Although not as bad as North NT or WA. Just a little sweaty, but I think I will live. (see photo 402 to 408)

 Anyway before I knew it, it was 4.30 and time to book into a caravan park. There was one quite near the centre, which is great, and I was into there and setting up. Quite nice in that it had many good sized mature trees around and mostly the grass plots to park on where excellent grass, and not the scruffy mostly dirt and dust with a few strands of tired looking apologies for grass, type parks I have been in for ages now. Amazing what a good decent rainfall can do for grass and greenery! It's a different world here, to the last four months I have spent, since leaving Melbourne. (It was reasonably green around there) (see photo 409 & 410)

The day after I arrived at Cairns, a Tuesday, I decided to make it a rest day. So I took the scooter off and had to give it a good clean up, yet again. Then it was into the town centre to do some catching up on emails to everybody. I then spent the rest of the day looking around Cairns, which as I have said is a pretty modern place with all the amenities one could wish for. Very clean and tidy and well laid out with very nice gardens and verges and lots of trees everywhere. Very well served with new modern shopping centres. I made enquiries about a trip to the reef and I will do this once I have been to Cooktown and Cape tribulation. I also did some washing and more cleaning of the home. A woman's work is never done!

Next day I am heading towards Cape Tribulation which is on the coast and going towards Cooktown. Now here's another example of the cockeyed way the Ozzies do things. This whole area of Queensland is very heavily into tourism and of course part of the lure of this part of Oz is not only the nearby reef, but also the beautiful rain forests of this area, and the lovely mountains. On top of this for those interested in history, Cape Tribulation is the first area of Oz where the white man (British that is) settled for any length of time. Captain Cook holed his ship on a reef in the area in 1770, and he thus named Cape Tribulation because of his troubles he suffered. As it took a couple of months to repair a little further up the coast at an inlet where he beached it on, which is now Cooktown. He and his crew had to stay for longer than he stayed in the other landfall he made, namely at Botany Bay. Many tourist will want to see the area for that reason and because also in the same area are the rain forests of the Daintree National Park. From Cairns the road runs up the coast to the Cape and is tarmacked. Yet the ongoing road from there to Cooktown which continues up the coast for only some 100K's is dirt road and so bad that it is only suitable for 4WD. So if your like me, you have to go South again back to a place called Mossman and then head up an inland road in a great circuitous arc for some 246K's in total. When the coastal road would be 161 K's. So the return inland road is going to give you an extra 161 K's of driving plus extra fuel cost. Not to mention that on the coastal route, an Aboriginal settlement that is on it, would benefit from better road connections, but then in Oz they don't count, especially in Queensland. But that is another story! (see photo 412 to 414)

Once you are on the Captain Cook Hwy going North the scenery is simply stunning. Inland from the coast is a range of quite high mountains, which if I am right form part of the Great Dividing Range. One mountain which stands out is Mt Thornton at 1375 Metres or nearly 4,000 Ft. A couple of others nearby are at around 1,000 Metres. So it's all pretty impressive and they are all covered in heavy rain forest. Mt Thornton looks just like an extinct volcano as it is pointed like one and its peak his shrouded in clouds.

The road goes across the Daintree River and a car ferry and not a bridge is what operates here. Reminds me of the similar cable operated ferry across the narrows at Poole Harbours entrance. (see photo 415) Then the road is into the rain forest proper and the road all the way to the Cape is narrow in many places and very twisty. At times it runs but metres from the sea, but a heavy strip of forest makes the sea hard to see through it. After a while I stop at a place called Jindalba where the Daintree Rainforest Environmental Centre is. They have a boardwalk which is halfway up the height of the trees, and a tower that is almost the full height of the trees. So you can take a leisurely walk through the dense rain forest and hopefully see a bit of wildlife. However here I am sorry to say I only saw one bird which was a green dove and far more colourful than the scruffy ones you see in towns. I also saw a couple of very large butterflies, which looked more like birds they were so big. (see photo 416 to 420)

I also visited Thorntons Bay and Cow Bay beach where you can see how the forest goes all the way down to the beach, so you can actually lie on the beach and be shaded by large trees that overhang it. This is supposed to be one of the few places in the World where you can see the forest going right to the sea. At Cape Tribulation there are a few shops and places to stay. (see photo 421) Actually dotted along the whole route are resorts and camping grounds if you want to stay some time in this area.

Anyway after a look round during which time I got a little scare. Walking along a concrete path I came round a sharp corner and nearly trod on a snake. There it was on the path at about 18 inches long. It was obviously more scared than I was as it shot off into the trees. Would have made a good photo had it stayed put. (see photo 422)

It was late in the afternoon and time to head back to Port Douglas where I have decided I will stay overnight, before tackling this inland road to Cooktown. The caravan Park I stopped at I am afraid was another example of the Great Tourist Rip Off phenomena. Nothing to write home about, no better than the one at Cairns which was $15 a night, this one is $27 and at that is at the top of the price range I have paid so far. Usually at this price they are very large and modern and run by big concerns, which this one isn't. Another rip off I am experiencing up here is the price of coffees at $3.50 and even one place at $3.80 these are more expensive than in Sydney, which up to now has been the most expensive for coffees.

I was woken up the next morning by a terrible screeching of birds that I did not recognise. When I got up I saw that this noise was coming from four fowl like birds about the size of a chicken, that were pecking around the grounds. They were dark brown/black in colour and they were obviously in two pairs. All the noise was because they were squabbling amongst themselves. Each pair obviously thought that this park was their territory and kept trying to chase off the other. So I got an early morning side show as these birds were really comical to watch. They ran just like a roadrunner, really fast. They would dash at their quarry and just launch themselves at them, whilst making these screeches and gobbling noises that woke me up. I found out later that they were bush fowl? (see photo 423)

Next day I had to fill up with diesel before I left and again I was ripped off at $1.24 a litre when I know in Cairns it is $1.06 and in the Daintree National Park I saw it for $1.09 and left it thinking Port Douglas should be the same as Cairns. I mentioned it and got a Cock and Bull story.

So whilst P.D is a nice place it is a rip off place because of all the International tourists who stay there are fair game to the Ozzies. (see photo 424, 425 & 426)

The road from PD goes inland through a nice range of hills and then joins up to the inland road to Cooktown. That road, some 234K's of it runs through some interesting landscapes and some not so interesting. There is a big difference in such a short space of time when you come inland, in that you are back to the dry typical Oz bush and even though there are hills and some quite high, they are not covered in lush vegetation. Further up the road you go through a couple of interesting hill ranges which are quite high, but mainly there is nothing to get excited about. (see photo 427)

The road quality is good, but at a place called Lakelands it reverts to the dreaded dirt, but good quality dirt if dirt can ever be good quality. I mean it was reasonably level, hardly any holes or corrugations, but dusty all the same, so more cleaning to be done. Halfway up the stretch, I called into a roadhouse to have a coffee. The coffee wasn't too bad, but another example of rip of prices. Instead of being cheaper than in an expensive town it was dearer at $3.50. OK they do not get as many customers but then their overheads are minimal as they are right out in nowhereland.

The dirt road goes back to tarmac some 30 K's before Cooktown and it must be said that this section is now being tarmacked and is scheduled for completion end 2005, but I would be surprised if they managed that, judging where they were at when I went through. A lot of traffic on it, and I still think that the coast road would have been better to have been tarmacked.

Cooktown is quite small and has an air of frontierism about it. It is possibly the last reasonable sized town before Cape York which is some 1,000K's away. Quite what all the people do there is the question, and there seemed to be a lot of spare bods floating around doing nothing. The pub was quite busy with Abo's and singlet attired white Oz males. The only three decently built buildings in town were an ex Convent (now the James Cook Museum) an ex bank also a museum, and a building called 'The Ferrari' building which somehow I think has nothing to do with the Formula 1 team. I believe it too was a bank.

Quite when people started to live at this spot I could not find out, but there must have been some early settlers in the locality because in 1872 gold was found nearby, and like many a place in Oz the gold rush that then came really kicked off the town and it quickly became the second most populated town after Brisbane. However the gold did not last too long but I could not find out exactly when the gold ran out. When it did the town rapidly declined, but obviously some stayed on.

Just how unimportant it became is I think amply shown by an incident in 1885 the Council sent a wire to the Premier in Brisbane requesting men and arms be sent to the town in case of Russian invasion (they were very sure this would happen in the late 1800's, in Oz) What they were sent was one cannon and three cannon balls, 2 rifles and 1 officer. Quite what they could have done with all that I do not know, but the cannon is on show in a park on the waterfront and is reportedly fired every year on the Queens birthday. How touching!

I took a trip up the large hill called 'The Grassy Hill' and there is a very steep and narrow track to the top. I thought the motorhome wouldn't make it, but it managed. At the top there is a magnificent 360 degree view which was also enjoyed by Capt Cook who went up to spy out all the reefs and to see if he could work out an exit route, when the Endeavour was repaired. So I stood in his footsteps as it were. (see photo 428)

I visited the museum named after him which disappointed me as the only artifacts to do with him on show were a cannon which he ditched overboard when stuck on the reef and an anchor to the boat, which both were recovered a few years ago from the reef at Cape Tribulation area. Also the trunk of a tree which they say he tied the boat to whilst it was beached. I wonder? That was the sum total of what you can see and do at Cooktown. Was it worth the 550K journey, I wondered. But then if you are a Capt Cook junky like me (I thought he was a hero and quite the best sailor the British had for ages) you cannot get much better than to see exactly where he committed one of his best feats of seamanship and good old Yorkshire common sense and grit! Eeh Ba Gum lad! (see photo 429 to 443)

So it was back to the dreaded highway and the dust, but no flies thank God. I appear to have left them back in the NT and the real bush. I headed to a place called Mareeba, just inland from Cairns. I went through there when I drove from Atherton to Cairns. I had noticed a big rain forest place in the high mountain at the back of Cairns, and I want to visit it tomorrow, then go onto see the Mossman Gorge, which I am told is fantastic. The park I book into is mediocre but the price is right at $14 (but only in cash and no receipt... another Oz tax fiddler, I bet!)

The next day I became the typical tourist by visiting all the touristy places and mixing with them all. First stop was to visit the Barron Falls and Gorge which is near to the village of Kurunda. This village is set up just for the tourists with a high street full of tourist shops. A pretty place and there are a lot of Aborigines living in it. (see photo 444) The falls are some 6K's outside it. The River Barron which rises around the Atherton area has cut a deep gorge through granite and a deep falls is part of that process. Not a spectacular falls as falls go as it is only two thin streams of water, but the rock face is quite something as is the depth of the following gorge. (see photo 445 & 446) Towards the last century they built a rail line up the mountain and to take the line as far as Atherton. This was initially to take away the lumber and tin from that area, and down to Cairns and the port. Now it is very much a tourist attraction as the route it takes through the gorge must be spectacular. I did not take the journey but I think if you make this journey it must be worth it, especially if you are a train buff. Although the locomotive is diesel, it would have been better had they had an old steam train.

Another way to get up from Cairns is to take what they call 'The Sky Train' which is a modern cable car system. Again must be spectacular to take, but I did not have the time to do everything.

After the falls I had a coffee in the village and then made my way a little further along the road to Kurunda Rainforest Station. This makes it sounds like some government run thing, but it is just a private rainforest tour but on Army Ducks (amphibious trucks). They also have a wildlife collection, which I did not go round. The duck tour was a little different I suppose, taking some 45 minutes the also acts as a guide and he explains what the different vegetation is, that you pass by. Very similar as the various boardwalks I had taken to date, except the mode of transport. There is a little dam into which the Duck goes and then out again. If it hadn't been for the Duck ride it would be cheaper to take a free boardwalk somewhere. The DUKW's as they were called in the Army are ex World War 11. and still going on their original engines (rebuilt of course). (see photo 447 & 448)

After this it was onto another gorge called the Mossman Gorge, which is outside the small town of Mossman, through which I have already travelled on my way to Daintree and Cooktown. Reached down an extremely narrow road barely wide enough for my home to get down. The Gorge was a let down as although it was a gorge it wasn't terribly deep and spectacular. The river was running through a boulder strewn bed with numerous little waterfalls. Thick and dense rainforest right down to the river. (see photo 449 & 450)

Next on the list was a crocodile farm I had passed on the way up to Mossman, called Hartleys Crocodile Farm, so it was back towards Cairns. Quite expensive at $26 but what the hell. They had fed the crocs at 11am so I would have to make do with a demonstration on how crocs attack people and a general run down on what they are all about. This took place in the amphitheatre which had a pool in it with a resident croc of about 3.8 metres long. The croc keeper spent about half an hour explaining all about crocs and getting it to snap at a dummy bait. Also showing how it will twist a person it has grabbed and take it into the water. Then he feeds it a couple of fish to show how quick those jaws snap shut. Very informative and a first if you have never been up close to any crocodile. (see photo 451 to 456)

They have several pools full of fresh water crocs and sea water crocs. An area with wallabies and cassowary's in and we get to see these being fed, plus a lecture on them. A very dangerous bird the cassowary, who will attack a human and is capable of killing him with its razor sharp claws on those big feet. Luckily they are only found in northern Queensland and even then are very scarce as they are diminishing in number, so are on the endangered list. So it is not likely you would come across one. Thank God for that I thought.

Next thing to check out was the Koalas, lovely things that everybody loves. Three of them sleeping on tree branches in an enclosure, one with a small baby. Nice to look at but totally boring creatures who spend 16 hours a day sleeping, due to the non nutritious diet of gum leaves they eat. They too are becoming scarce due to their habitat being taken over by man.

The whole of the day has been punctuated by rainy weather. Big black rain clouds have been over the mountains all day and as I get close to Cairns on my way back to there, the heavens opened. The whole of the mountains around Cairns had black clouds draping them almost down to ground level. So you can see why those rain forests are there. It rained all evening and I hope that tomorrow it will have stopped, as I want to go up in the Tiger moth plane, if nice. So we will see. This rain is the first real prolonged rain I have had since Melbourne. Up to now it has been short showers, so can't complain too much.

After a night of constant showers and still raining when I got up on Saturday morning, I knew that doing anything that day was out. I checked with the Tourist Info place to see if they knew what the weather forecast was for Sunday but they did not know. So I did not book any reef tour preferring to leave it to Sunday too see how it turned out. I spent all the afternoon thoroughly cleaning the home, five hours of it! It rained on and off all afternoon and evening and even all night. However it had stopped by morning so I went down to the tourist place again, but of course I could not book for the reef as that has to be done the day before. So I booked for Monday. I tried to get a flight on the Moth, but that was all booked out, so that's out as on Tuesday I will push off down the coast. Pity I did not book on Sat for a Sunday sail, as it was nice and sunny all day.

Anyway in the afternoon I went and checked out the Centenary Lakeside lowlands swamp park. Walking past the lake which was choked with weeds I saw a beautiful blue Kingsfisher atop a pole waiting for a passing fish. (see photo 457) Then a little further two small turtles sunning themselves on a half submerged log. The swamp was indeed very swampy and it was amazing the intensity of growth of trees and other vegetation there. A boardwalk wends its way through it all and whilst walking your in another World, yet bang in the middle of a large town. Many immensely thick trunked and tall paperbark trees, various palms and creepers. You then come to another park The Flecker Botanic Gardens. Fairly small in size but a staggering diversity of rain forest trees and vegetation of all sorts are contained within in it. (see photo 458) Whilst walking through I came across a bush Turkey but being a shy creature it quickly disappeared into the undergrowth before I could take a photo of it. Very interesting, and worth a visit if you make it here, and that was my Sunday.

I had a long conversation with the lady who runs the caravan park I am in, about when their busy period is, and it would seem that in Northern Qld it starts to get busy in April as it is cooling off here by then. So I have been lucky pretty well all the way round always missing the rush and the crowds. Apparently what happens in Oz is that in this period a lot of Southern NSW and Victoria people come up here as it's at the coolest, and in the summer hot and wet season up here these Northerners go South to Victoria. So everyone is chasing the 'Cool' and getting out of the 'Hot' or the 'Wet'. Funny old place, but if you do not like crowds you can organise your round Oz trip to miss all of this and be in places when it is less crowded.

I awoke on Monday after more rain during the night and black clouds and the definite possibility of more rain. I just hoped that what I had been told about it not raining on the reef when it rains on land, is true. I take my wet weather gear and scooter to the jetty for an 8am start. They take some time to get organised and it is more like 8.45 before we get out of the harbour. There are enormous rain clouds and it rains on and off on the two hour trip to the reef and the sea is running with up to 2 metre swells. However once we get to the reef the rain has cleared up and some blue sky is showing, and the swell has greatly diminished. So I am looking forward to snorkelling, however due to our boats size which is about 50 foot, have to anchor a little distance off the edge of the reef we are going to swim over. There is still a reasonable stiff wind and so the swell is still about a metre and I have to swim about 50 yards or more to get to the edge of the reef. I put my flippers and mask on and jumped in. I was very surprised at how warm the water was as I had expected that sharp intake of breath as you hit cold water. (see photo 459 & 460)

I start to swim towards the reef and found it quite hard going pushing against the swell and only slowly making progress. It became apparent to me before I got to the reef that I was running out of breath and in the circumstances as I was on my own (other swimmers were around but all over the place). We had been told that should we need assistance, to raise your arm.

Now as I have said before I had suffered a heart attack some three years before almost to the day, and when one has a heart attack, you lose the use of some of you heart muscle. When I was back in the UK I went to the gym 3 to 4 times a week and also did lots of walking and cycling, and this has the effect of building up your remaining heart muscle to compensate. I had always felt very good when exercising and had never felt short of breath. However the effect of motorhoming especially on my own has had the effect of nearly eight months of not enough exercise, and I have put on 8 pounds and my muscles in the heart have not been kept at top condition and also my leg muscles, the same. So anyone who has suffered any health problem should think about what the effect of doing such a journey will have on any exercise regime you have in the UK. I must say that when you stay in any big city you can go to a gym, but I have found Oz gyms too expensive on short term visits. OK if you sign up for six months, or more but on a daily basis just too expensive. Then when you are doing a lot of driving, you are getting no exercise. One way would be to do lots of walking, but I being on my own do not particularly like walking every day on my own. You could also take a push bike with you and use that for exercise. Ultimately it is up to you to work this out, but I tell you of my experiences to show you what can happen if you do not get into a regime of exercise.

I raised my arm and good as gold one of the young crew men who was already standing by in the water with a ring, shot quickly towards me and helped me back to the boat. I got my breath back quite quickly and felt fine, so it was suggested that the diving instructor would take me over to the reef on the ships dinghy and once over the reef he would stay with me and I would use the flotation ring to help with buoyancy and make everything easier. It all worked well and so I had a good half hour going over the reef, and this helped my confidence that all was well. I suffered no more shortness of breath.

We then had a good lunch and shortly after it was time to have another session on the reef. This time I did the same procedure except with the young crew member and we went to another part of the reef. I felt fine and everything went well. We saw all the things that you go on a reef to see, fantastic corals of all sorts of shapes and sizes and colours. All the hundreds of different coloured fishes that you normally only see in peoples fish tanks. Then we saw the 'piece de resistance' as it were. A very large Wrasse fish, which was about three quarters of a metre long and I was told can get to a meter long or more, and is very tall as well, and it has big lips to boot. In fact we went on to see another of these, and a lovely turtle of medium size. So I ended up having a fantastic hours swim with no problems and felt my money was well spent and I had realised my dream to swim on such a reef that has World Heritage classification. Something I should have done when I was much younger and living in Oz.

We had to set off back towards land and we could see that over the land there were all the massive banks of angry looking black clouds which were dumping buckets of rain onto Cairns. We had motored to the reef in the morning but sailed most of the way back, which is why I picked this sailing boat instead of sterile motor boat, which were more packed than this anyway. We had only eight of us plus three crew, so it was more intimate and the crew were very friendly and the food they supplied was excellent. Although I must point out that their full compliment can be up to twenty passengers, but this being slightly off season was responsible for the smaller number.

Tomorrow I head off down the coast towards Townsville were I would like to make it for the evening.

Chapter Fourteen

Cairns to Brisbane

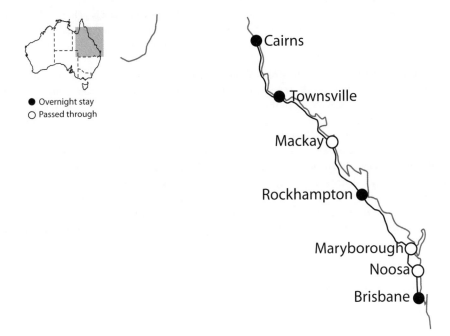

● Overnight stay
○ Passed through

The road south passes through mile after mile of sugar cane fields and the occasional fields of banana plants. The hills and mountains around Cairns continue for most of the way. Then about 30 miles North of Townsville it all suddenly changes. Gone are the cane fields and the lush green vegetation and in comes the standard dry looking bush. 'So are we out of tropics?' I ask myself.

The towns I passed through on the 320 K journey are small and nothing of real interest. Townsville is a large city by Oz standards of about 150,000 population and well spread out. The approaches take you through many industrial areas and finally you are heading down the main road into the city centre area, and past the hill that dominates the centre, called Castle Hill. (see photo 461 & 462)

My memory of my visit from Mt Isa back in 1966, is of this hill, of big weird looking Moreton Bay fig trees and of the large Magnetic Island just off the towns shore. It was here that I had to change trains and get a train to Brisbane. The town lies on the Ross River and is a town that serves the inland pastoral areas and tourism to the reef and has a busy port. (see photo 463 & 464) A town that like so many towns in Oz, it was founded in the late mid 1800's, to be precise in 1860, and primarily built up as a port. Now it is a town built like many Oz towns with all the modern facilities. Down on the beach front it has nice gardens and a modern marina. A ferry runs from the wharf on the river to Magnetic Island, and other boats run out to the reef. There are a few Museums you can spend time in, and a large aquarium which specialises in reef fish and corals. A bit pricy at $21, to get in. I stay at a caravan park on the coast which is OK and quite crowded unlike that at Cairns.

I spend a day buzzing around the place on my scooter, and first I went up Castle Hill What a view! You can reach the top either by a narrow road, but no Motorhomes or caravans allowed as too narrow. Or you can walk up the 'Goat Track' if your feeling fit. It is 300 metres high and the walk will be quite steep in places. You could walk up the road, but that is a longer walk but kinder.

I was going to visit the Aquarium but after I had done my emails and had a coffee and bought the UK papers it was time for lunch. After that I wanted to search for the manufacturer of my home so visited the library and post office and a home hire company. That took all afternoon, so I did not visit anything, not that there is anything of greatness to visit.

The next morning I am off early when disaster strikes. While filling up with fuel I find that my credit card that I am relying on to pay for everything and to get cash, is missing. The last time I used it was when booking into the caravan park and I think I chucked it into the bin with all the paper rubbish they give you when you book in. Luckily I am carrying enough cash to see me through to Brisbane where there is a branch of HSBC, and where I can get some more cash and a replacement card. I rang HSBC's London stolen card number and end up talking to someone in India. She cannot understand English place names especially Ozzie ones, so I am really annoyed. I think that a letter to HSBC telling them what I think of their call centres situated in countries where the staff cannot speak English, English.

On the point of Banks and what system you use on any trip to Oz. The ONLY British Bank with any branches here is HSBC. However they do not have many branches, only in the Capital cities. So much for their slogan that they are the Worlds Bank! When you are in places where they haven't any branches you cannot withdraw your money from your account unless you have a credit or debit card. I did estimate how much cash I would need and transferred it into my HSBC Ozzie account, so I could use what they call EFTPOS and we call a debit card. I also withdrew $700 in cash. However it is impossible to know just how much you are really going to need. In my case after I left Perth I found that I eventually ran out of credit in my account and then the cash went. So I then had to rely on my Mastercard, until this happens. My advice is either open an Oz account when you get here and transfer a large amount into it. Then you've access to an Oz bank throughout Oz. Bring two credit cards with you and keep one hidden in reserve in case you lose one.

After all this kerfuffle, I got going and was on the road out to the South at 8am. I had to change my plans now I had less money to play with. Instead of taking say four days to get to Brisbane I would have to do it in two as I needed to get there by Friday afternoon while they were open in order to order a new card and get some cash. So it was a full days hard driving today to get to Rockhampton, some 640Ks away for an overnight stay.

The road down to there is unremarkable and no remarkable towns en route either. South of Townsville the landscape is either cane growing, cattle country, or bush. Fairly flat all the way and the many mountain or hill ranges that are found from Townsville and to the North, are not found to the South. A few small ranges, but nothing too high. The road quality ranges from very poor for a major Highway to very good. The weather was overcast so that kept the temperature down and later on it rained for most of the afternoon. So by driving I wasn't missing anything anyway. I pull into the outskirts of Rockingham and into the first caravan park at about 6.30.

Of course on the way down I have passed many beach places that people holiday at and at Airlie Beach this is a jumping off place to take Reef trips and sailing trips around the Whit Sunday Islands. Well of course I have already done this so I am not about to repeat the exercises. Other beach places are of no interest to me as one beach is much the same as another, and I have seen enough different beaches now to last me a lifetime. Tomorrow it will be another six hour non stop slog of 600 plus K's, to get into Brizzy (Oz way of saying it) and a lot of what I will pass is in striking distance of there anyway. So I can go back if I want. The forecast is more rain anyway.

An early 6am start and the weather forecasters were right as it rained all day. On this final leg to Brisbane you pass through Gladstone, Maryborough, and Gympie, which are all working towns and all other towns are small towns off the main highway. They are all very small and mainly beachside holiday places. So I can say that on this final leg to Brisbane there is nowhere you would go out of your way to spend time in.

The countryside is much the same as before, a mixture of cattle country and cane country, with a bit of fruit growing. Plus the ever present bush. Mostly flat with occasional low hills and the lands nearer to Brisbane are quite pleasant and green. Approaching the outer fringes of Brisbane what you see is much like any big Oz city, suburb after suburb. You get onto a freeway about 75K's North of the city, so the last leg is quite a quick one. Although I must say I was not impressed by the quality of this motorway. It is a very dangerous piece of road because it has no central barrier, and a deep central ditch and an even deeper ditch to your left. Any accident causing you to swerve would be asking for trouble. Given that Queenslanders are not known to be very careful drivers and certainly they were all going at about 80mph which is faster than the limit of 100K's, you can see the capacity for accidents on this motorway, is high.

I book into a caravan site in the Northern district of Apsley, where there are three of them all in close proximity to each other. The one I picked is on the main Highway and is the closest to the centre of the city, which is about 15K's away. I went into the city centre straight away, to my bank, to sort out my card loss and to get more cash. The cash was no problem but I got nowhere with my card as I had hoped they would be able to expedite a replacement card. They were not interested, telling me to ring the UK again. (So much for the HSBC being the 'World Bank'!) So it will be another call to India I am afraid. Looking forward to that one. Goodness gracious me. I did call India again and this time got an Indian bloke who spoke better English and was told that now having notified them of the loss, I would have to deal with a different department the arrange a replacement. This was a in the UK and they only operated on UK time. They do make it easy for you don't they, these banks that are supposed to be Global. So I had to wait until the evening Ozzy time to do that, only to find that it will take two weeks and by that time I could be in Sydney.

Needless to say, I was not at all impressed by HSBC and after I got back to the UK I closed my account down.

Chapter Fifteen

Brisbane: Sights and History

The third largest city in Oz, which surprised me as I am sure it was nowhere near that big, back in the eighties. Much like all the other capital cities in that it is on a river, near the coast, and is a vast sprawling affair, with a smallish town centre or business centre. Built on the grid pattern with many tall buildings. The last time I was here was in the early eighties and it, like all the others (apart from Sydney, which was light years ahead of the others anyway) has made vast strides to modernise itself. (see photo 465 & 466)

Historically it was started as a settlement at much the same time as Melbourne, Adelaide and Perth and that is to say in 1824. They first settled in Moreton Bay at a place they named Red Cliff. The spot at which they landed had already been visited in 1790 by our busy lad Flinders, who I think must have visited just about everywhere in Oz as his name pops up everywhere I have been. Well this spot they picked turned out a bit like many of the first spots they seem to have picked. That is to say it wasn't suitable due to lack of good water and nasty natives attacking them. So they moved to a more suitable site on the banks of the river at where the centre now lies. Redcliffe (as it is now known) is now a trendy beach suburb.

At first Brisbane was used to transport to, all the difficult prisoners at Sydney. God they must have been bad blokes as if you think about it, the prisoners they sent to Sydney were not the actual cream of British Society. So the ones ending up at Brisbane were the bad of the bad.

The first thing I did was to study the map and the guide book, on what is to be seen in this city. Not a lot I found out. Not many historical sites to visit, probably because they have knocked them all down. I have picked out The Commissariat Stores (1829), The Treasury Building, the Old Windmill (1828 and the oldest surviving building), the Old Government House (1862), and I will see at the city info office if there are any other historical places worth a visit. (see photo 467 & 468)

On the Sunday I took a scooter ride to the nearby beach suburbs of Sandgate, Shorncliffe, Brighton and Scarborough. (see photo 469) I find it funny that in all the capital cities, there are to be found all these suburbs named after English towns. I think on the beach suburbs the only well known English seaside town I haven't come across is Blackpool. They all lie on the Moreton Bay and have reasonable beaches and some marinas. You can see across the bay, the Island of Moreton, which is quite big. Doesn't have any towns on it and is just a big natural park with beaches. You can take a ferry across from Scarborough. Talking about Islands, the whole Eastern coast from the Queensland border northwards has hundreds of Islands of all sizes.

Brisbane is full of houses that can be described as the typical Queensland type house. That is to say a wooden house with a tin roof and built on posts so that it is elevated. The space under is used for car parking, and utility rooms. Some of these spaces are left wide open, and some have been walled or covered in. I personally do not like wooden houses as I think they look distinctly third rate, and you only have to get one that is neglected and they look dreadfully scruffy. I have found that in the country areas they seem to neglect their houses more and so many country towns in Queensland are decidedly scruffy places. In the city, you get some that are well looked after and even tarted up withadditions that make them look quite OK. Others are scruffy and obviously rented out and therefore even more neglected. Having tin roofs doesn't help because they go rusty quite easily and then they look even worse. I always used to think to myself every time I visited Brisbane in the 80's when I lived nearby on the Gold Coast, that if all the people in Brisbane were to go out and bang on their tin roofs at the same time, you would hear the din back in the UK. It still has the same aura about it on the housing front. Although modern outer suburbs with recently built houses, you will find they are all brick now and with tiled roofs. (see photo 470 & 471)

The caravan park I booked into has a lot of bird life with Butcher birds and gaily coloured Lorikeets in gay profusion. The butcher birds are about the same size as starlings and go about in families like starlings. They are very noisy and quite unafraid of humans. The lorikeets are so noisy and go about in very large flocks. They fly around at manic speeds screeching all the time or settle in a tree and will eat whatever it is they eat in these trees, whilst giving forth a barrage of noise. They seem to have a daily routine in this park. Whereas in the Adelaide park where they also had many lorikeets, who stayed in the park all day, this lot seem to disappear for most of the day and reappear about 3 to 4 in the afternoon and only disappear somewhere, when it gets dark. As the park is owned by one of the big park owners, Top Tourist Parks, it is kept in a nice condition so no complaints there. (see photo 472 & 473)

Well as I have said, there is not a lot to see in the city centre from an historical point of view. I visited the few old buildings and was not impressed one bit. The current Parliament House is well made out of some local stone that looks like a pale sandstone, but it is not very imposing and it is in a crap position completely surrounded by high rises and the Queensland University buildings, which are next door to it. You would have thought they would have built it in its own imposing grounds. To look at it you would never think that it was a States place of governance. In fact I wasn't even sure I had the right place, and had to look to see if I could find a sign saying what it was. A little further down the road in amongst the university buildings there is the old government house, which is a small affair, and it was covered in scaffolding obviously being renovated and in true Qld fashion it had a metal roof! (see photo 474)

A building called the Commissariat Stores was built in 1829 by convict labour for government supplies, is now a museum. It is near the river, but is very plain and architecturally simple. So the only other thing in the city centre I wanted to check out was the Old Mill and Observatory, perched on a little hill. I presume it was once a windmill, and now it does not have the sails any longer. On the top of the building there is the small dome of an observatory. Once the hill would have commanded a good view over the city, but now you cannot see very far for a forest of high rises. It is not open to the Public which is strange as it is the oldest surviving building in the city and built in 1828. So for history buffs, a bit of a let down. The city centre is otherwise the same as any other Oz city centre and if your a man, you won't want to traipse around its shops which a repetition of shops anywhere. The upshot is that you can see all of Brisbane centre in one good long day, or maybe two if you are slow.

The only remaining sight I wanted to see was Mt Coot-tha lookout which is on the Ipswich Road about 6 K's out of the city. 284 metres high, which doesn't sound high, but is well high enough to rise well over the city and to give you stunning views of the whole city and well over to the coast, and to the South. So I would rate this the best tourist site to visit and is a must. You can also go up the tower of the Town Hall but this is not so high so you are not going to get as good a view. (see photo 475 & 476)

The street sign posting in the whole of Brisbane is crap, as are the signs informing you where you are going. That applies to the various suburbs or destinations out of the city. The number of times I got to an intersection, couldn't tell where it was as no street names and didn't know which way to turn. Whilst on the subject of Brisbanes roads I must point out that so far it has been the most bike unfriendly city of them all. In the city centre I saw no bike or scooter designated parking bays as in all other cities. These are not subject to a payment system so are free. I could find few nooks and crannies that I found in the other cities, where I could stick the scooter without attracting attention. So no marks out of ten on that one Brisbane! I stayed for only a week in Brisbane due to the smallness of the place and a lack of places to go to see.

Chapter Sixteen

Brisbane to Sydney

● Overnight stay
○ Passed through

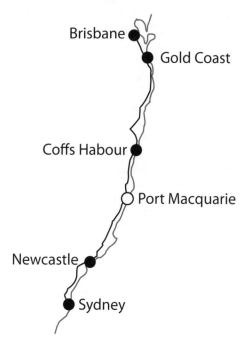

On the way out of Brisbane I hit the morning rush hour as I had to go into the heart of the city to get on the motorway South to the gold Coast, some 80K's away. Once over the river crossing and onto the motorway it was easy going. Quite a good motorway which runs all the way to the Gold Coast and the NSW border.

The Gold Coast area is the most well known holiday area in Oz. Not a Blackpool but more a Florida with mile upon mile of concrete high rises and an extensive man made canal system upon which sit thousands of bungalows with boats at the end of the garden. They all end up connected to the Nerang River which runs from the inland range of hills, to the sea. All this built since the Fifties, so all is fairly new. Then of course you have the world famous beach area of Surfers Paradise which is just a small area on the 35K coastal stretch which runs from Tweed heads on the NSW border and up to Southport just North of Surfers, where the Nerang River exits to the sea and into an inland bay called The Broadwater. They have built about four big theme parks and the whole are abounds with clubs, pubs and restaurants, and that is about it. Great for youngsters and beach bums or oldies who buy one of the expensive high rise flats, so they can sit there all day looking out to sea. I don't even like the sea here as it is always big surf and many a rip to whip you away, that's if a shark or a deadly Portuguese Man O War jelly fish doesn't get you first. You will not get a nice easy leisurely swim here unless you swim in the river or the Broadwater. So whilst it all looks impressive it is not to everyone's taste, including mine. (see photo 477 to 479)

It is some 22 years since I was last on the Gold Coast and it has changed considerably. New roads by the score, more sprawling suburbs where there were fields, even more high rise apartment blocks on the coastal strip. More canals, more everything, and it still resembles a building site with more new high rises going up. More huge shopping malls and centres. I stopped off for two nights so I could take a look at where I used to live and work. I expected the house I rented on a canal to have been knocked down as it was not a very well built house and being on a canal it could be worth more had a decent house replaced it. However I was surprised to find it was still there looking much the same as it did back in 1982. (see photo 480)

Then I took the road West to a small inland town called Nerang. The factory I rented there, was a tip being a corrugated iron effort which on hot summer days was like an oven. I thought that it would be bound to have been replaced with a more modern unit like all the new factories and units I was seeing newly erected all over the Coast area. I was flabbergasted to see it still there, like nothing had changed. Now it has a car wreckers as occupiers, which is maybe all it was fit for. Certainly for boat building it was unsuitable.

The road I used to take from my residence to it used to be a meandering lane through farmers fields, and now you just could not recognise it at all. It is a dual carriageway all the way through endless suburbs of houses, shopping centres, and the like. Similarly the main road between Nerang and Southport on the coast, which is one of the main centres of the coast area, has changed out of all recognition.

One of the first things to hit me about the area is the manic traffic here. It is rush hour all the time, and I am even not here in the busiest summer time, as this is the beginning of Autumn. The drivers here obviously don't have much time for scooter drivers either as I have felt threatened several times by their lack of consideration when passing. All are driving well over the speed limits, too. Many of the original roads are in poor order too, being bumpy and falling apart. So getting around is not proving very nice. You can tell that this place is the hangout of the rich because as soon as you start driving around it, you quickly notice all the posers cars. I have seen more Jags here than in Sydney, plus the BM's and Mercs and all sorts of sports cars. They even have a large Rolls Royce dealers here and an Aston Martin dealer. So there must be some serious money here. A lot of the fancy flats in the skyscrapers must cost a fortune as well, and the marinas are full of large expensive power boats. However it is also the playground of the working classes and apparently very popular with the Japs. Some 30 K's inland there are forests and gorges and mountains, but having had my fill of them I would be giving them a miss, but they are worth going to explore if you wish.

The Caravan site I chose was on the coastal road just out of Surfers, (see photo 481) not fantastic, especially the price of $25 a night, which is in the top end of pricing. I suppose I am paying a premium as it is a prime holiday area. The first night at the park proved to be the first time since starting the journey round Oz that I experienced a noise problem from other people also staying at the park. This park had more static cabins than spaces for overnight stayers in caravans or homes and as this is a holiday town they were full of families and people on holidays. When you get people of a certain type on holiday you can get problems as they lose any sense of responsibility and think that holiday times is one of drink, noise and to hell with anyone else. This is the problem I faced because next to my site there was a cabin with a man in his twenties or thirties who was an obvious yob with a drink and attitude problem. I was woken up at 12.30 am by him yelling down a phone, and then his drunken mates standing around his cabin also talking loudly. I thought that it would not last, but by 1.30 it had not shown any sign of ever stopping. When it had first started I went to the office to see if there was a bell I could ring to attract the owners. There was none, and the receipt for my payment did not have a number on it either. So I had no way to try and ring them to come and sort this problem out. As the spaces for homes and caravans was very small I could not even move away far enough not to be able to hear them and the noise was considerable. So I came to the conclusion that if I was ever going to get any sleep, it was to vacate because after all this could have gone on all night. We all know what drunks are like, and as these people were swearing and behaving this way it was obvious that if I tried to ask them to not make this noise so we could sleep, I stood the chance of getting my head kicked in. So I got the home ready to move and drove to a nearby street and parked there and did get some sleep.

The next morning after I had had my breakfast I went back to the office to explain what had happened and to complain that there was no method I could use to alert them what was happening. I asked for my money back. (I had paid $50 for two days) and I told them under the circumstances I did not feel like staying another night. The man who I presume was the owner refused saying that their policy was not to give refunds. I received no apology and it was even hinted that I was making all this up into a story. Quite why I would want to do this was not explained. I should have been forewarned that I was dealing at this caravan park with robbing shysters, by the events that presented themselves when I was booking in. First by the fact that their charge was $25 for what essentially was a substandard park, and by their asking me if I intended to use the aircon on my home. If I was I had to pay $5 extra per night as they used a lot of electricity I was told. No other park in the whole of Oz had ever tried this on, even in the hot areas where people where using aircon. This is an example of what you can come across with some Aussies who can only be described as SHARKS.

The Gold Coast is full of them and it reminded me of Florida and Los Angeles that are similar types of areas that also attract sharks, shysters and con men. I had experienced many examples of conmen on the Gold Coast when I lived there, so the place hasn't changed much. My advice is if you visit the place and want to stay at a park, don't stay at the Southport Caravan Park, stay only at one of the big name parks, or only pay for one night at a time.

So instead of staying for the second day as I had intended, I decided to leave the area because after all I knew it well having lived there for two years, and I pushed off leaving a trail of fumes. (coming out of my ears, until I calmed down a couple of hours later!) I will report them to the Gold Coast Council who may deal with them, and to the Caravan and Motorhome Club who may warn their members. (You will see that the Motorhome Club were not interested and the Gold Coast Council ignored my email. Make your own conclusions.)

As I drove slowly down the wide highway to Tweed Heads I tried to recognise what I was passing, which in some areas I did, but mostly not. (see photo 482) Tweed too had changed tremendously and I did not recognise it too much either. Another river exits into the ocean here and to get into NSW you head over it across a modern bridge. Whilst doing this I could see some sort of incident had happened on the four lane bridge, and when I got up to it I could see some dozy individual in a beat up old car had driven into the back of a nice new modern car, which was now sitting on his bonnet. Quite how this had happened god knows, as the traffic wasn't very heavy. Oz drivers for you! (see photo 483)

At this point you can take the main highway which goes a little inland or you can take the absolute coastal road (the Tweed Highway), which is what I opted to do. It goes through some very fertile looking land which is heavily farmed and is very nice to look at being gentle rolling hills. All very green and nice. All along the coast they have built and are continuing to build new developments of holiday homes and homes for all the year round living, so it is all quite new looking.

The whole coastal stretch from Sydney to Surfers is one long stretch of bays, inland bays and lakes and river after river that has run off the Great Dividing Range and down to the sea. Many of these rivers and very wide too, so you go across many a big bridge. (see photo 484)

The first town of any size you get to South of Tweed, is Byron Bay. This is an enormously favourite town with many and it is literally heaving with people. Quite why it is so I couldn't make out as it seemed to me to be a fairly ordinary town. Not ugly but a little on the scruffy side. It looked to me as if at some stage in the past they had given it a make over but since then it had been so busy that now it needed a new one and they didn't have the money or time. Still the people like it and it was heaving with people and cars. I had a look around and a coffee and tried to get out and back to the highway. Like so many Oz towns the signs were non existent, so that took a lot of wandering up and down streets before I saw a sign which was facing the wrong way for anyone to see it. (see photo 485 & 486)

The next town I hit was Ballina and whilst here I came across about 15 Cobra replicas who were on a Sunday ride out into the country. Having spent the last 20 years building Cobras I naturally was interested and had a good look at them, before continuing on my way. From a small town called Maclean (No they don't make the toothpaste there, but it is described on a billboard as the Scottish Town of NSW) You follow for miles, a very wide river which leads to the next bigger town you come across, of Grafton, which is a bit inland and is the areas supplier of farming supplies etc. A bit scruffy and industrial looking and the housing decidedly third rate.

Another good few miles on from Grafton, the next town of note was Coffs Harbour, which was a bit scruffy down by the harbour area, but not too bad further away. It was here that I took an overnight stop in a not too bad park which was full of holiday people many with children. It must be pointed out that this weekend was busy everywhere including on the road, with people taking a break, as in NSW it was a school holiday week. (see photo 487 & 488)

The next day I am heading for Port Macquaire and I go through Nambucca Heads, Macksville, then Kempsey where I was struck by the absolute decrepidness of the place. I saw house after house that looked as if the best thing for them was to torch them. Which prompts me to tell you that the Aussies or some of them, do live in the most grotty houses out, which I think I have commented on already. I took some photos of these to show you. (see photo 489, 490 & 491)

Port Macquarie I quite liked, nicely laid out, clean and tidy unlike Coffs and Byron Bay, situated on a river outlet as most of these places are. After a coffee it was back to the wheel and through Taree, Buladelah and towards Newcastle. I decide to take a road to a place called Stockton which is on the opposite bank of the River Hunter, upon which Newcastle sits and where there is a caravan park where I can stay the night and then go into Newcastle the next morning. It was full of weekenders but it was OK. (see photo 492 & 493)

Next day a Monday, I go over a huge new bridge over the Hunter (for wine buffs further up this river is the Hunter Valley where there is a wine growing region.) and into the city. This place is very industrial as this area is a coal mining area and unlike the UK's coal industry, this one is very much still alive as they export much of it to China were they fuel their power stations with it, thus polluting the earth even more. There was a steel works and smelters here and I think that it is in operation. At least there are plenty of plants around that look very industrial. So the city hasn't much beauty to offer or much to really see. So I am not long there before I set off down the coast road rather than following the main highway and motorway. This road leads me through some lovely scenery past the amazing sized inland lake of Lake Macquarie and through little places like Swansea. Charlestown, Budgewoi, Toukley and The Entrance. (being the entrance to the lake from the ocean, and very pretty (see photo 494, 495 & 496) Then onto Gosford and finally I join up with the motorway to North Sydney.

The motorway runs through some pretty spectacular scenery of forest parkland and the Hawkesbury River which if you remember I sailed to when I was back in Sydney last, on that wonderful three masted barque. Past another park, the Kuringai Chase and eventually I reach the boundary of Sydney where a signs tells me I am entering Sydney. So it is here that my journey, my odyssey around this great big land, finishes. I cannot make my mind up if I am glad it's practically over, the driving that is, or I am sad. I still have things to do before I can return to Blighty, like work out if I can sell the home or if it is better I ship it back. However first I have to find the caravan park at Lane Cove. I know pretty well where it is and I find it no problem It is just off the main Northern Highway down to the Sydney Harbour bridge, and is about 10/12 K's away from there.

Here I have to point out that Sydney is the WORST capital City in OZ for caravan parks. ALL the others have plenty of parks and many quite close to the centres. Not Sydney! Lane Cove is the nearest and the only other one is at Botany Bay, which is also some distance from the centre. When I am booking in I nearly fall over when they tell me that a site is $252 a week as it is a high cost time due to these school holidays. Funny though because the camp is hardly heaving at the seams with happy campers. It's just another excuse to rip you off again. I protested at the fact that this place is the most expensive I have encountered ANYWHERE in Oz including major cities. Well it's because it is

Sydney I am told. Thanks a bunch I think. I could stay at a backpackers for less and I was renting my bedsit at Clovelly for only $150 a week. I am told I am lucky as it goes down next week to $200 a week! That is still more than anywhere else, so it sets me thinking.

Chapter Seventeen

Sydney: Second Time Around

This caravan park is run by the Parks and Wildlife Service and is situated in one of their parks called Macquarie Park and is alongside the Lane Cove River, so it has quite a rural feel to it and we are surrounded by trees. No sound of city life at all, except we appear to be slap bang on the flight path to Sydney airport, at least when the wind is blowing from the South, which is most of the time. So one benefit is there is plenty of wildlife in the form OF so far, birds, and on my first morning whilst sitting down and about to start my breakfast, I spied a lovely big Kookaburra fly down off a nearby tree and to the back of my home. So I gingerly went outside and round to the back, and there it was calmly sitting on my scooter rack. It casually looked at me, not bothered a bit. So I went and got my toast and took a piece which I lobbed over its way. It landed just below him and he hopped off the rack and onto the grass to pick it up. I sat on the sloping bank which is at the back of where I am sited and he walked over towards me, so I threw another piece at him to get him interested. He ate that and came closer to me until he was just a few feet away, so I held a piece of toast in my fingers and offered it to him. No problem, he took it off me without a qualm. These birds are amazing, so tame. It never ceases to amaze me just how observant birds are. They are watching you all the time, because by now birds were flying down to me from all over the place, and I soon had four magpies and several butcher birds and I was feeding all of them my toast by hand and they were all taking it unafraid of me. I went back into the home and got a slice of untoasted bread and spent several minutes giving them all a feast, and by now about 8 ducks appeared from nowhere and they were taking the bread out of my hands. Magic, which I doubt I could repeat in the UK as the birds there are nowhere near as tame and unafraid of humans as here in Oz. When I was at the caravan Park at Coffs Harbour, I had a piece of bread which I could not use so went out onto the concrete apron next to my home, and started to break into into small pieces, throwing them onto the concrete. When I started there wasn't a bird to be seen, yet within seconds three Magpies were there gobbling it up. They have such good eyesight they can be sitting in a tree quite some distance away and they see it all. Later on one of the Kookaburras sat on a branch of a small tree near my home and the path to the toilets ran past this tree, so I got my camera to take another good photo, and I was able to get so close, it did not bother the bird at all. (see photo 497 to 500)

One good thing about this Lane Cove Caravan Park is as I've said, its location in a park. You would not think you were in the middle of a large city as trees and wildlife is all around you. Birds abound, and walking through the park following the Lane Cove River banks, you see many ducks and other wild fowl and something I have never seen in Sydney before. Namely a lizard called The Eastern Water Dragon, a rather fearsome looking creature. The first time I saw one I was quite taken aback and surprised as it was totally unexpected. I was walking very close to the banks of the river and the banks were covered in bushes and in front of the bushes on the land was open grassland. There in front of me were two of these creatures, one very large about two feet long and the other was much smaller.

They were both as startled as I was and dashed into the nearby bush, but not right into it, so I could still clearly see them, and I stood there looking at this creature wondering what it was. It wasn't a lizard but more like a miniature Kimono Dragon as it had a frill running along its back and head. It had splashes of colour around its legs and body of black and yellow. We both looked at each other for some time and then I carried on. I kept seeing the creatures, mainly sitting on logs or branches right next to the water. I then came across a sign which amongst other things told me that these were the Eastern Water Dragon. That figured as dragons is what they look like too. The next day I went down to the area where I had seen the biggest of these dragons, and sure enough they were there again, so I got some shots of them. (see photo 502)

I saw plenty Kookaburras too and I guess that this park is home to many of them. Later on back at my home the daily visits at 4pm by the flock of gaily coloured Rainbow Parakeets who are coming to the caravan behind me, because the lady there is putting out feed for them, is under way. She told me that one even hopped into her caravan the other day and almost went right in, they are so tame.

I have had my home advertised for sale on the web and in some motorhome magazines, but it is clear that I am not going to have enough time to sell it before my years visa is up. It is clear to me that selling a motorhome in Oz is a protracted job and not helped by the huge distances between the big cities.

Now my main job is to see if this home of mine will fit into a container so I can take it back to the UK, and I will have to go a shippers in a suburb called Alexandria, to measure one up. If it will fit then I can deliver it to the shippers within a week for shipment and if it will not then I will have to make arrangements for it to be sent on a RoRo ship.

After much measuring and working out what can be done, I was told by the shipping company that it was too tall for a standard container and still too tall for a slightly higher container. That was even if I took off all the aircon and vents that were sitting on the roof. However all was not lost as there was a system called a rack, which was a floor with flexible sides and top and mine would just about fit in that. So that was going to be the way I could send it back at the most economical price. I could send it by Ro Ro but I could not fill it with all my gear, and that would have to go separately, part container. That would cost extra and if it went on this rack, I could keep all my gear inside saving myself that cost.

Well before I sent off my home I wanted to see a few places I hadn't seen during the first time I was in Sydney. That would include the Rocks again to take photos of the old buildings still standing, plus a ferry trip up the Paramatta River to Paramatta itself. Plus a trip to the Blue Mountains which are to the West of Paramatta.

My first trip was to catch a ferry up river to Paramatta. This would give me a different perspective on the river and all its inlets and bays, west of the Sydney Harbour Bridge. This costs $15 for the return trip and that is quite cheap considering it is a 45 minute trip of about 22 kilometres. The scenery all the way to around Homebush Bay, where they built the stadiums and everything else, for the 2002 Sydney Olympics, is simply stunning. However thereafter it gets a bit drab as the river narrows and the land on either side becomes industrial. There are lots of mangrove swamps too, and by the time you reach Paramatta centre the river is only just wide enough for our quite wide catamaran, and just about deep enough, too. We made a tight turn in a space especially made to do this, in order to tie up at the ferry terminal. (see photo 503 to 509)

Paramatta has a few tall buildings but mostly it is fairly original and this town was the first town to be started after Sydney was settled in 1788. That same year they had explored right up to the Paramatta area and had found that the surrounding land was excellent for future farming. As the land around Sydney Cove was poor quality and unsuited for farming, so it was at Paramatta that many settlers came to in order to set up farms which would supply Sydney's needs for food. There are not too many original buildings left, but some of the slightly younger buildings they built from around the 1850's are still to be seen. Like the Town Hall, a small cathedral, barracks which housed the contingent of troops that had to be around to keep order. It was at these barracks that I experienced another example of Aussie nastiness. They are still used by the Aussie Army, although I cannot for the like of me understand exactly for what they can be of any use to a modern Army as they consist of about six small old buildings built in the early 1800's. These are in a relatively small area and considering that they are Australia's oldest surviving Army buildings, you would think that they would be open to the Public, especially overseas visitors. I walked in through a gateway which was open and was walking towards these old buildings, when I was yelled at by some female soldier who came running out of a building which was hidden from view by some bushes. I was brusquely asked what I was up to. I said that I only wanted to photograph these old buildings and I was told they were out of bounds to the Public. I asked if they contained State secrets which thus made them sacred. She was not amused. Funny people some Aussies and considering it was obvious I was a tourist and this was a place of historical interest, what did this girl think I was up to? As there are not too many places of historical interest to see in Paramatta, a two hour trip will suffice for there. (see photo 510 to 513) So it was I got the 2.30 ferry back to Sydney. (see photo 514 & 515)

My other photographic trips were around the Rocks, Sydney centre around the Cove and area of MacQuarie Street and the Sydney Heads at the opening of Port Jackson or Sydney Harbour. Then my last trip was out to the Blue Mountains and here I decided to take a leisurely organised coach trip. However as luck would have it I had to do it on a day that I normally would not have gone on as it was overcast and rainy. However as I had little time left because I was booked on the forthcoming Wednesday to leave Sydney back for Blighty, I had to go.

The Mountains are some 50 miles from Sydney and are not so much what I would call mountains but large hills of some 1,000 metres in height, which run mostly on a North to South line. In the early days they formed an impenetrable wall to settlers wanting to explore lands to the West. They have sheer walls, so present many vistas of photographic opportunities. However this day I went due to the rain there were low clouds that spoiled it for taking photos. We visited a number of viewing points, but some where spoiled by this mist and I was a bit disappointed, however we did descend into one of the many valleys to a spot were there was a nice grassy clearing in the thick tree growth. Called Euroka Clearing, here we were able to get close to a large group of wild Kangaroos, who were now used to gawping camera snapping tourists. I thought it strange that here I was after many, many miles of country and bush driving where I hardly saw any Roos, only a few miles out of Sydney and I was standing amongst a group of wild roos and not ones in a zoo, and this during daylight hours when roos are normally sleeping during the heat of the day. (see photo 516 to 520)

After this we made our way back up to the tableland, as the clearing is down at sea level and back to the Great Western Highway. We drove west to another lookout point called Govetts Leap where we should have been able to get a good view of one of the large valleys of the area. However as there was so much mist, you couldn't see very far. So we headed back along the highway to a hotel where we took lunch. A help yourself job where you could make a pig of yourself. All very good.

Then the next place we went to was Echo Point just outside Katoomba. Here we were able to get a good view of the famous Three Sisters peaks, rocky outcrops on a nearby range of cliffs. Named the three sisters by local aborigines in one of their tales about a Father and his three daughters. Nearby there is the Scenic Railway which is a funicular railway built during the last century to get coal miners down the cliff face so they could get down to the valley floor and tunnel into the high cliff faces to extract the coal that had been found there. Long since closed but made into a tourist attraction, together with a boardwalk around the semi tropical forest that is found around the base of the cliffs in the Jamison Valley. So you can go down on this railway which is reputed to have the steepest incline of any such like railway in the World, walk the boardwalk and come back up on a cable car called the Scenic Skyway. All very worthwhile and informative. (see photo 521 to 527)

At the end of the afternoon and before heading back to Sydney we pulled into one of the main towns of the Blue Mountains, the town of Katoomba which is very scenic with its tree lined streets full of twee shops and cafes. Reminded me of Blighty as it was a right old overcast rainy day as we all scuttle about getting wet. After this the coach drove to the Olympic Park where the recent Olympics were held, and we picked up a quick running catamaran ferry back to Circular Quay. This part of the trip was done just as it got dark, so we were able to see the Opera House and Bridge all lit up. Quite magical.

This whole trip I would rate as a must, preferably done on your own and taken over two or three days, as there is quite a lot to see around the whole Blue Mountains area. Places like the Jenolan Caves to the South, Mount Victoria the highest point, the Zig Zag railway out of Lithgow, and the Bells Line of Road which is the most scenic road in the area. Plus more which I haven't mentioned.

So had I not left it to last and given myself more time I could have seen much more, so don't make the same mistake.

Another area I just had to visit again to get some good photos, was The Rocks area around Sydney Cove. This is a spit of land, a small peninsular which we all will know as the portion of land to which the southern end of The Bridge is attached to. When Sydney was first settled, this area because it is made up of solid rock, made a good place to build the very first solid buildings on. So it is here that you will find scattered amongst the awesome structures of the bridge, which tower above and all around you, many of Australia's oldest stone buildings and business houses. I think it is a pity that over the years many of the original houses and buildings have been torn down and replaced by hideous modern ones. However you can still see a representation of the original buildings that thankfully have been left for us. On a Saturday visit the street market which is very touristy, if you like that sort of thing. Go up to the hill in the Rocks area that has The Sydney Observatory atop of it. Good views here of the bridge and harbour around Sydney Cove.(see photo 528 to 556)

Back at Lane Cove Caravan Park I was having some marvellous experiences with the local wildlife. As I have said many wonderfully coloured parakeets live in this park and about 4 in the afternoon they seem to descend onto the caravan park area. Filling the air with their screeches and swooping around all over the place. You only have to throw a few pieces of bread on the ground and they are onto them in quick order. Then if you sit or stand with pieces of bread in your hands, it won't be long before the cheeky ones are all over you. I had then on both outstretched arms and on my head and shoulders in their attempts to get at the feed. Now remember these are completely wild animals, but so tame and unafraid of humans. Maybe these park birds had got used to humans, but it was a thrill to be mobbed by them.

Similarly with the Kookaburras of the park, because they too would flock in from everywhere when the feeding frenzy started. So I would feed them from my hands with no problem. Mostly they would sit on a low tree branch in a row, and I had up to 12 of them at one time, and I would walk up and down the lines of them feeding them pieces of bread one after another. They would make no noises unlike the screeching parakeets, just sit there patiently waiting their turn for a piece of bread.

If I sat on the ground they would come up to you and patiently stand there waiting to be fed. In fact nearly all the birds that were common in that park would come close to you and take food off you.

Like the crows, sparrows, and magpies.

Another wild animal which is a frequent visitor to the caravans, is the Possum. A marsupial of the night. So when it starts to get dark out they come and when you are walking around at night you often see them. Some are quite tame, and will come to beg for food. The occupants of the caravan behind me, who had small children were fond of feeding one who liked bananas. Delightful creatures, but if you live in Sydney they can get to be a nuisance as they like to take up residence in your roof void. So in the dead of night you can get treated with scampering noises and squeaking, all night. Then it's time to evict them and close up any small holes which they have used to gain access to your roof. (see photo 557 to 563)

Back to the shipping back of the home, saga. Eventually it was worked out that my home would just about fit into the confines of a shipping rack. I would have to take off all the items on the roof and any external protrusions on the sides, front and back. I got a quote of just over $7,000 which made it feasible to have it sent back, due to the lowish price I paid for it. A similar home in the UK would cost me about £20,000. I paid £12,000 plus £3,000 to send it back plus some work done on it, made it a bit cheaper than I would have paid. Plus I knew it by now, condition wise and it is OK. So I booked for it to go on the next ship which meant that I would be leaving Sydney shortly, which suited me as I was running out of things to do to keep me occupied. The only thing left I could do was to set off for a completely new trip inland say down to the Snowies South of Canberra, and that wasn't on as I hadn't enough time left on my visa to do that. So it was a case of my removing the aircon unit sitting on the roof, two air vents and the rear main ventilation hatch. All very easy to do. Plus I removed all the lights on the sides and a grab handle.

I worked out I could drive it to the shippers yard in the South side of the city, on the way to the airport, on the morning I was due to fly out. My flight was not leaving until late afternoon, so that gave me plenty of time to do this and spend some time removing the last things which had to stay on in order to drive, like the side mirrors, and then get a taxi with my suitcase to the airport down the road.

By now the road tax had run out and with it my third party insurance and my MOT. But what the hell! It was just out of the question to get all those with the cost and hassle, and of course I would have to pay about $300 just for the third party insurance and get no refund, just so I could make a three quarter hour journey. So I took a chance and drove to the shippers without tax and insurance and I made it safely and saved myself all that hassle and money.

So it was that on a lovely day I winged my way out of Sydney after a memorable ten months of exploration, seeing sights most would die for, and on my way to Seoul and then onto Drizzly old London town.

Chapter Eighteen

Conclusion

Having done going on 25,000 Kilometres mostly around the perimeter of Australia I can now look back and ask myself 'was it worth it?' 'Did I enjoy it?' and a whole host of other questions that most would want answered. I must say straight out that I am glad I did it, because it was a challenge that had eaten away at me for years. I had spent quiet some time in Oz and hadn't seen many things that the country is famous for. Like Ayres Rock (Uluru) and the Kakadu Park. Another must I had passed before but never seen was of course 'The Reef'. Fancy that, I lived within sight of it and piloted boats to within sight of it and yet I had never been on it. Now I can say 'Been there, done that!' Add it to the long list of places I have been and sights I have seen.

On top of all that whilst such a journey can and is quite mind shatteringly boring, it is only boring in certain places. All down the East coast and along the Southern coast to Adelaide is interesting. The trip across the Nullabour can be said to be very boring because there is nothing much to see. The section from Perth to Darwin is exceedingly boring except for the few places where the boring hours can be said to be worth having suffered. Like Coral Bay and the fantastic Monkey Mia and Shark Bay a World Heritage Site.

The stretch from Darwin to Ayres Rock and then onto the tropics of Queensland is mostly boring except of course for Alice Springs, The Rock, and Mt Isa and then up comes the wonderful greenery of the Atherton Highlands, which makes all those kilometres you did on dusty, corrugated roads or even on blacktop never ending stretches, all worthwhile. So you tend to forget the boring bits and remember the good sights and the glimpses of wildlife and the interesting bits.

Then of course there are the six major Capital cities. With the exception of Darwin which I could have happily missed, they are all exceedingly interesting and it is in those places that you meet the majority of the faces of Australia. For Oz is the most urbanised country on the planet. Sydney is my favourite because I just love that Harbour. I only wish I was rich enough to be able to afford to live on its shores and be able to have a nice yacht to sail on it.

I did fail to see some places that I would have liked to also see. After arriving back in Sydney I would have liked to made a short stopover and then continued inland and down to the Snowies. In fact there is another journey one can make which is a big trip in itself and that is the travel from Melbourne up to the hinterland of Queensland but keeping inland. Meandering around by first exploring the course of the great Murray River and into its source in the Snowies. Then up to the wine growing areas of northern Victoria and southern western NSW. Through the great inland farming outback towns of NSW and on into their equivalents in Queensland.

Lastly other places I have always wanted to visit are the Opal fields of Cooper Peedy and the great mining town of Broken Hill, or a dusty ride along the evocative Birdsville Track. But those are all other dreams that may or may not be realised.

One regret I do have is that I made this trip on my lonesome and in my case I am definitely not a solitary animal, so all the wonderful sights and experiences one has had were not to be shared, except by the readers of this tome. My way of at least a kind of sharing. So I do think that such a trip is much better done in company. For myself I seem to have been destined in life to have seen most of what I have seen of the World without someone with whom to share the wonders, but it is infinitely worth it to see places on your own. So for fellow solitary wanderers don't let the prospect of doing such a momentous trip as this, on your own, put you off actually doing it.

Part 2

Chapter Nineteen

Exporting a Motorhome to the UK

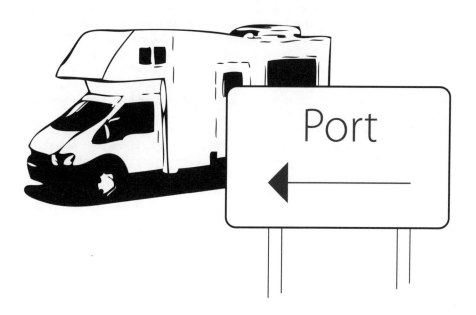

This is a story of the continuing saga of the exportation of my Motorhome from Australia back to the UK. But it could apply to it going to any EU country. Luckily for me having spent many years in the UK manufacturing cars which were exported Worldwide, and having imported some cars into the UK, I had some knowledge about the ins and outs of it all. But even so, I still suffered at the hands of shippers and their agents etc, when it actually arrived in the UK.

It took six weeks to get to the docks at Tilbury. I took on a shipping agent local to me in Poole to handle the importation and Customs clearance. Now this was a company that I had used for years with good service. However when it was owned by the old boy previous owner, no problems. Now it was owned by a much younger chap and quite frankly the service had gone out of the door. I had to keep chasing him. So getting a good agent is a must.

The first rumblings of maybe things were not going to go smoothly, concerned Customs. The rules are, concerning the importation of privately owned vehicles into the UK, is that if you have owned it for at least a year, then it is free of import duties, as long as you don't sell it for a year after importation. This agent was going on about my having to pay customs and I couldn't get him to even contact the Customs at Tilbury to check it out. Depending on what country you are going to import into and how long you have owned the home, is important. This is because you could end up paying more import duties than the whole exercise is worth. On top of this once the container gets off the ship, you will only have 5 days free 'on wharf storage', then you have to start paying at the rate of about £30 a day. So it will quickly start to rack up if everyone doesn't pull their fingers out.

In this case nothing was happening and the fifth day was quickly coming up. So I had to push the agent again and he blames the Customs for not having cleared it through their entry system. I ended up ringing them and asking them where they were with it. The bloke got the case onto his screen and cleared it there and then for me. So it pays to push and not rely on agents who can't be bothered.

The next thing that he fell down on was how it was going to be got out of the rack. Had it been in a normal container, it could have just been driven out. Now the system is that the unloading of containers usually takes place at the recipient's premises, so it is brought to them on a truck. In my case being a private individual, I had nowhere to do this nor did I wish to pay for the trucking down to me when I could easily go to it. It therefore cannot be unloaded on the wharfside and has to be picked up, so I was told, by a specialist unloading company and taken to their yard. More expense.

On top of this they will need to crane it out at the cost of £500, which I know from experience of craning yachts, is extortionate. I rebel, but they have you, because you cannot get it moved off the dock, so as to not have to pay the daily storage charges, unless you give the go ahead for the unloading firm to pick it up. Then they want paying up front for all their charges. So I ended up having to pay a fee of around nearly £900, but I paid my agent by card. Make sure you too pay by card and not cash or cheque.

I drove up to Tilbury with a driver and just trying to find the right company who is handling this, is frustrating. You get pushed around from one company to another and this entails driving backwards and forwards around Tilbury docks. Eventually I get hold of this unloading company and they take me to where the rack is, and it's not in their yard at all, but sitting there on the wharf alongside the ship that brought it to the UK. They have a large forklift and NOT A CRANE, to get it out of the rack. I know forklifts do not cost £500 for half an hour, but there is little I can do as I am dealing with workmen who don't give a stuff. 'Nuffink to do wiv me Mate, yule ave to talk to the office mate'

The home cannot just be driven off this rack as it has upright ends consisting of two pillars at right angles to the floor of the rack. So it has to either be lifted out upwards by crane, or in this case slid out sidewards on this forklift. They slide the long forks under the homes chassis, but they are below the actual chassis rails. So the gap between the two has to be bridged with wooden blocks. This would be no problem but they use stupid small bits of wood, which I thought looked inadequate and so they proved. These workmen like all workmen lacked the necessary between the ears. They had to move the home forwards within the rack, before starting to slide it outwards. They did not go forwards enough before starting to move outwards, AND they were not at right angles to the rack. So the outcome of that was that the home came out on an angle, the back end eventually crunched up against one of the uprights, and it all jammed solid. The forks continued sliding out and the stupid unsatisfactory wood blocks just collapsed as did my home, down onto the forks. Thus landing on its exhaust system. The whole weight of the home lands on these forks and it weighs about 3 Ton. I did not realise what had happened straight away as they moved quickly to reblock it and get it out.

On the drive back to Bournemouth I thought the exhaust sounded a bit loud but not roaringly loud. So it wasn't until I took it to my local garage and up onto their lift could I see what damage it had sustained. The section of exhaust immediately after the exhaust manifold had cracked and the home had also landed on the propshaft and bent that too. So new section of manifold and a complete new prop all at a cost of £600 plus. Of course the agent I used did not want to know, even though it was he who took on the subcontractors, but then I expected that. So as I had paid by card, I went to them and after a month of hassle I got a refund of the cost of the repairs. However I still ended up paying for a crane, when the sly bastards only used a forklift. Had I stayed in the UK I would have taken that up too with the company concerned, but as I was off to Europe to spend Winter in warmer climes, I let it go.

The moral of this story is that bringing back any vehicle especially a large one like a motorhome, is not without its hassle and problems. However I haven't lost out as I should, if I have to sell the home, be able to at least get back what I have paid out on it in total or near enough. Plus I have somewhere to live in, in the meantime.

I would advise that before you ship anything out of Oz get quotes from an agent in your country, first. Get it all sorted and clear before you move. Then there will be no surprises and hopefully no hassles.

Chapter Twenty

Melbourne for the second OZ trip, 2007

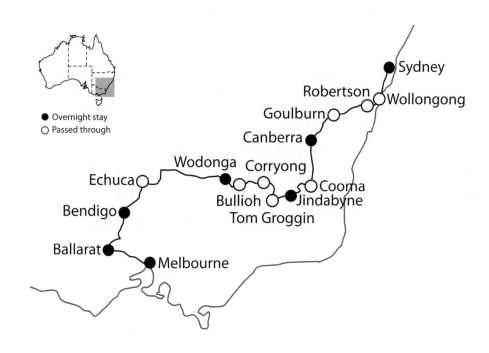

I arrived from Auckland by plane on December 17th after a three hour uneventful trip. After a not too long taxi trip from the airport I arrived at a caravan park in a Western area called Braybrook. I had booked a cabin via the internet when in NZ. The motorhome was due to arrive on the 18th.

From now on I had nothing but difficulties due to the useless politicians and their horrendous bureaucracy. It became one frustrating event after another and where I had thought I would get the home off the docks, all done and dusted in two days, my thoughts were all but dreams. The customs agent I took on to handle the clearance through customs etc, even thought it should get through within two or three days. However we were all dreaming.

I knew that there was a possibility that some drone from the Oz agriculture mob would decide that it needed cleaning. This even though I had had it cleaned on entry to NZ and I had hand cleaned the wheel arches again, and that at the docks on the way out of Auckland it had been inspected by the shippers. They had not said to me that it was dirty and they knew that there had been instances when the Oz people (named AQIS) had refused entry to a vehicle 'because it was too dirty' and had sent it back to NZ. Of course they didn't want this hassle, so I was reasonably sure that it would get passed.

The home arrived on the 18th and was on the dockside on that day and the AQIS inspection took place on that day little more than half a day after unloading, on the 19th. The so called inspector said that because I had camping equipment in my large toolbox at the back, it would have to be all cleaned in the toolbox. The vehicle could not be cleaned on the dockside as no facility to do this was dockside like at Auckland. It had to be taken to a facility to do this off the dock, and it had to be transported on a low loader as it just could not be driven. (I presume my camping equipment would have polluted all of Melbourne's roads had the wheels touched the floor, thus causing a major biological incident of International importance!) However one small point here is that I had no camping equipment at all! I did have a motorbike cover folded up and in that box and this constituted, in the thicko's so called brainbox , as a tent!

So my agent sorted out a towing company to go onto the dock to pick it up on the 20th but when they got there they were refused entry by the company that ran the dockside (called Patricks Stevedores) as this company supposedly did not have the right passes to get onto the dock. In other words they were not a favoured company. So my agent had to find another towing company but by the time he did that it was too late to pick it up on the Friday the 21st and as Monday was the 24th and both the towing company and the cleaning company, not to mention the lazy dockers, were all on a half day. So that meant I had lost the opportunity to be able to get my home so I could live in it over Xmas.

This also meant that for every day I was without it, I had to pay almost double for a cabin. That is to say instead of paying $39 a day for a powered motorhome site, I was having to pay $59 for the cabin.

It was now arranged to pick it up off the dock on Dec 27th and take it to the cleaning company called Pestex, which was some 4 K's from the docks. However I was worried about the security of my belongings on that home. I know that docks are notorious for thieves knocking off whatever they can get hold off. So on Xmas day afternoon I scootered over to the dock gates to see what I could see and also see if I could get in and examine it. I had bought a scooter within a couple of days of arriving to replace the one I had sold in NZ. Needless to say the people on the dock gate refused me entry saying I did not have these passes to get on the docks. This even though I had all the documentation showing it was mine and had been shipped in. I could see the home standing there and very vulnerable to theft off it.

So the first time I got to be able to inspect it was on the Thursday at Pestex, and straight away I went into the toolbox and sure enough where I had packed my Honda generator in the middle of the box, all there was now was a large hole with nothing in it. On a further quick look around I could see that the transformer for my freezer had gone along with the monitor screen for the reverse camera. Either these things had been stolen on the docks or on the boat. As for the cleaning, the bloke there said that another inspection had been done and another inspector had said that the chassis also now had to be cleaned. So it went from being OK on the dock to dirty enough to have to clean it, this over the Xmas period. The toolbox also had to be stripped and washed out even though I had done that in NZ before shipping it.

Quite frankly these Aussie AQIS idiots are a shower of paranoid dickheads who I believe only exist to stuff people around and cause them endless delays and to have to pay huge amounts of money, just to get their vehicle into the country.

The vehicle would be ready for pickup on the Friday but of course I had to pay my agent all the various costs it had been racking up. Like $410 to the docks for 6 days storage over the Xmas time when it could have been off within the first 3 days that are free. Then $450 just to take it 4 K's. The cleaning cost $300 plus and my agent $300. Plus various other sums to Uncle Tom Cobley and all. In fact I think every shyster in Melbourne got his cut off me, and the total I had to pay was a staggering $2,000 (just over), just to get my home into Oz.

Then on top of that, once I did get it to the campsite and could go over it at my leisure, I found a whole list of things had been thieved off it, too many for me to list here, but totalling over $3,000. I guess with the rip off fare I had to pay of $3667 for such a short journey (put this alongside the $5,500 fare from UK to NZ for a much longer journey) and you see why it was a rip off.

Of course all the hassles I have had with this home in NZ and now getting into Oz should warn anyone thinking of doing what I did with their own vehicle, of any sort. Needless to say I am hopping mad over it all and have sent stinging letters to the Tourism Minister in Canberra and the docks company as well as the AQIS mob, both in Melbourne and Canberra, as it is a government department. So I guess I will be spending quite some time engaged in battles with everyone from the shipping company to Ministers. Will I get anywhere? Well don't hold your breath.

Talking about the shipping company, I had gone to them to see if I could claim for the stolen stuff, off them, seeing as it was obvious that it was stolen on their ship. My Marine insurance that I took out in Auckland would only cover the actual home and not any tools etc. The shipping manager said he would do all he could to at least pay the full replacement price of the generator, which was $2300. All the other stuff would have to come out of that. As the selling price of the genny would be only $1,000 to $1500 if I had sold that separately, which is what I had intended to do anyway on reaching Sydney, If I got the full price for it, that would satisfy me. However as the days went on they showed to me that if I actually got that money I would be lucky. Remarks were made that how did they know that I had even had a genny in the home and they wanted an invoice for the replacement. I had to put them right over those things and they didn't like what I said. So I began to get very suspicious as to what their intentions really were. If you ever have to use this company who are called Wilhelmsens, a Norwegian company who run new cars all over the World, be very wary and make sure you get insurance to cover every eventuality as their seamen are unmitigated thieves. Wilhelmsens will tell you that you cannot have anything in the caravan or home whatsoever, but on pressure they relented for me, and said I could keep in tools, bedding and cooking equipment. Which in anycase, you should be able to leave in. So get another shipper if you can, like I did when sending it out to NZ, when I was able to put in side ANYTHING, and nothing got stolen. However from Auckland I did not have any option as few car carriers did that journey across the Tasman.

I ended up spending just about a month holed up in Melbourne, because don't forget that the axle had got much noisier whilst in NZ and I had decided to get it done in Melbourne. However, again because of the Xmas holidays and New Year, I could not even get it started until the 7th Jan and it would take 5 days. This was done at the huge price of $4747 and this included the rear brakes being rebuilt. At least this was cheaper than having it done in the UK and it did get done on time and I was at last able to leave Melbourne and get onto the road on the Saturday of the 12th January 2008.

Whilst I was in Melbourne, at least I had the scooter to get around and I spent time seeing a few places again, and getting reorganised with various things I had to do. (p.564) Like I had to see what the score was over motorhome insurance and get a Medicare pass again so I could go to the Doctors for free. Once again I found that I would be in a quandary as to whether to run it on its NSW plates or its UK plates (which it now had). I found I again could not get even third party insurance off any private insurance company, because it was British registered. Same again under NSW plates because the Rego had obviously run out back in 2005 when I exported it. If you remember in Oz States when you pay your Rego or road tax, it includes the minimum third party personal body injury insurance. Then by chance I found out that if I went to Vic Roads I could pay for this insurance if I ran it on my UK plates, and not the original NSW plates.

I have related previously re the first trip, that in Oz they have this stupid seven countries in one business, each with its own laws on all to do with motors. (and everything else too) So if your NSW rego runs out and you're in another State and on the move, how can you renew it? You cannot post it as you have no address to post it back and you cannot go anywhere in any other State to do it. You would have to go through all the hassle of registering it in the State you were in, and that would mean getting a fresh MOT done, even though the current MOT may have ages left on it to run. Now Vic Roads insurance would only be good on Victoria roads, and as I would be crossing over into NSW at one stage it would mean going into a NSW rego office and going through the whole hassle once again, because believe you me when I went through the procedure in Victoria the woman had no idea and it took ages to complete. So I will keep quiet about it and plead ignorance if any copper asks me in NSW if I have insurance. I will plead that I thought the Vic insurance would cover me and why shouldn't it? Anyway Oz Policemen do not seem bothered whether motorists have insurance as in some States it is not even a State legal requirement to have it, and that is something to think about. For if you are hit by some yob in a beat up old banger, and there are heaps of them on Oz roads, your bound to be faced with someone with no insurance at all, and no money or intentions to pay for his accident.

I had worked out that I wanted to travel inland and into the Victoria goldfields areas for a look round the areas where immense wealth had been generated in the mid 1800's. The road to Ballarat and then onto Bendigo was very uneventful with the usual Oz countryside that I had seen just about everywhere else in Oz. Quite flat and parched looking, so nothing of interest to report on what I saw. Whilst I had been in Melbourne, Victoria had suffered from many days of temperatures of around 40 to 43 degrees. I can tell you that anything over 30 is quite horrible and at 40 all you want to do is relax in an airconditioned room, like my motorhome. So that is what I did on those days.

Both Ballarat and Bendigo were similar kinds of towns, having been both built about the same time as each other. They both had nicely restored and substantial Victorian buildings. However all the rest of these towns were much the same as any Oz town. In Ballarat the main attraction is a place called Sovereign Hill where they have built a replica of what the original gold diggings would have looked like when alluvial gold was found. So on a hill near the Town centre they have built this very good replica of the beginnings of Ballarat as a town. (see photo 565 to 581)

At Bendigo the main attraction is the original town centre gold mine that was called 'The Deborah Goldmine' It was closed in 1954, but was then made into a show mine for tourists. You go down only to the 2nd level (it had 17 levels) and they take you on a tour of the tunnels which lasts for 40 minutes to an hour. They show you how the gold was mined underground from quartz in the ordinary rock. This as opposed to the original finds in creeks (Alluvial). Very good it was too and you need to allow half a day to run round Bendigo and to go down this mine. They do a much longer two hour tour as well and that is on the next level down. Not tours for those with claustrophobia. (see photo 582 to 585)

From Bendigo I motored up to the town of Echuca which sits on the Murray River and this is a nice place to visit to see the mighty and long river itself, with a multitude of various paddle steamers that you can go on for a little trip. Of course this river is OZ's longest river and starts in the Snowies and goes all the way to the coast just east of Adelaide. I had crossed the river on my last trip at a place called Murray Bridge. (see photo 586 to 591)

From Echuca I followed the Murray River Highway east towards the Albury/Wadonga twin towns, also on the Murray, where I booked into a caravan site for the night. The road all the way that day was along dead flat countryside with dry parched fields alongside. It was only when I got to the town of Cobram which is also on the Murray, that you started to see real farming in the form of fruit trees and vines and vegetable growing. All of this irrigated with water from the river, which is run into irrigation channels to feed all this farming activity. (see photo 592 to 594)

Then further east again (all this time I am following the run of the river even though you cannot see it from the road) I came to the town of Yarrawonga, which is on the edge of a man made lake, called Lake Mulwala. Here you can see hundreds of the original trees that were drowned, sticking out of the water, which is quite eerie. However the lake is well used as dozens of boats were on it when I passed. (see photo 595)

Albury is on the NSW of the river and Wadonga is on the South and Victorian side. Both are typical Oz towns which although neat and tidy etc are nothing out of the ordinary. So nothing to report with them, and it would be onto the Snowy mountain areas to the South, the next day. This caravan park was a Big 4 park but although this group is supposed to be one of the better groups, I thought it was like many and not up to scratch and not cheap at $25. It did not even have an internet machine, let alone Wifi. The park at Melbourne was also a big group park and it too had many minuses and the park at Bendigo was a bit of a dump. As I have mentioned many times before, too many parks in Oz and NZ are below standard and it is about time the pygmy brains in the Tourism Office of the Federal

Government, should bring in compulsory standards.

The next morning because I had been unable to keep tabs on my internet bank account the night before, I needed to go to my bank. They don't open until 9.30 and then I had to wait for over half an hour just to get to talk to an operative so I could access my account via the internet and make sure I had enough money in my day to day account. By the time I was all finished it was 10.30 and this meant that I got off to a late start. These are the kind of ramifications you have to put up with when you get campsites that are still in the dark ages.

To the East of Wodonga there is a lake which has been made by damming the Murray River. The road runs alongside it for some distance and by 11am I had got to the town of Tallangatta which in the 50's was right in the valley bottom where now is the new lake. So they moved the whole town further up to where it is now. I had a coffee and got on my way again. I am travelling into a range of low hills and I am travelling due east towards a higher range of hills called The Great Dividing Range which runs North South. In this range of hills are several National Parks of which the most well known one is the Kosciuszko National Park. During the winter this whole range of hills are covered in snow and in fact the area covered is greater than the European Alps. So various areas have ski slopes and little towns that thrive on this activity. I never had time to visit the area when I lived in Sydney, which isn't too far away, and in any case I don't like snow. So I thought I should at least visit it now. (see photo 596 to 598)

Eventually I reach a turn in the road as it begins to head South towards a place called Tom Groggin. Along this section of highway called the Alpine way, the road steadily heads upwards. It is not a fantastic road being narrow and windy and the land on either side is heavily wooded with gums and pine trees. (see photo 600 & 601) It was along this road that I started to notice that the temperature of my engine was easily rising to almost into the red, when I was climbing. This shouldn't have happened as there are to small electric fans that should kick in and obviously weren't. However I kept going because as soon as you went downhill again the temperature went down quickly. But when I got to a particularly steep section I decided I would have to look into it all. I decided to cut the cable running to the fans and take a 12V supply directly off the battery and to the fans. This worked proving that it was the auto cut in switch that was U/S but it meant that the fans would be constantly on. A little later on when I tried to open the bonnet, my run of bad luck continued because when I pulled the lever, the cable pulled out and the bonnet stayed shut. Another job to sort once I'm at a caravan park.

The road when it reaches Tom Groggin turns and runs East to Jindabyne, which sits on the edge of another man made lake, which in turn was part of the great Snowy Mountain hydro scheme of the 50's. (see photo 602 & 603) Once on this last stretch your immediately out of the worst of the hilly roads and the road improves too, by getting wider. Eventually you come to the resort of Thredbo where in the Winter they all come to ski down the slopes. The road that goes past the village is higher up the hillside, so you can look down into the village, and I could see it was quite small and would not be worth the effort to divert into just to look at houses and hotels etc. I took some pictures (see photo 604 & 605) and moved on and I quickly reached Jindabyne and I'm into the first caravan park I find on the lake shore. Here I find that this area could be called the 'Rip off area of NSW' The camp costs me $33 a night which is the most expensive so far, even more expensive than Melbourne, which when I was there was $29 and that was because it was the Xmas/summer holiday period. I wouldn't mind if this was a top 'quality' camp, but this wasn't. My pitch was just another dirty, dusty patch of dirt. I am getting fed up with these dirt patches, because for the money they expect you to pay you should get a pitch that is either concrete or tarmac. The toilets and other facilities were simply not up to scratch. These were just like last nights camp, old and tired and showers etc that are not up to International standards.

Across the road was a shopping centre and there the rip offs continued. A latte coffee at $4.00, way above what I have been paying elsewhere at $3.50, max but usually $2.50 to $3.00. Next I saw an Internet access shop and was horrified at the cost there of $12 an hour, when elsewhere in Melbourne it was $3.00 and even in Bendigo it was half that at $6.00, which I thought outrageous. You would think it was mid Winter and all these businesses thought we were all rich skiing types.

I tried on getting back to the home, to sort out the cable, but could find no way to get to it and it would probably mean having to lift it on a hoist to get up behind the rad and release the bonnet that way.

What with the bonnet cable problem and the fans and now these high prices I am rapidly going off this area. I had planned the next day to take the road up into the Mt Kozziosko (how the Ozzies say it) area, which backtracks where I have come from but slightly more North. I decide that probably it will be just the same landscape that I've already passed and the villages along there (it is a dead end road) will be just like Thredbo which I had past and not bothered with. I decided that I would the next day, just drive into the nearby Main town of Cooma and see if I can get a Ford Dealer to sort the bonnet, as I need to put in some oil.

I had also planned to head North and up to the Hume Highway, cross it and get level with Sydney but well inland. Then turn right to the East and head into Sydney from the West. This plan went into the dustbin too, because I realise that along that inland journey I will be passing boring landscapes of no tourist value and the same for the towns along the way, and what for. It would be hot and lengthy with no rewards but money spent for nowt. So my plan now as for me to head into Canberra, which is North of Cooma, and there I will try and catch up with someone in the Tourism Ministry. For there I want to try on register my disgust at what I have had to spend getting the home into Oz. I had put all that into a letter to the Minister and another letter to the head of AQIS. So far neither had even acknowledged receipt, so I feel it is time for a frontal confrontation. So while I am in the area I may as well take the chance with both hands and call in there.

Whilst the lake was OK it certainly was no Lake Windamere and the surrounding hills were no great shakes either. (p.606) I reckon with a good covering of snow to hide them, they probably would look much better. The trouble with a lot of hills in Oz is that they are drab as the trees (gums) are not a bright green and these hills were entirely covered with them, so no grass could be seen. Even there had been, it would be dry looking and yellow. So all round I am not impressed with this area, considering its notoriety as being a great place.

The next day I drove to nearby Cooma intending to see if they had a Ford dealer so they could look at opening the bonnet. It turned out to be a small place and I did not see any Ford dealers on the main road in or out, so I just kept going. The home had not suffered from overheating on the 60odd K's to Cooma so I thought I would chance the next 115K's to get to Canberra. The landscape to Cooma and then onwards all the way to Canberra was flattish and slightly undulating land, with low hills either side.

For what is a really quite smallish city, population wise that is, Canberra certainly spreads itself out. You begin to get into the suburbs some way off the city centre. As I had visited Canberra before, when I lived in Sydney, I was not seeing anything new. (p.607) Quite why they had decided to build a purely administrative city, inland and far from any large population, beats me. It has little going for itself as a tourist destination. I wanted to find a Ford dealer and a caravan site so I called into the main Information Centre which is on the main through the city. I then called on the cities Ford dealer and their response to my problem was abysmal. They did not deal with emergencies by the way the guy I spoke to reacted. They could see me only 10 days ahead, even though I said I was only passing through. He told me to try a garage across the road, which I did and they were a heap better in their attitude, telling me to come back at 1330 and as it was almost lunchtime this suited me. So I went back to the Lake Burley Griffen area and into a lakeside car park, to have lunch. (p.608(On driving back to the garage the heavens opened, but I was expecting it as the weather forecast on TV, the night before had forecast it, and they were right. Anyway the mechanic had it opened within 10 minutes and did not even charge me. The moral of this story is that Ford dealers are rubbish, and occasionally you get an Aussies who is a diamond!!

I then went some way up the main road out of town to a caravan park situated in Canberras show ground. This only cost $20 which is more like it and when I think about Jindabynes caravan park at $33, this place is as good with a bit more grass and less dirt. After setting up I got the scooter off and went back to the Info place to find out the address of the Tourism Ministry and there I went. I wanted to see if they had got my letter as they had not acknowledged receiving it. I got to speak with a secretary of the Minister who assured me she would check to see if it had been received and would ring me back in half an hour. Guess what….no phone call! That is governments for you, and their minions are just as bad. The lady at the info place told me as much telling me she had worked for the government and I should not expect any satisfaction. Well I knew that already, but I have to try. I resolved to call back the following morning and get her name and ask why no call?

I did get through to the Ministers Department at 9 am the next morning, and the woman I spoke to said straight away that they had got my letter. I did not make a fuss over why they hadn't rung me. As is usual with civil servants it was a pass the buck exercise. Of course even though my complaints had to do with Tourism, none of it was to do with this department. They make me mad. I was told that my comments were passed onto the relevant departments. Well I will not hold my breath and plan to approach several newspapers. (which I did to absolutely no response)

The manager of the stevedoring company who refused to allow my tow company onto the dock to pick up my home which resulted in 6 days of parking fees, is playing silly buggers with me and although I have asked him to email me any questions which he says he wants to ask me. However I know his game he just wants me to ring him at my expense and then there will be no evidence as to what was said. So I await what will happen if anything. Next stage is to contact their head office in Sydney.

I set off from Canberra on the freeway to Sydney and after some K's I am going past a massive flat area off to my right and this is bounded by hills all round. It is called Lake George, but it is completely dry. (see photo 609) Further on I reach the first town of Gouldburn and I call in there to get some food and have a coffee. They boast that it is the oldest inland town in Oz, and I guess it could be as it was founded in 1833 and was founded on sheep farming. It doesn't warrant me stopping for any time though and on I went.

The weather was overcast so it kept cool which was good for the motor and no probs on overheating. After Gouldburn I turn right and head towards Wollongong along the Ilawarrra Highway as I decided not to continue up the main Hume Highway and into Sydney from Liverpool in the West, but to get to the coast and follow that through to Sutherlandshire which is just South of the campsite at Ramsgate on Botany Bay. Once I get to Wollongong I am on familiar ground having once lived in Sutherlandshire.

I was glad I took this road as very soon I began to pass by much nicer countryside than I had seen so far. Very quickly the land became much greener than I had seen since leaving Melbourne, so much so that I could have been driving through English countryside. They call this land area, 'Highlands' (see photo 610) and I guess this is so because a few K's inland from the coast, there is a dramatic escarpment which rises some 1500 metres and I was driving along land sitting on this escarpment. There are only a couple of towns along here Moss Vale and Robertson after which you will reach to edge of this escarpment and the road dives down the side. A somewhat dramatic road with many twists and turns and very sharp corners. In fact the corners are so sharp that I had passed a notice saying the road was not suitable for caravans or other towed vehicles. However I was following a truck with a trailer and he went round the bends. To the sides of this plunging road were many tall trees and ferns, to the extent that it all looked quite like tropical rain forest. At the bottom you emerge out of these thick trees into flat grassy plains. From here you are quickly at the coast and heading North towards Wollongong.

North of Wollongong you have to climb up the Bulli Pass to get back onto another escarpment and to follow the Princess Highway into Sutherlandshire. Before long I am approaching the campsite on Botany Bay and by now the weather is breaking into light rain. Although I had passed this campsite hundreds of times I did not know what it was like. I was not that impressed on driving in as it seemed very cramped but I did not fancy driving on to North Sydney to the camp at Lane Cove. When I was told how much it cost per night I was very surprised at the highest cost to date of $40 per night. I mentioned it and was told that it was due to the very high taxes they had to pay to the NSW government which were on top of Council taxes. I was going to stay a week, but opted instead for four nights instead. Then I would go to Lane Cove. It didn't take me long to regret that decision because when I got there about 3pm it was empty but for two vehicles, but during the rest of the afternoon and early evening it filled up. As there were only sites for about 15 vehicles and each site was extremely small, it became evident that one would not get any privacy and indeed it was quite noisy especially as right behind me were three silly English girls who never stopped with their loud talking, and by 23.45, I'd had enough and had to do my policing act or not be able to get to sleep.

Chapter Twenty One

Sydney for the second time, 2008

Indeed this camp is not worth stopping at as their facilities are very sad and old and the men's was even quite dirty. There was no kitchen and in the laundry there was a kitchen sink with a hot tap, but no hot water or even any water at all coming out of it. Internet access cost $12 an hour which is nothing more than a rip off and higher than anywhere else. So it looks like Sydney prices have rocketed since 2004/5 when I paid $25 a night at Lane Cove and $3 an hour for internet.

So anyone planning to stay in Sydney for any length of time, and let us face it Sydney has the most to see out of all the big cities of Oz and you need a minimum of a week here, is going to have to plan to spend a lot of money on staying in a caravan camp. On top of this as they are some distance from the city itself, you will have to spend more money and time travelling into the city centre to get to all the attractions. Maybe it may pay to hire a small car to get around.

During the night it rained but when I got up it had stopped and I went to the nearby shopping mall at Miranda. I spied an internet place and low and behold it was only $3, so I spent an hour there. It spat drops of rain all morning but after lunch when I wanted to run over to Coogee Beach area to check on how much it would cost me to rent rooms etc, it started to tip down and never stopped all afternoon. I didn't have much luck seeing anything so will have to try again on another, dry day.

Back to the campsite and I see there are many more birds to be seen here compared with other places I've stayed at so far. Many small parakeets and a number of larger (and more noisy) Cockatoos (Cockies in localese) Plus crows who are exceedingly noisy with their raucous and tuneless screeching, and warbling Maggies. In Melbourne you did see the bright parakeets but they never would stop in the trees around the campsite but just flew overhead at a fast rate of knots. Here, like at Lane Cove they are seemingly tamer. (see photo 611 to 614) The weather forecast is rain for a week, wonderful and not what I want. We are getting the edges of the tropical storms that have been lashing all of Queensland and dumping much needed water and resulting in much flooding.

It rained heavily all Friday evening and all Saturday so it was a case of sitting in the home all day reading and catching up with things. In fact during the weeks that I was at Lane Cove the weather was very dodgy and we had many days of almost constant rain which made life a bore, as venturing out on the scooter was right out due to the intensity of it. I saw some more of the wildlife at Lane Cove and took more photos. (see photo 615 to 623)

During those weeks I was getting nowhere with all the problems I encountered at Melbourne with the importing of my Home. The stevedoring company refused to answer my complaint and the company that owned them didn't answer my letter at all. So I approached the Victorian government entity that owned the docks. They did reply but tried to wriggle out of any responsibility over the way a company they allowed to operate the docks. However I did get an answer off the boss of the guy I had made the complaint to.

My letter to the Tourism Minister eventually after three weeks got an acknowledgement that they received it, but after four weeks still no answering my points and complaints over the cost to bring in a vehicle which is extremely high and time consuming and did they not feel this would create an extremely bad reaction from intending tourists who would go on to spend a lot of cash in Oz?

The Agriculture department AQIS were no better, but eventually I got a reply off one of their minions that was a typical governmental whitewash, so I wrote back again to reiterate all the questions that I had posed and were unanswered.

The shipping company to whom I had made a claim to for the value of three of the most valuable items also took a month to say they would only offer half of the claim, which I did not accept. So I put in a fresh claim for the full amount of the 28 items stolen plus costs. So we will see what they now do. They will I am sure, ignore me.

However one good outcome so far has been that even though my Insurance company from NZ looked initially as if their small print would mean I was not able to claim for these three main items, I decided on studying the wording carefully that they did not really apply. So I wrote in a claim and after much arguing a toing and fro-ing, they eventually agreed to pay out. However they wanted to apply a $1,000 excess as I had not had a condition inspection done prior to shipping it. This was because I had trouble to find an insurance company and the home had gone onto the docks.

However I argued that the condition report only covered the body condition and did not cover equipment inside the home. I asked them to send me a copy of their condition report which they did, and after seeing it, it was exactly as I thought, totally to do with body condition. It therefore had nothing to do with the double excess they had imposed on me. I wrote back telling them this but they stubbornly stuck to it. So now the whole affair is with the NZ Insurance Ombudsman. No doubt he will have it for months and will find for the Insurance company.

What all this trouble tells one, is that Antipodean males are so macho that they will never admit they were wrong or apologise for crap service etc. The fact that you are a Pommie as they call us, is also I feel against us. So they will automatically want to tell you to get stuffed as you are no more than a whinging Pom. Of course you can never prove it. But the proof is that I have had no luck so far in getting the shipping company to pay me for all the stuff stolen. The Tourism Minister doesn't want to know about the problems entering the country. The Victoria minister for docks doesn't want to know either. The biggest bill of course was the one for cleaning the home and all that that entailed in costs. (over $2000) So far I have had no luck with anyone to whom I have complained to on this matter. The local AQIS manager doesn't reply, and the Canberra CEO of AQIS replied with a total whitewash letter. The trouble with the Insurance company is one I, to be fair, could encounter in any country as all insurance companies are bastards.

The only progress so far is that the local dock manager eventually agreed to pay me the $600 I claimed, and this I know is only because he has been pressured by others higher up that I have complained to. This of course is only a fraction of what I have lost so far. The theft claim is over £3000 and the AQIS cost is £2,000. I should eventually get most if not all the theft value.

I will in my summing up of this second combined NZ/OZ trip, cover this question of taking a vehicle to those countries and if it is really worth it in view of all the problems I have encountered.

Another problem besetting me is the awful weather, as we are having a summer that is definitely not a normal OZ summer. It has rained heavily every day for a week now and it is a real pain. They even forecast all next week it will also rain every day. The only thing that my problems of getting justice over the home, could be said to be a positive thing, is that all the emailing and letter writing gives me something to do whilst being detained at home because of all the rain.

I spent from about the end of Feb living in Coogee. When I decided it was time to move from Lane Cove, I got the Saturday Sydney Morning Herald as that was the only day you got a load of flats etc for rent, in it. Unlike the UK there are not many agents specialising in rented accommodation. Some Estate agents handle them, but strangely it is not as big a part of their business as with UK real estate agents. Plus you do not get any newsagents shops that allow cards in the windows selling stuff and renting out flats etc. So finding a place is quite hard work.

Another thing while I was there was the fact that like the UK, their housing market was going off the rails. People losing their houses and so many people looking for rented accommodation. It was no joke as for even a small one bed flat, hordes of people were wanting to rent it. So you turn up at an address to look at it, along with 50 others. So I started to look at adverts for sharing a flat, and eventually found one in Coogee but the guy was a Macedonian, and whilst he seemed OK, my experience with Slav types had never been good. I had to take it as I wanted to get away from Lane Cove which whilst nice, was too far in the northern suburbs.

Well the bedsit room was VERY sparsely furnished. A bed, a fitted wardrobe with some cupboards which were so high you needed a ladder. A desk type table, no TV, and only an office type swivel chair. Share the kitchen, which was very sparsely fitted out. No microwave, so I had to take the one out of my motorhome. The Slav guy was quite unfriendly and untalkative and when he did talk it was all crap. He was into Scientology and I guess that says it all. His head was just full of shit. He told me once that the Queen had a monopoly on the Worlds gold and that was a conspiracy to control the Worlds economy. He said she could monetarily break the USA, anytime she wanted.

However the most annoying thing I found with him was he was one of those most excruciating of people who are compulsive door bangers. He just could not close a door without banging it.

So it eventually after about a month, it came to a head when I politely asked him if he could not slam the door to his bedroom, which was always in and out like a YoYo during the evenings. It was right opposite my room. Well being a macho Slav he just could not take some upstart renter, having the cheek to ask him to do this AND IT WAS HIS GODDAM HOME ANYWAY!! The fact I paid him quite a high rent seemed to pass over his head. So I got my marching orders . I cannot say I was upset and at least I had a month to get somewhere civilised.

On the other side of Coogee there was quite a big 'Backpackers' hostel who said that they would put me on their waiting list and that I should be able to get in within my time scale, OK. I did indeed get a room and so I moved there at the end of my month. Rent was a reasonable $150 a week. The room has an ensuite and I share a large communal kitchen.

At this point I feel I should write about how one can get about the big cities of Oz in order to see all you wish, this when you do not have wheels. Sydney is the best endowed city with Public transport.

It has a tube like train service which covers quite a lot of Sydney, although not as much as Londons does. The bus service is comprehensive and good. The main roads are very good as a lot are dual carriageways and now there are a number of motorways to. Melbourne also has a rail network but not as comprehensive as Sydney's, but it does also have a tram service in addition. A good bus service is also in service.

Perth has virtually no rail or trams, but there is a good bus service, so it is mainly down to cars.

Brisbane is much the same and Adelaide is also similar, but does have one short tram line from the city centre to the beach suburb of Glenelg.

Hence why the car reigns in most places much like in the States.

Chapter Twenty Two

Selling the motorhome

I live at this place for about three months until May 2008 when I was at last ready to return to the UK. I had of course got to get rid of the motorhome before I could return, as there was no way I would be taking it back to Blighty again. The flat I shared with the mad Slav was on a busy main road, so I stuff a large 'For Sale' notice in the windows and it was surprising how many people rang me up, but they were all dreaming tyre kickers and time wasters. Similarly the same was the case at the Backpackers place. So I began to get worried about getting shot of it.

I had put it online in a number of free motorhome and caravan sales sites. They did elicit responses but again tyre kickers and many interstate who would not travel. A few did look at it yet even though I was asking a very reasonable $35,000 for it, and it did have many extras that you would never get on Aussie homes, like the big back box, a huge stainless steel roof rack, and a completely new kitchen set up with new cooker and fridge etc.

I found that although when I was looking to buy a home in 2004, there was then a number of caravan and motorhome dealers dotted around Sydney, now there were none… ALL GONE!

The nearest dealer I could come across was some 150 K's north on the fringes of Newcastle. Actually he emailed me from one of my adverts, and the salesman I talked to seemed OK. I told him that I was not going to be ripped off by a dealer and I outlined my auto experience to him to show they were not dealing with some ignoramus on vehicles. He assured me that it would be worth me driving up there with it to show them.

I did do this one day and when I got there I then had to deal with the owner of the business, an older archetypical Aussie male of the type I have met many times in the past. He looked at it and then launched into the typical car salesman waffle routine of how it was a load of shit and wasn't worth much. Even though I reiterated the fact that I was ex auto etc etc and I knew what it was worth, and that it was loaded and in A1 condition etc, his attitude just made me mad and I virtually told him he could piss off especially as his salesman had just wasted a day of my time and petrol.

I was not a happy bunny on the long drive back to Coogee.

I then thought that maybe a motorhome hire mob would be interested, so I looked up who they all where and started to visit them all. One bunch were a group of young English lads at Maroubra which is near Coogee, but they were no better and wasted my time. Then I visited all the hirers around the city area of Kings Cross. This area has a number of backpackers places and so is frequented by young European kids doing gap years and the like. Most of the hirers here hire out the cheaper camper vans, but some did have a few larger motorhomes and as most of the vehicles they hired out were not the new or near new homes, as the larger hiring companies hire out, my older home would not put them off.

Anyway I came across a company on William Street, that was owned by a Swiss bloke, so my having lived there got me into talking about things and about sports cars. He then said that his Father in law had just retired and was looking to buy a home and he would see if he was interested. I gave him a sheet of paper with all the specifications on it and emailed him some photos, and he came down to the Hostel one day. I took him for along drive in it and we ended up in Bondi Junction area where the son in law met us, and now the haggling started. I had asked for a price of $30,000 which was well under what homes were being advertised for, of the same age and size. The son was on my side as he knew that I was offering it at the right price, but the old guy only offered me $22,000 which was ridiculous. I stuck out and eventually we arrived at a sale price of $29,000.

For this I had to throw in my getting the equivalent of the MOT done on it. He would have to pay for the 'Rego' and any fully comp insurance, if he wanted that. So now I was to experience another example of the Aussie nightmare of governmental bureaucracy and garage rip off merchants and sheer incompetence all round by all. But all that I have been telling you about this motorhome and its history, about the purchase, repairs to and the selling of etc, is all of extreme importance to anyone intending to have any involvement with any type of vehicle in the antipodes. (see photo 624)

I had now to make enquiries about how I was going to get this pink slip (MOT) and I found out quite quickly that being a motorhome it was classed as a small truck, and that only a garage that handled trucks could do the inspection. I then found that the nearest place to Coogee that could do this was in an industrial area not far from the airport, called Mascot. Here there was a Hyundia truck dealer that had a truck repair garage. I went there to make an appointment and when the foreman saw I had a scooter rack attached he said that such racks were illegal but he would turn a blind eye that it was on. A date was fixed in about a weeks time.

I took it down and waited around whilst a young mechanic did the inspection in much the same way as a normal UK MOT test. He found a few minor things wrong which I knew I could do myself, but one thing would need a specialist to fix, but I cannot for the like of me remember what it was. However nearby there was a specialist company that dealt with replacing whatever it was. I went around and booked it in. However it again was a part that was not routinely stocked in Sydney, but only at Melbourne and it would take same days to get it up. This insane business in Oz of not being able to get all parts for all cars in the main towns of Sydney, Melbourne, Perth, Adelaide, and Brisbane, is a real pain in the butt. No matter what city you are in it is always only to be found in stock at another city a thousand miles or more, away. I was anxious to get things done as any delay in having it all tested and ready to hand over to the buyer, ran me the risk of him changing his mind.

When I had this job all done at the cost of a few hundred dollars I went back to the MOT garage for the retest. The other thing it failed on was the fact that in Oz the engine must be squeaky clean with no oil to be seen on the outside of the engine which could indicate an oil leak. I said to the mechanic that I had never seen a vehicle engine that did not have evidence of oil somewhere on the block as you can spill oil down the side when topping it up with oil. Plus what had this to do with the safety aspect of a vehicle. No answer was given, but I was told that what people did prior to getting the inspection was a steam clean of the engine. I looked everywhere to find someone who could do this and found few companies except out on the outskirts of Sydney, that had steam cleaning. I went back to this mechanic who then told me that they could do it there. Quiet why he did not say that in the first place I do not know.

So the engine was cleaned and the retest done, but when he went to see his foreman to get him to issue the pink slip (test certificate) the foreman suddenly announced that he had made some checks and that my size of vehicle was too small for them to test. Now isn't that just an example of how thick some Aussie companies are? Here we have a large group who sell new trucks and do MOT's and they do not know their own rules. He said I would have to use a garage that did trucks and cars and that he knew of a place that would do it, only it was about 20 miles out west towards Liverpool. He would ring them and make an appointment, which he did, for a couple of days hence. More wasted time. Of course I was keeping this buyer up to date with progress, or should I say lack of progress.

I drove out to this place and on arrival the tester comes to the Motorhome and straight away asks me to show him the manufacturers compliance certificate. Apparently when a vehicle is made up that consists of an original vehicle that is modified like a motorhome is, the manufacturer supplies a certificate that certifies it has been approved etc etc. I pointed out to him that the vehicle had already been on the roads since 1975 with several owners, had been tested endlessly since and that I was never given any such certificate nor could I get one as the manufacturer was in NZ. He wasn't interested, no cert no test. Why hadn't the last garage wanted this certificate was my immediate thought. I was livid at being pissed around by incompetents wasting my time, none of whom seemed to know the law on testing motorhomes.

I went to the government office in Bondi Junction where you get road tax and licences etc and demanded to see their manager to get what the law was on motorhomes. Even they did not know and had to ring some head office in Newcastle and speak to someone. It turned out that I could get it MOT'd at any normal garage that did cars. So I had wasted over a week pissing around with a bunch of tossers at two garages when all the time I could have gone down the road all the time. Now I just had to find a garage who had a lift higher enough (a high enough roof to allow my high vehicle to be lifted up so a bloke could get under to inspect it all for the second time) At least the first truck dealer did not charge me for the first aborted inspection. Luckily for me I found one in Bondi Junction itself, and the owner told me 'No Problems mate' I booked it in for this test to be done a couple of days hence and presented early one morning on the said day, hoping that this saga would now come to an end. It should have been ready late afternoon.

Of course nothing to do with garages and bureaucracy in Oz ever goes to plan, so it was when I went at the appointed time to pick it up. Of course whenever an Aussie tells you 'no problems mate' that really means there is bound to be problems, and so it was as it was not finished when I went to pick it up! He had tested everything he needed to WITHOUT putting it on a hydraulic lift! However he said he needed to check that the engine number corresponded to the engine number on the registration document (I was now showing my NSW plates) and had given him my NSW rego document. This is more of your Oz bureaucracy nonsense as what has the engine in the vehicle got to do with a safety check? It could be a replacement engine… then what? In that case I suppose you would be locked up for jiggery pokery of some imagined thought! Trouble was he said, that on a Transit the engine number is halfway up the side of the block on the manifold side and could only be seen from underneath, hence he would have to get it up the lift, and he had another car on the lift that he was halfway finished doing a job on it. It would be finished some time the following morning and then he would do mine.

More delay and more having to ring up the buyer with yet more excuses which I felt could put him off. We had made arrangements for the day after I should have got it back, for him to get the train down from Newcastle to come and pick it up. So now I had to ask to delay it more and we arranged now to wait until I did get it in my hands with the slip before ringing back to arrange another day. It was getting me down and I was really wondering if I would ever get shot of the blasted thing in this mad house of a country of idiots and bureaucratic nightmares, and all this just to sell a vehicle and get a bloody MOT. Which in the UK you do in a day with none of this nonsense.

Anyway with extreme trepidation I went the next day and thank God it was all done and ready. Huge sigh of relief and a quick telephone call to the buyer, who I must say was very good about all this, but then I guess he must be used to being fucked around over such matters. We arranged for him to come down the next day, he would visit a branch of his bank in Bondi to get a bakers draft made out, then go to a insurance shop also in Bondi to get his insurance on it, and finally to the Road Transport Offices to get the vehicle transferred into his name and a set of new rego plates as I had lost the one plate up in Queensland as you may remember.

The next day all this was done and thankfully without any further problems and I was hugely relieved to see him and his wife drive off into the sunset with my motorhome that had been my home for three years now and I cannot say I shed bucket loads of tears about this, either. Just a huge sigh of relief because now I was free to fly back to the UK.

One final story for you about vehicles and Oz garages who mostly seem to be villains and this I believe could be due to the fact that it seems that in Oz there is little protection for consumers, so they no doubt know they can get away with it. It has to do with the Melbourne garage who did my back axle rebuild. Now this was a Ford Dealers no less, and I deliberately went to a dealers as in the UK by using a dealer instead of a back street garage, as it should afford you some protection against shoddy workmanship and being ripped off.

I told the dealer that my axle was now whining a lot and that it needed to be rebuilt. I was given a rough price for the job and told that they could not be specific as it was down to what was the condition of the diff when thy opened it out. Fair enough. They had another dealer on the other side of Melbourne that specialised in rebuilding axles and it would go over there. Knowing what garages can be like I asked for all the parts they replaced to be kept and put in a box for me to check out.

The job was done, the price was higher than I expected partly because the whole of the back brakes needed also rebuilding. Fair enough. I paid and picked the home up when it was finished, along with the box or replaced inner parts of the diff and all the brake bits. I departed Melbourne in a cloud of dust, glad to get on the road after about a month of trials what with the importation saga, and now this repair job.

When I had time to inspect the diff parts I could see that the most expensive parts namely the crown wheel and pinion, was still in very good condition and certainly did not need to be replaced. Their cost was in the region of £800, so not cheap. Now the facility that did the rebuild, and which I called upon to inspect, had all the facilities to rebuild diffs. So it was not a case of 'we only supply whole replacement units so you pay top dollar and get a unit that has had all the internal parts renewed irrespective of the condition of your diff' because they could just replace the absolute necessary parts and with the C/W & Pinion part they could leave the original in and save me some money. As I was going to sell the vehicle why waste money?

So I resolved to try and sort this out with the dealer as I felt I had been ripped off. They had my telephone number and on splitting open the diff, could have rung me to ask what I wanted re the CW&P. To cut a long story short I got nowhere. So I sent an email to the customer services at the Ford Factory in Melbourne. Here it is the Head Office of Ford Australia and could deal with my complaint about the dealer. Short story is that first off they ignored my letters until I wrote to their CEO, then I got nowhere. They told me they had no jurisdiction over their dealers, which I know to be a lie, as I have worked in the past for Ford dealers.

So it is yet another story for you to ponder on and to be aware with all things automotive in Australia. Please forgive me for telling you all about the various sagas I have had with his vehicle, buying it, getting various repairs done, trying to sell it, all the shipping horrors to the UK, then from NZ to Melbourne and so on. But it is all to show you what a pain it has all been and IT COULD HAPPEN TO YOU. Or at least some of it could happen to you, and certainly the whole question of vehicles of any sort that you may want to take to Oz, or buy there and move around, has to be researched thoroughly beforehand and carefully weighed up. For things in Oz to do with vehicles are not at all as easy and straight forward as in the UK. Of course if you only buy a cheap banger you will not be bothered, expect maybe if it goes wrong and your then in the clutches of some Aussie garage shyster. To compare, I had no problems at all with getting the home UK registered, road taxed, MOT'd, and insured and there are ways to deal with shyster garages, in the UK.

PASSING THE TIME AWAY UNTIL DEPARTURE.

During the four months I was in Sydney after arriving from Melbourne, I kept myself amused by going on plenty of coastal walks, trips around Sydney on my scooter, having a more in depth look at some of the history of Sydney by reading up on it, shopping, going to the gym each day and so on. Saw the new Cunard ship Victoria that came in to Sydney Cove (see photo 624 to 631)

Then in April my lovely daughter came out for two weeks, for a holiday, as she had old school friends who were working in Sydney and living up the road from me at Bondi Beach. A favourite haunt of young Brits working and living in Sydney. I took her out on various trips during the day when her friends were working, and we took one trip up the Blue Mountains, for me a second trip. So we had some pleasant time wasting together. (see photo 632 to 642) I took some more iconic pictures of Sydney to add to others already on file. (see photo 644 to 647)

My Backpacker hostel was proving not too bad, the only blip there was the obnoxious Yanky bumpkin living in the room next to me, who had the usual loud voice that most Yob Yanks have. Also he was another one of these infuriating people who cannot got through a door without slamming it shut. My asking him to desist from that was met with the usual belligerent bolshy attitude that so many Yanks have, although he did not do it as often after our talk.

I was quite reluctant to have to come back to the UK and if I were rich enough I would prefer to live in Sydney but now the Aussie government has only eyes for Asians in its efforts to integrate with Asia. So if you have slanty eyes you are, in but if you are Anglo Saxon, we will only allow you in if your young and have work experience that we want, or if your famous and rich. All the rest can bugger off, especially if you are old like me, for you may fall sick at some time, and we cannot have that. We may have to spend some money on you. No matter that thousands of Aussies go to the UK each year and have FREE NHS service whenever needed. So much has changed since the Sixties and before.

So it was in early May I flew back to Blighty and its problems, but that is yet another different story on its own, worthy of another book!!

Part 3

Chapter Twenty Three

New Zealand trip.
North Island – Arrival, Auckland 2007.

After arriving back in the UK in May 2005, from my trip round Oz, together with my motor home, it wasn't long before the travel bug juices starting to work on me again.

So by August I decided to explore Portugal, a country I had never been to, and to then go onto Spain and see if that place was good enough to retire permanently to. It wasn't and so I was back in the UK by the end of February 2006.

I bought a motor-sailer but summer wasn't up to much so I didn't get much use out of it. However it did give me a purpose to life during the winter months as I spent hundreds of hours doing it up in anticipation of a better summer ahead. We had a marvellous April which was more like mid summer, but thereafter it went back to the usual dismal wet and cloudy English summer and my boat purchase was looking like a waste of money.

So it was no surprise that all this got me thinking of Antipodean climes, and why was I still in the UK? I made the decision to go and visit New Zealand for an extended tour, in the same way I had explored Oz. I started to make enquiries about the costs of airline tickets etc. But quickly found out that since my flight to Oz in 2004 the UK government had found yet another way to stitch up the travelling public by slapping on all sorts of taxes onto ticket prices. So as a consequence the ticket was going to cost me another 50%, whilst doing absolutely nothing for global warming. Such is progress!

My motorhome which was in temporary storage as I wasn't using it had proved impossible to sell in the UK. This was due to the huge number of homes on the market for sale and my reluctance to give it away. So I started looking at how much it would cost to ship to NZ. I researched values of motorhomes in NZ, on the net, and saw that homes identical to mine were selling for much higher figures than those in the UK. I quickly found that it would only cost £3,000 to ship it on a RoRo ship (Roll on Roll off ferry) and that included insurance. It wasn't hard to come to the conclusion that it made sense to ship it and avoid having to give it away in the UK and then have to buy a replacement in NZ at an inflated price.

I now needed to find out about any problems I may have getting it into NZ and here is where one starts to get into hair tearing territory. I don't know about you, but I find whenever you end up having to deal with governments and their civil servants, your going to end up getting high blood pressure. All governments are the same and I quickly found that NZ was no better than the UK or OZ. Their website simply didn't deal with any of my questions re taking your own vehicle or to how long you could stay for.

Re the length of time a Brit could stay for, I did find out quickly that normally you get a six month stay without having to get visa. Trying to find out how to be able to stay for a longer period was another matter and I never did get that question answered. So I decided that I would deal with that one when I was there. I needed to know if I would have to pay customs as all the info only dealt with someone taking in a vehicle, as an immigrant. It seemed no one in the NZ authorities had thought that anyone would want to take a vehicle there as a tourist. After many emails to various NZ government departments including London, I was getting nowhere fast. If you send say five questions to a civil servant you are lucky to get replies to three of them and even then they may still not actually answer all the questions properly and fully. A visit to their High Commission in London proved to be a total waste of time as they only dealt with immigration and I was told to email customs or their department dealing with transport. The upshot of all this was that I never got all my questions answered, but I did find that even though I was ostensibly only bringing in a vehicle which I would then depart with on leaving, I would still have to pay a customs duty AND, get this, I would ALSO have to pay VAT (they call it GST; Goods and Services Tax) Not only this, they would charge GST on the shipping cost AND the cost of insurance. So charges that you pay to someone outside their country which have nothing to do with the value of the import, you end up having to pay a tax on. The Kiwis are very adept at gross robbery!! I would get all this back if and when I left their country. So they said! So if you have designs to sell your vehicle in NZ you have to work out if it is going to be worth it money wise.

I booked the home on a ship leaving Portsmouth in mid August and arriving at the end of September. I reckoned that if I arrived at the beginning of September that would give me a few weeks to get settled in find my way about Auckland and get a scooter sorted. So I booked a ticket on Malaysia Airlines with a four hour stopover in Kuala Lumpur.

After spending a boring month waiting for the flight date to arrive, (the weather during July and August was so rainy that I couldn't get out for walks etc and I had managed to sell the boat) the appointed day arrived. The flight was

due to take off from Heathrow at 10pm which I felt was too late on. This, because I will have spent a whole day before take off, amusing myself and I would then have to try and sleep straight away, which I always find difficult on a plane. Heathrow was the usual bedlam and I had to spend quite some time queuing to get through check in. I was worried that they may not let me take on as hand baggage, my laptop. This because the bag it is in was slightly over the dimensions they said it would be allowed for had baggage. As it was they did not even look at it or weigh it and I could see other passengers on that flight had HUGE bags and suitcases, well over the hand baggage required size. So it shows you that some airlines are not keeping to their own stated rules on weights and measurements. I had to buy a dinner which was as usual, a rip off as they have you at airports, by the short and curlies. Still I was on the go at last and looking forward to another bout of TRAVELLING.

My seat was right at the back and only two wide and the seat next to me was empty, I did manage a fitful, on off kind of sleep. So when we got to K/L I wasn't too bad and I was lucky that the flight on to NZ was half empty. I moved to an empty row right at the back of the aircraft, and although the ridges between the seats were uncomfortable, I did again get a fitful doze for about five hours. This helped to break up the length of the 12 hour flight. At last we sighted the coast line of the North Isle and like they say it was certainly looking like a land of the 'Long white cloud' as most of it was covered in long rolls of white cloud. We came into line with the runway and swooped in over the entrance to Manakau Harbour. This large body of a natural harbour was bereft of moored boats, but it looked very shallow, and that would explain that.

I was somewhat apprehensive about how the processing through immigration would go, as what info I could get from London was again incomplete and difficult to get. I was eventually able to find out that on arrival I would have to show a return ticket AND show a flight out of NZ to OZ because my return was from Melbourne and not from NZ. This because I wanted to return to OZ and do a trip from Melbourne to Sydney along the inland route and through the Snowy Mountains, and this meant me booking a flight online. So it was to my annoyance that I wasn't even asked to show any return tickets or even that I had enough money to cover my trip or where I was going to stay in Auckland. I had also booked for a week at a B&B in the Mount Eden area, precisely because I was certain I would have to show a NZ address. They just looked at my passport and waved me through! Similarly it was the same with customs. I was disappointed, as I thought they may want to know about the wildlife and food and insects I had in my bags, that I wanted to sneak into Kiwiland. So they are more laid back than the Aussies and you do not even need a visa, which is nice.

A taxi ride took me into Mt Eden and the B&B, and it was about mid day when I got there. After dropping off my bags into my quite large room, I walked down the road to the nearby shopping centre to get some grub for lunch. Frau Deutscher was quite pleasant enough and had been living in NZ since the eighties. The room was on the large size with an en suite, but no heating apart from a small electric space heater that patently wasn't man enough to heat a room of that size. But this is Germans for you, they are hard as nails and used to Arctic Winters. When the evening came I found it a bit chilly so took to staying in the communal lounge instead.

I had booked for a week which was unwise due to the cost of $85 per night, which quickly adds up. The first night was OK as I fought to get my body clock into Kiwi time. But the second night I was plagued by a rotten dog next door that spent all night barking its' head off. So things in NZ aren't much different on that score to the UK, over dogs. I complained the next morning and expressed surprised that they should have this problem being as their guests would be seriously crapped off by such happenings. Unfortunately the Frau woman who was looking after the place for the owner was a timid creature who acted as if I had accused her of a heinous crime. It took me some time to get her to understand that all she had to do was pass on my complaint to the owner so they could have serious words with the dog owner. (who turned out to be Chinese which surprised me as I thought they had a more sensible attitude to dogs and ate them!)

My first job was to get mobile and find wheels so for the first few days it was all about getting a scooter sorted. I quickly found that to be able to find a second-hand scooter of more than 50cc was going to be impossible as not many scooters were advertised let alone the bigger ones. I was told that scooter and bike ownership in NZ is not very high. I would think that due to the high percentage of rubbish car drivers has something to do with this. It was the same in Oz. So I had to look at new ones. I wanted to get a 200cc or 250cc job but found that these were too expensive and in the end had to plump for a 150cc PGO which is made in Taiwan. I knew that it should be OK quality wise as the 50cc one I had in Oz was also PGO and that was fine. So I ordered one but would have to wait until the coming Monday before it would be ready and taxed etc for the road.

The weekend I spent walking into Auckland city centre so I could get some exercise and see something of the place on the way. It was about five miles and after two days of doing that my right foot starting playing up. Quite why remains a mystery as I had been doing just as long walks in the UK when it wasn't raining with no probs. Roll on the scooter.

I quickly found that Auckland centre hasn't much to offer a sightseer. It is quiet small in area and has no sites of real historical interest. So that leaves a city that is much like any other apart from the waterfront which is quite pretty. The Maritime Museum was interesting enough especially the Maori canoe exhibits and how the Polynesians spread out over the Pacific.

One thing that was immediately noticeable about Auckland was the huge number of Asians that were in evidence, just about everywhere. Since my last visit in 66 it has become a virtual Chinese outpost and some areas of the city all the shops have only Chinese descriptions written on the shop fronts, so you don't have a clue what they sell. You may as well be in China. It will be interesting to see what the situation is throughout NZ.

I did all the jobs I had to attend to in the first week, like visit the ASB Bank Head Office to facilitate to movement of my funds from the UK to NZ. One good thing is that the interest rate in NZ is way above the UK. I was lucky to get 3 or 4% in the UK, but in NZ the top rate for a year's investment is 8.4% and 7% on an ordinary savings account. That will help out a bit on the money front. I also had to get a jumper of sorts as it was proving really parky without one, especially once I got on a scooter. Being the land of sheep, you would think that they would be cheap here. Not on your life, they were incredible, price wise. On a Saturday and Sunday, they had a market in front of the Town Hall and I found one there for the equivalent of about £30, and even though it wasn't exactly what I wanted, it would have to do. I also needed a new waterproof boating jacket and deck shoes. I got these at about UK prices in a ships chandlers down on the yacht/marina area.

So now I was all togged out for the scooter and for handling this wet and parky weather I was experiencing in Auckland. It was like UK weather which I wanted to get away from.

I had a look at two of the North Shore caravan parks as the week at the B&B was fast approaching its end. One at a place called Northcote seemed OK and it had cabins at $47 night which was a saving per night of $41, and over 7 days that's a saving. What a mistake. It turned out to be a grotty hole with broken equipment in the communal parts like the kitchen and men's toilets. My mattress which was made of foam, was of such poor quality that the foam would compress to almost nothing when I lay on it. I had to take the mattress off the spare bed and double it up.

However the worst thing about the place was the noise. The cabins area I was staying in was used in much the same way as a motel and some of the people staying in them were to lowest of the low with large numbers of out of control kids. Also the place was being used by the local hoody gang, as a meeting place with their noisy loud exhaust cars. In and out all day long with those rasping exhausts, blasting away. When I brought it up to the staff they were obviously too scared to put a stop to it. After one night of being woken up four times throughout the night by screaming kids and inconsiderate yobs, I'd had enough. I went down the road to nearby Takapuna and booked into their site, which if nothing else was slap bang on the beach. A bit more expensive, but hopefully no yobs.

Well it was better in some ways but it still left something to be desired. I was finding out that caravan parks, at least in Auckland, have their fair share of yobs staying in them. Certainly staying in the cabins, which I suppose attract them, instead of staying in more expensive hotels. The amount of noise they make is nobodies business and it starts at 7am sharp. I was unfortunate that for the two weeks that I spent in these two parks, it was half term, so families were in abundance along with their manic out of control kids. Not much different than Brit kids, I thought!

I spent the two weeks up to the end of September, when the weather permitted; driving around looking at might be worth seeing. The suburbs are like any other you find, so there wasn't anything out of the ordinary. The coast around Auckland is very broken up with many inlets and bays and offshore Islands, so following shore lines enabled you to see some nice sights. Off the shore of Takapuna lies the volcano made island of Rangitoto with its prominent cone mountain. It is not lived on and only Waiheke and Great Barrier Islands, have people living on them. (see photo 648 to 653)

There are many good shopping centres and malls dotted around greater Auckland, with large up to date

Supermarkets. There are about six supermarket chains and Foodland seemed to be the largest and offered the largest selection of food lines. I found that I was spending a bit more on a weekly bill than I would in the UK. However not having my home yet meant that I was not cooking the type of meals I normally would and I think this was costing me more. Once I get back to my normal meals maybe the bills will come down? The caravan sites do have kitchens but no oven facilities and this precludes some cheaper meals, plus I did not have my pots and pans etc.

I must say that the roads of Auckland are pretty good quality compared to the rubbish in the UK. The surface quality was generally excellent with virtually none of the checker board quilt like surfaces to be found all over the UK. By this I mean, one hardly saw evidence of the millions of badly filled holes that we have to suffer in the UK. Nearly all roads are free of this and beautifully smooth to ride on. Also virtually no dirt in gutters or loads of litter, which is the hallmark of every British town and city. Vandalism of Public property seems to be non existent. I did see just a little graffiti on a footbridge over a railway line, but that was it. What will the rest of NZ be like in this department?

One thing that does annoy me driving around is the number of traffic lights and the slowness of their operation. As the towns and cities are built on grid patterns there are loads of junctions and all have lights. I think that this is because the drivers cannot be trusted to have a junction where one road has precedence. They operate on a system where every flow has a sequence, so you get two sequences each way. That is to say traffic will turn right first, followed by straight through. Then the other road gets the same, and that makes four sequences plus one sequence when pedestrians can cross all ways. Thus making a total of five sequences, every time. So one has to wait through all these to get to your turn and this makes for very slow progress, as lights are very frequent on any one route.

The general quality of driving seems to be on a par with Oz. They suffer the same lack of quality that the Aussies do and that is to say, they are sloppy and inattentive. Too many macho young males in hot noisy cars, going too fast and doing tyre burn outs, just like in Oz. So driving has to be done with much concentration and care.

I was astounded to learn in the press that Kiwi kids can get a licence at 15 and there was press coverage going on as to whether this should be raised, due to the number of accidents. Are they crazy? They should be putting it up to 18 and restricting what power of cars they can drive under the age of 25. Not only this, but I found that you do not even need to have insurance! More craziness. OK for me as I am saving a bundle, but if I get hit by some uninsured driver, I know I will be in for grief.

I also noted that many drivers are driving and using mobile phones whilst doing so. Another recipe for disaster. Then there are the high numbers of Asian and Polynesian and South Sea Islander drivers, and this means a higher risk of accidents as both of these peoples do not have a good records as being top drivers. I remember this fact only too well when trying to teach driving to Asians back in the 60's in Sydney and Perth. So I would say that driving in Kiwiland is going to be a similar experience to driving in Oz. We will see.

In the short time I have thus far been in NZ, there have been quite a number of shootings, stabbings and murders. So just like the UK! Whether it is a more violent society than in the UK remains to be seen, but the Maoris seem to have a preponderance to violence, maybe that is what makes them such good rugby players?

So far even though I haven't been far out of Auckland, it seems as if the countryside is much greener than in Oz, but then I thought this would be the case before I got here. They get more rain here than in Oz, and I see from the news that Oz is still suffering the draught it was when I was there in 2004/2005.

The cost of property in Auckland seems to be lower than the UK. For NZ$300,000 you will get quiet a large house on a large plot, whereas in the UK you will be hard put to get a 2 bedroom bungalow or flat for that. (On the South coast that is) However I am sure wages here are lower.

Eating out costs are a bit down on the UK, and there are no shortages of good places to eat in. Many Chinese, Thai and Indonesian restaurants are to be found and all the Malls have cheap eating areas or takeaways. Loads of coffee shops everywhere you go and a Latte costs $3.50 to $4.00 which is also down on the UK.

On the news side of things, TV news and what's in the papers is very parochial. World News comes last if at all. Each evening's main TV news on the State TV1 station, starts and goes on for at least an hour, with just local news. If you are lucky you will get a short mention of some World news. For instance, the Burmese problems with demonstrations by the monks, was in full swing and never got mentioned for days. Iraq or Afghanistan hardly mentioned. Also there are no general programmes dealing with World news and newsworthy items, like Newsnight etc. So there are no intellectually stimulating programmes that discuss the state of the World or even of NZ itself. However there is a surfeit of Sports programmes and discussion on the news to do with sport. Mainly rugby which they seem besotted with. Maybe this tells you a lot about the psyche of Kiwi men, I'll leave that to you. (I've always thought Rugby to be an excuse for legalised violence) Also, even on the TVNZ channel which is their BBC, they have adverts, and boy do they go on for ever. Really makes a meal of the evening news which runs from 6 to 7pm. Without all the adverts it would only last 30 to 40 minutes.

My boat got in on the 29th September with my motorhome on it. Back in the UK I had taken on a company near the Auckland airport, to cover the Customs clearance. I had a feeling in my water that somewhere I was going to get problems over this importation and sure enough things started off with a big question mark over how they would proceed.

On the Friday it landed, I rang the agents to see what amount of money I would have to pay out. I had already worked out what it should roughly be, for Duty and VAT, going on what I had found out off the info sheet London had sent me. I should have been given a depreciation of 70% on the $30,000 I paid in Oz and duty to be paid on that. Pus VAT on that figure, and the shipping and insurance cost. The figure I was given was some $3,000 more than my figure, so I'm wondered where it was all going to go. I went down on the Saturday to the dock area and could see it sitting there already. So it had got to NZ but in what shape, and had anything been stolen from it. I was on tenterhooks and couldn't wait to see it and check it out. I know from experience that sailors are thieves and even before it got onto the ship at Portsmouth there was time for things to go, not to mention it sitting there on the dock at Auckland for a few days.

On the Sunday it was rubbish weather and it rained in the afternoon. So it was a long and boring wait for Monday to come round and so be able to go and sort things and get it into my hands. For once it is in my possession I can then get on with organising to start this adventure and get out of Auckland and head South.

I did go on the Saturday to the Domain Museum, which is near the dock area. The Domain being a large park in the central area of Auckland. Much like the Domain in Sydney only smaller. An imposing and large building which reminded me a little of Liverpool's St Georges Hall. Only $5 to get in. It was quite interesting especially the Maori exhibits of intricate carvings and houses and a food storage house, also heavily carved. A huge 15 metre war canoe made in 1830 which held 100 men. A heavy representation of all the wars New Zealand had been involved in, from the Boar War. I was especially taken with the Spitfire and Zero fighter aircraft shown, which were both in very good condition.

Especially interesting was the hall on volcanoes, seeing as New Zealand has them in large numbers. They have a room which runs a large screen, which shows you what would happen if a large eruption took place in the Auckland harbour. You are looking out over the harbour and an eruption starts on the volcano Island of Rangitoto. There is a heavy rumbling sound first and then a huge bang and the whole house shudders when the eruption starts. It surprised everyone no end and from then it was watching how this shower of clouds, steam and dust, grew and grew, until the pyroclastic cloud expanded and was rushing towards the Auckland city shoreline. When it does reach it, there is another shudder of the floor and the screen goes blank and a sudden deathly silence… your DEAD! It showed you in no uncertain way just how hopeless it would be for everyone. No chance to get out of the way. Hope if it does happen… I'm somewhere else!

On the subject of natural forces, this brings to my mind the weather in NZ. I positively hate rain and I thought I'd seen enough of it before I left the UK. I know it is Spring here, but the amount of rain I have seen since arriving is no joke. As I sit here writing this in the caravan at Takapuna Holiday Park, it is bucketing it down in sheets and windy as hell, and has done so since just after lunch. It comes with a thunder and lightning show as well and you just cannot do anything. In the evenings it can be quite cold, much colder than I thought it would be.

Today being Monday I rang the shipping agents first thing about the Customs figure and thankfully was told that I was right about the quoted figure being too high. Quite frankly the bloke I spoke to didn't know anymore than I did about the rules etc. So now the figure is down to where it should be, that is about $4,000. What now remains is whether the Ministry of Agriculture and Fisheries require the home to be washed off so that I don't bring in any aliens from the UK (or outer space) I was told by the agents to contact MAF as they needed the home opening. I had left it locked up except for the driving cab. They wanted to see inside as well.

So in darkening skies I set off on my scooter straight after my lunch, over the bridge and onto the quay at

Auckland central. I went into the MAF offices and spoke to a girl who like many civil servants, didn't appear to know much about anything. Eventually it was ascertained that over the weekend it has been inspected and decided that it not only needed to be cleaned outside, but fumigated inside. I was told that this was so because of foot and mouth in the UK. So thanks to UK government incompetence I'm being messed around, kept waiting and will end up having to pay through the nose for massive clean ups. Not to mention that this will hold me up, and every day I'm held up, I have to pay more for the caravan I'm in over the cost of staying in my home, instead.

However the agent should have organised all this and I now know that they are simply were not up to scratch on organising these clean ups or anything else.

I had to meet the guy from good old Rentokil, who would do the fumigating and give him the keys, and just as I was leaving the dock... down came the rain. On the journey back over the bridge to the Northside and the park, I could feel that my brand new waterproof jacket (made by Gill in the UK) wasn't waterproof. I could feel water getting in at the front around my belly button. I tell you my bad luck is constant. I'm firmly convinced that a hex has been put on me by someone, early on in my life. I think it was that white witch woman I slagged off back in 1975, in Folkestone. But that's another story folks!

When I got back I was soaking and had to do a complete change, but worst of all, now I am going to have to have a go at the chandlers I bought the jacket off. Got to get it sorted because I have read that rain in the South Island is pretty awful, and if I'm scootering around or even walking, I need to keep dry.

So more boring days waiting for things to be done and if the weather keeps rotten, it's even more boring. To think that over in Oz they are crying out for rain right now. The Kiwis should trap all this excess water and make some money piping it over to Oz. Could be done as they pipe gas all over the place including under sea. Will have to have a word with old missus Helen Clarke (the Kiwi PM) and get some Brownie points.

Sitting around wouldn't be so boring if there were some decent programmes on TV. If you think UK TV is generally rubbish, it's even worse here. There are only four channels and I can get only one of them. Plus Sky if you have an aerial, but I think most of Sky is a waste of money anyway. Two are run by the government and like the UK called Channel 1& 2 but they have dreaded adverts on them. A lot of the programmes are British but mostly the rubbish ones. So I can go days and not look at it except for the news. This means my relying on reading, but here the price of books is about 50% higher than the UK. One thing is that there are heaps of book shops in each area. They must do a lot of reading, probably because the TV is crap. I'm getting some of my books cheaper from a secondhand bookshop and charity shops. Just topped up, for my reading ahead, with four books. So it means I'm laying out heaps to keep occupied.

Regards the Internet, I had hoped that I would be able to use my Wifi on my laptop, but everywhere I have gone I have not been able to find free wifi spots. Everyone is either charging you or encrypting their Wifi, or putting some sort of blanking device that stops you getting onto the net, even though it says their site is free. One place that is free is the library, but usually busy and you only get half an hour. I've been using internet cafes or shops, and they charge between $3 and $4 and hour or part thereof. Most of these are run by Chinese (the same as in Oz cities, computers must appeal to the Chinese) and they are full of chattering young Chinese kids, all manically playing away on computer games, and shouting to each other. The noise is deafening and I find it difficult to think about what I'm doing....must be getting old.

I've just read a book by some Kiwis who motorcycled along the Silk Road and they were saying that they used an internet café in some really out of the way places that you would never think would have such places. Just goes to show that in today's World the computer and the Internet is everywhere, even in the middle of Mongolia. It will therefore be interesting to see how I go on for internet access, in the more remote and less well populated areas of NZ.

One thing that is keeping me amused when I've not much to do is the resident wildlife on and around the park. We have a resident pair of Mr and Mrs Duck. A pair of Mallards who seem to like the grassland of the holiday park rather than the nearby lake. The female is definitely the boss and he just follows her where ever she wonders. She is also very tame whereas he is stand offish. Today I had a spare piece of bread and as they appeared at my open door in begging mode, I sat on the step and broke it up into small pieces feeding Mrs Duck by hand and even getting Mr Duck to take it. Later on I'm sitting in the caravan reading and in comes Mrs Duck cheeky as you like. I guess I'm in for some heavy begging from now on.

Shortly after the duck visit I was startled when a Swallow flew straight through the open door, did a circuit of the caravan, chirped and then flew out again. Didn't know swallows could be so cheeky or maybe it was a mistake. They fly manically over the waters edge inches off the water, and over the beach, but what they actually catch I can never see. There are so many sparrows to be seen everywhere that the UK authorities should ship some back to the UK to replenish our dwindling stocks. I see more Blackbirds here than even in the UK and there are even starlings. Apparently many UK and European birds where brought to NZ in the late 1880's supposedly to make the new Kiwi's feel more at home. They even brought Indian Myna birds here and you see them but not as abundantly as Blackbirds. They are about the same size but light brown in colour with yellow legs and feet and white patches on their wings.

One thing that surprises me about the half dozen holiday parks I have sussed out in and around Auckland, and that is the smallness of them. I would have thought they would be bigger. This one I'm on at Takapuna is quite small and I think it would be very quickly full each day, in the full height of the summer. Even now in spring it gets nearly full of motorhomes each evening. So if you ever do a trip like this and you do it in the full height of the summer season, you may want to make sure your going to get into somewhere before you arrive. One thing about this park is that it has excellent showers which unlike many, actually give you a nice hot shower, but like so many showers I come across, the shower head is set too low and the taps too high. Trying to get my head under the stream of water to wash off the hair shampoo, I only succeeded in butting one of the taps. Two days later I still have a sore bump on my forehead. Are all shower plumbers or installers, pygmies, I wonder?

Today being Tuesday the day started off nice and fine but like the last few days as the day has progressed it has got worse, and now in the late afternoon it is bucketing it down again. Thing is that the caravans that they have on this park which are the cheapest to rent, are circa 1950's or at best 60's. So they aren't made all that well and are very tinny with no insulation to keep out the cold or noise. So this rain beating down on the roof makes such a racket that you can't hear the radio or TV or hear yourself think. Luckily each evening it has stopped by the time I'm ready for bed, so I've been able to get to sleep OK.

On the Wednesday, first thing I rang the company who were supposed to fumigate and found they had done so and passed it onto the second company who are to power wash it. So rang them and the girl I spoke to was another wishy washy employee, who didn't know what was going on. Eventually she found out it had already been cleaned and was ready for pickup off the wharf. Now I had to go to my shipping brokers, Gills, who were supposed to be handling all this on my behalf. Yet I am having to do all the pushing myself. I actually rang the woman at Gills myself even before I rang the fumigators and asked her to chase everyone, but as I could tell she would no doubt not keep on top of things, prompted me to get on with it myself. After lunch it was on my scooter and off down the 20 odd kilometres to the airport area. The weather was heavy showers all morning and even though it was clear as I set off, but incredibly windy, I knew I would get soaked. Indeed I did have to go through a heavy shower.

The woman at Gills still hadn't got the cost of the fumigating, so she couldn't make up a complete bill. I had to intimate to her that she should ring again and start pushing. She did but was so laid back I was tempted to pull the phone out of her hands and give the other end an earful. Well after waiting some 15 minutes eventually we get the figure and I end up having to pay a total of $708.75 just to have the damn thing so called cleaned against alien bugs and the like. Can you imagine if all European countries adopted this ridiculous stance at all their borders with every vehicle that came into their country? Every vehicle gets held up for five days while bureaucrats go through the motions of trying to show how clever they are at stopping viruses and creepy crawlies getting into their country. I paid the total bill of $5,300 which included the customs duty and VAT and then I hightailed it down the motorway back into the city centre and the dockside.

Again the bureaucracy you have to go through just to get through the gates just makes you want to weep because of the stupidity of it all. You have to ask the guy on the gate house to please let you go and pickup your motorhome. Then you have to sign in and all that. Then you get a yellow vest to put over your waterproof coat AND a visitors tag. I asked if I could drive to where it was on my scooter "Not on your life" I'm told. "Why" I ask…"Oh your scooter doesn't have a flashing yellow light on top of it… it's for your safety your know" Well blow me down I'm thinking, aren't they just so thoughtful for you? Then he asks me "How are you going to get it out of here" Incredulously I told him

"I'm going to drive it out Mate!" I fully expected him to come up with the excuse that as it didn't have the required flashing light on it, that that was OUT. If it weren't so surreal you'd want to manically laugh at it all. But if you did they'd probably lock you up for being a demented fool. "You will get taken there in that small bus there" I am told, and so I am whisked off 300 metres down the wharf, in case I abscond off with some of the stacked containers.

I get the keys to the home, relatively easily and a note called a Release Note which will allow me out of the San Quinton dock gatehouse. Within minutes I am FREE and out on the outside, so I quickly park up nearby to load up my scooter. First I have to get the rack out of the inside of the home and fixed back on. I find that the pin that holds it into the tow bracket is missing. I cannot remember if I put it back into its hole or stashed it in one of the many places where I could have. I look everywhere and can't see it. Never mind nearby are a load of ships chandlers so I dash off on the scooter to one and get a stainless bolt and locknut. Rack on, scooter on and tied down and off back over the bridge to Takapuna Park.

Once there I spend some time inspecting everything and what a mess and what a farce the whole exercise has been, and at a massive expense. The washing place have taken up all the rubber mats in the cockpit, which are held in place with screws and angle strips etc. This to supposedly clean out all the nasty dust under the mats that has been there over the past ten years. Yet there is still dirt and rubbish still to be seen lying there on the steps and under the mats. They have just thrown them in a heap on the floor, all the screws that they have removed, are not to be seen. Plus they have nicked a pair of sunglasses that were draped over the rear view mirror. And they have soaked the expensive Aussies Merino wool seat cover on the passenger seat. The interior floor is covered in dust and dirt yet this is ignored. The large ally toolbox at the rear hasn't been touched and I know that in the bottom of this there is plenty of accumulation of dust and dirt…untouched. The roof which had a layer of black mould on it, now has a layer of dust on top of that… untouched. The shower floor is also dirty and dust laden… again untouched. My fridge and freezer are heavily covered in mould yet not touched. So exactly what have these people cleaned other than my cockpit floor? Tomorrow I will look under the vehicle and see what if anything has been done there.

The shipper has damaged areas on the drivers' side. A rubber rubbing strip has been pulled out of its holding ally strip, but I can put that right. They have also damaged the brand new stripes that I put on the sides recently and which run just above the rubbing strip. But I thought this may happen so brought with me some of the left over strips for repairs. They have stuck a sticker on the door which is going to be a devil to get off and not damage the paintwork. Why didn't they stick it to the door window? They have damaged the drivers side wheel arch return and left black stains on the paintwork on the door. I guess the straps that they would use to tie down the vehicle to the deck, where not correctly fitted and they have moved have rubbed against the arch, and damaged it. Lastly my rear view camera has been snapped off its bracket. The only thing that pleases me is that nothing so far seems to have been stolen.

The MAF inspector has somehow been able to open the side door, which I had left locked when I left it with the shippers in Portsmouth. He's left the interior in a complete mess. All the cushions that make up the rear seats have been taken out in order to get to the storage compartments under them. Pieces of wood that covered some of the compartments have been taken up. All these were then just thrown in a heap on top of the compartments. My 240volt strip light on the ceiling has had its plastic cover ripped off and split and just thrown onto the sink top. And my push bike has had a sticker saying "passed inspection" stuck onto one of the handle bar rubbers. This proved to be a dog to get off and left a sticky gluey residue on it. What Neantherdals, and I had to pay these bastards ($800) to do this inspection and commit their vandalism.

The upshot of all this is that to take a vehicle to New Zealand has proved to be a bureaucratic nonsense and time consuming, expensive nightmare. And there's more to come folks, to do with how they licence, MOT and give out a heap of other licences. But more on that later.

Just before I left the caravan and moved into my home, I had another visit by Mrs Duck, who invited herself in as I was sitting there. On the scrounge, but as it was a windy day and I had the door open but not on the hook, a gust of window slammed the door shut and that duck shot two feet backwards and deposited a large green deposit on my floor. This is known as 'shitting your pants'. Only in duck terms, as no pants, the floor will do. I opened the door and she shot out. That will teach her, the cheeky mareduck!

One thing I must warn you about in NZ and that is be prepared to be accosted absolutely everywhere by the most talkative people on Earth… Kiwi's! Since I've been here I have been drawn into long conversations by total strangers in all manner of places. On the street, in queues, coffee shops etc. They very quickly want to know all about who you are and were you are from and what your doing here. Today an older woman in her late sixties, accosted me. She was behind me in the queue of a warehouse type place that sells everything. I made the mistake of making eye contact, and was then regaled by how she was going to have a big clear out in her home, and was going to sort out her materials into the two large pink plastic storage boxes she was buying. Pus a load of other personal information on how she was a hoarder and how her daughter was always getting onto her to tidy up etc etc. I was glad when my turn came to pay for my pillow and make a getaway and before she invited me round to help her.

Of course on the campsite you are always getting people wanting to yakker on about this and that, and especially now that they see a motorhome with UK plates on it. They seem to find this incredulous, it's almost as if they think I've done a JC and driven it across the oceans to here. I then have to make the long spiel as to how I came to own it and how it got from Oz to UK and then to NZ. Now the owner of the site has taken to engaging in long conversations since he found out that I used to make kitcars. It turns out he has a British kitcar he's been trying finish for years. Then there's the guy who's been on the pitch behind me, boy he can talk for New Zealand. He is a Mini freak and British car and motorbike enthusiast. But then I think most older Kiwis are into Brit stuff seeing as once upon a time they were the only vehicles they had in NZ. Anyway I now know his full life history and all about his plumbing business and his bad back etc etc. Still it passes away the time.

Back to the motorhome saga. I knew from the fact sheet I was sent in the UK, that I had to now go to one of their MOT stations. They are not garages like in the UK but privately run business that do nothing but deal with registration matters and MOT inspections. I had to tell them that I was in the country with this UK registered vehicle. I had a form to fill in giving various details about me and the vehicle. So on the Thursday I went to my local one and a jolly Philipino woman dealt with it. She told me how she's soon off to LA to see her sister. I was dead chuffed to be told that. Makes you feel like your part of the family an all that! I got a small ticket to put in my windscreen which would tell a copper or parking warden that even though it was a bloody foreigner, they knew all about me. Of course this wasn't going to be free… Oh not on your life… $85 thank you, sucker!. God this government really know how to get their pound of flesh off tourists. But don't all governments all round the World? We are a cash cow for them to milk.

Back in the holiday park I could see that all the hire motorhomes or even privately owned ones, had three or four small stickers on the windscreens. So I collared an owner and asked him what they were all for. I tell you this place is a bureaucracy heaven for all those individuals who thrive on the stuff. I thought the UK was bad enough and that OZ came even above the UK, but now NZ is first, followed by OZ, then the UK. Sticker one is the equivalent of our road tax, sticker two is their distance ticket if they are on diesel, sticker three is their electrical compliance ticket, sticker four is their MOT certificate. They take up so much space that the left hand side of the screen is practically obliterated with them. This diesel thing is more bureaucratic rubbish, as they apparently sell diesel fuel with either no tax on it at all, or little tax. They then make you pay tax on how many miles you do. You go to a Post Office fill it yet another form and state how many miles you want to pay for. You give them your current mileage figure and they put this on the ticket and depending on how much you pay depends on what end mileage figure they put on the ticket. So you could get stopped and if your mileage is over the end figure… you get fined or have to go and buy more miles within 7 days. How do decent Kiwi's put up with nonsense like this? Then to this electrical compliance. All motorhomes have to be inspected by someone to make sure their electrical systems are up to scratch. My thoughts on that are that most motorhomes that you see are coachbuilt and have to pass a type approval test before they are even sold. So why do they have to be tested a second time. I can understand a home built motorhome conversion but not mass produced homes.

Well this is the rubbish you get from Labour run countries as they only want to control everyone's life down to the smallest nitty gritty. Since Labour got in the UK we have been going down the same Alice in Wonderland route. The Elf & Safe Tea mob springs to mind straight away, and guess what, Elf & Safe Tea are going strong in Kiwiland too, and come out with the same old nonsense as their Brit counterparts.

Back to the subject of driving around Auckland and all the traffic lights. As I have now done a lot of driving around I can tell you I'm absolutely cheesed off with all he time I'm spending stuck at lights while they slowly grind out all their sequences. I must have used more petrol stuck at lights than I'm actually using getting places. The traffic must be pumping out heaps of CO2 with all those idling engines. No wonder they are complaining that Auckland has real bad pollution due to traffic. Don't they know that the combustion engine works at its worst when idling? They should invest in new fangled traffic light systems that monitor traffic flow and how many cars are waiting. Then lights would operate to their maximum efficiency and make journeys quicker and more efficient.

At least the weather has bucked up and we have had a couple of decent days of weather. Will it keep up? Luckily it did stay nice all over the weekend and this enabled me to work on the home cleaning and repairing damage and repainting the steel scooter rack. I will finish off those jobs on Monday and get the uprights rewelded back on. Then it will be all systems go on Tuesday to head out into the great wide blue yonder!

Whilst I was working I had a very long conversation with a South African bloke and his wife who are over here looking at whether they will emigrate here. They like many whites of SA are looking to get out while they can. So they will join the long procession that has been steadily going on since the 80's. (I wonder why?) I remember back then quite a number of them pouring into Oz. They were very taken with NZ and will be back in 6 weeks. We will meet up when I am back in Auckland.

As I am a lazy cook and don't like taking more than 20/25 minutes to prepare a meal, I use precooked meals from supermarkets, a lot. The range of available meals here is not too bad. Foodland has the best and widest selection but not in all its stores. However one think I have noticed with those meals and indeed all mass produced and processed food stuffs is that they are not as free of noxious ingredients as UK manufactured meals and other foodstuffs. I am finding higher fat, sugar and salt contents. Also labelling that is either misleading or deliberately misleading. By this I mean they show you a lovely photo of say a full bowl of the meal in question with loads of it overflowing the bowl and if it has a meat in it or chicken they will show large chunks of that. The reality is that usually you get far less than they show and the meats or chicken are miniscule in quantity. Of course they do this in the UK as well, but it is definitely more prevalent here. So I am constantly let down with what I have bought.

I bought a smoked fish pie meal with mashed potato and found it had a high saturated content. I mean you eat fish because it is not supposed to have saturated fat in it. (a 500 gram meal with 26 grams of saturated fat in it!) Certainly the potato would not have it in it. I like to eat mixed nuts and fruit as they are supposed to contain good and essential oils needed by the body. Almost all the bags of various nuts are salted so when I saw a large bag of mixed nuts and fruit which did not say they were salted, I bought a bag. Yet I could taste salt on the fruit and so looked at the bag again. Sure enough on the list of ingredients, there was salt listed and of course in small print. So be warned if you like me need to avoid salt, saturated fat and sugar, be fastidious and thoroughly check the contents and ingredients lists.

An early start, well early for me and that was about 9am, it saw me in a big queue waiting to get onto the bridge across to Auckland central and onto the South Motorway. You would think most people would already be at work by that time. However once on the bridge the traffic eased and it was a fairly quick run to get well on to the run out of the city heading south. A lovely motorway with three and four lanes for some distance and not too heavy traffic. The southern suburbs are like any other big city so nothing to report there.

Once the outer limits were receding, the surrounding countryside looks remarkably like that of the UK. Low undulating hills, mostly of volcanic nature, richly covered in very green grass. Could have been parts of Wales or Scotland I was travelling through. The road remained dual carriageway for some distance before it went to double lanes, and in parts it would revert back to four lanes again. The traffic was very light by now and it was some time before I even came to a town or village of any size. This was Rangitiri beside the river Waikato, which was quite wide. I stopped at a coffee stall in a lay-by for my mid morning victuals, it was run by a lady in her thirties and I underwent the Kiwi interrogation once more. I think I should buy a tape recorder and record all the necessary info they all want to hear and this would save endless repetitions of who I am and where I've come from and where I am going.

About midday I arrived at the outskirts of Hamilton, which is a reasonable sized country town. The northern outskirts through which you pass to get into the centre are not very eye catching, being endless commercial outfits selling all sorts with the occasional shopping centres. A mish mash of horrible competing sign posts, advertising all manner of businesses. All looking very Americanised in appearance and an eyesore. Then your into the centre and going along Victoria Street which is the main drag. At the end of it I parked and walked back the way I had come to have a look see. The Rough Guide book I am following said that this town did not have much in it to see. The buildings on this main road were mainly late 19th century ones but not architecturally beautiful. I came to the Le Grande Hotel and opposite was the La Commune Café, so I guess that was their French quarter. The number of café, restaurants and pubs on that street all practically empty, made me wonder when they did get busy. But then I read that there were many students, so maybe they are the patrons of all these places at night time.

The Waikato River runs just parallel this street and has gardens on its banks, so that was eye pleasing. The whole air of Hamilton was, I thought, a little bit sleepy feeling, with not that many people about, even though it was nearing lunch time. I did not tarry long and got going again and made my way to the banks of Lake Rotoroa which is not a stones throw from the central area. Here I had my lunch in a car park on the banks, and watched all the ducks and geese with their young ones.

My next Port of call would be Otorohanga where this motorhome of mine was made, by Caravans International Munro. I had lost one of the rear mudflaps way back in central Oz when the back end went down a dip and it got trapped and ripped off. One couldn't miss the place when I got there as it was right on the main road. However my luck wasn't in as they were just in the process of moving the whole shebang to Hamilton!

On the way out of this small town I came across tourist signs saying Kiwi House so went to have a look. It was a little zoo type place which exhibited the Kiwi bird and other native birds and reptiles. As the Kiwi is very shy and nocturnal I doubted that I'd ever see one on my travels. After paying the first exhibit is two large glass fronted enclosures roofed in and almost completely dark. No matter what I did I could see no Kiwis, another exhibit you never get to see. I did the rest of the show, which did not impress me overly. Many ducks and various birds that were duplicated many times. One bird of interest was the large indigenous flightless parrot the Kakapo. On my way out the girl who took my money asked if I'd seen the Kiwis and on being told I hadn't, she went into the enclosures and got them out of their hiding and running around. So mission fulfilled… seen the Kiwi, totally overcome with excitement!

After this it was back on the road and I hadn't gone very far out of Otorohanga when I noticed that I had a car then a police car behind me. I had noticed quite a number of Police cars going the other way since I left Auckland, so they patrol this highway in bigger numbers than you would get in the UK. No matter, I was in open 100K country and doing my usual 80K cruising speed. The car behind me could have easily passed me as traffic was very light and the centre lines were broken, so overtaking was allowed. So I was not in any way alarmed about anything, yet I couldn't understand why this car did not overtake. Then the police car is behind me giving me his flashing lights and siren. I was not pleased as I knew I was 100% doing everything within the law.

The copper asked me did I know why he was stopping me. "No I replied" "You were holding up the traffic" as if I had had a mile long queue behind me. I was told that this was a 100K area and I was doing 80K. "So what, that is my cruising speed and it was up to the car to have overtaken me" I replied. He couldn't overtake, I was told. I argued that that was incorrect as the centre lines were broken. No reply to that but I was told that I could have pulled over and let it past. I pointed out that despite the fact that this road had a widish hard shoulder, it was bordered by an UNBROKEN white line, and that unbroken white lines are not meant to be crossed. Then I was asked "You haven't got New Zealand plates, where are they?" "So what I said, I do not need them" Then ensued a long and repetitive conversation whereby this uninformed copper who obviously did not know International Law as regards the movement of vehicles, could not believe he was in the wrong.

I was getting a bit pissed off being stopped, firstly for going too slow, the first time in my life, when I know that there is no law which says you have to do the maximum, and as I was not doing say 40 or 50K's with half a mile of traffic behind me, which would have been unreasonable, he would have had a point. Then having to put up with being questioned over something the guy was 100% ignorant about. My tone of voice obviously told him I was not happy and he being one of those coppers who think you should be licking his boots and not showing him up. I pointed out to him the ticket on the screen which showed that the vehicle was registered on the Land Transport system. He then wanted my licence and disappeared to his car with it, no doubt to confer with his base.

Meanwhile all the time he was waffling away to me, his partner was sniffing around the motorhome like a dog on heat. "Bugger it" I thought these bastards are going to try and dredge something up that they say is wrong with the vehicle to get back at me for daring to argue the toss. I thought for sure they would make a big deal about the scooter rack. They would say it wasn't legal etc etc. Or find something else. After about five minutes he comes back and then goes on about how it is not normal to see foreign plates in NZ and that is why he stopped me and was in other words trying to justify his actions, but it went on and on to the point where he was over the top. Eventually he gave me my licence back as he'd obviously been told that I was correct, and I then asked if I could now go.

What really annoyed me was when he said in amongst all his waffle, that I would have to be prepared to be stopped many times… JUST BECAUSE I'M DRIVING ON NON NZ PLATES.

It just goes to show you just how isolated some in New Zealand are, in respect of the rest of the World. They are simply not used to, what in the rest of the World would be taken as normal. I could have registered it in NZ, but what if I decided at the end of my stay, to take it out of the country again? That exercise and cost would have then been a waste. So you can make your own mind up on this one and what you would do if you were thinking to bring a vehicle over, rather than buy in NZ.

I drove on for a shortish distance to a place called Waitomo where there are lots of caves and sink holes. Besides it was now around three in the afternoon and if I went into any of these caves, it would then be time to stop overnight, anyway. It had started to drizzle by now and I first of all went into the Caves Museum, but this was a waste of money even though it was only $5. It only gave info on caves that I already knew from my many caves visited in Oz. Then it was time for a coffee and after that, time to retire into the holiday camp that was opposite. A Top 10 site which I knew should of good standard, which it was. The rain eased off but it was still cloudy and damp. I decided that tomorrow I would not visit any caves as they were too expensive at $30 plus, as I would only see similar to what I've seen many times before. I would get on and drive towards the coast at a place called Marokopa and then southwards following the coast. It is supposed to be a scenic drive, so we will see. Most of all I hope it is less eventful, with not a copper to be seen. When you really need them they are nowhere to be seen!

Left the campsite at 9am and headed west towards the coast. The land is very hilly and the road winds about a lot. Some very scenic views to be had of rolling, green farmland with many hills and mountains. (see photo 654 to 657) A few kilometres along this road and you come to the entrance to a walk, to a natural stone bridge called Mangapohue Natural Bridge. A well made track goes into the hillside and follows a narrow river. After five minutes walking along a deep rock gorge with heavy foliage of trees and ferns much like a rain forest, you come to a high piece of the rock which bridges the two gorge sides. Apparently originally this had been a cave and the roof had fallen in, but left some of the roof which is now the bridge. (see photo 658 to 660)

A few miles further on it is the Marokopa Falls. Here you have to walk some half kilometre into a forest, to the falls, which whilst not on the scale of Niagara, are nice enough a view. The walk back if your not fit could puff you out, as it did me, as it is all uphill to get back to the road. As I have not been walking or cycling on a daily basis for over a month now, my fitness has gone all to pot.

I was amazed when I came across a large area of gorse bushes complete with many flowering yellow flowers (this being Spring) It reminded me of the New forest heathlands, and I wandered if they had been introduced into NZ. If they had they were doing a good job, as they were strangling the forest slopes. (see photo 661 & 662)

Before I left Waitoma I was worried that the road that follows the coast and which is shown on the map as being unpaved after a place called Moeatoa, may not be a good gravel road. So I had asked the girl in the campsite office and she told me that most of it was now paved and it was all OK to travel on. When I got to the coast itself at a place called Marokopa there was another campsite there and whilst purchasing a newspaper off them, I asked the girl there if she could confirm the roads condition. No problem, I was told it was all paved except for a bit at the end.

A river which I had been following for some miles reached the coast at this place and it was obviously a holiday weekend type area, in addition to this holiday campsite. Here there were quite a number what I call weekend shacks, most which were not occupied, although some were by Maoris. In fact there seemed to be quite a few Maoris living around there, and some in shacks that were no bigger than a small shed. There was a lot of activity going on too, with a field next to the rivers mouth, full of parked cars and loads of Maoris milling about and being ferried over to some buildings on the opposite bank. It looked like they were having some tribal get together. As it was lunch time I pulled into this field and parked up away from them to have lunch. I must say that so far I have found that quite a number of Maoris are unfriendly and look at you in a way that says they do not like you. It was so with some of them that were coming into this field to park and going past me. I think quite a lot of Maori men just look naturally very aggressive and not at all radiating piece and goodwill to all men, off their unsunny faces.

After lunch off I went down this scenic route following the coast but inland and down towards New Plymouth. For about the first four miles the road climbed quite steeply and of course was winding about. On the map it said it was paved, until a place called Moeatoa, however this was wrong and so were the two girls who had advised me previously. For within six miles it had turned to gravel, but very good gravel. Smooth and well maintained, so no probs. But it does show you that you can't rely on the map or what people tell you, even when they are locals, because the Marokopa girl told me that it was only gravel at the other end of the stretch but this was not so.

Anyway this road was very picturesque, running through hilly country with occasional valleys and alongside rivers in them. Some of the hills were very densely covered in trees. The gravel road after about ten miles reverted to tarmac and remained so to the end. Everywhere there were sheep and also some cattle, and as there was very little flat land that could be tilled to grow crops, one can understand why NZ has so many sheep if all the land is like this. The particular nature of this hilly land, covered as it is with many bumps of hills reminded me of the shape of egg containers. It's like looking at eggland. On can imagine millions of years ago that this land was a heaving cauldron of volcanic activity, bubbling away and making all these little hills and the bigger cone shaped hills that were obviously old volcanoes. I was surprised at the number of ducks of various shapes and sizes that there were to be seen. Many of them actively flying about. I suppose the number of streams and rivers attracts them along with meadows to graze on, and for the first time I saw what appear to be NZ version of the ubiquitous magpie. Bigger than ours and the Oz ones, but with very similar markings.

On the map they show several names of settlements along this stretch of road. However most of the time there was no town or village or even any houses. Talking of houses they appear in rural areas to be mostly very basic. Hardly any of brick, mostly shack like wood things, many in need of a good paint. The designs of most where also very basic, and many were just like shoe boxes in shape. So I would say that those farming these lands do not appear to be loaded and able to afford decent housing. I will keep a look out on this score as I go around other rural areas, which will mean most of NZ.

Once the scenic road rejoined the main highway 3 that ran inland from Waitomo, I was able to make better time as it wasn't narrow and windy. Lunch time, I had reached a place called Urenui at which there was a holiday camp on the beach. So I snuck down to there for lunch. Strange place it was, because it was deserted. It had several parallel streets running down to the beach, on which there were many holiday shacks of various designs and sizes, all deserted. Even the camp shop and office was closed. I parked up alongside the beach and wondered why they built such a place at this particular spot. At this point a river exited the land and the beach was strewn with wood all along it, washed up from the sea. The sand was jet black volcanic, the waves looked strong and dangerous and unsafe to swim in. Had my lunch and got under way for New Plymouth not far away.

On approaching the outskirts I saw a Warehouse place and snuck in the see if they had slippers my size, which I'd been unable to find anywhere in Auckland. Was in luck, so I now have something comfortable I can wear when I'm in the home, instead of my shoes all the time. Going into N.P it looked just like any other Antipodean type town with the usual length of parallel streets bisected with cross streets, and with the same style of buildings as well. So I just drove up and down, not wanting to park up and walk around, as by now it had started to pee down. There is a largish quayside and port area where containers are unloaded. Like most port areas it wasn't very scenic and while I parked on one street to look at the map, I clipped a damn stupidly situated parking sign pole, which was too close to the kerb. Knocked back my left side mirror and ripped off my radio aerial. I was not best pleased. Trouble with many Kiwi gutters I have noticed is, they have a very steep camber down into them. So a high sided vehicle like a motorhome, leans over towards the pavement when you park. Then some silly sod of a council worker parks a pole too close to the kerbstone. Now I've got to pay out for a new aerial and couple this with the fact that this morning I forgot to take down the TV aerial at the back of the home, and the cable dragged along the road messing up the plug on the end. Not my day today for communications equipment mishaps.

I tired very quickly of N.P and what with the rain and all, decided to carry on out of town to further down the coast to another suitable night stop.

South of N.P is the high mountain/volcano called Mt Egmont, named by my old mate Cookie (Cpt, deceased) Some 7500 feet high, but today the top cannot be seen due to all the wicked rain clouds. The land since joining Highway 3 has levelled out somewhat as between the Mountain and the coast is, by NZ standards, classed as a plain. Even so I saw no evidence of crop growing, just more cattle and plenty of sheep.

When I had gone some 12 K's I came upon a campsite at Oakura. Situated right on the beach, and at $14 a night, a snip. By now the rain is coming down in sheets and the waves pounding on the shore make a real racket. Hope I will be able to get off to sleep. The place is practically empty of people as this would be strictly a summer camp place for beachies. At least today I wasn't accused by some Kiwi cooper of some heinous crime.

TV reception on the sets aerial was rubbish, but I was able to catch the news. (I couldn't use my outdoor aerial, because of the messed up coax plug) It is now four days since France beat the All Blacks at rugby and they are still bleating on every minute about it. Of course some are trying to blame the British ref for allowing a forward pass. If I were in Oz I would have been assaulted by now over something like that! It's on the radio and TV, non-stop. Anyone would think that they had just been beaten in a war. It is pathetic, and they go on about sport too much here for my liking. The newspapers, radio and TV all feature it too much. When I was in Auckland I listened mostly to the BBC overseas as one Auckland organisation relayed it all day. Since I've been out of Auck you can't get it, but tonight I raised it on shortwave. So caught up with what's happening in the World that way.

I reckon it will now be a two day stint to get to Wellington. The only Kiwi radio stations I will listen to are their equivalent to BBC and that is Radio NZ their national radio station. Also Coast Radio which plays classic records going back to the 50's. The only thing is that they seem to keep switching the positions on the dial, as you move about. Which is a nuisance, having to have to keep hunting around for them.

Today it was plenty of clouds, but no rain. This Surf Highway runs along the coast through many small towns that if you blink you've missed them. Many are a bit seedy and almost deserted of people. You wonder what the people of these places do for a living. The thing with NZ houses as with many houses in Oz is that many of them are wood, devoid of style or nice design and with horrible corrugated iron roofs, many which are rusty. When these go rusty together with the unpainted or pealing paint sides, they just look awful. Some of these little settlements are made up almost entirely of the shacks and the shops not much better. However as I progressed further down the coast things got gradually better. Better quality houses, and some of the towns quite clean and having good designed and modern housing stock.

Again like in Oz, many Kiwi houses especially in the country, seem reluctant to get rid of their old and dead cars. So they get put out in the rear or even the front gardens. A great number of these rusting cars are old Brit ones. Many years ago the only cars they imported were Brit ones, and even in 1969 when I passed through Auckland, they were still driving around in some unbelievably old cars. Then import duties on cars were prohibitive and they drove cars for ever. So that explains the many old Bits ones still lurking around in peoples gardens. Shortly after leaving Auckland I passed a small scrap yard in one small county town and it was full of old Brit classics. Fair tore at my heart to see them forlornly rusting away into oblivion and the great car yard in the sky. Mind you I have seen some right old classics driving around still and mostly in immaculate condition.

Another thing I have noticed every now and then are large scruffy factory type places either on their own in mid country, or on the edges of little towns. No signs to say what they were once used for, but whatever it was, they are now defunct. Why they don't pull them down, but I am getting the message that Kiwis do not like getting rid of stuff. Having said that though, they do seem an inordinately neat and tidy people. The highways are always in such general good condition, as I have said before, but also the sides of the highways are all neat and tidy. No heaps of litter like you see at the side of every Brit road and highway. The grass verges are all neatly and regularly cut and hedges trimmed, again not like many of the jungles at the sides of Brit roads. All the road signs are in good nick and clean and readable, not like many of the mouldy never cleaned Brit ones. I even saw a maintenance man cleaning one of the sticks they space out along the sides of their roads. These have reflectors on them so you can see the edges of the road. The towns as I got further south were also incredibly neat and tidy with excellent housing stock.

One such town was Wanganui and was so far the prettiest town I had come across. Whilst it was of the same layout as all NZ towns, that is a square of parallel streets, a lot of the buildings in the centre were of late 1800's, early 1900's and all had been tastefully restored. The streets had been nicely laid out, parking wise, with neat pavements and nice street furniture. So I spent a little time and my lunch break time in this town. I got a replacement roof radio aerial and fittings to repair the broken one, courtesy of that errant signpost incident. Cost me $30 in all so thanks a bundle New Plymouth Town Council! (see photo 663 to 668)

Wanganui sits on the quite wide river which bears the same name and is NZ's longest navigable river. Was once a bustling port, but not now. So I guess once it was quite a rich little town hence all the substantial buildings.

After lunch I travelled onwards to the South and Wellington. The traffic has been light all day and I've been cruising along at my steady 80/90K's. The flattish plain continues and got even wider, but even though I now saw some fields had been ploughed over, there were still no signs of crops, yet I did pass one medium sized gain silos. Where the grain is grown, I know not.

At one spot a hawk of some sort flew right across my path at windscreen height. So I got a good view of it. Reasonable sized and with light brown feathers. I will look up what it was when I get to Wellington.

As I got closer to a medium sized town called Levin I had two other Motorhomes up behind me and one in front. So it was a procession through that town but right at the outskirts we came across an accident with the police blocking off the road at a junction. There had been a head on and a Chinese family were sitting at the side of the road. As I've said before, Asians make dreadful drivers on the whole, so I wasn't surprised. Coupled with the fact that as I have already said, NZ drivers aren't great either. Today I have lost count of the numbers of drivers weaving about all over the place. We all had to turn left and then after some yards, make a U turn and go back to the highway and that way we missed the car blocking the junction. This way I was able to shake off the other RV's as they seemed to find doing the turn somewhat difficult. Hate travelling in convoy anyway.

Another 20 odd Kilometres and I had reached a town called Otaki, and as it was now 4pm, it was time for me to call it a day. I knew by previously scanning the map, that there was a campsite on the beach here. This time I had to pay $20 and the site is no better than last nights stop. Why there are such differences in prices beats me. I was paying $20 for a much better site at Takapuna in Auckland. What can you do? You end up having to pay, but I had my pennyworth to the receptionist, to no avail.

I repaired the radio aerial so I have something to listen to again, whilst driving. I also repaired the TV aerial but the reception for TV1 was rubbish again, as last night I had the same bad reception. Here I am not far from Wellington and last night not far from the largish town of new Plymouth, yet reception of their number one station is rubbish. Mind you, yet again there is nothing on worth looking at so I am not missing a thing. As I got the weekly Express and Telegraph, I have plenty to read. It has started to rain again, so I hope it is not raining tomorrow. (see photo 669)

Not actually raining full pelt but lots of black low clouds, so it doesn't look good. On the road it drizzled on and off all the way to Wellington, which I reached by 10.30 as it was only 70K's away. I went straight to the only park near the city and even then its' about 12 K's out in the suburb of Lower Hutt. It's a Top 10 park and reasonably big but I was shocked at the price of $25 a night. Again they know they have you, a big city where everyone is going to end up at because this is where you have to get the ferry across to the South Isle. This is the most expensive so far and when I saw the state of the pitch they allocated to me I was not a pleased bunny. It was like a mud pitch the grass all churned up and puddles. When it is like this you constantly tread in mud and wet into your home. I looked around and saw many of the pitches were similar but there was a row of pitches with all nice pristine grass. I returned to the office but all those pitches are booked I was told. I managed to get a pitch that was a bit better being mainly gravelled instead of all grass. But still not upto scratch and especially at $25 a night. There is another park a little further out and I will have a look and see what the score is and if better I will be out.

The rain had got worse as I arrived and after setting up and getting my scooter off the rack, I togged up in all my wet gear and took off to find the local shopping mall. This turned out to be a huge place and I stocked up on what I needed in the food area.

In the afternoon I went back to the central area of Hutt to find an email place. I could find only one and guess what… yes, it was owned by a Chinese. Worse still he was charging $5 an hour which like the park is the most I've had to pay, but again he has a monopoly. I caught up with all my messages as quick as I could and vowed to also find a cheaper internet place.

I didn't feel like scootering into Wellington because of the weather, and made do by doing some jobs like cleaning all the cow shit that my scooter and push bike had collected on the way down. Can't think where it happened as I don't remember anywhere where it would have been on the road.

This park is also full of Mallards as it sits next to a river and they know how to scrounge, like those up in Takapuna. No sooner had I stopped the home when I arrived on my pitch than one female was into the inside of the home. Trouble was I couldn't get round her to shoo her out so she just kept going further into the home until she panicked and tried to fly through the windows at the back. I was forced to grab her to get her out, which wasn't easy, and out she went. But not without her leaving her calling card on my seat cushions!

Funny how it is always the female ducks that are so forward. During the late afternoon I saw one being gang raped by about six males. One had her head in a beak hold while he and all the others tried to have it away. I don't think any were successful and eventually she broke free and flew off rapidly. They don't mess about these male Mallards! You should see how they mate when they are on water. Back in Christchurch UK, I saw the female with her head being held underwater and for a long time. How she kept her breath for so long was amazing. So tomorrow I will go the Wellington centre and look around there. It should be a quick run in as a motorway runs to it. I will check on the ferry prices.

The next day was free of rain but cloudy and very windy. A quick run along the motorway got me into the town centre within 10 minutes. I called at the ferry terminal first to check on prices. It will cost me $220 each way, yet if I were carrying a passenger there is a special on at $350 return. Doesn't make sense to me. Maybe I should pick up a hitchhiker and save $90.

I parked up in the Lampton Quay area and started walking around. I was primarily searching for an Internet place as well as general sight seeing. The place seems quite small for a capital, and the guide book says you can easily walk around all of the central area in a few hours. First thing of note I saw was a London double decker bus stood at the side waiting to get passengers for round the town trips. Amazing where those things turn up in the World. (see photo 670)

After tramping around a number of streets I eventually came across an email place at $3 an hour, much cheaper than yesterday. So I caught up with the ones I wanted to send yesterday. Spent all morning having a good look around. In the docks area there was a large Chinese destroyer in for a friendly visit. Looked very impressive and upto date.

Then I had a good look at the NZ Parliament building which was well built. The new Anglican cathedral next door, which wasn't, as it looked like a concrete modern pile and very unimpressive inside with a large damp patch showing up on one of the columns. Round the corner was the old cathedral which looked more like an ordinary church, and built of wood. Inside it was very cosy and with an excellent ambience. Built in the late 1800's, they nearly scrapped it but for the fuss kicked up by the populace. Used a lot now for weddings, which just goes to show you what people think of the new one!

Back to the scooter to get my packed lunch which I then had in a little gardens nearby. Then it was on a scooter tour of a wider city area, ending up on the nearby Mt Victoria lookout. There I took a string of photos. The whole of the bay is ringed by hills so Wellington sits in a kind of bowl of flatter land that clings to the shores, but many of the suburbs have houses on the hill slopes. Not my kind of place to have a house, perched on the side of a steep hill, especially in an earthquake zone. Most of the houses are made of wood, which I found strange as I would have thought city folk had made enough money to build in better materials than wood.

I doubt if I will stay the whole week as I will have exhausted things to do before my booked week is up.

This day being Sunday I am not inclined to rush out anywhere and I will take it easy. It is a lovely clear day with little cloud for a change, but still windy and the forecast is for high winds. About 10am after a leisurely breakfast I scootered over to the local Mall. I needed to get me a tin of beans for lunch and a newspaper. The rest of the morning reading the newspaper, which unlike a Brit one like the Telegraph, which takes me most of the morning to thoroughly read, this one is read in half an hour. The rest of the morning I potter about, watch the antics of the many ducks. One female has only one leg and she hops around with great difficulty, yet she still has a male with her. There is a bird that you hear making a single note whistle and I think it is a bird I see flying around like crazy usually in pairs. They sit in the row of trees next to where I am parked and I never see them on the ground. Bigger than a blackbird with a little white, loose bib.

After an early lunch I went into Wellington and spent an hour on the internet, then wandered over to the main museum called the Te Papa, which is on the waterfront. Large modern building with a lot of floor space which I thought was grossly underused. All the halls were in semi darkness, which I found annoying as it made viewing things that much more difficult and hard to read the description tickets when your having to wear glasses to read. The exhibits were mostly natural history and evolution of the earth. A few rooms on the immigration of white peoples, and a lot on the immigration of Scots. I suppose they felt at home here with all the mountains. Overall I wasn't enthralled. But the thing that did enthral me was, IT WAS FOR FREE. Had I had to pay I would have been feeling cheated.

Then back to the park for a shower and get ready for dinner after the news when I may be lucky and get to see some Rugby action on the news as earlier I had heard that England had beaten the French in the world cup. It was nice they beat the Aussies, then they beat the Frogs… heaven, not that I'm really interested in rugby. However the Kiwis and Aussies are so pumped up about how they will thrash the Pommies, that it's nice when we make them eat their words. With the French I dislike them so much that it's always a pleasure to beat them at anything. I think in a life before I must have been a soldier in Wellingtons' army.

The next two days the weather was foul yet every morning I awoke to a wonderful blue sky and thinking I was in for a good day. Yet by lunch time it was all dark clouds and rain starting and all afternoon it pored down. Plus a roaring wind. Certainly not weather to drive a scooter round in or try and look around. I did manage to get one morning, walking around the Botanical Gardens, but like a lot of Wellington it is not a park that is flat but one that sits on the side of a hill. So you have quite a hike up steep paths and eventually after much winding about through mostly wild bush, at the top. Here there are buildings; toilets, a café, a cable car station and a museum of cable cars. This so called cable car is not what I call a cable car system, but a funicular railway. Cable car systems usually are cars suspended on a cable. This one goes down into the city centre below. After this walk it was becoming obvious that we were in for more rain so it was a mad dash to get back to the park before it started. Then having to spend another boring afternoon stuck inside a motorhome.

I am finding that a Kiwi Spring is proving to be a bummer for bad weather unlike Oz which has mainly calmer weather and warmer. Maybe for anyone wanting to visit NZ it would be better for them to come a little later than when I arrived. Probably from November onwards. Today there has been an earthquake down in the South Island around the Queenstown area and a slide cutting off the Milford Sound Road. Somewhere which I intend to go so hopefully we will not have anymore while I'm there.

Hurrah, the next morning was wonderful fine weather. Blue skies not much cloud, but still windy. So see photo I went off into Wellington, did some emailing and then took off after a coffee to the area around the airport and its southern end called Lyall Bay. Here you can see right across the Cook Strait and the peaks of snow covered mountains on the South Isle. I then followed the coast road round to Seatoun which is a coastal suburb on the channel which leads off the Cook Strait and into Wellington Harbour.

Then it was back to the holiday park for lunch. Unlike yesterday and the day before, today it stayed fine, so in the afternoon I went off for a nice long ride over the hill pass behind the park and into the valley of the Wainuiomata River. Following a road called Coast Rd which doesn't actually follow the coast itself, but goes along this valley which eventually reaches the coast at a place called Baring Head. The river wends it way along the valley floor and on either side are steep hills covered in a lot of yellow gorse which I found HAD been introduced into NZ to act as hedge making material. Like a lot of things introduced into countries, it has run out of control where it has taken hold. I had a wonderful fast run along a road that considering it really goes nowhere, was in great shape and condition. Absolutely no traffic allowed you to indulge in some TT style riding. It terminates at a place called Orongorongo, which I thought may be a few houses on the beach, but which turned out to be a cattle or sheep station, which you were advised at a gate baring you, was private…'keep out' On the way back before descending the hillside and back into the Hutt River plain, from a vantage point you can get a wonderful view of the upper end of Wellington harbour and Petone, the River Hutt and Lower and Upper Hutt towns.

Whilst in the valley I couldn't help noticing that all the houses of the town of Wainioumata and around it, where all of wood. As I have mentioned before the vast majority of houses in NZ are made of wood. see photo A lot of these wood houses are not of what I would say, a pleasing design. Some houses made for people of money are of complex and pleasing designs. But the houses made for the poorer sections of society can look awful and can be completely devoid of any pleasing design. Certainly all of the houses in this area smacked of it being a poor area. Many were little more than boxes and some quite small, so when you get a house which is no more than a small square box, it looks

more like a shed or shack, than a proper house. see photo On top of this if it has peeling paint and the roof, which on most of these wood houses is made of corrugated iron, is rusty, then you have a bit of an eyesore.

Another thing I have noticed in NZ about a lot of house is that whilst many are on large blocks, the gardens are very bare. That is to say Kiwis do not seem to be into gardening, and most gardens are just of lawn and a few shrubs etc. Being like this also labels an area as being poor when most of the gardens look quite bare, because you think that these people cannot afford to buy plants and the like, to make them nice.

Of course Australia suffers from the very same sort of substandard wood housing and so does America. I well remember when I lived and travelled around America, how shocked I was at the absolute low standard of much of its housing. How so many people in what is supposed to be the richest country on Earth, lived in such squalid, abject hovels. Worse in the South and in rural areas, but even big cities could have areas of these wood hovels. So ever since those days, I have always equated wood housing with poverty and lower standards. I have even, in Sydney, owned such a wood house, and whilst it was in good condition I always felt it wasn't as good as a brick house. Cold in the winter and hot in the summer.

Thursday and it was back to the miserable dark and rainy type of weather we had been having. It had rained most of the night pelting down on the roof, but I had hoped the morning would be free of rain, but not to be. Not only is the rain a pest but it is decidedly chilly and I am constantly surprised as to how chilly it can get. Yesterday a group of four young Brit women pulled up next to me and they had come up from the South Isle and they said it was quite cold down there, it was even Long John weather... wonderful. So much for my getting away from lousy UK weather.

I didn't feel like going out but there was the need to book the ferry for Friday and last night I had found out that this weekend is a Public Holiday being Labour Day. I suddenly realised that the ferry may get fully booked and I was kicking myself for not having booked it earlier in the week. So I phoned them up and luckily there were still vacancies so I booked on the 1pm ferry. I don't know how long it will take but as the distance is not huge, probably no more than 2 hours or so.

This morning it is going to be a question of reading, watching the antics of the birds and ducks and hoping it will clear for afternoon, because then I have to go the local mall for a supply of food. I got the Dominion Post newspaper, which is the Wellington paper but like the Auckland one it is very poor value for money at the equivalent of 50p but as there is not much happening in NZ most of what is in it I find rather parochial and they hardly discuss World news. It is much like the TV news and it has like UK papers these days, far too much advertising. I had picked up a number of NZ Readers Digests in another caravan park for future reading, but these have turned out to be almost devoid of any interesting articles. In the UK or US editions there are usually articles that I find interesting. Not in these, so they did not provide the required material for passing the morning away and went into the bin.

Never the less I had to do my washing and as with other camps these cost $4 for a wash and $2 for dry. Tomorrow I need to get all the tyres checked and next to the camp I see on the other side of the river there is a big tyre depot, so I will go there. I found that all the petrol stations these days have these stupid machines that do not have enough power to inject 60psi that you need on a light truck tyre. Plus you can't see the pressure it is at or hear when it has reached the desired pressure. So a tyre place is the only way I can get it right. I called in yesterday to check they would do it and they were very friendly and said they would gladly do it for nowt. Now that what I called service. Another job I must do before leaving is to fill up with water. At least it is drinkable here unlike in Auckland and its horrible chlorine taste. Then on the way to the ferry to fill up with diesel which is much cheaper than the UK at the equivalent of 45p a litre. Unleaded is 64p a litre, again cheaper. The diesel as I have said before does not have either any tax on it, or as much as it should, and you pay more according to mileage. I am hoping that I can get away with this.

In the area of Lower Hutt shopping centre there is a shop I noticed on the first day I went into that area. You couldn't really miss the two union jacks on the awning. It specialised in selling UK products. You get these kind of shops practically anywhere where Brits have settled. This was quite a large shop and yet the amount of goods on sale was very small. It looked quite bare for its size. The biggest selection was of sweets but what I was interested in was UK tea as Kiwi stuff is not very good. It did have amongst its meagre stock of foodstuffs 80 packs of Typhoo which is exactly what I use in the UK. I checked what I paid there and found that it was 140p and so I went in one day and checked his price. He was really trying to make a killing because his price was 440p practically, three times the UK amount and that is comparing retail prices. He would surely get stock at wholesale prices which would then mean he would be making over this figure in profits.

OK he has to pay transport and duty, but this could not amount to much on one packet. Needless to say I never ever saw anyone in his shop and I went passed it many times.

Well thank God today, Friday, is OK weather wise as I didn't fancy going across the Strait in the kind of weather we've been having of late. Took my time getting prepared to leave the campsite as I want to keep connected to power for as long as possible. I've got the house battery fully charged and want to see how it handles a few hours off charge while I wait to get on the ferry and whilst on the three hour crossing.

At 1015 I left and went round the corner to the tyre place and they kindly checked all my tyre pressures for me and I couldn't see any Brit place doing that for nowt. The guy was extremely friendly and informed me his father was a Pommie. You seem to get this a lot from Kiwis telling you their parents or whatever are from the 'old country' You never get that from Aussies as they seem to want to not be seen to be pro British. He chatted away about the South Island and extolling its virtues. The following are a collection of pictures of all over Wellington and the surrounding areas that I saw during this stay:- (see photo 671 to 710A)

Then it was into the ferry terminal where I dropped off the home on the quay, and then went into the city centre for a coffee and to waste an hour up to midday, when I have to be with the home to drive on. I may as well have taken longer as I had to wait up to 12.45 before I was able to drive onto the ferry, and it is supposed to be off at 1300. It actually set off at 1315 and as soon as we got away from the quay and partly into the bay, it was darned cold on that deck. So I was glad I'd put on my fleece on top of my pullover. The harbour bay is protected a bit, so once your out through the entrance and into the Strait channel you then get the full force of any wind. Actually today has turned out gorgeous, OK it is cold in that wind, but then it always is when your at sea, but the sky was clear of cloud and the sea state was calmish. A bit of a swell but not that much meaning we had a nice trip over to the entrance of the Tory Channel which leads into Charlotte Sound. On the way there you an see several quite high mountains going south down the coast of the South Isle, and they had snow on them due to all the cold weather we've been having. Once in the Channel you have hills on either side it is like a Fiord and very nice scenery too and it's like this all the way to Picton. (see photo 711 to 729)

Chapter Twenty Four

South Island

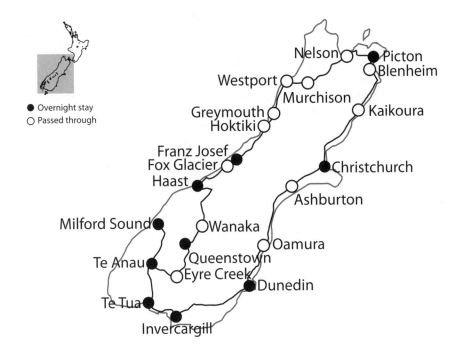

● Overnight stay
○ Passed through

Nelson
Picton
Blenheim
Westport
Murchison
Greymouth
Hoktiki
Kaikoura
Franz Josef
Fox Glacier
Haast
Christchurch
Ashburton
Milford Sound
Wanaka
Oamura
Te Anau
Queenstown
Eyre Creek
Dunedin
Te Tua
Invercargill

Picton as you approach it, it is obviously only a small place, but a very agreeable place when you get to walk round it. It is obviously a place where everyone would know everybody due to its size. Beautiful surroundings make it an ideal place to live if you like the outdoors and water. It is surrounded by national parks for walking , hiking, and camping. Then all manner of water pastimes like sailing, fishing, kayaking, dolphin watching etc can be undertaken. I would think that the whole sound is fairly well protected from the worst of the winds that the Cook Strait gets. (see photo 730)

I booked into the Top 10 Park which is the only one there and it certainly had better pitches than the Top 10 at Wellington. Once set up, I walked the short walk into town and had a quick look around. Whilst doing this I passed of people of both sexes and all said "Hiya, how ya going" just shows that in small places all the natives are extremely friendly and even in Wellington that would happen so much. Not that much to see as you can walk right round the centre in 10 minutes. They have an old boat set up on the shore line as a café and restaurant. It had been what is called a scow. Built in 1905 its design is flat bottomed for river work, but apparently in World War 2 the Yanks requisitioned it to supply various Islands in the Pacific. It apparently had a chequered career doing that up to 1944. Now it is well past it and you can see it is riddled with rot in paces and probably has more holes in its woodwork than a piece of Swiss cheese. Still it looks the part and they have tarted it up OK. (see photo 731 to 738)

I've noticed lately that there are quite a few French and German youngsters knocking about and it is VERY noticeable how these two races of people NEVER say Hello or even acknowledge you, let alone strike up a conversation… heaven forbid. I'm talking now about on campsites and places like on the ferry. Miserable bastards!

One tip I must give you once again, as I've covered this in my ramblings on Oz. Kiwi toilet paper is the same as Oz paper… like gossamer paper. You have to triple or even quadruple it to be safe. Why these two countries cannot produce the lovely thick and soft paper like we have in the UK, I do not know. So be warned otherwise you will end up doing an Arab job in your cleaning up in the loo.

Saturday was another nice day and after getting some eye drops and a newspaper it was 'hey ho onwards we go' I had no idea how far I would make it today as it depended on what I found on the journey to do and see. As it happened it turned out… nothing. The scenery all the way to Christchurch was all very nice and again it reminded me of parts of Wales. No large towns only very small ones, and of no interest, so no stopping there. Once you got close to Kaikoura you could see the mountains of the Seaward Kaikoura Range, the highest being Manakau at 2609 metres high. All the peaks in that range were covered in snow, so looked impressive. But to be brutally honest, no better than what you see in Switzerland or the French Alps. (see photo 743 to 746)

Just before Kaikoura I spied some seals basking in the sun on some volcanic rocks. The road was following the shore, so I stopped and took some snaps. The seals were so close to the roaring traffic whipping by them, but they were unconcerned. (see photo 738 to 742)

After Kaikoura the road and passage all the way to Christchurch was uneventful and once I got within 20 K's of the centre I stopped and booked into a caravan park called Pineacres. What a dump which I couldn't see until I got inside, and to make matters worse it cost $20, what a rip off. It seemed to be a trailer trash type of park mostly full of a motley bunch of full timers living in all sorts of hovels. The facilities were rubbish too.

I had to park on a small so called grassy area that took two vans but was really a scruffy bit of dirt wit a few tufts of grass. I was the only motorhome there that night. I quickly unshackled the scooter and roared off to find a better place for tomorrow.

I first went into the city centre and had a quick latte and walked a few blocks, then back out towards a few other parks. The first I got to was another Top 10 which turned out to be a top rip off at $29 a night. No thank you, I thought. I then tried to find another one on my map but it took some frustrating riding aimlessly about as many of the junctions had no names of the streets at them. Bit like the UK I thought, and even the road surfaces aren't as good as the usual for NZ, so definitely a town like a Brit one. No wonder they are always saying that Christchurch is supposed to be a town most like a Brit one! The first park I came to looked OK but was $20, so went onto the next one just down the road and that was $14 and looked OK quality wise but again full of trailer trash full timers. I will stay tomorrow at that one and scooter around looking at some more. Got to be one somewhere that suits me better and a bit closer to the centre. At least there was no rain today. Spent the evening listening to Radio NZ playing impossibly old songs, which I quite like. Songs from the 20's and 30's, 40's, 50's and 60's. Songs you never get the BBC playing, which is a shame as some of the old songs are a change from a lot of the rubbish doled out on the radio these days. They are even playing the sound track of an old Abbot and Costello Show, who I used to really like as a kid

Sunday started off with real nice weather, clear sky hardly any clouds and warm if you were out of the wind. Once I got out of the rubbish campsite I decided not to waste my time going to the $14 a night place but to go to a campsite on the map, which is in a coastal area called Brighton. On the way I took a wrong turning because of inadequate signing again. When I eventually got there it turned out a nice site, situated where the river Avon (like its UK counterpart) meets the sea. Or in this case a wide estuary. The woman who dealt with my booking in, was British too.

Approaching the city centre from a different suburb, when in the afternoon I went back to the centre, showed me that some of its housing stock is a bit scruffy. I guess there will be areas that are up to scratch but so far I've not seen them. Walking round the centre I felt that it too had an air about it, of slightly, not 100% on the ball. Too many scruffy edges to it, and building works going on in various places. Even the Cathedral in the dead centre had its interior off colour with building/renovation work going on. Also as I said already, the roads aren't as good as Auckland or Wellington, more like some UK city, uneven, patched up and with signposting missing. The ambience of the city, I wouldn't say is like an English city as the architecture of the older buildings is typical early Antipodean Colonial. As are the houses, being as they re mostly wooden, which you do not get in the UK. Even the trams don't look like typical English trams as I remember them. However all round so far its OK, don't get me wrong. I think I will find plenty to do for a week or two so I can pass away some time while the weather gets warmer, because it was quite cold when you got into any breeze or when I was on the scooter. I guess any wind coming off surrounding mountains with snow on them, makes it cold.

The Labour Day holiday Monday was again a lovely day, so first thing I went for an early morning walk along the shoreline of the estuary that the park sits on. The tide was out but on the remaining water there were dozens and dozens of black swans feeding in the shallow waters. The wind coming off the water was chilly so my walk was for only half an hour. After this, a trip to the supermarket, which like in the UK is open no matter what, which is a big change from years ago in NZ when they closed at midday on a Saturday. It was whilst in this particular supermarket I saw another example of how Antipodean birdies are unlike UK ones. That is to say they are either smarter, more cheeky or more tame. A pair of sparrows were gaily flitting about in the fruit and veg section from shelf to shelf looking for eats. Now to have got into the store they would have had to negotiate TWO automatic doors. However as I have recounted when I was in Oz, this doesn't present any problem to these birds. When I was in Wellington I was in a coffee shop which was a bit gloomy and had a small entrance door yet there was pigeon nonchalantly walking about the floor some distance away from the entrance.

In the afternoon I went into the centre again and walked around the Botanical Gardens which was quite well attended with people. Very nice too with trees from all round the world and various kinds of flower gardens. They also have a lake with attendant ducks and it was whilst walking along the banks of this lake watching the ducks that I witnessed and incident which quite shocked me. I think one thinks of ducks as being nice creatures, but as with the other day when I related the incident of a gang rape of a female duck, today I saw just how there is a dark side to male Mallards. I could see a group of five males who appeared to be going through the same motions as I saw before. Holding the head of a female under water whilst they attempted to mate. However this female wasn't fighting and it became quickly apparent that she was dead, no doubt drowned. No doubt that with the onslaught of so many males holding her under water for so long that she had succumbed. What shocked me was that this gang of male Mallards were not giving in and for a good five minutes I witnessed male after male still grabbing her by the head in a frenzy and attempting to mate even though it was obvious she was dead. They had grabbed at her head in such a frenzy that they were ripping out clumps of feathers and her head was almost bare of them. They were still at it as I walked away wondering how many female Mallards were dispatched in any mating season in any one area. I also wondered if they set upon females that were hitched with a partner which is what you see most of the time. That is to say that most females are in pairs, but there are always more males than females, yet I never saw this behaviour in the UK on the River Avon in UK Christchurch. Are Brit ducks better behaved? Are Kiwi male ducks suffering from the Ocker syndrome that many Antipodean males suffer from, I wonder?

I saw in the river some lovely examples of trout fish and several quite large eels, bigger and fatter than the eels I have seen in the UK River Avon.

On the Tuesday we had gale winds in the South of the South Island reaching 150Kph. It was windy here too but not that bad. What a windy place this is proving to be. I went to the local Doctors to get a prescription for my tablets and that cost me $58 so be prepared for this. Even the locals have to pay this, but the upside of this is, is that you can get to see a Doctor with hardly any waiting, and this a day after a long weekend. In the UK you'd have a queue a mile long. Of course I had to pay but it wasn't too bad at $15 for 3 months supply.

Wednesday was another nice sunny day but by midday the wind had got up nevertheless I decided to visit the port of Christchurch which is to the south and on the other side of a range of hills. Taking the road which goes over these hills in a circuitous route but affords great views. Once on the top you get great views of the whole of the Christchurch plain and the city. Also the mountains to the north and west and then on the other side you get the views of Lyttleton Harbour. This is an inlet of some length and of some depth. So as Christchurch had no place on its coast where a port could operate, this harbour became the port for Christchurch. Once on the Summit road the wind was wicked and it was quite scary being buffeted on that narrow road with steep drops down hundreds of feet with no safety barriers.

Once at Lyttleton one wondered why you bothered. Nothing worth seeing there, however the views on the way did make it worthwhile. On the way back I took the coastal road through the little coastal suburb towns of Sumner and Mt Pleasant.

Back at the camp I had time to study a pair of Paradise Shelducks who are constantly around the camp, waiting for scraps to feed on. Bigger than Mallards the female unlike most ducks is actually more colourful than the male, which is a drab dark brown. The camp is surrounded by tall fir trees and I was surprised to see this pair fly into a tree to settle on a branch. I've never seen ducks fly onto a tree, although I constantly see Mallards in the UK settle on top of house roofs. Also the calls these ducks make, sound more like a seagull than a duck. In fact when you hear them at it you'd swear there were seagulls around.

I put out some small pieces of the bread like base of a Pizza I had the night before, the male duck came along with his female and scoffed the lot while she just looked on. She only moved into the spot where the bread had been when he moved away, but hardly anything left. So in this type of duck the male is king. Whereas with Mallards the male is very much under the thumb and it's the female that gets in first and he has to wait. I put out some more bread and along came the resident Mallard pair and before they had much time to start along came the resident female magpie. So it came to a battle as to who was going to get to feed. The magpie kept trying to edge into the pile of bread but both ducks would shoo it away. To show just how clever these birds are, eventually the magpie managed to get the male duck away from the female and on his own. Now she was able to just aggressively fly straight at him, this unnerved him so he flew off, So now she turned on the female again just flying straight at it and it too took fright and flew off.

No she had all the bread to herself. As she had a young one to feed she would fill herself up and then fill her beak with as much bread as she could, then fly off to find the young one. This young one when it is alongside its Mother makes such a whining noise to get food, you wouldn't believe. The Mother picks up a piece of bread and puts it into the mouth of the young one. The baby is obviously just too lazy to pick it up itself and all the time this high pitched whining goes on. No sign of a male magpie, he's probably to smart to put up with all this and keeps away.

Now it's Sunday and the past three days have been generally fine and sunny but changeable as regards the temperature. One day would have chilly wind then the next would be nice and warm even if there was a wind, then a chilly wind again. Boy was that wind chilly when it blew from the right direction, whatever that was. I didn't do anything real exciting as there isn't anything around here to do that is. On Friday I had a local engineering works fit a modification to my scooter rack in order to make it a bit stronger. If I got stopped again by a young eager cop I wanted the bike rig to look well strong enough. They were very accommodating and did it right away and at a very fair price. The foreman was very friendly and chatty and we talked about classic planes.

Then on the Saturday I visited The RNZAF museum which was fairly near. What they had here was OK but it was quite small with no more than a dozen aircraft including a Spitfire. This looked almost brand new and the placard said it had been delivered in 1945 and had hardly been used. Must be worth a fortune if it had its engine, still apart from the planes on view the rest was tableaux which depicted the various WW1 & WW2 theatres of conflict. UK, Europe, Malta, the Middle East, Malaysia, Korea, all featured. Pictures, various uniforms, posters, ammo and guns etc. In fact it was all very similar to the exhibits at the larger museum at Auckland. Great emphasis on the two wars and especially the Second World War. Again quite what any visitor from Germany would think, I know not. Had the exhibits covered much more ground then it would not have stood out so much. I looked at the visitors book but saw no comments about how lovely it all was, from any Germans! Plenty from Yanks and Aussies though. The tour of the museum didn't last more than an hour.

One day I took a walk up the long concrete pier at Brighton and at the end met a chap fishing, so I got talking to him about what he could catch there and what bait etc he used. Turned out he was from Oregon, retired and spent 6 months in NZ and Oz and the other 6 months in Oregon for the summer there. Whilst talking to him some, Neantherdal Kiwi male starting berating him for fishing there when it wasn't allowed. Which it patently was OK, as posters said it was. He looked like a Hells Angel without his bike and the sort you would think wouldn't give a toss what you did, but he obviously had some demons in him. Even though he was put right and the poster pointed out to him, he never apologised and just wandered off muttering to himself. Which brings me to the subject of weirdo's.

I had in my notes and comments on Oz, explained that that country was full of male weirdo's and outlaw replicas.(minus the guns… I think) Here it's not as bad but they are definitely alive and well and should be avoided and treated with caution.

Following is a large selection of pictures of Christchurch and all the surrounding areas I visited. (see photo 749 to 777)

Now that I have exhausted all the things to do in Christchurch, Monday I will move off and onto the road to Dunedin, which I should easily reach in one days travel. On the Monday it turned out to be a nice sunny day which is good and so I set off out of Christchurch on Highway 1, heading south. The whole journey was made along a coastal plain of some width and along the whole 379 K's there were always a range of mountains off to the right some 20 to 30 miles away. So it wasn't a trip of great beauty and interest apart from just a few places.

The land was the usual fields of sheep and cattle and a few places where for the first time I saw evidence of crops growing. Very flat and the road mainly quite straight and it wasn't until I got to Oamaru that it changed to undulating small hills, and some small forests of pine trees on slopes. This made it a bit more pleasing to the eye, and I could see that the dreaded yellow gorse bushes were in strong evidence. I bet the farmers hate this pest as you can see how it eats up grazing land. It must be a constant battle to keep it in check. Mind you when it is in bloom as it was when I passed, it looks nice but it is a horrid looking shrub without the flowers. (see photo 778 & 779)

At a place called Moeraki there are some round boulders on the beach which are on the tourist list of must sees. I had seen pictures of these and they turned out smaller than I thought they'd be. They reminded me of the 'Devils Marbles' seen in the NT of Oz, however they were much bigger in size. These were quite strange in that they had patterns all over them much like you see on a football made by the different leather panels stitched together. There seems to be hard sections of rock and in-between them is a substance that looks like an amber resin, but could be another type of weaker rock. (see photo 780 to 784)

As you get to the northern edge of Dunedin you come to where a hill suddenly dips down and into the city. So you come round a corner and suddenly there is Dunedin laid out below you. (see photo 785) Driving through the city I was on the lookout for the universal Motorhome/caravan sites. IE a large blue sign with either a caravan or a motorhome silhouette and a tent sign with an arrow pointing to where it is. Dunedin must not be at all concerned for tourists because unlike all other places I have gone through to date where all camp sites were very well sign posted, here I had no clue as to where I should go. I knew from my road map that there where around four sites in Dunedin. I motored on hoping to see some signs and as it became obvious that I was now on the road going out, I stopped. I dug out two pamphlets I had on various sites of Top 10 and Kiwi sites, and it was only because of them that I was able to work out in which direction I had to go. However even that job was made more difficult because I came across several major junctions where no road name signs were evident. So poor points on these two things, Dunedin Council. Eventually I got to the beach area of St Kilda. Also nul points to the park there as when I mentioned this to the completely disinterested female who booked me in, she couldn't have cared less. You would think that a business that is way away from the main road would want to make sure that it prospective customers would be able to easily find them. The signs I did see where not the International standard sign my eye was on the look out for, but small brown ones in hard to see places and only then about half a mile away from the site itself. The site itself was a bit on the scruffy side and nowhere near as good as the South Brighton site at Christchurch, which was family run and this looks like it is run by employees. So there you are, it shows you that some of the best sites will be owned and run by a family who put in the effort to make them nice and give them some ambience,

Now talking about ambience, Dunedin itself turned out to be a nice little town with oodles of ambience, better than Christchurch in my opinion. The centre was fairly compact and wouldn't take long to walk round. Made up of only four main streets all running north/south and parallel. I cruised up and down them in about 15 minutes on the scooter and thought that the fact that many of the older building where still there and were mostly all in lovely condition, gave the place this nice ambience. Trees in the streets also help make them look nicer. Plus I think someone on the Council may have made sure that the signing on shop fronts was kept more low key than in other towns. I think that where you get towns where shopkeepers are allowed carte blanche to put up whatever signs they like, you then get a huge number of garish and hideous signs, many in dayglow type colours. Everyone is trying to catch your eye and get your business. There is nowhere worse for this, than a lot of American towns and cities. Although I was in business in one city, in LA, where they had an enlightened council and where they did allow these kinds of signs. In fact you could not even erect any signs on poles on the highways edge, of the type you see on TV and films showing typical US towns.

All the next day I pootled around the place shopping for food and looking for an internet place and some book shops to replenish my reading, which is completely out. For a University place I found a distinct lack of Internet places and found only one. I did find a number of bookshops where you can buy secondhand books and also swop them. I also took many photos. On the question of food I have been finding that the further south I have got, the worse the ready made meal situation has got. The best was Auckland and it has got worse ever since. Also the best supermarket, Foodtown, hasn't been seen since Auckland. Another thing I have noticed in the South Isle is that the newspaper I have been reading from day one, The New Zealand Herald, is now I am at the end of the South Isle, unavailable. In Christchurch you could get it in some of the bigger newsagents but had to pay an extra $1.20 for freight! This I find astonishing, as the paper is hardly worth the normal $1.30 let alone another $1.20. In this day and age when newspapers are printed via the computers, this newspaper could be printed in the South Island cities where they are sold. So if you like reading the news and keeping up with what's going on then, you will find like me, that in NZ you are in a desert. Their papers are terrible, with little news except parochial local matters and absolutely full of adverts. (even worse than UK ones who are bad enough on this score) World News hardly figures. I get most of my news from the UK Weekly Telegraph and Express which are printed in NZ and cost the same all over NZ. Or off the Net on Google or Yahoo Home page.

Another thing I have observed since being in Kiwiland is their propensity for waffling on about a subject ad nauseum. I have mentioned already, about them banging on about their All Blacks Rugby losing out on the World Cup. They went on for two weeks plus. Then the next subject to receive the treatment was when their police arrested a bunch of Maoris they caught carrying out semi military exercises out in the bush with weapons etc. Anyone would think they had caught Bin Ladin himself, so we were subjected to endless goings on about it, from all sides. After two weeks they were still banging on about it. I doubt if the Maoris have anywhere near the ability to be able to turn themselves into credible terrorists. Then one of their government opposition politicians bopped a minister after a slanging match had taken place during Parliament and he'd been apparently abused. Again this has dominated every minute of radio, newspapers and TV. I have come to the conclusion that there isn't enough going on in NZ to keep them occupied, so when some little thing does happen, which anywhere else would blow over in a couple of days, because nothing else comes along to elbow it aside, they just keep up the interminable waffle. No wonder Kiwis are adept at collaring perfect strangers to get them into a conversation. I don't know about the Land of the Long Cloud, it should be 'The Land of the Long Tongue' Maybe it comes from the history of watching all those Maoris sticking out THEIR long tongues during their 'hakas'

The day was nice and warm even though there were plenty of dark clouds around. It would definitely rain in the evening (it did) and it was forecast to rain the following day. (it did, but only spots) I spent the morning shopping for more food and checking out where all the bookshops where. Being a university town there a more of these than most towns. I traded my books that I had read in against another five books to take up the east coast as I doubt that I would be able to find any used bookshops up there. New ones 'Yes', but in NZ as I've said, they cost much more than the UK.

After I had finished I still had about an hour left of my afternoon so I decided to start going down the road towards Portobello which is on the Otago Peninsula along which I had planned to explore for the wildlife. The road hugs the Otago Harbour inlet and it snakes in and out for miles so when I got about a third of the way, at a place called Warwick Bay, I decided to head up onto the range of hills and the south side of the inlet. I could then follow this along to top and back to the campsite at St Kilda. Up there you get a fantastic view of the whole of this long inlet and down to where Dunedin sits at the end. So I will go back when the weather is fine again and revisit this road so I can take some snaps. I want to get right to the end and hopefully see penguins and albatrosses.

Dunedin is a town that sits partly on a small coastal plain and is surrounded on three sides by hills. A substantial part of the towns suburbs sit on the sides of these hills. This gives the town a snug feeling of being wrapped around by the enclosing arms of the hills. The town centre sits at the extreme end of the long narrow inlet called The Otago Harbour. To the South East runs a peninsular, funnily enough called the Otago Peninsula, and it was to this that the next morning I hurried to. Mind you I nearly abandoned my plans as when I got up at 8.45 it was black clouds and spits of rain. However by 10 am it was clearing and the rest of the day was beautiful with mostly clear skies, but a little chilly.

I rode along the crest of the quite tall hills that run up the spine of this peninsular and taking shots of the various scenes. I was heading for a so called castle called Lanarch Castle. Built by a rich bod in the late 1800's so he could act as the local laird. When I got there they wanted $30 to go in and around the house and $20 if I just wanted to look around the gardens. I had seen photos of the place and could see that by UK or European standards it was quite a modest affair. In the UK I will not go round rich men's houses on principle. My attitude is, who wants to gawp at the opulence of man who had or have more money than they know what to do with. I was more interested in the architecture and just wanted to take a photo from the outside, but not at $20. So I passed on that one and motored onto the village of Portobello where I had got to the day before. There I had a coffee and read the local newspaper in 5 minutes flat.

Then on down the winding coastal road until I got to the sign advertising the Penguin Reservation. This is a privately run place owned by the farmer on whose land these penguins nest on. He has built up a special reserve for them and you get a guided tour. First you have a 15 minute lecture in a special little theatre room when you get told all there is to know about all the various species of penguins in the World. Then we all hop into a bus and off over the farmland to the nearby coast. The land next to the beach has been laid out with many little wooden boxes for the little blue penguins to nest in. This way it allows you to be able to see the little blighter sitting on its nest. I was there at the right time as eggs had been laid and now it was hatching time. Had they been in their normal burrows into the ground you would not see anything. The other penguin that also nests there is the bigger yellow eyed penguin, which is an endangered species with only around 4,000 in total around NZ. To see these they had built a larger inverted V shaped cover for them to nest in. We did get to see one standing outside its shelter whereas all the others were sitting inside and difficult to get a good decko of. After all this excitement it was back to base in the bus.

Then a quick run down to the end of the peninsular to the Tairaroa Head where they have the Royal Albatross Centre and Colony. (They had a photo of Prince Charles crouched in front of two of the birds and the caption 'A Royal with a Royal bird' How nauseating…he gets everywhere on these freebies. Whereas the likes of you and me have to pay. Here is where this particular type of albatross hatches its chicks and brings them up. It was nesting time and because of this they would not allow you to walk up to the places where they nest. Later on in November when they actually have hatched, you could. So one had to make do with just watching them wheeling about overhead. However that is not to say they are there in huge numbers, it is a matter of waiting 'til one shows up overhead and they are not round for more than a few seconds before they are gone out of sight. So getting a picture of one in the air was a devil of a job, especially with these new fangled digital cameras which I do not like much. They have their good points but also some horribly bad ones. Try catching a snap of a wild creature that only pops up every now and then and then only for seconds. That is up in the sky as well, and not so close to you. The camera will not stay on permanently so you have to switch it on, wait for it to automatically switch into photo mode, then get it into full zoom, and while doing this keep it trained on the wheeling about bird that you can't even see on the screen… IMPOSSIBLE! Then if it is bright day, when you look at the screen, what do you see?… the reflection of your own face! When you don't want it to happen, the batteries run out of power and even though I paid for LONG LIFE BATTERIES, they didn't last any longer than el cheapos. Maybe a more expensive model would be better?

At this same location there are the remains of a Victorian fort built in the late 1800's in response the jitters of that age, the possibility of a Russian invasion. The exact same as I had seen at several locations in Oz. Here they wanted Mucho Dollars to go round this place. So I gave that one a miss, having already seen very similar in Oz for free.

After filling myself up on my prepared lunch I had brought with me, I headed off to the next 'Tourist Highlight' This on the map was headed 'Lovers Leap and the Chasm' I had to head back along the High Road and turn off down to the coast at a place called Sandymount. This turn off road was a gravel track and after going about 5 K's I reached the end of it only to see a sign on the walking track down to the spot, which told me that due to 'Lambing' the track was closed. So I had slithered around on this dusty track for nothing and for the lack of a sign to tell me this, at the main road turn off. A not too happy bunny, headed back to distant Dunedin for a fortifying cup of coffee to calm me, and to see if there were any emails for me.

Although I must admit I enjoyed the switchback ride that this whole road to and from Dunedin and along this peninsular. It was for a bikey, a thrill drive to test your skills, and when up high, it was a bit scary with the drop off to one side, of several hundreds of feet down and no barriers whatsoever. The Kiwis I think must feel that barriers are for wimps, as I have noticed a distinct lack of them EVERYWHERE in Kiwiland. Even when you do get them, they are so low that a biker hitting them would just sail right over them and to his death. They also like these wire barriers which are also a death knell to bikers and one was cut in half on the motorway out of Auckland recently when he went out of control and hit one. I was crossing a long bridge over a river, in the m/home and saw that the barriers they had to stop you dropping into the quite wide and deep river, where about a foot high. Again a biker would just topple over them and certainly no car or trucks would be stopped. In fact I saw many barriers just made of wooden posts with planks of wood as a barrier. Obviously safety is not an important issue in Kiwiland, and bad accidents are a daily story on the TV and papers.

Back to Dunedin and its port, I had taken a tour of the wharfs and I saw that not one ship was to be seen, and then I was told that bigger ships tied up at the place near the head of the inlet called Port Chalmers. So if it is nice tomorrow I will take a trip up the north western side of the inlet, to it.

One thing I have noticed about Dunedin now I have scootered all around the centre and that is that it is a city of smells. Nice ones like the beautiful waft of chocolate you get from its big Cadburys chocolate factory which is bang in the middle of town. This would send women chocolate lovers into a constant frenzy of longing everytime they visited town to shop. I have also smelt a perfume smell and the smell of coffee beans, as well as various food smells.

Also I have noticed that it is a city of many old cars. I would say that it has more old cars still on its roads than all the other places I have so far come through. Cars going back to the sixties, like Marinas and Hillman Avengers and Hunters, Triumph 2.5's, many early Minis and so on.

Then to its houses, these I find are of better stock in general, than those of Christchurch. More brick houses and the wood ones of a generally nicer design, also in better condition. So all this gives a nicer feel and air to the place.

The natives are generally nice and talkative, and talking of that I can't help mentioning that in the camps I have been in so far, the tourists that are in them are definitely not talkative. If they are French, German etc and even Brit, no one seems to want to talk to others. For instance I am the ONLY Brit registered vehicle to be seen ANYWHERE, so I stand out. Plus I am the only motorhome that has a scooter/bike rack with one on it. (In Oz many homes had like me scooter racks on them) Yet not one person has stopped to have a talk to me in any camp I have stopped at. Not even fellow Brits. The only people that will talk to you are native Kiwis travellers, that are in the camps, or working there.

So much for interaction between fellow travellers, and it is not me because I have tried to catch their eyes but when they always keep their eyes averted it is difficult to get a conversation started.

On the Friday I pootled around during the morning doing various jobs and after lunch I set off along the Port Cameron road. A totally uninteresting stretch of road full of trucks going to and from the docks. Didn't take long to get there and once there I couldn't quite believe I was there. That because there wasn't much to the place. A short main street housing a motley selection of mainly older buildings. Some had or were being done up, but still it had an air of faded life about it. The shops were a funny selection too as a lot of them were arty farty type paces and this I read was because some arty farty types had settled there in recent times and were trying to make it into an artists retreat!

The port itself was small and as far as I could see could only accommodate three vessels and that day there was a fancy large modern tour ship, the Rhapsody of the Seas. Next to it was a largish container ship. On the wharf next to the tour ship was a large pile of wood chips and the rest of that wharf was full of logs, presumably for chipping. This type of wood chip I think goes to making up paper. From a nearby lookout point I was able to see the whole town and docks below. So that was it and with nothing else to see, I wanted to see if I could find what on the map was supposed to be New Zealand's tallest tree. It was shown to be just off the road that connected P.C to Waitati where when on my way into Dunedin I had stopped for a coffee.

On my way along that road I had hoped to see a sign directing me to it and on the map it showed a track that ran alongside the area where the tree was supposed to be, so I went down this track. However it was obvious that I could not get to this tree as the track ran along near the top of a ridge and to my left where the tree aught to be, there was a pest control fence. So back to the road and down into Waititi.

Where I went into the local plant nursery where I could get another coffee, so no better place to ask about this tree. I was told that it was in a wood which normally could be reached from the town, but as the powers to be were making the whole area into some refuge, hence the fence, you couldn't actually get there yet. That explained why there were no signs anywhere. The lady I spoke to said it was a singularly unimpressive gum tree that wasn't even a native of NZ, so I wasn't missing much anyway.

After a nice coffee it was back onto a road back to Dunedin and rather than take the main highway which I had come in on, I took a minor road running through the hills. What a bumpy badly paved road it was too. So I was at home with it because it was just like being back home in the UK, being thrown and bumped all over the place. At least there was very little traffic on it.

On Saturday I thought I should try and get a supply of my anti cholesterol tablets as I had only two days supply left. I had the prescription I had got back in Christchurch and with this I fronted up to the nearest Pharmacy, only to find out that the doctor had omitted to put some reference number on it so I would therefore have to pay full wack. I said why couldn't he ring the doc and get this number. That could only be done on Monday. I later found that the doctor has to write to some central government agency to ask for permission to issue this number that would entitle to patient to a subsidised cost. So once again we have the spectre of the NZ government not caring about tourists, because obviously a tourist who is on the go, cannot wait while some doctor corresponds with a slow government agency. Also would the tourist get permission to buy the drug at a subsidised rate in any case? I doubt it.

In the afternoon I planned to visit the Settlers Museum in town and while in the town I would visit a bigger pharmacy and see if I could swing it without having to wait on Monday morning, and to check on this bureaucracy re numbers, as I wanted to get off without delays. I went to one place and they had only one months supply and they again said I would have to pay full wack of $120. At still yet another place, although they had the full supply it would also cost me $120 per months supply, so times that by three! $360 for 90 tablets I nearly had a heart attack at that.

In Europe I could buy ALL my heart tablets without any prescription and these like the others cost no more than Eu20 to Eu30 a months supply. Even in Oz I had no probs and the costs where not much different than Europe. So why is NZ trying to rip people off with a charge for 30 tablets of approximately Eu50? You need to look into this obvious problem and costs for any medication you may be on and that you may need to replenish whilst in NZ. I could only get three months supply in the UK but didn't think I would have to break the bank to replenish any of them or to even have to pay to get a prescription.

In this last week I saw in the media that fireworks would be on sale in order that Guy Fawkes Night could be celebrated. I was astonished that here in NZ they would even think about this British tradition let alone copy it. After all it happened long before the Brits even found NZ. I must say that I believe it should be banned in the UK because now with so many youngsters that are out of control, one has to suffer interminable bangs for a week before and a week after. Also quite why the Brits want to celebrate something that happened so long ago and which really has no meaning these days, is beyond me. I mean who likes Parliament and all those pigs in it with their snouts in the trough of our taxes? So few people have any time for politicians and fewer even bother to vote for them, so I would have thought that many these days would have preferred that Guy Fawkes had been successful.

At least in NZ they only allow fireworks to go on sale four days before the fifth and then only to adults and judging by the feeble noises that I heard in the evening of the Saturday. The fireworks that get sold are not like the ordnance on sale in the UK. I mean the strength of fireworks sold now in the UK is a menace to society, peace and safety. The explosions one hears sound like World War 3 has broken out, hence my hate of the whole thing. They certainly do not celebrate this in OZ, so I must ask around as to why it goes on in NZ.

On my last day in Dunedin, a Sunday, I had planned in the afternoon to go to a supermarket and get enough provisions for at least three days. In the morning I was going to clean up the interior, read the Sunday paper and have lunch. All went well until lunch time at 1300 hours. By then it had got increasingly darker and then started to rain. It had got increasingly colder and I decided to not go to the supermarket and get drenched on the scooter, but to call there first thing in the morning in the motorhome and on the way out of Dunedin.

So the afternoon was a bit of a misery and I even ended up having to put my small electric fan heater on. I am dreading what the weather is going to be like on the East coast as every time I hear the weather forecast it always seems to rain, snow, hailstones and cold. If this is normal weather for very late spring in NZ I would definitely suggest that you leave coming here until later. Over in Oz the weather is up in the late 20's each day and that is why I made a miscalculation as to what it would be like in NZ at this time of the year.

Late afternoon I thought I would go and have a shower and the men's block that I had been using nearest my pitch proved to have rubbish showers with only lukewarm water. Which seeing as the air temperature is damn cold, makes the exercise really annoying. I only washed my hair, dried off and shot over to the other block where at least the water was hot. This brings me to comment on the state of the average shower in campsites. Some are very good but most I would say are rubbish. Water that never gets hot enough and shower controls that do not work very well. On top of this I have noticed that Kiwis being a rural type, I can only surmise that most were born in fields, seem to love toilet blocks that are open to the blowing gales and freezing airs. Also I have yet to come across a door to the men's toilets that has an automatic closing device on them. So you get a gale blowing into the block due to lazy blokes who will not close the doors after them. Roll on the summer if we ever get one.

On a completely different subject, the quality of Kiwi caravans and motorhomes. Compared to European build standards they do not compare. The average Kiwi motorhome a just a square box with little or no style. The interior fittings like the wood cupboards and drawers etc are way behind in quality and style. Their caravans are light years behind and I am amazed at how many old caravans one sees on caravan sales lots. So far I haven't seen many caravans being towed or on the sites I have stayed at so I am inclined to think that they may be only used in numbers as a static home left in one position all the time. However one guy turned up next to me on my last day, with a small Caravan that looked like it was out of the 50's or 60's… couldn't resist snapping it.

Anyone contemplating hiring a motorhome of sorts for their stay in NZ, will have to be prepared to pay a lot of money as in OZ. That is for a full sized home, smaller van type conversions would be cheaper and the even smaller campervans, which are the small Hiace type vans that are really only a bed on wheels, are the cheapest. These are favoured by the young as they are the cheapest and they don't mind slumming it as they are at least better than a tent.

The van conversion types are made up from the larger Transit and Merc vans, with side windows and two long seats at the back which convert into a double bed. Together with a toilet up front and a small kitchen area with cooker, fridge, sink etc. Too constricted for a long stay but I suppose OK for 2-4 weeks or so.

Even though the weather is rubbish there are still plenty of people on the move and one sees loads of motorhomes and vans on the roads, wherever you go. Each night there are twenty odd homes in each park I have stayed at. So there are plenty of mad bastards out there like me, braving this crap weather.

Monday, and the weather at least in Dunedin, when I got up was nice. Blue skies with some white cloud. Filled up with diesel, got provisions, went to the chemists and got ripped off for $88 for a months supply because as I just knew, they couldn't get a number off the doctor that gave me the prescription. So I had to pay full wack. But get this, as I have said above, in town the chemists were wanting $120 for 30 tablets, so big deal I save $32. I fume but what can I do, I will try and sort it when I am back in Wellington. The following pictures are all of Dunedin and all the places around it that I went to. (see photo 786 to 821)

So on to the road south and for a while it is good weather and easy going, but it didn't last. The countryside was fairly uninteresting for some while and any town I went through was only small, until I got to Balclutha. A bit bigger but not worth a stop. At this place you can either continue on Highway 93 to Invercargill along an inland route, or turn south and follow the scenic route more or less along the coast. I took the scenic route and before long the weather started to turn and for the rest of the journey all the way to Inv, it was blustery to howling wind, rain showers, and at one stage I saw my first snow and hail showers. Also it was very cold and down to 9 degrees but with the wind chill factor, below that.

The scenery changed to very hilly and the road became winding and up and down. The scenery is alternating between bush and farmland along with thousands of sheep. The first place I wanted to stop and have a look at, a listed scenic point, was a place called Cathedral Caves, which was supposed to have very high roofs like a cathedral. When I got to the spot the sign on the turn off said it was only open at 5pm at low tide, and a gate was across the entrance to the road leading to it… First disappointment.

Then I drove onto a spot called Niagra Falls, which according to the map was the Niagra Falls of NZ, so I naturally thought that it may be worth a look, even though I knew it wouldn't be anything like the real Niagra, but maybe better than any other NZ falls. When I got there all that there was, was a café called The Niagra Falls Café and no signs at all to guide you to any falls… 2nd disappointment, and maybe a con?

A little way down the road I stopped at the info centre in Waikawa and spoke to a gnarled old lady to ask her about the next scenic spots I wanted to visit namely Slope Point, the most southerly point in NZ. She said that there wasn't much there to see but people went there just to say they'd been there… much like Lands End or John O'Groats. (see photo 822)The road from Waikawa onwards was only gravel, but after about 30K's went back to tarmac. She also said to call in on Curio Bay and see the Fossil Forest and maybe see dolphins in the bay. So it was to there I went first and boy was it cold when I stopped and got out of my nice warm cab. (I had the hot air going) It was blowing a hooley and the sea was rough. The bay a bit more sheltered had no dolphins, so maybe they don't like rough water? The place where the fossils were supposed to be turns out to be a ledge of rocks at the bottom of a small cliff, on which they had some steps down. However you can't walk on the ledge until the tide is out and it was in. 3rd disappointment. I speak to some Dutch women and tell them they are my favourite European race. So I get effusive calls of 'have a good journey' (see photo 823 to 830)

After having my lunch I move on my bumpy and wind torn way. Some times the gusts are so strong I fear the home is going to get blown over. Eventually I reach Invercargill and drive up and down their main roads. The place is much bigger than I expected it to be, and the buildings in the centre are much more substantial and older than I thought they would be. Many have dates on them from the 1860's. I wanted to park along one of the streets, but everywhere they have pesky parking meters which I find odd as even in Dunedin and Christchurch you could park for free even if it were only for 30 minutes or so. The local council here must be a shower! So I park in the Pak N Save supermarket car park. I do a quick walk around as it is real blowy and freezing and showery. However one good thing about most NZ towns, like in Oz, they have substantial awnings over the shop fronts and right over the pavements. So you can walk some distances in the rain without getting wet. Found an internet café after my afternoon coffee, and after that went back to the supermarket to get some more provisions as I do not know what shopping is going to be like henceforth.

After this I attempted to find a motorhome/campsite as several where shown on the map, but I saw absolutely no signs on any roads pointing you towards any. Yet another dozy council that doesn't think about tourists. I eventually find one and on mentioning this to the owner, she told me that their council didn't want to know about putting up signs around the town, and they had a job to even get permission to put up the small sign they had outside their camp entrance, which I barely saw. Are you getting the picture about Tourism NZ? At least in some places that is.

The campsite was a little gem, (only space for about 20 units) very well turned out with nice pitches, and beautiful newish toilets. In fact they had only been open 2 years, and I was only one of two people staying there that night, so I wonder if it is because of the difficulty of being able to find them. How can good sites get enough business with unhelpful councils? Two sites that were marked on the map had closed down and were not there, I wonder why? (see photo 831 to 833b)

Thankfully the wild weather that went on during the night with strong gusts of wind blowing my home around, had more or less gone. After filling up with diesel I got onto the road (S/H 99) heading to Te Anau and the lake there. From Inver you can take the inland S/H 6 all the way or take the scenic rout S/H 99 which is what I took.

Out of Inver the road passes through flat land covered in sheep and this is the case until you get to Riverton on the coast. Thereafter it gets slowly more mountainous the more you go to the west. I stopped at 11am for a cup of tea at a small bay called Monkey Island. This was a very small island 50 yards off the beach, apparently called thus as in the mid 1800's they landed supplies for the new settlers in the area on this place and used a small monkey winch (never heard of one of them) to winch the supplies off the ship lying just off the Island.

At Te Waewae the road heads away from the coast to the North and the land on either side becomes mountainous and most peaks have snow on them. Eventually I reach a historic bridge at a place called Clifden. It is the spitting image of the Clevedon bridge in Bristol and whilst there taking snaps of it I talk to two women sitting at a bench having a snack. They are a mother and daughter from Melbourne Oz, so we get into things about that place and the immigration issues there and in the UK. It is a small world, suffering from similar problems. (see photo 834 & 835)

By lunch time I arrive at Manapouri on the lake of the same name. I have lunch in a layby over looking the lake. There is nothing in the small town of worth as it is just a collection of houses and motels all looking to have been built in recent years. On my way out I pass a house with a collection of Brit cars mostly various models of Moggy Minors. What an odd place to find such a collection and they all need restoring. Must be a homesick Brit living there. (see photo 836 to 839)

It is only 22K's to Te Anau so doesn't take long to reach there. It all looks quite new and there didn't seem to be a building older than 20 years. Plenty of hotels, motels, campsites and a small centre with a selection of shops etc. Obviously very much a touristy place, with many coaches about. It is early afternoon so I book into a Top 10 park which only costs $18 which I thought very good seeing as it is a well frequented place where they usually stick up the prices. An excellent site with everything in top order and all looking fairly newish. (see photo 840)

I had a walk around the shore of the lake and the weather was wonderful and warm. In fact since leaving the south shores it has got warmer, less wind and clearer skies. Hope it keeps up for tomorrow as I am off on the 120K's trip to Milford Sound and that road is supposed to be hilly, windy and narrow with loads of traffic. Should be interesting. (see photo 841 to 845)

During the last few days I have noticed a number of Harrier Hawks flying around near the roads. Unlike in Oz where you get similar hawks all over the place, practically on every tree along any road out in the countryside. They feed on road kill and I am surprised not to see more hawks in NZ as there is plenty of road kill to be had let alone all the wild life including loads of young lambs.

I woke to another lovely day, so I am very lucky as I expected this coast to be rainy. I set off for Milford sound a two hour drive away. For some distance the road is fairly flat and basically follows a valley formed by the River Eglington. In places the valley is very wide and flat. There are mountain ranges on either side of this valley and I would say all of the peaks are 5,000 feet plus. By the time you get to a place called 'The Divide' the road has started to slowly climb until you get to a tunnel called 'Homer tunnel' and as tunnels go I would say it is 'Third World Country' standard. Low roofed, narrow and for some reason best known to the authorities, quite dark. I could hardly see where I was going and I feared that my quite tall roof may hit the sides if I met anything coming the other way thus forcing me over to my left where the roof curved downwards. Luckily nothing came the other way. After the tunnel it was a switch back ride down into Milford some 8 K's away. The only thing that is at Milford is the terminal for all the scenic boat trip boats. I booked on the midday boat and off we went. (see photo 846 to 856)

The fiord (it is really a fiord and not a sound) is quite something with mountains on both sides of 5,000' to 7,000' The boat trip lasts almost two hours and goes to the mouth of the fiord at the coast, and back. Of course all this I recorded with endless shots on the camera. The boat was full of Chinese and Japanese all jabbering away and this was the butt of many comments by us racist Anglo Saxons, as we are wont to do. A couple of waterfalls of some height, fall down into the fiord and on the way back along the northern side we stopped in a little inlet and there were two little yellow crested penguins standing on a rock. They created such a rush of Asians to get to the bow of the boat to snap these little creatures and if you have ever been in a rush of Asians you will know they are very gentle. So it was all pushing, shoving and elbows, plus all the squawking about 'penguin, penguin' etc etc in their own high pitched way of excitable talking. Thus prompting another round of naughty comments. A little further on it was three lazy, sleeping fur seals, lying on a rock. Good warm clothing on this trip is a must as the wind whipping down that sound was something, (up to 70 knots in places) and chilly. Had it not been a lovely sunny day, I can imagine it would be freezing too. (see photo 857 to 872)

After the cruise there nothing else to do in Milford, there are no shops, only a café, and I don't think anybody lives there. At least I saw no houses, unless there were a few hidden away. So it was back on the road to get back to Te Anau. Even though my next place of call is Queenstown which is more or less level with M.S, there is no road across the mountain range, or tunnel. So you have to go back to Te Anau and then head eastwards and then northwards. Of course this is good for the pockets of the Kiwi government as more petrol is used and that means more taxes, but not good for the atmosphere with all the extra exhaust fumes.

The ride back was uneventful apart from once again going though The Homer Tunnel. I was dreading meeting one of the huge tour buses that ply that road, coming the opposite way. Luckily once again I did not meet any vehicle at all. (see photo 873 to 877)

After another night at the Top 10 Park I was lucky yet again, with the next morning and the weather. It was a beaut day, all day. The road all the way, was a long quite flat road and following a valley with the inevitable fields of grass and sheep. You could say that NZ is the Worlds largest lawn, for the land that is farmed which is an enormous amount, is all short cropped grass so that it looks like a lawn. Not a perfectly flat lawn, but lawn nevertheless. One thing I have noticed is that despite all this grass, I have only seen one rabbit. I wonder if the Kiwis have managed to get rid of most of them. I've seen more rabbits in the UK.

So it was like this all the way to a place called Kingston which sits on the extreme southern end of Lake Wakatipu, upon which Queenstown sits on, half way up it. The road clings to the eastern shore and twists in and out and up and down a bit. So it isn't a quick ride along that section, made even slower by my getting behind the first caravan I've seen on a NZ road, I do get by it eventually, although I have plenty of time as it isn't even lunchtime yet. I get into Queenstown at 11.30 and go straight to the Top 10 campsite which is within walking distance of the centre. It isn't a huge site and isn't quite up to the one at Te Anau, especially in the toilets side of things. Quite frankly for the number of people they could hold, the lack of toilets was terrible. They had only three multisex units for half the park and queuing was the order of most times. However it is OK otherwise, but, and I was expecting this, at $25 a night it is the most expensive I have come across to date. Because Queenstown is a destination that a lot of people who come to NZ, head for, especially youngsters, I guess they think they can charge what they like. (see photo 878 to 880)

I walk into town and it is full of youngster from every country imaginable. I hear Yanks, Brits, Germans, Italian, French, Spanish, and of course the hoards of Japanese and Chinese. It is a town that now has been upgraded from the old one that was originally here, to only cater for all these tourists. So I felt it was a bit of a contrived place with no ambience or atmosphere of its own. A bit sterile you might say. All, or the majority of the buildings are new and lots of building still going on. As I am past all the mad things that go on here, which is strictly for the young thrill seekers, I would only stay one night and I only wanted a quick look around and to do two things. Firstly to take trip on the famous old steamer up the lake, and then to go up Ben Lomond Hill for an aerial view.

So a quick walk around ten to book the steamer trip, get lunch prepared to take with me and I then catch the 2pm trip up the lake. It was built in 1902 and is the oldest surviving steam ferry still in good working order. The engine was very similar to the one in the oldest working paddle steamer, the Waverley which works the UK coast with trips in summer.

It is only a trip that lasts 1.45 hours and when I got back I walked the short distance to the gondola ride up to Bobs Peak on Ben Lomond. There they have a large café/restaurant and a jumping off point for the paragliders who take people down to the town below, in tandem. I didn't fancy doing it but I was curious as to what they charged. I found this to be $185 which is about £75 and I reckon it is money for old rope as it doesn't take more than a 10 minutes flight. Then the pilot or whatever you call him, hops on a gondola, back up for the next one. There were a number of young blokes doing this so I guess they all make a good living at it. But for me, not on your life, especially when you see how they loop around and drop like a stone towards the end of the flight. Plus the cost for me is too much for my pocket. If I were young it would be great as you like that sort of thing when your young and foolish.

I had a good coffee, took a load of pictures and then it was down to bottom again on one of those scary gondolas that I always feel is going to part from its cable and plunge me to my death down the steep sides of the mountain. Funny because I feel OK even in a small plane, but not in gondolas. The next day it would be off to the west coast again through Haas Pass. Will the weather hold out I wondered, because so far I have been pushing my normally slim luck. (see photo 881 to 901)

Another lovely start to a day saw me up and running and out of Queenstown and on my way north towards Wanaka. You can take two roads, one (S/H 6) through a place called Cromwell and approach Wanaka from the east, or a more direct minor road through Cardrona which I took. The turn off onto that road came up pretty quickly and straight away you knew you were on some road for it went straight up and into a number of hairpin bends. You were climbing up the side of a pretty high mountain and at stages I was down to second gear and some of the bends were TIGHT. In fact at the beginning there was a notice saying it was not suitable for towing vehicles. When I reached the top there was a large parking area and a plaque which said this was the highest sealed road in NZ at 1075 metres. You then went down the other side into a valley and from then on it was a pleasant run into Wanaka, which sits at the southern end of Lake Wanaka. It is quite a long lake too and Wanaka is another one of these very new towns that looks like it was finished yesterday. I only stopped for a coffee and then up highway 6 towards Haast on the coast. (see photo 902 to 906)

The road first of all follows the southern end of a lake called Hawea which is adjacent to L.Wanaka, then it switches over to follow the northern end of L.Wanaka. From then on it follows the valley and river Makaroro for some distance. The road rises a bit and passes through a constricted valley area called the Haast Pass, which is the lowest pass in the Alps area. It then picks up the River Wills which runs into the Haast River and that goes out to the west coast at Haast Beach. At around the beginning of where the road starts to follow the Haast River there are some seriously high mountains Mt Brewster and Mc Farlane at around 8,000 feet. As you near the coast you can feel the difference in the air, as it starts to feel fresher and cooler and the tops the mountains instead of having white clouds around them, the clouds change to dark rain clouds. (see photo 907 to 909)

I've noticed that since leaving Queenstown that there are virtually no farms that stock herds of deer. Whilst seeing deer herds along the south eastern coast and even more in the Southlands area right up to Te Anau, for some reason after Queenstown none to be seen. I often wondered what they used the meat for I presume they are kept for their meat, but I have not seen venison advertised or in supermarkets. Maybe they are exporting it.

The closer I got to Haast I found that the roads were not as good as previously. More repairs done to them and a lot less even or level, meaning the home bounced up and down a lot. This is disconcerting as it tends to shift things around in the home and it also puts a strain on the scooter rack that I don't like.

A soon as you leave Haas Beach (nothing there to stop for except to fill up on diesel) and start to follow the coats the vegetation changes completely to what you had been passing before. It is an exceptionally dense and ugly bush like forest and looks half dead and very windblown, with some swampy areas. It is so dense as to be impenetrable and the early settlers and explorers who first journeyed in this area, must have suffered a nightmare to get around, hacking their way through that lot. It was once coming into this area that I saw my first wild parrot or rather parakeet. It was about budgie sized and of a very dark green colour.

I also noted that from then on the amount of dead possums in the roadway was incredible. They obviously don't know the highway cross code, silly buggers. But then the Kiwis don't like them and want to kill them all anyway, for they say they are an introduced pest that is killing off indigenous wildlife. I like possums, even if they are pests, but I also like the creatures they are killing off… what a dilemma to be in. (see photo 910 to 917)

The road meanders between the coast and a little inland with nothing to report of significance except that always there are high mountains inland and on your right. Eventually you reach a place called Fox Glacier (no relation to Foxes Glacier Mints, I don't think) which is on the edge of two large glaciers that everyone goes to see and be on. However the day I am passing the glaciers, as I have said, there were lots of rain clouds swilling around the mountain tops, so I can't see them. 20 K's past Fox is the township or settlement of Franz Joseph (an early explorer) and it is here that I pull into at 4.15pm, a campsite for the night. Whilst parking I am approached by the first Brit who makes comment on my UK number plate. He is parked behind me. So I get some conversation out of a fellow Brit traveller, and after him the guy next to me who is also Brit, also gets talking. So a great deal of swopping of notes especially the second guy as he has just done a circumnavigation of Oz, like myself and he has brought his motorhome over from Oz, and has registered it in NZ. So I get some ideas off him as to what he had to do. (see photo 918 to 920)

I partake, in the evening of a little treat for myself, of a meal out. The campsite has its own bar and they do meals. I fancied fish and chips and for the equivalent of just over £6 I got a good plate of two reasonable sized fish and a good helping of chips and salad.

One downside to this campsite is the great number of midges that suck your blood, must be the dampness with all the rain they get here. Another minus is the fact that again like the last camp, there are simply not enough facilities in the toilets. Only one toilet, one urinal, and one shower together with three hand basins. All this for a guessed total of around 40 motorhome pitches. There aught to be a regulation number of facilities per 10 people.

The next day the weather is the same with dark clouds over the mountains tops. So out goes the flight over the glaciers and Mt Cook, I was going to treat myself to. So I will have visited the south Island and not been able to see the mountain named after me!! The Brit guy I was talking to has been waiting for 3 days to take a flight and was hoping to get off today, but I am not willing to kick my heels around for days in a place with nothing to do. So I take off for the nearby car park where I can park the home and take a short walk to where I can at least see the nearby Franz Joseph glacier. However after doing this I am disappointed because the glacier is quite small from what one can see of it and the ice is all dirty looking. The notice boards show that 200 years ago in 1750 it was enormous and even in 1850 it would have been considerably higher and longer and then worth seeing.

I had asked the girl in the office at the camp what was the red stuff I was seeing on lots of rocks in and around rivers. It looked like someone had been going round painting the boulders with red lead paint. Apparently what it is, is a red lichen which you can rub partly off. I took a picture of the boulders in the river that runs away from the glacier and that are covered in it. (see photo 921)

After the 30 minutes of walking I got back onto the road up north, and I must say that the whole days ride was quite boring. The scenery was nothing to talk about, being flattish coastal plains and mountains to your right covered in bush. Few towns, if they could be called towns, were on this coast and none worth a stop. So quite frankly you could say that you would not be missing anything if you missed out the whole of the west coast bar Milford Sound. Mt Cook can be viewed and flown over from the east side. The farm land you pass by has mainly all cows on it. I guess with the heavy rainfalls they get lusher grass more suited for cows who need more grass than little sheep.

Like elsewhere where there are mountains, there are lots of rivers running off them and down to the sea. The bridges over them along this coast are nearly all rickety affairs of one narrow lane width. Traffic has to stop and give way to the traffic coming the other way. There are signs which will tell you whether you have to give way, or you have right of way. Trouble is very often you approach the bridge from round a bend and do not see if anything is on it and very often there is something on it yet you have right of way. So you end up giving way, anyway. Then I'd not been going long and I had a car up my backside, when coming round a bend there was this car stopped right in the lane I was in. I had to slam the brakes of because I couldn't see if anything was coming the other way. I had visions of the car behind slamming into me. Thankfully they didn't and I resorted to giving HER a good blow of my air horns. Shortly after SHE overtakes me, so it wasn't a case of her conking out or something like that. Probably stopped to adjust her face or makeup!

One thing I have noticed on the whole of this coastal highway is the complete absence of trucks and this makes me wonder how these little towns get their supplies delivered. I didn't even see any cattle trucks, which I seen plenty of before and elsewhere. Probably the narrow bridges will not take them as they seem to have weight restrictions. All day saw many motorcyclists going the opposite way. I must have passed a hundred of them in total, so the weekend must be the townies men on bikes weekend away, for a thrash down a windy coastal road, for their thrills. A macho boys away weekend!

I was making for the town of Westport to stay overnight before making the final stretch up and back to Picton, to catch the ferry back to Wellington. The description that the writer put into the travel guide book I have, I think said it all about this town and the rest of the other towns along this coast. 'Westport is one of the West Coasts more dispiriting towns.' Hit the nail right on the head there. I arrived at 4pm and everything bar the town's café, was closed. I had hoped a chemists was open so I could get a supply of one of my heart tablets. The town was practically deserted. It used to be like this in Oz in the 60's when everything shut on a Saturday at 12midday until Monday morning. Well at least it didn't rain and I had a half decent cup of coffee, and then after this, into the campsite a few miles down the road at Carters Beach. Another Top10 place and not too bad at $19 for the night. At least the toilets were sufficient.

The next day, Sunday, I was off with yet another reasonable day weatherwise. From Westport the road to Picton cuts inland and heads in a north easterly direction. For about the first 100K's was through the mountains of the Lyell Range.

The road followed a river for most of the way. And in fact this was the case for most of the whole way up this west coast. If you weren't following a river you were up in the mountains or on a flat plane. As for towns there was none of note or size. The first I came to was Murchison, which was eminently forgettable and the rest were just names on a map and a few houses. So there was nothing really to report, as the scenery was much the same as I've already passed through.

Approaching Nelson things got a little livelier and a real town started at Wakefield a suburb to the south of Nelson. Nelson itself was OK but still quite forgettable and it was here I stopped in the Woolworths car park to have lunch, after I had got a few provisions. (see photo 922 to 934)

It was some 60K's after Nelson and on the last leg to Picton that things went pear shape. At a place called Havelock I experienced the first time since I've been driving in NZ a cockup with Kiwi signposting. I had noticed that there is a distinct lack of signs telling you how far away the next towns are, and this makes it difficult to know if you are on the right road, if your not passing through any towns. Which was the case here. Also most countries mark there highways with the highway number, at regular intervals, so again you know that your still on the right road. Not the case in NZ. So when I got to this Havelock place I knew that the road split and the main highway that I had been following since Westport namely S/H 6 for some unknown reason the powers to be in NZ did not carry this highway right through to Picton, but headed it south again to Blenheim.

The road that turned off, just outside Havelock and did go to Picton suddenly becomes a minor road (our B road). This is crazy because Picton is the one and only port of entry/exit from the North Island and this minor road turned out to be a nightmare and the worst road I had had to travel on in the South Island. The sign that I was on the lookout for, on leaving Havelock, which I expected to say 'PICTON' actually said 'Queen Charlotte Drive' which I thought was just some fancy road and I continued on expecting to come across a main junction, saying 'PICTON' As the road I was gaily bowling along never went through any towns for 20K's I saw not one sign giving a place name or 'to Picton' I was getting sure that I was on the road to Blenheim which is 40K's south of Picton, and when I eventually came to the first settlement of Okaramio I knew that indeed I was on the wrong road, so a frustrating ride back towards Havelock, and when I got to the junction where I should have turned, I could see why I had made the error. You come round a corner and have seconds to read the sign and under the 'Queen Charlotte Drive' there was in small print ('the scenic drive to Picton') (should have said 'the crappy drive to Picton!) (see photo 935 to 939)

I was not too happy and especially so the more I drove along that goat track which was narrow, very badly surfaced and was one hairpin bend after another. Bear in mind that anyone coming into Picton and wanting to drive down the West coat would have to use this road. Conversely, those like me coming up the West coast and wanting to get to Picton the catch the ferry, would also have to use it. Indeed the majority of traffic I encountered going both ways was motorhomes, most of them too large for such a narrow road. Once back in Picton I booked into the same park I had stayed in four weeks previously after having booked on the 8am ferry tomorrow. (see photo 940 & 941)

Chapter Twenty Five

North Island continued

● Overnight stay
○ Passed through

Next day after an early rise at 6.30, which I am just not used to, so remained sleepy for ages after, I was on the ferry and on my way back to Wellington. When we got there a strong wind was blowing and the place was living up to its name of Windy Wellington.

I was quickly out of Wellington and up to the Lower Hutt shopping centre to stock up on a load of food. After this it was up Highway 2 and on the way to Napier which is supposed to be worth a visit. I had got into a stretch of road that was winding its way up a steep mountain side, and I could see a cop car up ahead of me. Also in front of me was another motorhome which was driving exceedingly slowly up this hill and then even slower down the other side. We passed the cop car which had pulled over and then tucked himself behind the two of us. After a while the slow guy pulled over onto lay-by to let the cop through, so he's behind me, and then he wants me to stop. 'Here we go again' I thought another cop who can't recognise a UK plate. Sure enough, but this time he was nice and was quick enough as soon as he was told I was from the UK, and I was on my way again. However this is a bit of a bind and I shall get really hacked off if it keeps going on, so I am going to stick a sign in the back window for the cops. Which I did and which they would be blind to miss, so I wondered what the result would be from then on.

The scenery en route towards the Hastings/Napier area was much the same as I've already passed through so nothing exceptional to report. The whole journey was along flat land after the above mentioned hills. When I reached the town of Eketahuna I saw a Cobra sitting in a petrol station forecourt. I stopped to have a look at it and see if it were a real one or a replica. Turned out it was a real one, a 289 Cobra and the bloke said it was the only one in NZ. He struck me as a bit of a snob (the owners of real Cobras have a thing about replicas of them!) and wasn't at all talkative especially after I told him I had spent 20 years making replicas. So that encounter didn't last long. (see photo 943)

Shortly after this I reached Pahiatua and into the motorhome camp there. A very basic place and really just a large field with a load of poles with electric supplies on and basic toilets and a kitchen. No one was in the office and a notice told you to find a spot and someone would collect the rent later. Well no one came to do this and even though I called twice still no one was their. So the next morning I just had to leave after a free nights stay. I was worried all day about this!

I completed the 150K's to Hastings and arrived at 11am just in time to partake of a coffee. After refreshment I got onto the road out and towards Napier. I could see a motorhome place halfway between the two twin towns, which would do nicely for two days of exploring the two places. It was a fairly basic place and most of the pitches were occupied with full time residents. However it was OK and not too expensive at $15 a night and the owners were nice and talkative.

Once you start to get near Hastings it becomes clear that this part of NZ actually has farms that grow things. Fields were showing a growth of crops, start to appear in numbers. Then groves of trees appear and I was told by the campsite owner that this whole area is called the fruit basket of NZ. There is also wine making in the area.

After lunch I got the scooter off and went into Hastings. First I had a good walk around the town centre which is not all that large, having a look at the art deco style restored buildings. Hastings and Napier had built such buildings in the 30's and both places are known for these buildings, although Napier is supposed to have the better collection. Both suffered from an earthquake in 1931 and as all the buildings collapsed, that meant rebuilding both towns completely and they used the then current craze for art deco. So Napier now has what is supposed to be the largest collection of such buildings along with Miami Beach. (see photo 944 & 945)

When I finished in Hasting centre I rode out to the area known as Havelock North and up the nearby hill called Te Mata. Panoramic scenes are to be had from the top so it is worth a visit up there. (see photo 946 to 951)

During the night a foul gale blew up and this just shows how changeable the weather in NZ really is. During the day you couldn't wish for nicer weather. Sunny and nice and warm. Overnight within hours all that changes and it rained quite heavily most of the night. All day on the Wednesday it blew at gale force but although the sky was full of black rain clouds, the rain mostly held off.

First thing in the morning, I went to a local Car Museum that was shown on the map. I had expected a pukka normal museum but this was no normal museum. A huge almost new looking shed that would have filled a football pitch was absolutely chockablock with British cars with hardly any space in between each car. A guy in his 60's let me in (for $10) and I could see that really this was no museum but one mans obsession with British cars.

Mr Hope the owner had spent his life as a mechanic but what made him start such an enterprise I do not know.

About three quarters of the space was taken up with dozens and dozen of cars that were in top condition. Some were in 'like new' condition and others were in very good original condition and some were restored. The rest of the space was taken up with dozens more cars that were in various states of wear from heavily neglected and looking like they had spent many years deteriorating in some paddock, to how they ended up after many years of hard use and needing restoration. Many of these cars were two high (one on top of another)

I would say that practically every model of British car that was ever made from 1947 onwards, plus some pre-war cars, were represented. Some models were present in large numbers such as the Morris Minor. There must have been at least 25 of these, representing each Moggy variant ever made. Many of the cars had been donated so hadn't cost the owner, however many obviously had been bought, including some expensive makes and models such as Jaguars and a Rolls plus a Bentley. The units that housed all these cars must have cost a fair bit too. Quiet how a mechanic could have made enough money to do all this, was a question I was dying to ask but thought better of it. I would think that some classic car experts back in the UK would love to get their hands on this collection. I jokingly said I thought that Lord Montague would love to buy this lot off him and he said there was no way the collection would ever be sold to anyone. It was a great pity that I had forgot to take my camera, and I didn't fancy going back again.

After lunch I took a windy ride up the coast and into Napier. There were more buildings still standing from the 30's and built in the art deco design, than to be seen in Hastings.

A nice, smallish and compact town with many of the buildings in very good order. A long Marine Esplanade, with rows of tall Norfolk Pine trees looked good. However the beach was a big disappointment being a dismal looking affair made up of grey gravel. In fact the gravel pathways of the Esplanade gardens looked better than the beach. I spent two or three hours running around on the scooter and walking around the centre, and then rather than going back to the campsite early, I went into the marine zoo (even the Duke of Edinburgh and Rolf Harris had been there, so I was keeping up a tradition) to see the sealions and dolphin etc. They also had penguins and gannets, who have a colony nearby at Cape Kidnappers, which I did not go to. Then with still more time to pass I went to the Aquarium, but this was not good value compared with others I have been to. (see photo 952 to 975)

The next day I got on the road and northwards towards Gisborne and that section of highway passed through countryside that was much the same as seen in many other places, a mixture of hills and plains. No towns or cities of any size were passed through and indeed only one settlement was passed through and that was Wairoa. So the 220 K's was passed in a quick time, and I got to Gisborne in time for lunch. A reasonably largish town of similar style to most Kiwi towns, so nothing much to report there. However the towns real claim to fame is that Capt Cook landed at this same spot when he first sighted the land now known as New Zealand. He was sailing westwards and one of his cabin boys Nick was the first to sight land. So down on the beach area which I must say is somewhat a depressing area as it is covered in warehouses and sheds there is a park/reserve area on the beach, with a statue of Cook and one of Nick. Considering the historical importance for New Zealand of this area, one would have thought that the whole area would have been the number one historical and tourist area of the land. As the inscription on the globe which the statue of Cook is standing on, says, that this landing was the first time a white man had landed and it was the beginning of what is now modern New Zealand. (see photo 976 & 977)

After having my lunch at the beach, I motored over to the other side of the river to the area where there was another memorial to Cook at a site where he actually landed. This was even worse than the other area, as it is completely surrounded by large port sheds and a large log storage area. The grassed area and gardens were not in top condition either. The obelisk that had been erected in 1908, to commemorate the landing had a picture of the opening ceremony and you can see that back then the shoreline was only feet away from the obelisk. Yet now you have all the reclaimed land upon which the unsightly Port facilities are now on. (see photo 978 to 983)

I continued onwards to explore the north east coast of NZ and I had no idea exactly where I would end up for an overnight stay. Shortly after leaving Gisborne I experience an example of just how bad and stupid some Kiwi drivers are. I am in mountainous terrain so the road twists and turns all the time and I went round a corner into a short straight to be met with about 5 cars and an idiot overtaking them all. Luckily there was a grass verge wide enough for me to come off the road and onto. He slammed on his brakes and pushed his way back into the traffic, but it could have been so different.

Not long after this I get my second example of Kiwi brainless driving this time over one of those stupid one lane bridges I have mentioned about. I was approaching such a bridge where I had right of way. A car coming the other way should have stopped as I was right on top of the bridge, yet it was approaching at a speed without decreasing so I knew it wasn't going to stop. I had to screech to a halt and the resulting space I left was only just big enough for the Neantherdal who was driving, to get through. He looked a right crim, the type that looks like they have spent a life in jail, and the worst aspect of his actions was that he had kids in the car. It seems as if this part of NZ suffers from some dysfunctional people.

As it was, because there were no places worth stopping for, as I passed through no towns, I eventually reached a place called Tikitiki. If you look at a map of the stretch of country I passed through that afternoon, you would see many places were there are place names. However all you get at these places are a few houses and no town. In fact this corner of NZ is quite sparse in population. The further north I got the less houses and farms and less land being farmed. It was also obvious that Maori people were in the majority and quite frankly some of the houses I saw were very scruffy. Houses that you wouldn't believe people would live in and many with lots of rusting cars and other machinery lying around in the gardens of these houses.

I had wanted to stay in a caravan park at a place called Te Puka, but it looked a dump so I motored on. The next site on the map was Te Puia Springs, but when I got there I could not stay as it wasn't actually a proper caravan camp but three spaces behind a pub, and they were taken. So I had to drive on to Tikitiki.

When I got there although I saw a sign saying 'Motorhome camp' but all that was there was a small overgrown field and the gate was shut. A run down house sat to one side of this area but I could not tell if anyone actually was living there. Since Gisborne I haven't seen too many other motorhomes or campervans on the road I thought that maybe lack of business meant it had closed down. I cruised up and down the short 'High St' to see if there was another place, but nothing. Next door was a garage and I asked a bloke outside it, if it was still open, and he said it was. At this time another motorhome arrived from the other direction and was opening the gate and going in, so I tucked in behind it. It turned out that it was open, but we were both apprehensive because of the dilapidated condition of the whole place. A young girl appeared saying that it was open and that the toilets did work and there was electricity on the posts. As it was getting on and I was tired I decided to stay and got hooked up. However what it showed is that up in this part of NZ, things were not the same as elsewhere. The cost of $10 for the night, was I thought no more than it should have been for such a run down place.

One thing I have noticed in NZ is that very often TV reception is bad or none existent even in places you would think would have excellent reception. I thought that here in this out of the way place I would be lucky to receive any reception. I did however manage to get enough of a signal to at least hear the news. However the same thing applies to radio reception. As I have already mentioned 20 to 30 K's out of any town of size, and you have no radio, and it was the same here except for a Maori speaking radio station. I thought I would try and get BBC World on shortwave. Something I have not managed to receive so far. So I was quite chuffed when I got a weak signal which was definitely BBC World. I had the idea to connect the aerial to my roof rack and this would give me a huge aerial and luckily I had in my tool box, a crocodile clip with a length of wire attached. Hey presto it worked like magic and I immediately got the station on really loud and clear.

In the evening the weather broke and it rained most of the night and on top of that I was woken sometime during the night by the sounds of wildlife having some sort of fight. Sounded like Tasmanian Devils having a go somewhere in the nearby trees and bush, which the campsite was surrounded by. In the morning the rain had stopped but there was heavy black cloud about. On my way out of this little settlement I could see many of the houses, and the building that had been a pub and another large building, were all empty and trashed. The road had definitely deteriorated the more I had got away from Gisborne and it was very uneven in places, especially on corners. I did not come across much traffic going either way, and certainly no trucks, whereas further back I was seeing many logging trucks. What I did see was a lot of cyclists, which hitherto I have seen only now and again. This section of road is very hilly and isolated so these cyclists were a brave lot. Another thing is I now hardly see any dead possums on the road. Maybe they are better at crossing the road in this part of NZ.

Once I got round the extreme top on the North Isle and started to go along the northern coast and towards the

Bay of Plenty the coast line became more rugged with the mountain sides coming down to the sea. So the road was hugging the mountain sides and sweeping in and out of the bays, as well as up and down all the time. I took it slow as I was in no hurry. But again as there were no towns as such there was no reason to stop at all until I saw a pretty white wooden church at a place called Raukokore. (see photo 984 to 986)

It had been built in the late 1800's and quite how it would get enough people to support it I don't know as there are not all that many houses around. I looked inside and the notice on the door tickled me pink. 'Please excuse the fishy smell but we have a penguin nesting under the font feeding fish to its young. Please close the door after you because of possums'. The penguin obviously was a religious one.

The first decent sized town I got to was Optiki (see photo 987) but nothing worth stopping for so I pushed on to the next nearby town of Whakatane which was quite a decent size. Got some provisions here, and had a quick drive around the centre, and then onto the road inland towards Lake Rotorua. This place is bigger again and you can tell that we are back into tourist country because I am seeing loads of motorhomes and campervans. I need to stop here overnight and according to the map there are several camp sites. Coming into the outskirts of Rotorua I could smell a funny smell and at first thought my toilet was the cause, however I discounted that because I hadn't used it for a year or more. Then I wondered if my fanbelt was breaking up as it smelt a little like burning rubber. It wasn't until I got to the park in the centre of town and saw a great cloud of white smoke I realised that I'd read that the whole place smelt of sulphur because of the geothermal activities… silly me.

Trying to find just one of the many caravan parks that appeared on my map didn't come easy, once again. While I drive along the main road where they are supposed to be near, there are absolutely no signs saying where they are. I get some way out of the town of Rotorua before I see a little sign saying Motorhome sites, but it is badly sited and not in the usual large blue and white International standard. Obviously here we again have a local council not into the subject of motorhomes and caravan sites and their clear and frequent direction signs.

This whole area I am now in is the volcanic area of NZ with active geysers and mud pools etc and this is why I have made my way here. I also want to see Lake Taupo which is an old volcano that has got filled with water. The campsite I booked into was poor quality again but unlike only $10, I get stiffed for $25. Always the same in areas where loads of tourists go to, but the quality does not always get better to match the higher prices.

First thing in the morning and I am up and off into town to have a look around. I went to the town centres park where the map said there were plenty of geothermal pools etc. Indeed there were and I saw many pools of hot steaming water and others of bubbling mud. A very neat and compact town and very clean, with lots of trees in the streets which make it quite pretty and I had no problem parking while I caught up on the emails, which included two emails from African fraudsters trying it on the way they do. How do they get your email address is what I want to know? Then it was an excellent cup of coffee and onto the road towards Taupo, 70K's south and on New Zealands largest lake. This lake was a result of a volcano erupting 1800 years ago which was a larger eruption than Mt St Helens and Krakatoa together.

However first I wanted to visit the Maori village of Whakarewarewa, which has a lot of geothermal features. I thought I would have to pay, as all these places around this general central area of NZ seem to charge like wounded bulls to get to see what are natural phenomena and I think this is a bit of a rip off. If they can let you see such things in the central park for free, why are companies allowed to take over other places and charge you? When I got to the village the entry payment booth was unmanned and people were just walking in and so I got to walk round for free. I saw more of the same as I had just seen in the park but these were intermingled amongst little houses in which Maori were living. In one part of the village there was a little cemetery and the bodies had been buried in long concrete boxes which sat above ground. There was steam hissing out all around these concrete coffins and I wondered if they steam cooked the bodies as well! I could see a geyser about 100 metres away across some ground and people looking at it, but I could see no way to get there, so I asked a Maori woman if I could get there. No she said it was belonging to another geothermal site Te Puia next door and they charged $50 entry. Indeed when I drove round there it was a heavily developed commercial site and they did charge $50 minimum! However there was a car park nearby and by looking through the railings and using my zoom lens feature I could get a good picture of the geyser as it erupted, which it did constantly. (see photo 988 to 1011)

The road down to Lake Taupo was good, even if it did get a bit bumpy in parts. Mainly straightish and the countryside is a mixture of heavy plantations of pine trees and rolling fields. I saw evidence of recently cleared forest and or bush and many huge piles of branches and detritus from the forest floor. You see this quite a lot around NZ and I wondered what they do with it all. To burn it all off would send lots of fumes into the atmosphere and yet to leave it in piles, it would take for ever to break down.

Just before I got to my destination I saw a sign for Haku Falls and though I've seen more falls than you can shake a stick at, I thought I may as well waste some time there. Actually they are not natural falls but a cutting made to allow the Waikato River to drop and power turbines and a notice said that on this river there were 8 such places generating some really high percentage of NZ's electricity. The spectacle of this narrow cutting with an impressive amount of rushing water going through it is heightened by the fact that a footbridge goes over the rushing torrent. (see photo 1012 to 1015)

Taupo was a smaller version of Rotorua situated right in the north eastern corner of the lake. After getting some food I needed at the local supermarket, I drove along the lakeside road leading to the south of the lake. The lake itself looks like an inland sea so quite impressive. I saw on the map that some way down the road I should be able to see an 'earthquake gully' and 'echo cliffs' However no sign of either so black marks to Kiwimaps. Good job I intended to go down that road anyway.

When I got back to Taupo I was just in time for my afternoon coffee break and then it was back to Rotorua to spend the night before heading back to the Bay of Plenty area on the north coast. I thought I would try the Top 10 park in the town centre that I had seen. No luck as it was full and this is the first time that has happened to me. However this apparently is a popular weekend destination for Hamilton and Auckland people, and it was nice weather so hence my bad luck. So I headed for another one I saw as I did not want to go back to the one I'd been in the evening before. Room at the inn this time but at a cost of $30, the most I have had to pay to date, and I said so. I was told that due to the demand etc etc that was the cost. The park will be full because of the demand, however it never did fill up. It shows that in all the World over, if a fast buck can be made out of the hapless tourist, then they are sharks meat. (see photo 1016 to 1018)

One thing this campsite did have was its own bubbling brook running along a boundary line. It was covered in bushes and other growth, but you could hear it making all sorts of hisses and bubbling sounds and through some breaks in the growth you could see mud bubbling away and some clouds of steam. A house next to this stream had clouds of steam wafting up from one corner of its back garden. So in this area you could buy a house with its own geothermal attraction.

During the early hours of the morning I was woken up by the screeching of these Takahe birds which are running around all over the place in this campsite, unlike others I have stayed at. They peck away at the grass but I can't see actually what they get to eat from it all. If another Takahe bird gets too close they start a fight as if to say 'bugger off this is my pecking patch'. When this happens they emit a gull like screech and that is what I was hearing and I watched for some time while having breakfast, their antics over these pecking rights.

After my bird show, I got going and headed back the way I had come an up to the top northern corner of Lake Rotorua, but this time I took the road to Te Puke which is an unfortunate name for the area where most of NZ's Kiwi fruit is grown. I was soon in this area and was struck by the number of fields that were bounded by the huge 'neighbours from hell' hedges. I suppose they are to protect the Kiwi vines from cold winds etc. (p.1019) I only found out back in Hastings that Kiwis grow on vines that look just like grape vines. I took a photo of the vines with young fruit on them and found from a young man tending the crop that they are picked about March time.

From Te Puke which is no great shakes to look at as a town, it is but a short hop to the next coastal town of Tuaranga which has an impressive harbour area. I was surprise to see a number of large ships tied up at the wharfs, when Auckland is just round the corner. On the seaward side of the harbour area is a longish strip of narrow land which has at its end a hill of about 250 metres which they call Mt Manganui and in fact the whole of that peninsular is called that. Apart from the commercial dock area the rest is quite upmarket stuff and being a Sunday it was full of people having breakfasts and coffees in the shopping street cafes. It is obviously a beach area for people with money and its closeness to Auckland probably accounts for this. I read that it is also a place for retirees. (see photo 1020 to 1023)

I drove round to the other side of the harbour to the town of Taurangua and this is a bit less up market, but quite a

largish working town with lots of business and commercial areas. This was to be the last town of any size before Auckland, but before getting back to where I had started from, I would go up to the area known as the Coromandel Peninsula after a British naval ship that called to this coastal area to replenish its supplies. It too is an area that is visited by Auckland weekenders.

This was quite evident by the fact that the roads were full of them and in fact even down at Lake Rotorua they were very evident. Many bunches of motorcycle maniacs, cavemen in hotted up yank tanks, three wheeler gorillas, and hoons (Kiwi for boy racers) in all manner of hot hatches, all making a nuisance of themselves on the roads.

The road north of Tuarangua roughly following the coast, went through a number of small towns that were instantly forgettable. I stopped at one, Tairua, for lunch. A pleasant enough place at the seaside. (see photo 1024 to 1028) From then on the road twists and turns as it goes through hilly pastures, and finally I reach a hamlet called Kuaotunu and as it is four o'clock and time for coffee and I have had enough, and there is a campsite here. I pull in, not a top site but much like a lot of the Kiwi second rate campsites one gets. It cost only $14 but later when I wanted a shower I found I had to put a $1 in a box only to find that I only got a lukewarm dribble of water which only lasted the length of time it took me to wash my face and hair. In the six weeks I had been on the road I only found one place that had decent showers. So the Kiwis are much the same as the Brits in this department. In fact I've only been to one country where they consistently have good showers and that was the good old US of A. Bully for them for that's all they are good for in my judgement.

Monday and I am heading first of all to Coromandel itself, (see photo 1029 & 1030) which I reach in about three quarters of an hour, across the usual Kiwi countryside. The little town reminded me of a Wild West town, out of a cowboy movie. It started because gold was found nearby, so that explains it. I get a paper and some apples and I waste no more time to head on down the coast to the next town of Thames. (see photo 1031 to 1033) The road winds its way along the coast and is exceeding poor, considering the traffic on it. The peninsula is visited by tourists and Auckland weekenders so quite why they didn't bother to make this stretch of road better than a medieval goat track, beats me. Some sections were narrower than the width of two passing wide vehicles and seeing as large trucks used it, made it a scary bit of road to be on.

I stopped in the town which was quite busy, for my morning ritual coffee. Then some petrol and I headed along highway 2 towards Auckland and this road was fairly straight and wide for a change. Before long I hit the main drag into Auckland which is called The Southern Motorway and this enables me to very quickly get into Auckland and over the bridge to Takapuna Beach campsite, where I arrive at 1300 hours in time to make my lunch sandwich. (see photo 1034 to 1039)

I got the same pitch I was on before, and next to me was a young couple with a small motorhome and we get chatting. They were from Berlin and had just done the South Island like me and it turned out that we both agreed that Kiwiland is overrated and all too much the same wherever you go. It made me quite seriously consider not exploring North of Auckland, as they said they did it and it was quite a rough area with hardly any towns of any size and with rough people to boot. I had plenty to do to keep me occupied for at least a week, and I decided to think about it.

Well it didn't take me long to work out that I wasn't going to explore north of Auckland and the deciding clincher for my decision to not even stay in New Zealand for any longer than I had to, was when the owner of the camp site told me after a week that I was really only allowed to stay on a campsite for a maximum of two weeks. That he would allow me to stay only up to the 22nd of December as after that he was fully booked up for the whole of the coming Christmas period. I thought that it would probably be the same story at the only other campsite nice enough to entertain staying at and I did not feel like taking a chance of finding vacancies at sites well outside the Auckland area. I simply did not feel like wandering around over the Xmas period trying to get into various sites. So my mind was made up to cut short my visit to NZ and go over to Oz earlier and go this side of Xmas.

I would have to make a visit to the Oz Consulate to get a year's visa as these were not available on the internet. Their place is in an office tower near the ferry terminal in downtown Auckland. So it was off to there I went one morning and what a shock I got when I got there. A relatively small room crammed with rows of seats and about 40 odd people of mainly Asian or Polynesian background where waiting. I took a numbered ticket and saw that there were at least 35 people in front of me. After nearly two boring hours of waiting, it was at last my turn. I explained that I wanted a year's visa and I was then told I had to supply a bank statement showing I had enough funds and also to write a letter saying why I wanted to visit Australia!

It was not so much that I had to supply this info, but more the fact that why didn't they put this requirement on their website, which I had perused before going to their consulate. Also why did they not put that fact down in writing on their visa application form which I had to fill in whilst waiting? It would have saved me that boring wait. I gave him my current passport AND my older passport which showed I had had a years visa in 2004 and had left the country OK after nine months.

The next day I went back with the documents they required and again had to wait about an hour to get to the counter. I asked how long it would take for me to get the visa, and was shocked to hear him tell me that they were taking at least two weeks. They would phone me when my passport was ready for pickup. So this meant that I now had to kick my heels for yet another two weeks and this was going to bring me right up to the busy Xmas period regarding flights to Oz. Also there was the question of what to do with my motorhome.

I had had to pay around $3500 in duties and taxes to get it into NZ and if I sold it there I would lose that but if I sent it to Oz I would get it back. If I tried to sell it in NZ I could see that it could take me ages as the market place for them was obviously overloaded. The fault for this lies with the many companies that hire out campervans and motorhomes. They sell them on after 2 to 3 years and thus overload the market which is really only a small market anyway with only 4 million people, many of whom already have a RV. So trying to sell it in NZ did not really make sense for me as I certainly did not now want to stay any longer than I had to. The weather was proving very unsettled with constant rainy days and Auckland as a place was a bit boring and as I have said the countryside of NZ had proved to me to be much the same wherever you went. So there wasn't anything to keep me occupied.

I therefore looked to see what it would cost to get it over to Oz and considering the closeness of the two countries you would have thought it dead easy to get a vehicle over to Oz. I certainly didn't find lots of companies vying to get my business and in fact I only found one company Wilhelmsen who are Norwegian shippers and who run a RoRo service. They primarily carry new cars around the World and this ferry is one that runs from Europe to Oz and stops at Auckland every ten days. However they obviously feel they have a captive market as the cost was going to be $3667 and although that wasn't much more than what I would get back off the Customs, I felt it was a rip off. Consider that it had cost $6800 to have it travel all the way from the UK to NZ and now it was going to cost as much as more than half of that for just a four day journey as against a 30 day journey, Not to mention the difference in miles in the two journey's.

However all round it would be better and it would mean that I would have my well proven home for use in Oz and I could take up to a year to sell it and would stand to get just as much as if I sold it in NZ. Maybe it would also sell quicker, who knows. Also one more factor made it more sense to sell in Oz and that was the fact that being an Oz registered home (I still had the Oz plates and rego document) it would obviously attract no customs duties going into Oz. So I booked it onto a voyage leaving Auckland on the 14th December and I found that I would have to visit Customs to register it as leaving the country which I found odd. Just another example of just how bureaucratic NZ is yet when I got to their office to do this, the girl who served me hadn't a clue. On top of this I could hardly understand anything she said. Which I find is a constant factor in NZ when you get Asian people in jobs where they are having to deal with the Public, yet they can hardly talk in understandable English.

Later on I found that in order to get my money back I would have to get the customs agents who handled the import and who I found to not be so organised doing it, to write a letter to the Customs giving their authorisation for the money to come direct to me. Now if you do not find that incomprehensible, I do. After all it is MY MONEY not the money of the customs agent and therefore I should be able to ask that it is repaid to me and certainly not to some third party. I could just imagine that this money would disappear once I had left the country and it would be a job to get it back. Quite frankly it was just another example of barmy NZ bureaucrats and their barmy rules.

I already had booked a flight to Melbourne for around June time, back in the UK, before I'd left and when I tried to change this to around the 17th December or onwards, all flights were fully booked. So it meant I had to see if I could get a flight on another airline and luckily I was able to do so but at a higher cost than the one already booked with Virgin Blue, which is a budget carrier, hence them being fully booked. I hoped that I could maybe get a refund or a credit at a later date and once I was in Oz. So I got a flight to arrive Melbourne on the 17th a day before my motorhome arrived.

Now I had to hope that my visa would be forthcoming before I was due to fly out and the two weeks would be up on the 12th December. I was taking a big risk in having my motorhome go on its way to Oz before I knew that I was getting a visa. What would happen if for some crazy reason they said I couldn't have a visa at all. The Aussies are such a pain and I think the way they treat Brits and Europeans over them being able to visit their country, defies decency and logic. If the Kiwis can allow Brits (and Europeans) to come to NZ without a visa, why is it the Aussies require one? More importantly why is it that it takes a minimum of two weeks to get the lousy thing? Why cannot a Brit or European be able to get a year's visa on line? It really gets up my nose when tourists are going over there to spend their money into their economy and this is how they treat you. Putting you into the position that for two weeks you are sweating as to whether your going to get this piece of paper or will you end up in some horrible situation where your home is over there and your stuck in NZ and stuck in hopeless weather with constant rain and Christmas coming up when it would be difficult to stay somewhere.

On top of this there was the question of my scooter, which I would have preferred to take with me to Oz to save having to sell it and buy yet another one over there. After looking into it I came to the conclusion that due to good old Antipodean bureaucracy, even though this make of scooter was sold in Oz, I would no doubt have some difficulties getting it through Oz registration. I would no doubt end up having to pay to go thro' hoops and would also have to pay 10% customs duty. So it just wasn't worth it and on top of this the shipper would not allow me to leave it on the scooter rack.

In fact the shipper was as big a pain as the NZ and Oz government Johnnies, because of their own brand of bureaucracy. According to their 'RULES' of shipment, you could not leave ANYTHING personal in the motorhome. Quite what 'personal' covered they did not say and what one was supposed to do with all the things one carries in ones home on wheels, I simply do not know. I suppose they expect you to go to the expense of having it all boxed up and then you pay them heaps more for them to carry those as well. To Hell with the fact that you have paid them through the nose to ship your home, which should carry everything in it as normal. Also why was it the case that the shippers who took it to NZ from the UK could allow whatever you wanted inside it, yet another shipper acts in this way. Someone in the agents office told me that I could leave bedding and crockery and cooking utensils inside and that I should hide other stuff so it looked like it was empty. So what I did was put all that I wasn't going to take on the aircraft, into the lockers under the rear berths. I then screwed the lids down to make it look like that they were not storage places at all. I tell you all this is utter madness and it annoys the hell out of me.

The only bright spot on this horizon of annoyances was the fact that the German lad next to me wanted to buy my scooter. He being a bike man back home and who was staying on in NZ as he and his wife had got jobs in hotels, they preferred to have two wheels than a more expensive car. Although it meant me taking a $1200 loss on the cost, it was more than I would get from a dealer and quicker no doubt than having to try and sell it through the papers or on Ebay. So that was at least done and dusted OK.

One other thing had happened regarding transport and that was my motorhome had started to make a transmission noise during the trip round NZ. In fact I had noticed even back in the UK when I did two weeks in Devon and Cornwall. I couldn't make out whether it was a diff noise or from the gearbox. Knowing what I know about dealers I felt that I couldn't rely on what they said if I took it to one. So I decided to use the services of the NZ AA organisation. At least that way I would get an unbiased 2nd opinion.

What a waste of time and $30 because the guy who was not a young inexperienced bloke, couldn't pin point what it was. He wasn't experienced in Transits and that did not impress me, nor the fact that I still had to pay for a non explanation/opinion. So I was forced to ask a dealer to have a listen and he came up with an opinion that it was a bearing in the axle. At least that opinion was for free, but I would get it done in Oz…if I ever get there OK. However the price they quoted was outrageous at around $3,000. So I will have to see what an axle specialist would charge for a recon unit, which is what I would do in the UK. So it will be interesting to see how all that goes when I get into Oz and through with the nuisance Xmas holidays.

Miracles of miracles because I got a phone call from the Oz Consulate saying my visa was ready for pickup, so they'd got it done in 12 days and not the 14 days. However I am still not impressed because I feel that there should be some fast track way some people should be able to get a visa. For instance:- A rich person goes to say New Zealand thinking they will take a holiday for two months, yet after one month they are bored with the place, have seen all there is to see and decided on a whim to spend more than three months in Oz. When they see that this will mean kicking their heels around NZ for up to two weeks, they could say 'cancel that idea I will go elsewhere because I want to go immediately.' Oz loses a person who could spend a great deal of money. It seems very short sighted for the Oz authorities to have no fast track system for people who want immediate access to the country. Even if it means paying extra for it, it would put them in a better light than of now. In my case it means I can now get out of this crappy weather for sure in a weeks time.

Tuesday came and time for me to get the home down to the docks. I had packed as much as I could of my clothes and personal effects that I would need in Melbourne until I got my home, into my suitcase Everything else that was left over including things like documents, books and items that I would want to carry in my suitcase, all went into the lockers under the rear seats. I was able to cram them full and all the overhead lockers were now empty. I then screwed the lids down and countersunk the screws and put filler over the screw heads. I was trying to hide the fact the lids were even able to hinge and that anything could be under them.

The problem was that the shippers agents were saying that when I took into the docks, it would be inspected for having personal effects in it, and also to see if it were dirty and required yet another power wash. All this gives you the willies as you're apprehensive as to whether this inspection will be a harsh one or an easy going one. You imagine that the crockery, cutlery and pans will be objected to. Then the bedding and then the ruse to hide all the belongings will be rumbled. Then where do I stand? Ones imagination starts to run riot and this doesn't help your already fevered mind which is upset by all the bureaucracy, and the costs involved.

I park the home outside the gate and go and see the Maori guy I'd talked to before. I've got my bright yellow cycling vest on which is an obligatory item for all people moving about in the wharf areas. He tells me that I should drive to a spot a few yards inside gate and wait for a van which I will have to follow to where I have to go. This I do for about ten minutes and just as I'm wandering if I've been forgotten, along comes the van. We only drive about fifty yards and I'm directed to park in some bays on my right. This is what I mean about all the mindless bureaucracy as I could have driven there without a van taking me there. As this van did not stop and had driven off and as the Maori on the gate never told me where I had to go or what I had to do, I was at a complete loss as what to do now. I went into the building there and was confronted by a lot of stevedore types standing around, so I asked one guy if I were at the right place to leave a motorhome. I was told to go to the cabin a few yards away and see them in there. The sign outside it, said it contained 'Tally Clerks' whatever they were or did. A queue of rough looking drivers was standing outside and there was no one inside the cabin. I asked one of the men if I had to join the queue and I was told that we had to wait as the tally clerks were on their 'smoko' The docks being heavily unionised which is the case in all Antipodean docks, drop all their work for these smoke breaks or smoko's Eventually two blokes turn up in a pickup and we are in business. I tell the clerk why I'm there, he takes the customs export paper off me and then messes around for five minutes and then asks me for the MAF clearance. This gives me the willies once more as I wasn't expecting to have them look it over. I explained that the shipper had told me that I would not probably have to have it cleaned as it had only recently come into the country and someone would inspect it from the shippers just to make sure. He appears to accept this explanation to my relief.

Then he tells me to go to the home and he will escort me to a place and this he does. This place is a huge warehouse with a lot of new trucks in there. I am to park it there with the keys in it and someone will be along later to inspect it and all being well it will be locked up until it goes on the ship. No wonder the shipper didn't want personal effects left in it as there it was, open to all, and for how long? I feared only for the portable freezer which was worth a bit. However what could I do? I could only keep my fingers crossed.

So now I have to kick my heels for almost a week until the next Monday and a flight time of 1430. However one thing I do have to do straight away is go to the Customs House and see that the importing agents have sent that letter authorising payment direct to me, of the duties I had paid. I also needed to see if they would send that payment to my new Oz bank account and not to my Kiwi account, which I would close on the Monday. After much head scratching I was told they could, but it would cost me $60. God they do know how to stuff it to you these Kiwi government departments. I said that in that case, could they make sure they get it into my Kiwi account by Monday. They thought they could, so I will see what happens.

Back at the Takapuna campsite, I am now in one of those 50's style tin boxes that passes for a caravan and that will be my home until Monday. After lunch I visit a local insurance broker to get a quote for marine insurance and that turns out to be another expensive Kiwi rip off like the cost of the shipping. It had cost me $750 from the UK to NZ which was a 5 week trip of about 18,000 miles and now it would cost $425 for a four day journey of about 1500 miles. Is there no such thing in this World as a 'fair go mate' that these Antipodeans are always going on about?

When I got back to the campsite I saw the German couple were back again. They had gone off to a campsite north of Auckland for the week and said they would be back on the Saturday when they would pay me for the scooter. They had already paid me a deposit of $500, so I knew that it was at least sold. Apparently they had got a telephone call from the hotel that the girl was going to work for, to come in about some matter. So all is still well on that front. On the push bike front, even though I have advertised it in the local supermarket for over week now, I doubt if it will sell even though it is cheap at $95, being as it is a lightweight, hand built job. If it doesn't sell I will donate it to the Sally Army. I would have packed it into the home, but no way would they accept it or even on the rack at the back. Pesky shippers!

A few days on and I got a phone call about the push bike from a young woman, who when she turned up to look at it, was from Liverpool. However she was overweight and as it is a man's bike cocking her leg over the crossbar was too much for her. She really needed a woman's bike, so a sale chance down the drain. A reminder of how fat Brits are these days! Amazingly the Sally Army for bureaucratic reasons couldn't take it and I ended up leaving it with the campsite owner to give away. What a waste on my money thanks to those Swede shippers.

On the Friday morning I went to my bank and as I thought, no cheque had been paid in from the Customs people. I had to make arrangements for my account to be transferred to Oz as this was the last working day I had to do that. I sent an email to them explaining that as they had had enough time to refund me and into my Kiwi account, I now required them to send it to my new Oz account and I did not expect that they will take out that $60 cost. I wonder what cock-ups over this will ensue from here on. I hate to think what messing about I will be put to over getting this money.

True to past experiences, they did not send the money to my Oz account in good time and when I got to Oz it took several emails to eventually get it, so that was a relief just to get it, and at least they did not charge me the extra $60. So good of them!

So it was that I caught the plane and after a short two and half hour flight, it was into Melbourne that I flew. Little did I know of the bureaucratic nightmare I was to be in for, over the importation of the motorhome, which let us face it was an Oz vehicle and not some alien from Mars trying to get in illegally. If all British motorists who were coming back to the UK after a drive round Europe were subject to the same over the top actions of Aussie bureaucracy, there would be riots and movement between the UK and Europe would grind to a stop.

Chapter Twenty Four

Postscript

My motorhoming odyssey was round two countries that couldn't be more different. One, Australia is a huge country of vastly differing geography and weather, with more to see, and more interesting and larger cities. It also has a more rich history and is now a rich country with good employment covering industry and mining. Their farming industry which used to be number one is now declining due to draught and other factors.

Because of its size it takes the visitor much more time and effort and cost, to get round and see most of the interesting stuff. Even then, unless you spent two years doing this, you still cannot due to its size get to see absolutely everything. One thing that you have to take into account that all the travelling you have to do does get VERY boring and momentous, when driving from one interesting spot to the next which can be hundreds and hundreds of miles away.

Whereas New Zealand is a small country both in size and population, with few big cities and even then the two biggest, Auckland and Wellington are only small compared to say Sydney or Melbourne. The rest are all just towns. The countryside is all very green and sweet but all of a muchness, which borders on the boring after a while. One can drive round the whole of the North and South Islands in relatively quick time, compared to Australia. So you can do the whole of NZ in a much quicker time.

Apart from the geography of the two places the main question for anyone intending to make a long term trip around both places is the business of all the government bureaucracy you can encounter. That is why I have taken some time to highlight it all. Then there is the thorny question as to how you make this trip. This is going to entail you in having to get involved with some form of transport, and that is where you can get some real aggro. Again I have taken much time and words to describe all my encounters on this front, so that you can be forewarned.

Of course if you are rich you will not be bothered at all. You just go there, buy a new or secondhand vehicle, do your trip, sell it at a great loss, and be on your way back. Or you may hire something at a great cost. If you do both countries one after the other, you won't bother taking your bought vehicle to the other, you just sell in one and buy another when you get to the other country. However if you are not rich you can get it in the neck like I did.

I blame of course the governments of both places. I have travelled greatly around the World and have always thought that the British were an over bureaucratic lot and I despise our ruling classes because of that. I do not need to tell you that both Australia and New Zealand were started by British bureaucrats and so they suffer from the 'British Disease' and with interest. For they have increased with interest the levels of mind boggling bureaucracy. So what should be an easy thing to do, namely buy and sell vehicles and move them from place to place, it is a bureaucratic jungle, which will cost you much in money and time and will assault your mental well being until you feel like screaming and putting yourself into a mental home.

You can see that most of my miseries were thrust on me in Australia and being the type of person I am, and that is to say I will not allow myself to be shat on especially by creatures from the deep, namely shiny arsed, creepy civil servants, whom I dislike with an intensity that is indescribable. So once I started to get it in the neck on my arrival at Melbourne, I had to complain at my treatment, for I had as you can see lost a lot of money.

I wrote to every person involved and kept writing to ever higher slimy civil servants, even up to the Ministers involved in Canberra. I got nowhere at every turn, which is on par with what you get in the UK when you try to get justice and satisfaction against ANY UK government department. I then complained to their relevant Ombudsman and when I found out that the Aussies had a Privacy Ombudsman who dealt with complaints against anyone who rode over your rights to privacy when you wrote to government departments or even to private companies. If any of those then discussed your complaints or letters with others not involved, you have a case.

Well of course I had had my privacy invaded by all the parties involved in my importation of my motorhome through Melbourne's docks. The shipping company, whose employees stole over £3,000 of my belongings, the stevedoring company Patricks who stitched me up for about $800, and the government department AQIS who stitched me up for over $2,000, all got together and discussed me as a person. Wilhelmsens mistakenly sent me a copy of a letter I had sent to Patricks and then had openly said that they had all decided I was a madman and wanted to sue them all. Of course I was mad because I had the temerity not to put up with their actions and had complained. Of course I had never even mentioned the words SUE as I could not afford the time or money to take anyone to court.

I put all this into the Privacy Ombudsman and after over about 18 months, all I got out of it all was $750 from Wilhelmsens. No apology from AQIS (par for a government department) and no recompense for the damage to my home or money they stitched me up for. Patricks also did not apologise or pay up, apart from their overcharging amount which they did refund. So through all my pushing and complaining I did get back about half of all the money I had lost for just wanting to bring back in a vehicle I had taken out of the country. Bugger that I had already spent thousand upon thousands of dollars in their country as a visitor, but that apparently does not matter to the Aussies.

Would I do it gain? Yes for seeing the countries, but NO if it meant I would have to repeat all the crap I had to put up with over the vehicles. Maybe it would have been better to have cycled round?

You the reader have to make your own mind up about it all, if you are contemplating any kind of trip to Oz or NZ, that involves what I got involved in, namely buying a motorhome or expensive vehicle and moving it about between countries.

As a last word on the subject, today I read in the Times of a UK man and wife who wanted to emigrate to OZ. Both had degrees, and both had much experience in IT and other top areas. They applied to the Oz Immigration people in London filled in endless forms etc, and had to pay a total of £3,000 to a government entity to process their work application. Now 18 months later they are no nearer getting a visa even though they have skills the Aussies say they want and have come to the conclusion that they will not get a visa and have been ripped off. Draw your own conclusions on that one, but as far as I am concerned the Aussies in London seem to be just as bad as when I first had to deal with them in 2004. So be forewarned about what can happen to you as soon as you have to deal with them and you will if your trip is longer than three months.

THE BEST OF LUCK TO YOU, TOO!

You can email me for information you wish to know which is not covered by this book, that is only to do with travel in these two countries. I cannot answer any questions to do with emigration. Just go to the website on this book at .co.uk where you will find an email facility. Do not expect an immediate answer, but I

email enquiries to
sailerboy63@yahoo.co.uk